HABITUAL OFFENDERS

HABITUAL OFFENDERS

— A True Tale of —

NUNS, PROSTITUTES, AND MURDERERS IN SEVENTEENTH-CENTURY ITALY

Craig A. Monson

THE UNIVERSITY OF CHICAGO PRESS

Chicago and London

Craig A. Monson is the Paul Tietjens Professor Emeritus of Music at Washington University in St. Louis and the author of *Nuns Behaving Badly* and *Divas in the Convent*, also published by the University of Chicago Press. He lives in St. Louis.

The University of Chicago Press, Chicago 60637
The University of Chicago Press, Ltd., London

Printed in the United States of America

25 24 23 22 21 20 19 18 17 16 1 2 3 4 5

ISBN-13: 978-0-226-33533-9 (cloth)
ISBN-13: 978-0-226-33547-6 (e-book)
DOI: 10.7208/chicago/9780226335476.001.0001

Part opening illustrations (pages 17, 143, and 183) are details from figures 14, 23, and 3, respectively. See the figure captions on pages 57, 181, and 12 for full source information.

Library of Congress Cataloging-in-Publication Data
Names: Monson, Craig (Craig A.), author.
Title: Habitual offenders : a true tale of nuns, prostitutes, and murderers in seventeenth-century Italy / Craig A. Monson.
Description: Chicago ; London : University of Chicago Press, 2016 | © 2016 | Includes bibliographical references and index.
Identifiers: LCCN 2015039579 | ISBN 9780226335339 (cloth : alkaline paper) | ISBN 9780226335476 (e-book)
Subjects: LCSH: Murder—Italy—History—17th century. | Nuns—Crimes against—Italy—Bologna. | Criminal Justice, Administration of—Italy—History—17th century.
Classification: LCC HV6535.I83 B658 2016 | DDC 364.152/30945411—dc23
LC record available at http://lccn.loc.gov/2015039579

⊗ This paper meets the requirements of ANSI/NISO Z39.48–1992 (Permanence of Paper).

Contents

ROME

BOLOGNA

Figures

Acknowledgments

The re-creation of this story would have been impossible without access to many archives and libraries and without the generous assistance and patience of their staffs: in Rome, the Archivio di Stato, Archivio Storico Capitolino, and Biblioteca Cassanatense; in Vatican City, the Archivio Segreto Vaticano and Biblioteca Apostolica Vaticana; in Bologna, the Archivio di Stato, Biblioteca Comunale dell'Archiginnasio, Archivio Generale Arcivescovile, Biblioteca Universitaria, and Biblioteca Arte e Storia San Giorgio in Poggiale; in Modena, the Archivio di Stato; in Florence, the Archivio di Stato; in Venice, the Archivio di Stato; in Paris, the Archives Diplomatiques du Ministère des Affaires Étrangères; in Princeton, New Jersey, the Marquand Library; in Austin, Texas, the Harry Ransom Research Center. I am, as always, especially indebted to the library system of Washington University in St. Louis and its interlibrary loan department.

The research was made possible by generous support from Washington University, a Paul Oskar Kristeller Memorial Research Grant from the Renaissance Society of America, and a travel stipend to the Harry Ransom Research Center at the University of Texas, supported by the Andrew W. Mellon Foundation Research Fellowship Endowment.

Jane Bernstein, Lucia Marchi, Dolores Pesce, Anne Schutte, Steve Smith, Carolyn Valone, and Elissa Weaver all read the entire draft and offered extensive suggestions for its improvement, as did the University of Chicago Press's anonymous readers. Lucia Marchi scrutinized my Italian and Latin translations and shared many fruitful discussions of possible literal and implicit meanings of thorny passages. Antonia Banducci, Liza Dister, Shannon McHugh, Anne Schutte, and Riccardo James Vargiu tracked down elusive sources and acquired copies for me. Emanuela and Maria Teresa Gozzini warmly welcomed me to Castello di Gorlago (home of Donato and Alessandro Guarnieri and their family), offered generous hospitality, and shared their family history.

I also thank Randy Petilos and the staff of the University of Chicago Press, Alice Bennett, Erin DeWitt, Natalie F. Smith, Kevin Quach, Joan Davies, and James Adcox, for their willingness to take on another of my projects.

The many others who liberally offered help and advice include Francesco Cifarelli, Federica Colaiacomo, Kaye Coveney, Robert Kendrick, Jim Ladewig, Tomaso Montanari, Margaret Murata, Colleen Reardon, Luca Salvucci, Milena Schaller, Michael Scherberg, Gianvittorio Signorotto, Chiara Sirk, Candace Smith, Simone Testa, Betha Whitlow, and Gabriella Zarri. ∗

Cast of Characters

Primary characters are marked with asterisks; secondary characters are in italics; ancillary characters are in roman type.

Agosti, Ottavio. Donato Guarnieri's cousin, who came to his aid in Venice and Bologna

Albergati-Ludovisi, Cardinal Niccolò (1608–87). Bolognese archbishop, 1645–51

Arnaldi, Monsignor Alfonso. Bolognese archiepiscopal auditor for criminal matters, 1644–45

Barberini, Cardinal Antonio (1607–71). Youngest nephew of Urban VIII, brother of Francesco and Taddeo, Bolognese papal legate during the abduction of the convertite

Barberini, Cardinal Francesco (1597–1679). Oldest nephew of Urban VIII, brother of Taddeo and Antonio, cardinal nephew under Urban VIII

Barberini, Maffeo. See Urban VIII

Barberini, Prince Taddeo (1603–47). Nephew of Urban VIII, brother of Francesco and Antonio, father of Carlo

Bertolotti, Taddea. Servant and nurse of Count Alessandro Maria Pepoli

*__Braccesi, Giovanni__ (d. 1685). Antonio Barberini's secretary of briefs, accused in the abduction and murder of the fugitive convertite

Conti, Suor Lucina. Prioress of the Convertite, 1644

Dioni, Suor Eufrasia Maria. Conversa at the Convertite; La Generona and La Rossa's personal servant

Falconieri, Cardinal Lelio (1585–1648). Bolognese papal legate, 1644–48

Galeazzo, alias Monchino (d. 1644). La Rossa's servant in the world and subsequently her convent messenger

Galliani, Bartolomea. Possenti family servant

Guarnieri, Colonel Alessandro. Older brother of Donato; implicated in the abduction and murder of the convertite

***Guarnieri, Captain Donato** (b. ca. 1620–27). Brother of Alessandro; captain in the papal army during the War of Castro; accused in the abduction of the convertite

Innocent X (1574–1655). Giovanni Battista Pamphili, reigned as pope 1644–55

Lomellini, Cardinal Girolamo (1607–59). Governor of Rome during the case of the convertite

Machiavelli, Sergeant Major Benedetto. Sometime governor of the Fortezza Lagoscuro; befriended Donato Guarnieri in Ferrara and Copparo in March 1644

Machiavelli, Isabella dall'Aglio. Sister of Dionisio Tomassini, mother of Francesco dall'Aglio, aunt of Diana and Domenica Tomassini; owner of the house on via Santo Stefano where the nuns' bodies were discovered

Malvasia, Marchese Cornelio (1603–64). General of the papal army during the War of Castro; Carlo Possenti's patron

Mariani, Galeazzo. Former soldier, acquaintance of Ferdinando Ranuzzi and Carlo Possenti; scarred by Possenti in March 1644

Mazarin, Cardinal Jules (1602–61). Prime minister of France, sometime ally of the Barberini family

Negrini, Negrino. Accomplice of Ferdinando Ranuzzi, implicated in the abduction of the convertite

Pallada, Andrea. Carlo Possenti's friend, who provided the convertite's first hideout

Pallada, Doralice. Wife of Andrea

Pamphili, Cardinal Camillo Francesco (1622–66). Son of Olimpia Maidalchini, cardinal nephew of Pope Innocent X, 1644–47

Pamphili, Giovanni Battista. See Innocent X

Panzacchi, Federico. Friend and confidant of Andrea Pallada

Pasi, Catterina (b. 1630). Daughter of Suor Silveria Catterina and Antonio Giovannoni

***Pasi, Suor Silveria Catterina, known as La Generona** (1604–44) (Cornelia in the world). One of the convertite who fled the convent on April 1, 1644; subsequently murdered

Pepoli, Count Alessandro Maria (1617–44). Provided the convertite's second hideout

***Possenti, Carlo** (1613–46). Canon of Santa Maria Maggiore in Bologna, chaplain general of the papal army during the War of Castro, vice duke of Segni; accused in the abduction of the convertite

Ragazzi, Giulia, known as La Fratina. Favorite prostitute of Donato Guarnieri

Raguzzi, Carlo. Army friend of Alessandro and Donato Guarnieri and Carlo Possenti

Ranuzzi, Count Ferdinando (1622–46). Implicated in the abduction of the convertite

Regi, Giustina (b. 1616). Sister of Suor Laura Vittoria, daughter of Lucrezia

***Regi, Suor Laura Vittoria, known as La Rossa** (1614–44) (Gentile in the world). Daughter of Lucrezia, sister of Giustina; one of the convertite who fled the convent on April 1, 1644; subsequently murdered

Regi, Lucrezia. Mother of La Rossa and Giustina

***Rossi, Giovanni Domenico or Giandomenico** (1598–1674). Lieutenant governor of Rome, prosecutor in the case of the fugitive convertite

Santi, Giulia. Housekeeper of Count Alessandro Maria Pepoli

Tomassini, Diana. Daughter of Dionisio, sister of Domenica, niece of Isabella Machiavelli; lover of Count Alessandro Maria Pepoli

Tomassini, Dionisio. Father of Diana and Domenica, brother of Isabella Machiavelli; maggiordomo of Count Alessandro Maria Pepoli

Tomassini, Domenica. Daughter of Dionisio, sister of Diana, niece of Isabella Machiavelli; lover of Count Alessandro Maria Pepoli

Urban VIII (1568–1644). Maffeo Barberini, uncle of Francesco, Taddeo, and Antonio; reigned as pope, 1623–44

Timeline

— 1644 —

THURSDAY, MARCH 17. Papal forces defeated at Lagoscuro, the last battle of the War of Castro

SUNDAY, MARCH 20. Palm Sunday; Donato Guarnieri last spotted at convent of the Convertite

FRIDAY, MARCH 25. Carlo Possenti returns from Ferrara to Bologna for Easter

SUNDAY, MARCH 27. Easter Sunday

TUESDAY, MARCH 29. Carlo Possenti last spotted at Convertite before returning to Ferrara

THURSDAY, MARCH 31. Peace treaty signed in Venice, ending War of Castro

FRIDAY, APRIL 1. Suor Silveria Catterina (La Generona) and Suor Laura Vittoria (La Rossa) abducted from Convertite; taken briefly to Count Ferdinando Ranuzzi's, then to Andrea Pallada's apartment on strada Maggiore; discovery of La Generona and La Rossa's flight from Convertite; archiepiscopal investigation begins

TUESDAY, APRIL 5. Archiepiscopal investigation temporarily halted

SUNDAY, APRIL 10. Feast of Our Lady of Borgo di San Pietro; nuns moved to Count Alessandro Maria's apartments at Palazzo Pepoli

MONDAY, APRIL 18. Archiepiscopal investigation resumes

FRIDAY, APRIL 22. Nuns removed from Palazzo Pepoli

SATURDAY, APRIL 30. Archiepiscopal investigation abandoned, incomplete

EARLY MAY. Nuns, dressed as men, spotted at Inn of the Torretta in Ferrara

MONDAY, MAY 9. Freak blizzard strikes Bologna

SUNDAY, MAY 15. La Rossa spotted near voltone dei Caccianemici about this time

EARLY JUNE. Guarnieri leaves Bologna for Gorlago

FRIDAY, JULY 29. Urban VIII dies; Possenti moves to Rome with Giovanni Braccesi

THURSDAY, SEPTEMBER 15. Giovanni Battista Pamphili elected pope, Innocent X

— 1645 —

SUNDAY, APRIL 9. Palm Sunday; Possenti leaves Rome for Segni as vice duke

WEDNESDAY, JUNE 21. Nuns' bodies discovered at Casa Machiavelli on via Santo Stefano; investigation in Bologna begins

SUNDAY, JUNE 25. Bolognese legate informs Rome of discoveries at Casa Machiavelli

MONDAY, JULY 17. Possenti arrested in Segni

FRIDAY, JULY 21. Giandomenico Rossi first interrogates Possenti in Rome

TUESDAY, JULY 25. Rossi arrests Giovanni Braccesi at Palazzo Barberini in Rome

WEDNESDAY, JULY 26. Rossi first interrogates Braccesi in Rome

FRIDAY, AUGUST 4. Guarnieri arrested in Venice

WEDNESDAY, AUGUST 16. Rossi leaves Rome with Possenti and Braccesi, bound for Bologna

FRIDAY, AUGUST 25. Rossi arrives in Bologna with Possenti and Braccesi

SATURDAY, SEPTEMBER 2. Rossi first interrogates Possenti in Bologna

FRIDAY, SEPTEMBER 8. Guarnieri leaves Venice in Venetian custody; Rossi first interrogates Braccesi in Bologna

TUESDAY, SEPTEMBER 12. Guarnieri delivered to Torrone in Bologna; Rossi first interrogates Guarnieri in Bologna

THURSDAY, SEPTEMBER 14. Possenti's first confrontations with accusers

THURSDAY, SEPTEMBER 21. Guarnieri's first confrontations with accusers

THURSDAY, SEPTEMBER 28. Cardinal Antonio Barberini flees Rome for France

WEDNESDAY, OCTOBER 11. Guarnieri confronts nuns at Convertite

SATURDAY, OCTOBER 14. Rossi interrogates Braccesi (first time since September 9)

SUNDAY, OCTOBER 15. Barberini family in Rome received under protection of France

MONDAY, OCTOBER 30. Possenti confronts nuns at Convertite

WEDNESDAY, NOVEMBER 15. Rossi sends transcript of investigation to Rome

— 1646 —

TUESDAY, JANUARY 16. Francesco and Taddeo Barberini flee Rome for France

FRIDAY, JANUARY 26. Rome authorizes torture of Possenti

SATURDAY, FEBRUARY 3. Possenti subjected to the strappado

SUNDAY, FEBRUARY 4. Possenti subjected to the vigil; dies the following morning

SATURDAY, MARCH 10. Rome passes sentence in the case and authorizes torture of Guarnieri

MONDAY, MAY 21. Rossi interrogates Braccesi (first time since October 23); Braccesi disappears from trial record

SATURDAY, JUNE 2. Guarnieri subjected to the strappado; Guarnieri released from solitary confinement

MONDAY, SEPTEMBER 17. Innocent X agrees to reconcile with Barberini family

WEDNESDAY, DECEMBER 19. Rossi banishes Guarnieri from Papal States

THURSDAY, DECEMBER 20. Guarnieri released at Tuscan border

Introduction

This book came about through the accidental convergence of traditional scholarly method (archival research) and twenty-first-century technological innovation (googling). In the summer of 1989, when I began to explore convent music in Renaissance Bologna, I spent weeks picking through chronicles and diaries, searching for details about nuns' music. Although such information proved thin in those histories, the documents offered diverting testimony about day-to-day happenings that captured chroniclers' attention. One June morning, a notice having nothing to do with music found its way it into my notebook. (This was the era when researchers carried pencils and notebooks into archives, not laptops.)

> 1 April 1644, two nuns fled the convent for reformed prostitutes. Nothing more was known about it. Then on 23 June 1645, their cadavers were discovered in a storeroom under some bundles in the house of Don Carlo Possenti, a canon of Santa Maria Maggiore, almost opposite the Baraccano, and you could see that they had been strangled because they still had the garrotes around their throats.[1]

After that I kept an eye open for further references to this fugitive pair, nicknamed "La Generona" (after an ex-boyfriend, Bernardino Generoni) and

"La Rossa" (after her flagrantly red hair). Rumor had it that these *convertite* (as reformed prostitute nuns were called in Italy) had been lured from their convent not only by the prominent local priest, Carlo Possenti, but also by Captain Donato Guarnieri, a head-turning young mercenary in the papal army during the War of Castro. Whenever other chronicles yielded details of their crimes, I copied them out, more for diversion than for any other reason, since they had nothing to do with music in convents.

Two decades later, with retirement looming, caught up in some late-life crisis, I took a break from music history and assembled a short collection of similar cases of transgressive convent behavior, *Nuns Behaving Badly: Tales of Music, Magic, Art, and Arson in the Convents of Italy* (2010). Although La Generona and La Rossa's story seemed perfect for the book, the scant gleanings from my old notebooks did not add up to a chapter.

By then, of course, I had graduated from pencils and notebooks to the computer. I had also ventured onto the World Wide Web, if not much further than eBay and e-mail. Like my students, I had also discovered Google. Some months after *Nuns Behaving Badly* appeared, I tried googling "Carlo Possenti," the miscreant priest who had allegedly lured Bologna's fugitive convertite from the cloister. Amid multiple citations about a nineteenth-century Italian engineer and politician of the same name and sites offering me a chance, quite remarkably, to chat and make friends with Possenti, I happened upon Claudio Costantini's *Fazione Urbana: Sbandamento e ricomposizione di una grande clientela a metà seicento*.[2] Buried in this remarkably detailed and exhaustively documented study of papal politics at the time of Popes Urban VIII and Innocent X, I ran across a brief discussion of the case of Bologna's missing convertite as it related to Innocent X's persecution of Urban VIII's nephew, Cardinal Antonio Barberini.

The outrageous misbehavior of two extremely ordinary women in a northern Italian convent had evidently set off a chain of events that reached south to Rome and the papal court and north to France and the court of Louis XIV. Cardinal Antonio Barberini fled Rome, disguised as a barrel maker, to seek asylum in France, followed shortly thereafter by his brother Cardinal Francesco and other family members.

Particularly intriguing, in a footnote Costantini made passing reference to a transcript of the investigation of the crime, surviving in the state archive in Rome,[3] which definitely piqued my curiosity. I had not ventured into an Italian archive since the early 1990s, however, before the advent of the euro and before my favorite economical pilgrims' hotel on the Janiculum Hill had

FIGURE 1. Processo. The bound transcript of the case of the murdered convertite. Courtesy of the Ministero dei Beni e delle Attività Culturali e del Turismo, Rome, ASRM 64/2014 (further reproduction prohibited).

been turned into condominiums. I tried to persuade a friend in Rome to drop by the archive, see what the call number might yield, and order a photocopy of the document if it looked interesting. She firmly pointed out that this was something I really should do myself. Of course she was right.

A few weeks later, I flew to Rome for the first time in eighteen years, checked into a bed-and-breakfast costing three or four times what I paid in 1994, and found my way to the state archive, not far from Piazza Navona. Within the hour a staff member delivered an unwieldy parchment-bound volume more than eight inches thick (fig. 1): 2,200 pages of testimony from more than 180 witnesses. Rather than a chapter, this had the makings of a book. Clearly there was much more material than I could deal with in the three weeks before my return flight. Another technological innovation had come on the scene since my last archival expedition, however: the digital camera. I learned that I could now photograph documents myself. Over four days I photographed the entire manuscript. Once more than 2,200 images were uploaded onto my laptop, I could digitally manipulate them so that impenetrable scribal hands often became legible.

My exploration of other leads over the next two years led to other archives in Rome as well as in Bologna, Florence, Venice, Modena, Paris, and even Austin, Texas. I usually visited the collections myself, but in some cases I managed to cajole colleagues and obliging students into undertaking investigations on my behalf. Thanks to digital imagery, they could send me hundreds of additional pages, until by now the relevant documentary material is approaching 5,000 pages.

What I originally envisioned as a chapter, then as a slim volume with half a dozen chapters, has swelled to seventeen chapters. It recounts happenings from Segni, south of Rome, to Compiègne, north of Paris. This wealth of primary sources permits me to reconstruct an unusually detailed microhistory of crime and punishment in seventeenth-century Bologna, one that puts faces on people "of the ordinary sort" from Italy's backstreets and back stairs, seldom encountered in historical narratives. In re-creating the case of the missing convertite, I examine such issues as life strategies among prostitutes, prostitutes turned nuns, maidservants, and other marginal women; self-promotion among "new men" making their way at the papal court without benefit of exalted birth; and the lives of mercenary soldiers, bandits, and others negotiating the boundaries of respectability. I construct much of the narrative from the viewpoints and in the words of these lesser members of the social order, often barely visible (or audible) in history.

Such ample material illuminates all stages of papal justice, from extrajudicial evidence gathering to tracking down alleged perpetrators, to interrogations of witnesses and their confrontations with the accused, to the uses of torture. It also sheds light on aspects of the judicial process sometimes less apparent in such records. Irene Fosi, Giancarlo Angelozzi, and Cesarina Casanova have pointed out, for example, that often witnesses' "own words" in trial transcripts of this period represent notaries' subsequent refinement, tidying up, and standardizing of what witnesses actually said.[4] Although some of that occurs here, 70 percent of this transcript appears to be the unredacted original, copied on the spot in the prisons of Bologna and Rome, including autograph affirmations of testimony scrawled in the document after interrogation sessions. It thus offers a plausible representation of "what happened" at the moment and of "who said what" in their own words.

Additional documents bound into the record reveal further intriguing aspects of the case. Love letters recovered from La Generona's cell suggest her ambivalence about her relationship with the possessive young priest for whom she fled. Another incriminating letter, confiscated from Carlo Possenti's desk at his arrest, becomes an important element in the prosecution's case and eventually a faintly smoking gun. Mandates for the arrest and detention of persons of interest, from prostitutes to booksellers, chambermaids, and tavern keepers (but very rarely aristocrats), and the record of when and how witnesses were released on bond after weeks or months of detention illuminate the realities of being compelled to testify. Notarial annotations, papal directives, and petitions on behalf of defendants elucidate the uses of torture in a legal case involving unparalleled prosecutorial license: not only to extract confessions and intimidate witnesses, but also to demoralize the accused. They also illustrate the less familiar practice of torturing a star prosecution witness as a means of confirming his accusations, which a defendant had vehemently contested.

Testimony "authenticated" by being read back and then confirmed by witnesses, face-to-face with the accused, but also preliminary and follow-up interrogations elucidate prosecutorial strategies in interesting ways. In the case of convent testimony, for example, interrogators' careful leading questions, planted early on, prompted more useful subsequent testimony after the convent gossip mill had continued to grind for several weeks. Other witnesses commonly tailored their "truths" to suit interrogators' or (especially) their own interests.

Other sources reflect public opinion as the case proceeds. Among the most interesting, if not always the most reliable, are Roman gossip sheets (*avvisi*), which disseminated the news of the day, commonly in manuscript copies passed from hand to hand and from scribe to scribe.[5] Tidbits from avvisi often found their way into ambassadorial dispatches to Venice, Modena, Florence, and Paris. These dispatches convey more detailed, sometimes secret information (quite often in cipher). Occasionally this information derives from well-placed sources: papal intermediaries or even the pope himself. Both avvisi and dispatches shed light on extrajudicial actions undocumented in the investigation's official transcript. Comparing their information with the trial record also suggests how misinformation leaked at high levels of the papal bureaucracy could mislead or impart a positive spin to public opinion in what was, after all, also a piece of papal political theater.

Private communications, preserved in the Vatican Secret Archive, between Cardinal Camillo Francesco Pamphili, the young papal nephew serving as Innocent X's right hand, and the archbishop of Bologna, papal legates in Bologna and Ferrara, and the papal nuncio in Venice also take us behind the scenes at the highest levels of the case. They illuminate secret strategies and aid in reconstructing a backstory to the investigation as documented in the official investigative transcript.

It is ironic that the prostitutes turned nuns, whose death provoked this cause célèbre and who should be the main characters in the story, remain among the most frustratingly elusive. In the remnants of the convent archive, preserved in Bologna's state archive, only a few scraps of information surface to shed light on the lives and characters of La Generona and La Rossa. (In La Rossa's case, a solitary original convent document confirms that she was ever there at all.) We therefore come to know them chiefly through what family members, former lovers, and scandalized cloistered sisters later chose to reveal (or fabricate) about them. I reconstruct their earlier careers as women of the world against the realities of female poverty and prostitution in seventeenth-century Bologna. Re-creating their subsequent cloistered lives puts faces on the least reputable of convent women, who rarely appear in scholarship on female monasticism, even though most seventeenth-century cities in Italy and other Catholic regions had their convents of convertite.[6]

This account unfolds in much the same way as the official transcript records the judicial discovery process. Readers learn details of the crimes in the sequence in which investigators discovered them. The unfolding therefore is not nicely chronological, since some later offenses came to light before earlier ones. To further complicate the narrative, for a time interrogations were under way in both Bologna and Rome—in Bologna, at both the archiepiscopal court and the rival secular tribunal, the Torrone. In the interest of clarity, a simplified time line appears at the beginning of the book.

At the discovery of these crimes, there was no CSI Bologna ready to ferret out clues using a sophisticated system of forensics. Although physical evidence (letters, clothing, jewelry, furniture) played a part in the case, witness testimony remained the method of proof in its formulation and prosecution. Circumstantial evidence or the testimony of a single eyewitness was insufficient for conviction: conviction and condemnation required the testimony of two eyewitnesses. Perpetrators of these crimes therefore did their best to avoid (or eliminate) eyewitnesses. If partial proof was sufficiently compelling, however, it could justify torture as a means of obtaining a confession.[7] In the absence of eyewitnesses to the present crimes, prosecutors labored long and hard to establish, through witness testimony, partial proof that was persuasive enough to persuade higher authorities to authorize torture.

Several chapters therefore re-create exchanges between persons of interest and their interrogators. Notaries present at every stage in the case were required to take down witnesses' responses exactly, distinguishing between information that witnesses volunteered on their own and their answers to the interrogator's direct questions. In the present case, the notary occasionally notes the witness's manner of speaking, changes in emotion, and facial expression (something that should "always" have happened but often did not).[8] In multiple instances, the prosecutor perceived such changes as important indications of guilt.

My presentation of "what was said" obviously reinterprets the notaries' own mediation between interrogators and witnesses. In notaries' transcripts, witnesses' statements appear in the vernacular and the first person and almost invariably repeat questions as part of their answers. Prosecutors' questions and all descriptions of judicial procedure are recorded in Latin and in the third person, often highly abbreviated. Re-creating such questions as direct speech, I have omitted witnesses' rephrasing of them in their answers. As in modern-day interrogations, questions get asked and answered repeatedly, over days, weeks, and months. I often combine details from a witness's different answers to the same question (sometimes from different days) into single encounters between interrogator and witness, while indicating the folio numbers for the various responses in the notes. At times I have combined answers to several questions into a single witness response. I have also simplified run-on sentence structure and omitted numerous details that are "redundant" or "irrelevant" to my construction of the narrative.

Witnesses often present others' words as direct quotations; at other times they describe what others said. I often re-create such interchanges as direct speech. When speakers, particularly from nonhegemonic classes, introduce dialect or less refined speech, or if witnesses remark on others' rough language in describing their words, I occasionally search for ways to differentiate such speech in English. I have preserved witnesses' highly repetitive, respectful form of addressing the interrogator as "my lord," however, since the absence or omission of the phrase can be revealing.

In a hundred days of interrogations spread over two and a half years, almost a hundred persons of interest were called to testify; in addition, eighty nuns were deposed at the convent of the Convertite. Thus, as in any complex legal investigation, the number of names to keep straight is daunting. The difficulty is compounded in this case because names are often very similar (for example, Bolognese nuns' vicar, Monsignor Ascanio Rinaldi, and Bolognese archiepiscopal criminal auditor, Monsignor Alfonso Arnaldi). That reality is inescapable and irremediable. Readers may perhaps find consolation in the knowledge that the papal nephew and the archbishop of Bologna, both at the center of the case, confused various persons of interest. To simplify matters, very minor players (from stable boys to cardinals) remain nameless in the narrative, their names relegated to the notes. To help readers sort out the others, a cast of characters that distinguishes primary, secondary, and ancillary figures appears at the beginning of the book.

Given my approach to historical narrative (reworking characters' words, as described above, reimagining their actions based on archival documentation, and suggestively reconstructing the scenes and the nature of those actions),[9] the detail in the original sources left little need for me to make things up. To clarify how rarely I was left to my own devices, the notes provide some sense of just how much appears in the original. The richness of the primary sources offers fascinating insight into far more aspects of seventeenth-century Bolognese life than could be included here. I try not to indulge myself too far in the detail I include. But one can leave out only so much. For both seventeenth-century investigators and twenty-first-century readers, the devil is in the details.

For any who might be interested in following the wanderings of the nuns and other characters or in discovering where the action took place, I have included GPS coordinates for most locations.

In 1569 La Generona and La Rossa's Ancient Observance Carmelite convent of SS. Filippo e Giacomo delle Convertite (fig. 2, A) was formally founded at the corner of via delle Lame and via del Rondone in Bologna, after informal peregrinations around the city earlier in the century. It was one of Italy's many monastic refuges for repentant prostitutes who had saved up enough to pay the requisite dowry. By that date the spirit of Catholic reform had inspired similar institutions from Genoa (1500–1510) to Rome (1520), Palermo (1524), Vicenza (1537), Naples (1538), Messina (1542), and Treviso (1559). Alternative institutions such as Bologna's Opera dei Poveri Mendicanti (1560) and the Casa del Soccorso (1589) received fallen women or women at risk who could not afford the price of admission to the Convertite.[10]

SS. Filippo e Giacomo was home to fifty women by 1574, when the convent took in a very modest £250. (At the opposite extreme, the Clarissan convent of SS. Naborre e Felice took in £8,720 that year.) By 1614 the population of the

FIGURE 2 (*opposite*). Filippo de' Gnudi, *Disegno dell'alma città di Bologna* (1702), detail. *A*, SS. Filippo e Giacomo delle Convertite; *B*, via del Rondone; *C*, via delle Lame; *D*, Capuchin fields (the surrounding wall was built after the nuns' flight); *E*, Riva di Reno canal; *F*, Canale Navile. Reproduced with permission of the Biblioteca Comunale dell'Archiginnasio, Bologna.

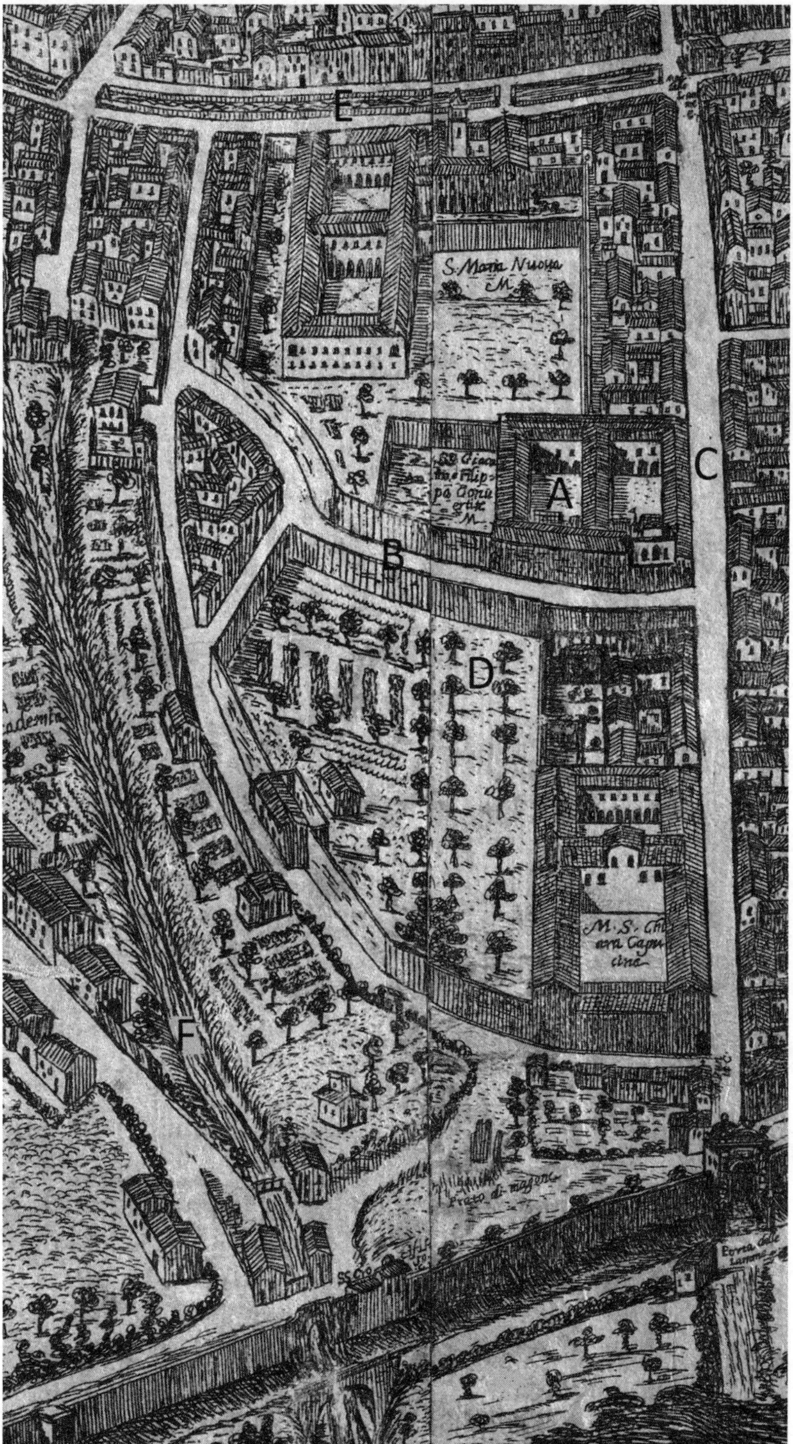
E
S. Maria Nuova
C
A
B
D
F
Prato di magone

Convertite had more than doubled to 128, a number that remained constant down to La Generona and La Rossa's time.[11]

Although this is not a history of great men, a few play roles at the margins. The story begins in the final months of the papacy of Urban VIII, Maffeo Barberini (1568–1644), who had occupied the throne of Saint Peter since 1623. With Europe at war throughout his reign, Urban struggled to mediate between Spain and its emerging rival, France. In 1635 France declared war on Spain; the conflict lasted until 1659. Concurrently the pope also tried to support the Habsburgs in their ongoing campaigns against the Protestants in the north, which were settled only in 1648, after Urban's death.

Spain, which controlled the southern half of the Italian peninsula as well as other island and mainland territories, remained the dominant power in Italy. The rest of Italy was fragmented into a number of independent polities, many too weak to maintain true independence: the Papal States, the Venetian Republic, the Grand Duchy of Tuscany, the Duchies of Savoy, Parma, and Modena, and the Republics of Genoa and Lucca. Lesser states struggled to find their own advantage in the balance between Spanish intimidation and French enticement to form alliances against Spain. As Urban VIII once observed, "It is certain that in this wretched Italy, if the Spaniards could be driven out, the French would establish their supremacy, which could be worse than the Spaniards', owing to the fickleness, insatiable greed and capricious nature of that nation."[12]

Violence involving the major powers broke out periodically on Italian soil (for example, the War of Mantuan Succession, 1628–31; the Piedmont Wars, 1639–42, 1647–49, 1655–59; the Neapolitan revolt, 1648). Comparable altercations were acted out in miniature by partisan groups on the streets of Rome, where the local governor struggled to keep order.[13]

Throughout his reign, Urban remained strongly committed to the Church Militant, most notably through his fortifications of Rome and its environs and of Bologna, but also through his pursuit of the War of Castro, which looms large in this story. He also promoted the Church Triumphant through ardent artistic patronage: lavish building and public works, the support of artists, writers, and musicians, and the funding of learned enterprises. In his pursuit of these initiatives, however, Urban more than doubled his predecessor's apostolic debt. By the end of his reign, the heavy taxation he imposed as a result earned him the epithet "Papa Gabella" (Pope Tariff, or Pope Tax). After years of such taxes and crippling inflation, the Roman populace greeted his passing with a mix of relief and fury, captured in one complaint, "They have sucked the blood out of our veins to enrich themselves, their relatives and their followers."[14]

"Our" included not only the Roman populace, but also rival noble families and other princes of the church holding grudges against Urban and his family. Urban's successor, Giovanni Battista Pamphili, was among them. As Pope Innocent X he turned against the Barberini family, purportedly for malfeasance during Urban's reign, but also, as we shall see, for alleged involvement in the death of a favorite relative.

"They" implied Urban VIII's own relations. The pope's promotion and enrichment of his kin set an egregious standard for papal nepotism, which heightened enmity with Italy's other powerful families. Urban promptly elevated his oldest nephew, Francesco Barberini (1597–1679), to the cardinalate to fulfill the role of cardinal nephew, at the pontiff's right hand; Cardinal Francesco soon became one of Rome's most powerful figures. In 1627 Urban named his youngest nephew, twenty-year-old Antonio (1607–71), a cardinal despite the youth's total lack of clerical experience and the presence of his brother and two uncles in the college of cardinals.

Urban's remaining nephew, Taddeo (1603–47), destined for the secular world, did not suffer from a lack of papal munificence. Thanks to his paternal inheritance and avuncular generosity, by the early 1630s Taddeo Barberini had become prince of Palestrina, gonfalonier of the church, governor of the Borgo, and prefect of Rome, with landholdings estimated at 4,000,000 scudi. Apostolic openhandedness enabled Taddeo's cardinal brothers to enjoy comparable wealth.[15]

Antonio Barberini plays the most important role in this story. Indeed, were it not for Innocent X's attempts to implicate Cardinal Antonio in the crimes, other sensational matters would probably have eclipsed them in a few weeks. Urban VIII's youngest nephew was high-spirited, bold, and arrogant, with a liking for fast company whom he sometimes shielded from prosecution for lawless behavior.[16] Cardinal Antonio was also openhanded. In the words of the contemporary highly informative if gossipmongering work *The Scarlet Gown, or a History of All the Present Cardinals of Rome* (1653, a translation of the slightly earlier Italian *La giusta statera*), "From his birth he was ever bountifull, and hath with donatives and magnanimitie drawn many to his devotion; whilst being possest of the goods of fortune he hath also made others partakers thereof, and hath prodigally spent his own. He hath not been a little taken with the beauties of women, on whom he hath wasted great sums of Gold."[17]

Based on contemporary artistic representations, papal historian Ludwig Pastor described Cardinal Antonio's appearance as "aristocratic and elegant." Artists may have shown him in the best light, however (fig. 3), for others

FIGURE 3. *La maschera trionfante* (Bologna, 1643). Cardinal Antonio Barberini as he looked during the War of Castro. With permission of the Marquand Library of Art and Archaeology, Princeton University.

found him unimpressive. *The Scarlet Gown* called him "the crookback." The traveling Englishman John Bargrave also confirmed his "crookt shoulder" in the 1640s. Comparably unflattering descriptions circulated in the mid-1640s, at the time of our story.[18]

Urban VIII initially kept young Cardinal Antonio busy in the north, out of his older brother Francesco's way, by sending him off on various legations. After 1633, when his uncle appointed him papal legate at Avignon, Cardinal Antonio became an ally of France. For the duration of Urban's papacy and beyond, Cardinal Antonio fostered French interests in the ongoing political struggles with Spain. The relationship was formalized with his designation in 1637 as France's co-protector (a sort of ecclesiastical lobbyist) in the college of cardinals.

Cardinal Antonio's colleague, Giulio Mazzarino (1602–61), who found a place in Antonio's entourage in the early 1630s and for a time served as his *maestro di casa*, subsequently entered French royal service and became a French subject, Jules Mazarin. In 1641 Mazarin received a cardinal's hat on Louis XIII's recommendation. Late the following year Cardinal Mazarin rose to be chief minister of France and primary adviser to four-year-old Louis XIV and his mother Anne of Austria, the regent. Mazarin would subsequently play a key role in the Barberini family fortunes as they figure in this story.[19]

The important post of papal chamberlain, which fell to Cardinal Antonio in 1638, required his presence back in Rome, where he moved into Palazzo Barberini with his entourage of 128 members. This inevitably exacerbated abiding fraternal conflicts with his cardinal brother, Francesco.[20]

But fiercer quarrels between the pope and his Barberini nephews and Odoardo Farnese (1612–46), Duke of Parma and Castro, began to smolder in those same years. In the early 1640s they flared into the First War of Castro. Faced with Farnese's financial mismanagement and unpaid debts related to the duchy of Castro, seventy-five miles north of Rome (fig. 4), as well as the duke's impudence and saber rattling, in late summer and early fall of 1641 Urban VIII organized an army to protect the northern Papal States. His lieutenant general also managed to take Castro (near 42.5° N, 11.7° E) in October without much of a fight, before the customary winter break in hostilities.

In January 1642 the pope excommunicated Odoardo Farnese, attempted to sequester his property, and, with encouragement from his nephews, resolved to take the war to the duke's own backyard. When Urban called for war to protect the north, Venice, Tuscany, and Modena, perceiving such advances as a bit too close for their own comfort, proposed an alliance with Parma against

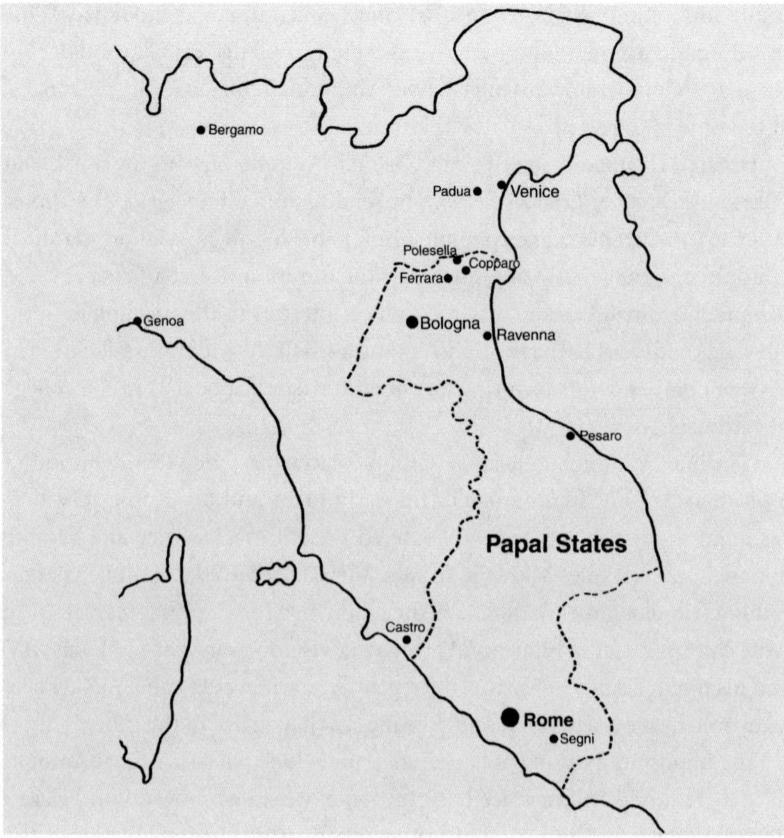

FIGURE 4. The Papal States and northern Italy.

the Barberini clan; France, Spain, and the Holy Roman Empire supported them from afar.

In September 1642 Farnese boldly invaded the Papal States. After menacing Bologna, he bypassed the city on his way south, largely unopposed. Ten days later Urban commanded the churches of Rome to join in "the cause of Saint Peter" on high. God turned a deaf ear, declining to put down the mighty and scatter the proud who were advancing toward Rome. As Urban's generals exhorted their troops to stand their ground, the Almighty chose instead to scatter the papal force.

The Duke of Parma advanced to within a hundred miles of Rome by early October, when Cardinal Antonio Barberini rode out to confront him at the head of another papal force. Perhaps because the invaders' kit bags already bulged with spoils and because winter was once again waiting in the wings, Farnese's troops began to slip quietly homeward. By mid-October their commander opted to follow their lead.

Papal forces' recent unimpressive showing and the prospect of Venice, Florence, and Modena joining Parma against him gave renewed urgency to Urban's determination to strengthen his northern positions. In December 1642 he appointed Cardinal Antonio Barberini legate not only of Bologna, but also of Ferrara and Romagna and ordered him to oversee military action together with his brother Taddeo. In the meantime the married men among Urban's troops had been sent home barely in time for fall planting. Bachelors in the papal army followed Cardinal Antonio north to Bologna, in time to sow wild oats during the ensuing carnival season, shortly before the preliminaries to this story properly begin.[21]

BOLOGNA

1

AIRING DIRTY LINEN

Easter arrived early in 1644. Although the days seemed warm for late March in Bologna, persistent overcast still shrouded the usual paschal signs of spring or ecclesiastical renewal in the days leading up to March 27, Resurrection Sunday. For the aging Pope Urban VIII Barberini (r. 1623–44) and his nephews, the political climate would also make this Easter especially bleak.

Bologna's central piazza (modern-day Piazza Maggiore) and the streets running out from it in all directions seemed congested nevertheless, not so much with the faithful intent on their Easter duty, hastening to San Petronio (fig. 5, G) or its nearby rival, the cathedral of San Pietro (fig. 5, O), but with soldiers loitering around an unsightly barracks hurriedly thrown up in the piazza. They had been drawn into the papal army and to the second city of the Papal States by the War of Castro. This prolonged Barberini feud with Odoardo Farnese, Duke of Parma and Castro, had dragged on since 1641, devastating the countryside and depleting papal coffers. The war had continued to disrupt daily life in Bologna, particularly during the past two years, as Cardinal Antonio Barberini, Bolognese papal legate and enthusiastic militarist, co-directed military operations out of the Palazzo del Legato (today, Palazzo Comunale, fig. 5, H; 44.493840° N, 11.342440° E) or on the battlefield.[1]

On Thursday after Judica Sunday (March 17), as the papal choir intoned

FIGURE 5. Joan Blaeu, *Theatrum civitatum et admirandorum Italiae* (1663). The southeast quadrant of Bologna. A, Porta Maggiore; B, strada Maggiore; C, Palazzo Bargellini; D, Santo Stefano; E, Palazzo Pepoli; F, voltone dei Caccianemici; G, San Petronio; H, Palazzo del Legato and Torrone; I, San Procolo; J, San Domenico; K, via Santo Stefano; L, via Fondazza; M, voltone del Baraccano; N, Porta Santo Stefano; O, San Pietro; P, San Giovanni Battista Celestini. Reproduced with permission of the Biblioteca Comunale dell'Archiginnasio, Bologna.

"Wherefore all that Thou hast done unto us, Thou hast done in true judgment," papal regiments clashed with Farnese's Venetian allies at Fortezza Lagoscuro (44.8731° N, 11.607° E) on the river Po, thirty-seven miles northeast of Bologna. On that day God did not judge in the Barberini's favor: two hundred soldiers fell on the battlefield and another hundred were captured. Cardinal Antonio himself barely escaped, thanks not to the troops of God's holy representative on earth, but to a particularly fleet-footed horse that carried the fleeing prelate to safety. After such a disastrous Easter season, Urban VIII and his nephews finally conceded. A treaty ending the conflict was signed on March 31, Easter Thursday.[2]

In the early hours of Easter Friday Leonardo Peri, better known as Leonardo Ortolano (Leonard the gardener) prepared to take back his fields (fig. 2, D): not battlefields, but the dormant gardens of Bologna's Capuchin nuns della Natività di Maria Vergine on via delle Lame, on the northwestern outskirts of Bologna, within sight of the city gate called Porta delle Lame

(44.502331° N, 11.333295° E) and nearby Canale Navile (fig. 2, F), the waterway to Ferrara and Venice.

Like other open expanses in this least-developed corner of Bologna, the Capuchins' fields showed scant evidence of field-workers' labors. A tangy haze from early morning fires, fortified by mists rising from nearby canals in this watery district, veiled modest orchards and skeletal trees, bare except for a few desiccated remnants of last autumn's foliage stubbornly retained. Dawn revealed gardens whose bare earth scarcely contrasted with the greening, threadbare carpet of sprouting weeds. Gray heaps of dead branches, brambles, and canes testified to Leonardo's preliminary efforts, still too soggy for the fire.

As the gardener settled a cloak around his shoulders outside his lodgings in Borgo del Rondone (Swallow's or Swift's Borough), south of the Capuchins, he noticed a small crowd idling near the large gate in the high wall that hedged in the side street outside his door, known as via del Rondone, (fig. 2, B; 44.500489° N, 11.334963° E). It marked the border of another women's community, the Carmelite nuns of SS. Filippo e Giacomo (fig. 2, A; 44.500384° N, 11.33444° E), better known as the Convertite, a refuge for reformed prostitutes. They had claimed the corner of via delle Lame and via del Rondone in the 1560s and founded a convent there. Back then the area seemed appropriately remote from the respectable palaces of Bologna's elite, nearer the city center.

Nevertheless, the entry to this retreat where "women of the world" retired to a quieter life of prayer and contemplation seemed unsuitably astir. To make ends meet, the repentant sinners took in laundry, which drew a steady trickle of servants laden with baskets of their betters' dirty linen. Ever since the War of Castro came too close for comfort, the convent portals seemed busier still, with idle soldiers turning up with their shirts (stained with food more often than blood), in search of a little conversation in the convent's public visiting room, the *parlatorio*.

But never at this hour. Had someone fallen victim to hooligans on the dark street during the night, the gardener wondered? (Foul play happened often enough with so many footpads and foreigners about.) Nothing had disturbed Leonardo's rest, however, or broken the Great Silence of the Carmelites or Capuchins, safe inside their walls.

Leonardo spotted a cause for the commotion: articles of clothing lay scattered along low parapets bordering his field and the street. He moved quietly to gather them up, lest they fall into the hands of some loitering opportunist. He shook a little debris from two long sleeveless garments of mud-colored serge, open at the sides. There were tunics of similar coarse weave and hue as well as two lengths of thinner black fabric and, in stark contrast, pieces of white linen limp from the dampness. In the gloom he also made out two pairs of wooden slippers, decorated with red and black ribbons that stood out against little drifts of sodden leaves. These had to be nuns' vestments, but not those of his employers, the Capuchins. They looked like those worn by sisters behind the wall across the street.[3]

"Look there—the gate's open too!" a bystander exclaimed. By then Leonardo's wife had come out to join him, always curious about any fuss. The pair approached the Convertite's wide carters' gate: the door was indeed unlocked, the bolt barely thrown. Leonardo gave a good hard pull on the bell cord dangling beside the portal to summon a nun gatekeeper—clearly not at her post near the door—from somewhere in the hidden recesses inside the wall.[4]

It was still not much after first light. Still half asleep, Suor Paola Costanza Torosanti, the *portinara*, or gatekeeper, on duty that week, hurried along the wall of a shadowy upstairs hallway until she reached the staircase, then padded down to answer the clangor that jarred everybody's last sweet moments of rest. Crossing the dusky courtyard, she hiked up the hem of her habit to negotiate a muddy corner where she knew a lazy nun often emptied slops from an upstairs window. Then she was startled from her doze: the heavy timber doors of the inner gate were unlocked. She dragged one open wide enough to slip through. The inside bolt on the outer doors several feet ahead of her was also unsecured, and she detected movement outside through gaps and cracks in the boards. She manhandled a door open just enough to discover Leonardo Ortolano and his wife, their arms draped with what were obviously Carmelite nuns' garments. "The gate were open. These were outside, so some nuns must have run off."[5]

"She didn't fall over dead (God forbid!)," Leonardo later recalled. Instead, Suor Paola Costanza, now wide awake, turned and hurried back up the stairs and down the corridor to fetch the prioress. By the time she reached her door she was fighting back tears. "Two sisters have run away, and I don't know how, because I've still got my own keys to the gate!" Prioress Lucina Conti rose stiffly from her kneeler, hastily made herself presentable, mustering whatever dignity she could, then opened her door.

"Look—look here: these are my keys!" Suor Paola Costanza blurted out.

"But how can the sisters have gone if you still have your keys?" the prioress asked mildly. Then she accompanied Suor Paola Costanza downstairs to make sense of it all.

"When I left the house I found these clothes over on the wall," the gardener explained, gesturing across the road toward the Capuchins' fields. "Then I saw that this here gate of yours were open, so I figured right then that some of your nuns must've run away. I rang to give you these clothes."[6] Closer examination revealed a single letter *S* embroidered on the front of one damp wimple and an *L* on the other. Oh, those two: Suor Silveria Catterina Pasi (commonly known as La Generona) and Suor Laura Vittoria Regi (called La Rossa). The prioress also spied some keys, not hanging on a nail in the parlatorio where they should be, but half buried in the unswept debris at her feet, between the inner and outer gates, as if tossed in through the gap above the outer threshold. Rifling through one bundle of cast-off clothing, Prioress Lucina discovered more keys: to Suor Silveria Catterina's cell.

She turned and headed briskly across the courtyard and back upstairs, with a few senior nuns who had filtered down to join her. "Suor Silveria! Suor Silveria! Suor Laura!" Her former mildness had given way to indignation, carefully contained yet unlike anything ever heard through the cell doors along the corridor. Behind the prioress, Suor Paola Costanza quietly secured the gates. A bit late, of course, once the sheep had strayed.[7]

Upstairs, the prioress unlocked the first door on the right side of a vaulted corridor and entered Suor Silveria Catterina's two-room suite: it had been picked clean. In one room the dim early light revealed a walnut kneeler, an ordinary armoire containing a few majolica plates, and a walnut chest with various cooking utensils and a bed warmer or two. In the adjoining room investigators discovered a few low stools and benches, dwarfed by a more imposing walnut armoire emblazoned with a coat of arms. Inside they found little of note besides four baskets of crisp, folded linens, ready for collection. Suor Silveria's parchment certificate of profession lay abandoned in another basket, half hidden beneath scattered sheets of paper, blank or delicately painted with oval miniatures of saints, birds, and flowers.

In a back corner of a lower shelf Prioress Lucina spotted a small paneled casket. She worked to get it open: empty except for two creased sheets of heavy paper, marked on the outside with bits of hardened dark red sealing wax:

> My Lady,
>
> I would like at least to know what game this is we are playing. For me to write and for your ladyship not to respond! Enough! Because if someone is present, you want to do and say something, but as soon as I turn my back, it is goodbye. Wretched is he who too readily believes and puts his trust in a woman who has nothing else to do—or so it seems to me—but to

mock first this one, then that one! Deliver me, O Jesus, save me! I would see her more compassionate, more mindful, more diligent in writing, and—what matters most—more heedful of her word. This is my third letter. Let us see if there is any power in the Trinity. But I will hold my peace, lest I say too much. All the more so because a few words speak volumes to one who truly understands. Console me then, my lady, by your grace, with your letters. And I kiss you there, that fairest part of you.

Rome, February 13, 1644

Your ladyship's most affectionate and most indebted servant,

Desiderio Desiderato

Lucina Conti unfolded a second letter.

My Most Beloved Lady,

At last! After waiting so long, I now feel the greatest contentment that I can have in this world, which is to hold your letters! Even though distance deprives me of that sweet sight of you and of your conversation, yet I remained thoroughly content to behold the sweet remembrance that you keep of promises made. And I pray God to make the outcome of that promise follow quickly. I give you good news about myself: that I am well, and I hope to receive good news about you with your answer. I therefore pray you to remember me, your servant, and to honor me with your commands. And I salute you with all my heart.

Rome, March 4, 1644

My Most Reverend Ladyship's most affectionate and most indebted servant,

Desiderio Desiderato[8]

This second letter was less than a month old. In rooms picked so clean, how could Suor Silveria Catterina have overlooked these egregious testimonials to mischief and inconstancy? Has she cast aside this pathetic, lovesick "Desiderio Desiderato" as carelessly as the letters she overlooked? Or does this sickeningly sweet talk of promises made and promises kept bespeak her rejection of far greater sacred promises and of those who had accepted her, whom she ought to hold dear?

The prioress stuffed the letters back into the casket and returned it to the shelf, firmly closed the cell door, and locked it. Then she reluctantly sent word to the convent's lay administrator.

Prioress Lucina could have saved her messenger a trip. In no time such a delicious convent tale mingling favorite themes in the public imagination (flight from the cloister and fantasies of sexual impropriety), spiced in this case by the character of its protagonists (relapsed convertite), spread far beyond Borgo del Rondone.

Sunlight already softened shadows under the porticoes in the parish of San Martino Maggiore (44.497293° N, 11.346101° E), twenty minutes' walk east of the Convertite, when Giustina Regi, younger sister of the fugitive Suor Laura Vittoria Regi, heard quick footsteps on the stairs of the lodgings she shared with her widowed mother, Lucrezia. "Oh, don't you know—Suor Laura Vittoria has fled!" the breathless Lucrezia Regi exclaimed as she burst in, then fell in a dead faint. Once a quick splash of vinegar had revived her, Giustina pointed out how improbable that rumor sounded. But Giustina would walk over to SS. Filippo e Giacomo to see for herself.

She hastily navigated the streets and alleyways leading to the broad thoroughfare along the Riva di Reno canal (fig. 2, E). She hurried past women already washing laundry on the broad steps at quayside until she came to the church of the Madonna del Ponte delle Lame (44.498396° N, 11.335767° E), looming astride the canal at the intersection with via delle Lame (fig. 2, C). There Giustina spotted a servant from the Convertite, rushing toward her.

"Alas! It's true."

"How did they escape?"

"Last night, through the carters' gateway—oh, what a terrible business this is! You won't find out much if you go there, except that they've fled. That's certain. And all the poor sisters are topsy-turvy."

By the time Giustina followed the servant back along the Riva di Reno, she could barely contain her anger and frustration. There was nothing to do but go home, confirm the family's public disgrace, and try to console her mother.[9]

Bologna's archiepiscopal police captain, or *bargello,* ever alert for violations of church law, may have crossed paths with Giustina on his way to or from SS. Filippo e Giacomo, where he confirmed rumors spreading around the city. He promptly informed Bolognese nuns' vicar Monsignor Ascanio Rinaldi, overseer of all matters concerning the city's two dozen female monasteries. Nuns' Vicar Rinaldi dispatched the archiepiscopal auditor for criminal matters, Monsignor Alfonso Arnaldi, to the scene, plus a notary and appropriate witnesses.[10]

The clerical sleuths first peered at the convent's inner and outer gates. They retrieved the keys, still lying in the dirt, and examined them. They questioned the distraught gatekeeper about how keys might have fallen into the wrong hands. Arnaldi next commanded the prioress to summon all the nuns to the refectory and make note of who failed to answer the bell. (To no one's surprise, La Generona and La Rossa were no-shows.) Then he and his witnesses followed the prioress up the stairs to inspect the fugitives' cells. (In the meantime the assembled sisters had plenty of time to compare notes about the case, which explains the uniformity and rampant hearsay in their subsequent testimony.)

Even in their present state, the opulence of Suor Silveria's private quarters might have given Monsignor Arnaldi pause. The examiners perhaps remarked upon the impropriety of a coat of arms on a nun's furnishings (particularly this sort of nun) and confiscated the telltale love letters, which the notary copied into his transcript. (The originals found their way into the massive record of the affair, where they survive to this day; fig. 6.)

The clerical visitors climbed another flight to Suor Laura Vittoria's cell. Furniture crowded the more modest space, which was obviously shared. An imposing bed dominated the room, overshadowing a second, ordinary bed *alla Romana* (akin to a couch). In a chest they discovered an especially lamentable vanity: a looking glass. Torn up, partially burned papers were scattered on the floor. Auditor Arnaldi commanded his notary to gather up the charred scraps, but he could make nothing of the scant handwriting that had escaped the fire.[11]

Only then did formal interrogations begin. Episcopal visitations followed regular protocols. An interrogator began by questioning those in authority, then summoned the nuns by seniority (the common convent method of enacting hierarchy and subordination). He worked his way down through the professed nuns to novices and *converse* (the convent servants). All the while, the notary hectically copied everything down.

Perhaps Monsignor Arnaldi viewed this as unfamiliar, indeed, treacherous territory: SS. Filippo e Giacomo was not the usual sort of monastic institution. Episcopal visitors regularly complained of immodest necklines on convertite's habits and of gambling with cards and dice. One clerical visitor had to issue the inconceivable command, "The sisters are not to use foul language or filthy words, one to another." That same nuns' vicar also complained, "It is reported that some sisters have three or four cats, and that one has as many as seven."[12] A stickler for ecclesiastical protocol might judge Monsignor Arnaldi's investigative procedures irregular: the auditor seemed to improvise. Some interviews were perfunctory, and he suggested names and events

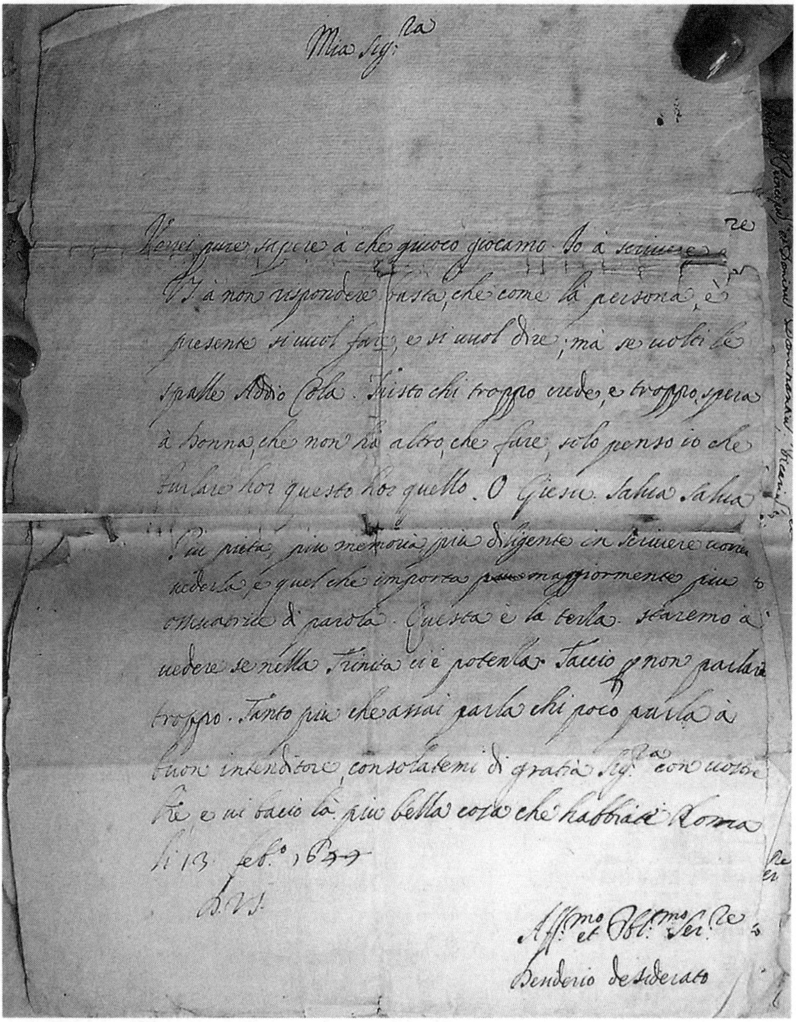

Mia Sig.ra

Vorrei pure sapere à che giuoco giocamo. Io à scrivere V.S. à non rispondere basta, che come la persona è presente si vuol fare, e si vuol dire; mà se volti le spalle Addio Cola. Visto chi troppo crede, e troppo spera à donna, che non hà altro, che fare; solo penso io che burlare hor questo hor quello. O Giesù. Salva Salva

Più pietà, più memoria, più diligente in scrivere [illegible], e quel che importa maggiormente più [illegible] di parola. Questa è la [illegible]. staremo à vedere se nella Trinità ci è potenza. Taccio per non parlar troppo. Tanto più che assai parla chi poco parla à buon intenditore, consolatemi di gratia Sig.ra con vostre [illegible] e vi bacio la più bella cosa che habbiate Roma li 13 feb.o 16[illegible]

V.S.

Aff.mo et Obl.mo Ser.re

Desiderio desiderato

FIGURE 6. Processo. Love letter signed "Desiderio Desiderato," discovered in La Generona's cell. (The two halves, separated by several folios, have been rejoined in the illustration.) Courtesy of the Ministero dei Beni e delle Attività Culturali e del Turismo, Rome, ASRM 64/2014 (further reproduction prohibited).

to lead witnesses more and more overtly as things proceeded. The prospect of interviewing 130 nuns perhaps prompted Arnaldi to abandon established methods and to interrogate his witnesses very selectively, without concern for time-honored principles.

The auditor commanded the prioress to send him any sisters especially familiar with the fugitive Suor Silveria Catterina and Suor Laura Vittoria. He then took his seat in the public half of the parlatorio and waited for his first witness to appear beyond the grilled window that marked the boundary of monastic enclosure. She was neither the prioress nor the *vicaria* (vicaress) nor the bursar, but an aged *conversa* (lay sister) named Suor Eufrasia Maria Dioni. As Suor Eufrasia fidgeted, Arnaldi chose to ignore every inquisitor's standard opening gambit, "Have you any idea why you have been called?" (This question sometimes provoked unanticipated useful responses or, just as often, a disingenuous "I wouldn't know, my lord.")

"How long have you resided in the convent of the Convertite?"

"I've been a conversa here these twenty-seven years."

"What tasks do you fulfill?"

"I serve all the nuns in common. I just do whatever they tell me."

"Do you wait on certain sisters more than others?"

"I serve this one or that one indiscriminately, depending on what's asked of me. But more particularly, I look after my companion of twenty-five years, Suor Paola Emilia, who's been sick in bed these four months."

(This cat and mouse game with a supposed star witness was going nowhere, the notary may have observed, as he waited for the auditor to get somewhere.)

"Do you know the erstwhile Suor Silveria Catterina and Suor Laura Vittoria, and how long have you looked after them?"

(The tight-lipped Suor Eufrasia, doing her best to appear guileless, perhaps wondered if he already knew that she was the pair's personal servant.)

"Yes, my lord, I've known them since they arrived at the convent," Eufrasia responded a shade more politely, but with a noncommittal stare. "And I've always waited on them in the ways they commanded me to."

"What sorts of tasks have you undertaken for them?"

"I've bleached laundry and cooked meals."

"Whose laundry did you do?"

"Oh my, there are so many of the sisters' own things, you see, as well as stuff sent here from outside!"

"Whose laundry do these sisters take in?"

Eufrasia shrugged slightly. "I wash what they give me, and I couldn't say who owns what." After a pause, "I do know that what I washed and dried yesterday, those things came from Count Uguzone Pepoli."

"Can you remember *anybody else's* washing that these nuns gave you to launder?" (The auditor did not hide his dwindling patience.)

"They give me so much laundry to wash that I couldn't possibly know whose it is. I do recall that some of it belongs to Signor Giovanni Braccesi. And it's certainly true that they get so much laundry from so many different people. But other sisters work for them, too, you know."

(In Bologna, the preeminent Pepoli family that Eufrasia mentioned needed no introduction, and Giovanni Braccesi was Cardinal Antonio Barberini's right-hand man. Was she attempting to lodge an understated warning with this nosy cleric about convent friends in higher places? Clearly, she was doing what she could to divert attention from herself.)

"Where are Suor Silveria and Suor Laura?" Arnaldi held her eye as if to say, "Enough beating around the bush." "What happened to them?"

"I don't know where they are. I do know I haven't seen them this morning."

"Well, surely you must at least have heard what has happened to them!"

"I don't know anything else about it besides what's being said publicly around the convent: that they've fled."

"Well, then, who told you that?"

"I first heard it from a sister who came banging on my door and uttered these very words: 'Hey, don't you know those sisters you look after have cleared out?'"

"And how did you respond?"

"How would you like me to respond?" Eufrasia snapped. "Not at all, except to rush out of my cell, lamenting such a disgraceful calamity."

"Do you know who comes to the convent to visit with Suor Laura Vittoria or Suor Silveria Catterina?"

"Oh my, so many come that I wouldn't even know what to say!" Eufrasia replied with another of her exasperating little shrugs. "A priest, Don Carlo Possenti, came, and Signor Bernardino Generoni. But it's been a while since that one visited, and he came here respectably."

"The priest, Don Carlo Possenti—which nun does he visit?"

"Suor Silveria. But I don't know a lot about that, because I, personally, am not one to hang around the parlatorio."[13] Suor Eufrasia arranged her face in a prim expression.

Clearly this one knew more than she was telling. By now the sun was well up, so Arnaldi dismissed her for now and awaited his next witness, who with any luck would be more forthcoming.

A portinara who proudly claimed thirty-seven years of convent life proved the opposite of Suor Eufrasia: she had seen plenty and was more than willing to share whatever she knew (and possibly more). "During my time as portinara, to be sure, I've seen so many—oh, so many—people come to call on that Suor Silveria and Suor Laura Vittoria! I've heard that a certain Signor Guarnieri, an army officer, I believe, who's called Captain, he frequents the place. And Don Carlo Possenti comes here for Suor Silveria Catterina."

"Who comes most often to pass things in and out of the convent?"

"Oh my, I've watched things pass in and out so many times, and especially laundry. Servants come to pick it up five or six times a day. It's true that lately a certain Galeazzo has waited on those two a lot. He was Suor Laura's servant when she was still in the world. And there's also another servant named Leonora. But I've never heard anything from those sisters themselves about who visits them, because they're so thick with each other that they never discuss their doings with any of the rest of us."[14]

The afternoon's final witness, yet another portinara, confirmed the endless stream of gentleman callers for Suor Silveria and Suor Laura. "More than any others, I've seen a certain Captain Donato Guarnieri, for Suor Laura Vittoria, and Don Carlo Possenti, for Suor Silveria Catterina."

"How long is it since you've seen this Captain Guarnieri and this Possenti, and what did they want?"

"In good conscience I'd say that I haven't seen Captain Guarnieri since maybe around Palm Sunday; Suor Laura also said he'd gone away. Possenti has been here after the Easter holiday, if I'm remembering right. But, you see, I see so many people that I just can't keep them all straight in my head."

"Did you ever see the two nuns remove any property from the convent?"

"Just yesterday they sent a large container of linens to the Guarnieri house. Formerly there were large amounts of clothing in their cells, but now I've heard there's nothing left except large furniture. And there were summer and winter coverlets and lots of fabric, more than religious women keep. And now they say that none of it's there anymore."[15]

Whatever light reached the parlatorio had begun to fade, and the lingering late winter chill was creeping back into the unheated room. Monsignor Arnaldi abruptly dismissed the portinara; the notary collected his growing stack of ink-covered pages. Another portinara silently observed from her post near the gate as the two clerics left the parlatorio and disappeared along via del Rondone, among any die-hard curiosity seekers outside.

First thing on Saturday morning, April 2, the auditor summoned the prioress herself.

"Do you know the reason for your present examination?"

Finally, the time-honored opening gambit. Judging by the lack of "my lord" in her response, it took much of Prioress Lucina Conti's accumulated experience in dealing with men, in or out of clerical garb, to control her response to the patently obvious.

"I would imagine you might want to examine me about the investigation of the two nuns," Suor Lucina answered, eying him with an unwavering stare. "Which is to say, Suor Silveria Catterina and Suor Laura Vittoria." Prioress Lucina demonstrated why episcopal visitors should interview her first. She was forthright, less defensive, adequately respectful, appropriately well informed, and certainly firm in her opinions. Her straightforward confirmation of the "facts" (as she construed them) contrasted with the previous day's vagueness.

"I am certainly aware that various people unknown to me came to chat with those two. Among them all, I know that the Guarnieri bunch and Don Carlo Possenti visited them. I also heard that once a foreigner named Filippo Ximenez came to visit. Possenti got into a shouting match with him, because the priest didn't want Ximenez to have anything to do with Suor Silveria. Possenti also spoke uncivilly to Suor Silveria and abused her, and he even threatened to shoot her with a pistol through the parlatorio grate. He slapped Leonora, Suor Silveria's servant, in the face and called her a pimp, expressly forbidding her to deliver anything from Suor Silveria to that foreigner."

"Do you know what went on between these nuns and this Possenti and Guarnieri?"

"Now, I don't know exactly what they all did together, but I do know that they shared an intimate familiarity, and that they were at the grates of the parlatorio every day. Most particularly, when Captain Donato Guarnieri went off to war, he turned his belongings over to Suor Laura Vittoria. He told her he was going off to battle and, should he be killed, was giving it all to her. This was before Christmas, during the military strife."

"Tell me about the ones who waited on these two."

"You mean Galeazzo, Suor Laura's former servant, and Leonora. But nobody more than that Galeazzo, who came to the sisters every day (so to speak) to carry away this and that."[16]

Monsignor Arnaldi therefore expanded his search beyond the convent parlatorio. He immediately dispatched archiepiscopal policemen, called *sbirri*, to compel Suor Silveria's servant Leonora to appear. Leonora was typical of myriad faceless Bolognese women surviving on the margins. A widow with three mouths to feed, she eked out a living as a weaver in Bologna's once-thriving silk trade. Whatever handouts came her way at the Convertite supplemented that paltry income.

Nuns confined within their walls developed symbiotic relationships with the likes of Leonora, their unofficial, often illicit links to the world. They ran errands, carried messages, summoned relatives, in return for a coin or two. Leonora's testimony initially stressed her role in Suor Silveria's convent laundry business. "Suor Silveria sends me to various places: to Count Uguzone Pepoli, to Cardinal Antonio Barberini's man Signor Marcantonio Castrodini, to Cardinal Donghi for laundry, to the Colonel, to Signor Filippo Ximenez."

Arnaldi had to be impressed by Suor Silveria Catterina's illustrious clientele. He already knew that her thriving enterprise extended downtown to the palaces of the rich and into the corridors of power, but not that it also included Cardinal Giovanni Stefano Donghi, who served as commissary resident off in Ferrara. "The Colonel" was Colonel Alessandro Guarnieri (as the notary indicated in the margin), another member of that family increasingly in investigators' sights. Clearly, curial investigators would have to tread lightly in their pursuit of justice, with the toes of so many powerful men in their path.

"Did you ever meet this Guarnieri or speak with him?"

"Yes, my lord, I spoke with *both* of them: that is, with Colonel Alessandro (he's the one with the wife) and also with Captain Donato, his brother. I had frequent conversations with the two of them about things like delivering laundry, and about getting stuff for carnival like swords or men's clothes, which they—the Colonel and his brother—said they didn't have. And once or twice I took letters to Captain Donato. But I don't know what they said because they were sealed and, besides, I don't know how to read."

"Did you see any of these men at the convent, speaking with these nuns?"

"Oh my, yes, my lord, I saw just about all of them. And especially the two Guarnieri brothers with Suor Laura Vittoria and Ximenez and Possenti with Suor Silveria. I saw Possenti on Easter Tuesday, if I'm getting it right, when he told the two sisters he was going to Ferrara."

"Who visits them most of all?"

"I haven't seen anybody who is more their intimate familiar than Captain

Donato Guarnieri with Suor Laura Vittoria and Don Carlo Possenti with Suor Silveria."[17]

Saturday's testimony had improved on Friday's unproductive start, and barely thirty-six hours had passed since discovery of the crime. Before breaking for Sunday, curial investigators ordered the arrest and detention of this much-discussed Galeazzo. If he knew as much as the nuns thought, his examination would usefully open Monday morning's business.

Galeazzo was an even more marginal figure than Silveria's servant Leonora. By age twenty-five, the life of this military casualty with only two ragged shirts to his name (counting the one on his back) had been in decline for years. An outsider with few friends, he lived hand to mouth, alone, near piazza San Domenico (fig. 5, J; 44.490031° N, 11.344503° E). After he joined the papal army, his right hand was injured in battle. Henceforth he was sometimes identified as Monchino (Stumpy or Gimpy), a nickname shared with other walking wounded.

Galeazzo had met Laura Vittoria when they were both children and she was still Gentile Regi. As a woman of the world, half a dozen years his senior, Gentile became his chief preoccupation. His tendency to dog her path like a lovesick pup proved useful once she remade herself as Suor Laura, the convertita, who could use someone in the world always at her beck and call. Galeazzo haunted the convent gate and the parlatorio, hoping for a few coins and the occasional smile or kind word. The convent's secular administrator finally had him and Leonora banned as public nuisances, but Suor Silveria Catterina undid that damage at the next change in convent administration.

Once darkness fell on Sunday, April 3, the archiepiscopal bargello and his sbirri, backed by reinforcements from the papal legate's constabulary, went to arrest Galeazzo at a soldiers' rooming house. The bargello stationed men strategically at intersections and darkened alleyways to block every escape route, then rushed the building with the necessary backup. Alerted by unusual, subdued commotion in the street, Galeazzo spotted them coming, even in thick darkness. He dashed up the stairs and out onto the roof tiles. There his pursuers cornered him, high above the street. But with a desperate leap he cleared the alleyway into the darkness, landing on a roof on the other side. His pursuers could only peer after him as he scurried across the tiles into the night. "Despite our best efforts to find him during the night, we failed to capture him," the sheepish bargello reported first thing Monday morning. "But I shall do everything possible and in my power to find him."[18]

That misadventure set the tone for week two of the investigation, which produced not a single break in the case. The convent bursar's testimony mingled hyperbole with few fresh details about the pair who had emerged as prime suspects. "I've seen a tallish man dressed in red who they say is called Captain Donato Guarnieri come here to speak with those two sisters more times than I've got hairs on my head, and also a Don Carlo Possenti, who's here constantly. And I've often seen them arrive together. Because of the intimate friendship they share, it's said here that they fled with Possenti and Guarnieri. And Possenti last came to see them either Monday or Tuesday after Easter, I heard."[19]

Having failed to snare Galeazzo on Sunday night, authorities tried hauling his mother in on Tuesday morning. She had no clue where he was, and that was fine with her. After this frustration, her interrogator took the rest of the day off. This became a pattern. The nuns waited anxiously through the week, but the parlatorio remained empty of inquisitive clergy. Monsignor Arnaldi turned up again only on Saturday, April 9, just long enough to recall his less-than-stellar witness, the conversa Eufrasia. For a week she had languished in solitary confinement to improve her recollective powers. Arnaldi was wasting his time. By then the fugitives had not been seen for ten days.

On the day when Suor Eufrasia took the stand a second time, Cardinal Girolamo Colonna, absentee archbishop of Bologna, wrote from Rome with his own thoughts on this disturbing news. But another fallow week passed before the archiepiscopal notary entered his letter into the record on April 15. Three days later, now eighteen days after the nuns' disappearance and after a nine-day hiatus, investigators returned to SS. Filippo e Giacomo, back to square one. Once again they charged Prioress Lucina Conti to send in the nuns likely to be well informed in the matter of the wayward sisters. But the prioress was running out of suggestions. Only five nuns made their way to the parlatorio as April drew to a close, with multiple appearances by the determinedly closemouthed Suor Eufrasia, who last faced Arnaldi on April 25.

"So, are you at last disposed to speak more truthfully than in the past?" Arnaldi intoned solemnly. "Do you have anything to add to or retract from your testimony?"

"There's nothing more to say than what I've already said." (By now Eufrasia saw no need at all for an occasional "my lord.") "And I told the truth."

"You've said who provided Suor Silveria's living expenses. Why, then, don't you do so for Suor Laura?"

"What do you want from me? I don't know how they manage things like that."

"That's incredible, when otherwise you should know everything there is to know, given your intimate familiarity with those two."

"I said, I don't know who provides for Suor Laura."

"Where, then, could all of Suor Silveria's and Suor Laura's money come from?"

"I don't know. They work for it, just like I do."

"Do you still deny that when your companion, Suor Paola Emilia, was on her way to testify you told her, 'Don't you go near that business, so you won't do me any damage'?"

"I tell you, I never said that! And if I ever did, may I fall over dead!"

"What if I were to bring in other credible witnesses who have testified that they heard you utter those very words, witnesses who say that you were an accomplice in the crime?"

"Bring on your witnesses! They'll only come in here with their false lies! Because they can't bring the truth! Only Suor Paola Emilia could!"

Eufrasia's mix of defiance and self-assurance perhaps left Arnaldi wondering if she had discovered that frail Suor Paola Emilia had loyally confirmed her friend's every claim the previous week: "With the sacrament in my mouth, I can swear to it all!" she had declared.[20] Had Suor Eufrasia been a servant in the world rather than a conversa, Arnaldi could easily have extracted what she was trying to conceal. But Rome was specific on that score: "Torture: nuns are not customarily subjected to the strappado, though they may be threatened with it."[21]

A month after the nuns' disappearance, Suor Laura Vittoria's mother and sister were also commanded to appear before the archiepiscopal tribunal. They had recently been released from eight days' detention in Bologna's notorious Torrone prison, where they underwent similar interrogations before secular investigators. Sbirri at the Torrone even tried to extort money from them, supposedly to cover expenses for the search for Suor Laura Vittoria. The women made no mention of fending off assaults by their jailers, which were so common that perhaps they went without saying.[22] When they came before Monsignor Arnaldi, both mother and daughter focused their testimony and invective on Carlo Possenti.

"Everyone who comes up to me to talk about it says it must have been a priest they call Possenti who took them away," claimed the mother, Lucrezia

Regi. She had encountered him herself a few days before, when she had gone out to buy some salad greens. "Good evening, my lady," Possenti exclaimed. "What's going on with you, Madonna Lucrezia? You don't look so good."

"How can I look good, what with all my troubles?" Lucrezia hissed.

"And what troubles might those be?" (As if he didn't know, according to Lucrezia.)

"How can I not have troubles, after what's happened to my daughter, who has fled the Convertite?" Then Lucrezia cursed him and wished him every misfortune.

"Oh, just leave it all in God's hands," Possenti preached. "He will put things right."

With that they parted.

"I don't know his character well enough to tell when he's speaking the truth and when he's teasing, but I'd say he was mocking me."[23]

Giustina Regi took her mother's place before the tribunal. Her red hair might have signaled her emotional volatility to interrogators. "I would pay with my own blood to discover whoever helped these sisters! Because he's just going about his business, eating and drinking." Giustina had no doubt as to the culprits. "It's said publicly that it was this Possenti and Donato Guarnieri. I was in the church of San Martino when I overheard somebody say, 'Oh, what rogues that Possenti and Guarnieri were, to spirit away those sisters!'"

The volatile Giustina, too, had recently crossed paths with Carlo Possenti. Two or three days after her release from the Torrone, she was out eating some eggs when she recognized Possenti passing by. "I've got half a mind to call him out and question him, just to see the effect on him," she said to herself. She hailed him and he returned her greeting. "So what do you have to say about these nuns who ran off?" Giustina asked. At first, Possenti blushed hotly and looked aside. Avoiding Giustina's eyes, "he mumbled into his mustache, as the blood drained from his face, 'those two, they were such a pair of ne'er-do-wells!'

"They should arrest him and throw him in prison, that lord and master of this world!" Giustina threw back in the face of her interrogators. "My lord, if I knew any more about all this, you may be sure I'd say so, because with my own hands I'd do my worst to him!"[24]

The impertinent woman glared at the archiepiscopal authorities as if awaiting some response to her challenge. They abruptly dismissed her. When she had gone, they gathered their things, left the empty chambers, and closed the book on the case. Tomorrow, after all, was May Day. Even prelates could not ignore that.

By April 30, 1644, a month after Suor Silveria Catterina and Suor Laura Vittoria's disappearance, everyone from the Bolognese curia presumably agreed that they had done due diligence in "such a painfully difficult business," as Archbishop Colonna put it. The record of the formal investigation for 1644 ends on April 30 with Giustina's outburst. In Rome, records of the Sacred Congregation of Bishops and Regulars, the final authority in matters of monastic discipline, contain not a word about the business of the Bolognese fugitive convertite, which suggests that the cardinals of the congregation were never properly informed.[25]

Many in the long queue of persons of interest, whose names appear and reappear in the month's testimony, had never been summoned to testify: not the oft-cited Count Uguzone Pepoli, or Giovanni Braccesi, both of whom Suor Eufrasia named within minutes of the opening interrogations on April 1. Perhaps local investigators agreed with some nuns that those two were more concerned with their laundry than with those who handled it. More likely the clerics recognized the personal risks of approaching men in positions of privilege, too important, too busy, and too powerful to be bothered about any connections to Suor Silveria and Suor Laura. As for ordinary, more defenseless players, snaring them was no simple task, as the elusive Galeazzo demonstrated. And who would pay the considerable costs of tracking them down and compelling them to testify?

But what about Don Carlo Possenti and Captain Donato Guarnieri? Virtually every convent sister and servant dropped these names. Most of the nuns had witnessed or (more commonly) heard about the pair's suspicious behavior and, in Possenti's case, astounding clerical misbehavior. One has to wonder, as many in the piazza, in the church of San Martino, or on via delle Lame must have wondered, why the local priest and the foreign soldier had been ignored in archiepiscopal efforts at due diligence. Perhaps Cardinal Colonna's deputies believed they had adequately pursued "every possible avenue to recapture the nuns and to discover their accomplices and the perpetrators," as the archbishop had commanded, and had gone as far as expected in the circumstances, as "the gravity and seriousness of the case and its substance demand." They therefore suspended the matter "until such time as God should shed some light on it," as Archbishop Colonna suggested.[26] In the meantime, the curia had more pressing matters to address than a cold case involving two reformed, then relapsed, prostitutes, who by April 30 had not been seen in a month.

Not been seen by these clerics at the archiepiscopal palace, at least.

But there were others in Bologna, those who quietly and invisibly waited, watched, and served in shops and taverns, in kitchens and corridors, back stairs and below stairs in the palaces of families of quality, or who idly waited and observed from Bologna's porticos and piazzas, from boats and docks on the Canale Navile, from barred windows in the Torrone. They might have had a different view and might have told a different story. But apparently they had not been asked and were not talking.

At least not yet.

2

A TALE OF TWO SISTERS

The record of Alfonso Arnaldi's investigation constricts a broader view of the scandal that broke in Borgo del Rondone on April 1, 1644. Beyond the parlatorio at SS. Filippo e Giacomo, what people called the *pubblica voce* (we might call it the word on the street, the court of public opinion, or even the public imagination) swirled around the figures of Suor Silveria Catterina, "La Generona," and Suor Laura Vittoria, "La Rossa." Within hours of the nuns' flight, the populace from Bologna to Ferrara was talking of little else.[1]

Sbirri slipped away from the Torrone in pursuit of phantom leads, returning empty-handed. Sightings of the wayward sisters proliferated after the archbishop's bargello offered twenty-five doubloons to anybody who discovered the pair. A squadron hurried off toward Ferrara after the nuns were spotted near Bondeno (44.88622° N, 11.423° E), twenty-eight miles to the north. On the sbirri's return from this wild-goose chase, the vice legate sent them off to the Canale Navile: La Rossa had just been apprehended on a boat bound for Ferrara. But this La Rossa turned out to be La Bruna: the wrong woman of the world, with only a partial resemblance to the fugitive.[2] Little wonder, then, that when the bargello reported a sighting of La Rossa, dressed as a man, looking down from a shadowy window near the voltone dei Caccianemici (fig. 5, F; fig. 7; 44.492236° N, 11.345210° E), the vice legate heard just one more cry of wolf.[3]

FIGURE 7. Bologna, voltone dei Caccianemici, where La Rossa was last seen alive in mid-May 1644. Photo: Luca Salvucci, Bologna.

Farther afield, the proprietor of Ferrara's tavern at the Sign of the Torretta later recalled a striking pair of foreigners who visited between Easter and early May. Although the short-staffed establishment was overwhelmed with thirsty men-at-arms, the harried barkeeper could not fail to notice the duo in matching male attire of Spanish yellow, garnished with lace, complete with boots, swords, and spurs. The innkeeper's wife pointed out that their walk, talk, and lack of beards betrayed that these were not real men. The mysterious couple's accents marked them as Bolognese. They claimed to be sisters—highly implausible, since one was taller than everyone in the tavern, with bright red hair, and the other was shorter than most and "round like a plum" (as the innkeeper put it), with brown hair. As the pair feasted in the courtyard on the first fennel of the approaching summer, one soldier at the bar sneered, "They're just two common whores from Bologna." After the enigmatic duo vanished the next morning, many assumed they continued their pleasure outing in Venice. "I've heard that the two nuns supposedly stayed at my inn," the innkeeper remarked. "They couldn't have been anybody but those two ladies."[4]

But before long, darker rumors began to pass among Bologna's shoemakers, chambermaids, barbers, and booksellers. The nuns' bodies were discovered in the crypt of the monks of San Giovanni Battista Celestini (fig. 5, P). Their remains also turned up in a dark corner of one of Santo Stefano's seven churches (fig. 5, D). Particularly credulous chin-wags whispered that La Generona and La Rossa had been found in the cellars beneath the Palazzo del Legato with their throats slit (fig. 5, H).[5]

Then overnight Bologna had more pressing problems to think about. On May 9 the Bolognese awoke in the midst of a blizzard: before midmorning, almost eight inches of snow buried the city. Limbs in full leaf sagged under its weight, cracked, and fell from trees all over town. Lifeless birds littered snow-clogged streets as if frozen in midflight. Snow gave way to ice and freezing fog that laid waste tender crops. Three days of rain turned valleys into lakes. When the water receded, farm animals' bloated bodies dotted the countryside.[6]

At least the depredations of men were finally ending. After solemn mass at the basilica of San Petronio in early May, with Cardinal Legate Antonio Barberini officiating, and a festive *Te Deum* sung amid salvos of musket fire in the piazza and trumpet blasts from the Palazzo del Legato, peace was formally proclaimed, ending the War of Castro. The city endured one last invasion when the holy father's regiments marched back to Bologna, where most were disbanded. Discharged soldiers drifted north toward Germany and Bohemia or caught ships from Genoa to Spain or Malta, in search of other conflicts. By late September Bologna finally saw the last of them, "at which all the people rejoice and the territory breathes a sigh of relief," as an official wrote to Bologna's ambassador to Rome.[7]

What of the quartet of players who piqued public curiosity and enriched gossip in churches and piazzas until nature's distractions struck close to home? Like their contemporaries, we are bound to wonder about that transgressive pair of female outsiders who briefly monopolized the pubblica voce, only to be forgotten in a few weeks. What of their alleged male accomplices, who still prompted speculation when spotted promenading, free and unmolested, through the piazza and in the shade of the city's arcades?

WOMEN OF THE WORLD

> Amongst other things that I heard of these kinde of women in Venice, one is this, that when their Cos amoris [whetstone of love] beginneth to decay, when their youthfull vigor is spent, then they consecrate the dregs of their olde age to God by going into a Nunnery, having before dedicated the flower of their youth to the divell: some of them also having scraped together so much pelfe by their sordid facultie as doth maintaine them well in their old age.[8]

Although Thomas Coryat was describing Venice's courtesans shortly after 1600, the righteously indignant British tourist might have been speaking of Suor Silveria Catterina and Suor Laura Vittoria. The challenges they faced and their life choices, at least until the moment they chose to flee SS. Filippo e Giacomo, were typical of any number of women "of the ordinary sort" in any number of Italian cities.

Aut virum aut murum oportet mulierem habere ("a woman should have a husband or a [convent] wall") pithily summed up noble and upper-class women's life choices for hundreds of years after it was coined in late medieval times. In the 1500s, on the other hand, Pietro Aretino recognized virtues in other options open to lower-class women. In his *Six Days: An Argument between Nanna and Antonia* (1534 and 1536), the prostitute Nanna and her friend Antonia ponder the pros and cons of the opportunities available to Nanna's daughter Pippa. After considering the roles of wife and nun, Antonia proposes the best alternative, "My opinion is that you should make that Pippa of yours a whore." Aretino's rhetoric was about the most "honest" career path for Pippa, given Italy's moral hypocrisy, especially among the elite and the clergy. For many women living on the edge who took similar maternal advice to heart, the choice was about making the most of the one natural resource that might ease their personal situation.[9]

A seventeenth-century Bolognese woman who fell below the equivalent of today's top 2 percent was often expected to help her family make ends meet: unlike patricians, ordinary women worked for pay. The death or disappearance of a male breadwinner could tip the balance of a lower-class family's subsistence into crisis. In cities such as Bologna, Milan, and Venice after 1600, 20 percent of households confronted that precarious reality. Leonora, Suor Silveria Catterina's servant turned messenger, the widow with three mouths to feed who haunted the parlatorio in hope of a few coins, puts a face on that statistic.[10]

With subsistence and survival in the balance, poor women left moral niceties to those who could afford them. They turned to prostitution to help their families get by or to improve their own lot in life. After all, one charming night of another's delight was worth more than two or three unlucky days of spinning silk.

Suor Laura Vittoria, known to the world as Gentile Regi, came from such a family, consisting of her widowed mother Lucrezia and her sister Giustina, two years younger and married, but with her husband nowhere in sight by 1644. Clerics perceived such ungoverned households of women as potential sinks of promiscuous immorality. Of almost a hundred women the Bolognese archiepiscopal curia investigated for alleged prostitution in the late 1600s, for example, only eight had a man around the house.[11] Word on the street claimed that both Gentile Regi's mother and her sister were also prostitutes, but nothing suggests that their neighbors ever denounced them to the city's registry of licensed women of the world. Not a single Giustina appeared on those lists between 1627 and 1645; of the half dozen Lucrezias, none appears to have been Gentile Regi's mother.[12]

Like many other Italian cities, Bologna maintained such lists in order to track and tax public prostitutes, whose livelihood was legal, if lamentable, and subject to government oversight. Men in authority remained ever mindful of the danger that other men posed to the imperiled virtue of their own wives and daughters. In cities such as Florence and Venice, lawmakers also worried that unmarried sons without a means to dampen raging hormones might solve the difficulty man to man. So legislators turned a blind if disapproving eye toward prostitution as a necessary though evil way to divert men's illicit impulses.

Gentile was born in 1614 to a Domenico Regi, who had passed out of Lucrezia Regi's household by the early 1640s. Gentile grew up near the southern edge of downtown, in Borgo delle Tovaglie (44.488636° N, 11.342063° E), not far from the basilica of San Domenico (fig. 5, J; 44.490031° N, 11.344503° E). Even today the modest houses and shadowy low portico along via delle Tovaglie (fig. 8), hedged in by the high wall of the monastery of San Procolo across the narrow street, conveys a feeling of marginality and constraint.[13]

Perhaps Lucrezia Regi introduced her daughter to the family business, a common enough reality among sex workers. But young Gentile Regi eventually struck out on her own. She lived not in the parish of San Martino where her mother and sister resettled by the 1640s, but in Borgo delle Casse, ten minutes away (around modern-day via Maggia and via delle Casse).[14] Gentile was a common-enough name in the registers of prostitutes, but none of them appears to be Gentile Regi. Men from all over town and from all levels of society seemed to know her, if only by sight. There was the bargello, mentioned earlier, who recognized her near the voltone dei Caccianemici. Admirers pointed her out to Cardinal Barberini's secretary of briefs, Giovanni Braccesi, although by then they called her somewhat ungenerously "a rather old courtesan." Count Ercole Bentivoglio presumably had more than a passing knowledge of her since, some sisters said, he provided her monthly convent provisions.[15]

It is no wonder so many men recognized Gentile, because this head turner would catch any man's eye. The bright red hair that prompted her trade name, La Rossa, flagrantly proclaimed her identity. Her extraordinary height—close to six feet—made her even harder to miss. "In the convent where there must be 130 nuns, only one might have been her equal," a conversa remembered. Or, as an admiring guard in the piazza put it, "She was a man-sized woman, tall, very grand—and white like a snowflake!" (Nature bestowed on Gentile a much-admired naturally white complexion that was always a cause for comment.)[16] So she stood out in (and above) the crowd: long-limbed but nicely proportioned. She must also have deployed her notably long, elegant hands to advantage, for they, too, rarely escaped notice.

A single inharmonious feature also made La Rossa immediately recognizable: a scar marred her lily-white complexion. It began below her left ear and ran several inches down her cheek before disappearing under her jaw. Although it had healed and faded since she received the wound in her late teens, the mark rarely escaped notice, even when hedged in by a wimple

FIGURE 8. Bologna, via delle Tovaglie, where La Rossa grew up.

during her convent days.[17] Indeed, it was a similarly scarred face that provoked the misidentification of La Bruna, the prostitute arrested on the bark to Ferrara.

We can be quite certain that La Rossa's scar was a work-related injury, particularly because another long scar on her right forearm and the missing tip of her right little finger suggest defensive wounds. The *sfregio*, or scar to mark a vendetta, was sufficiently common among prostitutes that a didactic print by Giuseppe Maria Mitelli, *The Whore's Unhappy Life, Divided into*

FIGURE 9. Giuseppe Maria Mitelli, *La vita infelice della meretrice* (1692), "Ottobre." A prostitute receives a *sfregio*. Reproduced with permission of the Biblioteca Comunale dell'Archiginnasio, Bologna.

Twelve Months of the Year (1692, fig. 9), incorporates just such a slashing for "October." As Aretino's Balia puts it, "The *fregio* and the sign of the *mal franzese* signify the perfection of the art of bawdry. And just as the wounds that soldiers pick up in battle make them appear more valorous and gallant, so the fine scars of little knives reveal more than a pander's passing marks: such things are the pearls that adorn us."[18]

Suor Silveria Catterina's history from her days as Cornelia Pasi, on the other hand, remains elusive, partly because she had lived behind convent walls for a dozen years before this story begins. We know only that Cornelia was born in 1604, the daughter of a Ludovico Pasi and his wife, Domenica.[19]

Rumor said that Cornelia had been a woman of the world for about fourteen years before joining the Convertite: she must have fallen into sin in her early teens. We know nothing of her life during the next decade. She would have been the sort of woman described today as "cute": five feet tall at most, with dark chestnut hair and a long face. Her fair complexion set off lively dark eyes. But everyone agreed about her most attractive physical attribute: perfectly white, even teeth. Even after a decade of convent life, Suor Silveria

Catterina still remained that rare sight in religion, and an oxymoron in the public imagination: a smiling nun. Her perfect dentition, even as a forty-year-old, reveals that she recognized a value in keeping her teeth when all about her were losing theirs, even when, theoretically, it should no longer have mattered.[20]

But nice teeth alone would not draw gentleman callers to the parlatorio, as Suor Silveria did, despite her monastic habit and approaching middle age. Refined interpersonal skills must have played a part in her abiding allure. Reminiscence by Giovanni Braccesi's page, on the verge of manhood, offers a hint of her method. Dispatched to the convent to retrieve his master's linen, the youth did not forget the flirtation of the nun old enough to be his mother. "She asked what Signor Giovanni was up to, and I told her things were good. And she replied, 'He never lets us see him—that awakens longing.' So I answered, 'He's got things to do,' and so he couldn't fix that. Then she replied, 'Kiss your lord's hand for me.'"[21]

The full range of Cornelia Pasi's and Gentile Regi's personal charms also surpassed those of the everyday prostitute. One of their eventual sisters in religion remarked disapprovingly, "Oh, they were two skilled, subtle-witted sisters, who knew how to read and write." Another commented, with a shade more admiration, "Suor Silveria and Suor Laura Vittoria knew how to read and write well; they knew how to do needlework, and Suor Laura Vittoria could do embroidery." More akin to nuns in Bologna's exclusive, upper-tier convents, both these convertite were adept at embroidery and lacemaking.[22]

Suor Silveria Catterina also practiced the genteel art of limning (judging by those oval miniature paintings left behind in her cell). A servant also remembered delivering a harpsichord to Suor Laura Vittoria, when she was planning to entertain some gentlewomen in the parlatorio. Men would have been no less attracted to La Rossa's keyboard skills, judging by Niccolò Martelli's compliment to the Venetian courtesan Tullia d'Aragona in 1546, "People are amazed when they hear your beautiful white hands play any instrument so delicately." This array of talents suggests that, although the two may not have held a candle to such renowned courtesans as Veronica Franco in Venice or Nina Barcarola in Rome, they outshone those wives waiting at home for the Bolognese aristocrats and wealthy merchants whom Cornelia and Gentile entertained late into the night.[23]

About 1630 Cornelia Pasi's life began to change: she gave birth to a little girl she named Catterina. The elusive father did not vanish without a trace. At the time of Suor Silveria's convent escape, this Antonio Giovannoni was

FIGURE 10. Bologna, Piazza San Salvatore, with a pharmacy on the corner opposite; the parish of La Generona's keeper, the apothecary Bernardino Generoni.

a monk at the Capuchin convent of San Bartolomeo in Imola, twenty-five miles away.[24]

Within the year, Cornelia entered into an arrangement with one Bernardino Generoni, a *speziale* (a grocer or apothecary) from Bologna's close-knit expatriate community from Bergamo. Generoni lived above his shop in the parish around the church of San Salvatore (44.493805° N, 11.339551° E), a few blocks west of the piazza. (By an interesting coincidence, a pharmacy still occupies the corner of the ancient building right across the piazza from San Salvatore, looking much as it may have looked in the 1630s; fig. 10.) From then on Cornelia was called La Generona.

Women of the world who entered into such relationships sometimes came to an understanding with their keepers, who promised them a future bridal or convent dowry and in the meantime provided a certain security.[25] Cornelia may have had outside encouragement to abandon the world. After two years together, Bernardino Generoni began to urge her to withdraw to the cloister. The ever-loyal Leonora took credit for persuading Cornelia to become a nun, and the veteran convertita Suor Paola Costanza Torosanti agreed to sponsor her. Generoni promised to cover all monastic costs for the present and future. He would prove almost as good as his word.[26]

A final, potentially more sinister reality might have motivated Cornelia's retirement, however. The prioress described Suor Silveria Catterina as "bald." Another observer remarked, "As near as I could tell, she had slight scars of the pox." Hair loss and pockmarks identified survivors of smallpox, of course. But ever since the early 1500s, both were also associated with an evil invariably mentioned in the same breath with prostitution: syphilis.[27]

BEHIND THE WALL

On October 28, 1632, La Generona appeared in the church of SS. Filippo e Giacomo. Perhaps the chapel aroused misgivings: its modest size (with only a single pair of side altars) was far less imposing than the churches she commonly frequented. (Bernardino Generoni's magnificent parish church of San Salvatore had as many as nine altars, for example.) But the Convertite chapel looked to be in decent repair, after reasonably recent refurbishment in the modern style. In the year of Cornelia's arrival the convent also hung an impressive new bell in its campanile to remind residents in Borgo del Rondone of its spiritual presence.[28] From above the chapel's high altar, a dying Christ on the cross, flanked by Philip and James, perhaps seemed to observe the latest convent arrival (fig. 11). An inconsolable Mary Magdalene clutching the cross, the paradigm for every repentant woman, ignored her, forgetting everyone but Jesus. La Generona would now be called on to do likewise.

With indecorous haste (a potential convertita should have undergone three months' probation), the party reassembled in the church just ten days later. By then Generoni had agreed to provide a dowry of £1,000 (less than a fifth of what patrician parents paid at upscale convents).[29] On November 7, Cornelia Pasi received a novice's habit and her new name in religion. Although Bologna's repentant prostitutes tended to favor patently virtuous

FIGURE 11. Bartolomeo Passerotti, *Crucifixion with Saints Philip, James, and Mary Magdalene*, formerly above the high altar in the church of the Convertite, now in the parish church of SS. Filippo e Giacomo.

names (Patience, Innocence, Hope, Clemency, Prudence, or Constancy), Cornelia chose Silveria Catterina.

For the next year Suor Silveria Catterina lived under the watchful eye of Suor Paola Costanza Torosanti, who forever regarded her as her *creatura*. Then, on November 20, 1633, the novice took her solemn vows. A busy pair of nun sacristans, who saw to what seemed like an endless succession of such chapel services, recorded day-to-day ceremonies in narrow ledgers called *vacchette*, bound in old parchment recycled from medieval manuscripts. Among perhaps a dozen such vacchette to survive four centuries is the one sacristans kept in 1632–33 (fig. 12). On a leaf sandwiched between dozens of blank pages of creamy white paper, the sacristan recorded the late October expenses "for the acceptance of Signora Cornelia." Immediately below, she noted the cost of Cornelia's clothing ceremony on November 7.

In late 1633 the sacristan once again leafed through the still largely blank pages until she found last year's record for Suor Silveria Catterina. There she chronicled her final rite of passage and the newly professed nun's donation for charity. Instead of hundreds of lire spent for a blaze of candles and silver gilt on the high altar, for double-choir music, and for trumpets blaring in the street outside, which characterized such occasions at elite convents uptown, the sacristans at SS. Filippo e Giacomo recorded for each of Cornelia's modest rites of passage a mere £5: for a single large processional candle and a pair of short, heavy candles. Suor Silveria Catterina in turn offered a charitable donation of one zecchino—a single gold coin.[30]

Barely a week after taking her solemn vows, Suor Silveria Catterina took her place among the professed nuns in the parlatorio to affirm legal documents. After 1633 her name appears in some sixteen documents, listing nuns in order of seniority. She gradually works her way up from the very bottom until January 1642: no lists have come to light for the two years before her flight. A search through the convent archive yields no further trace of "Suor Silveria Catterina Pasi." She remains only a barely legible name, hidden among a hundred others. What we can learn of her therefore depends on what those who knew her chose to reveal (or to fabricate) when authorities summoned them to testify a dozen years later.

We do know that about 1635 little Catterina joined her mother at the convent. At more conventional monastic houses, cloistered aunts customarily took in young girls. While the Convertite likewise found room for aunts and their nieces, the young Catterina would have encountered other mothers and

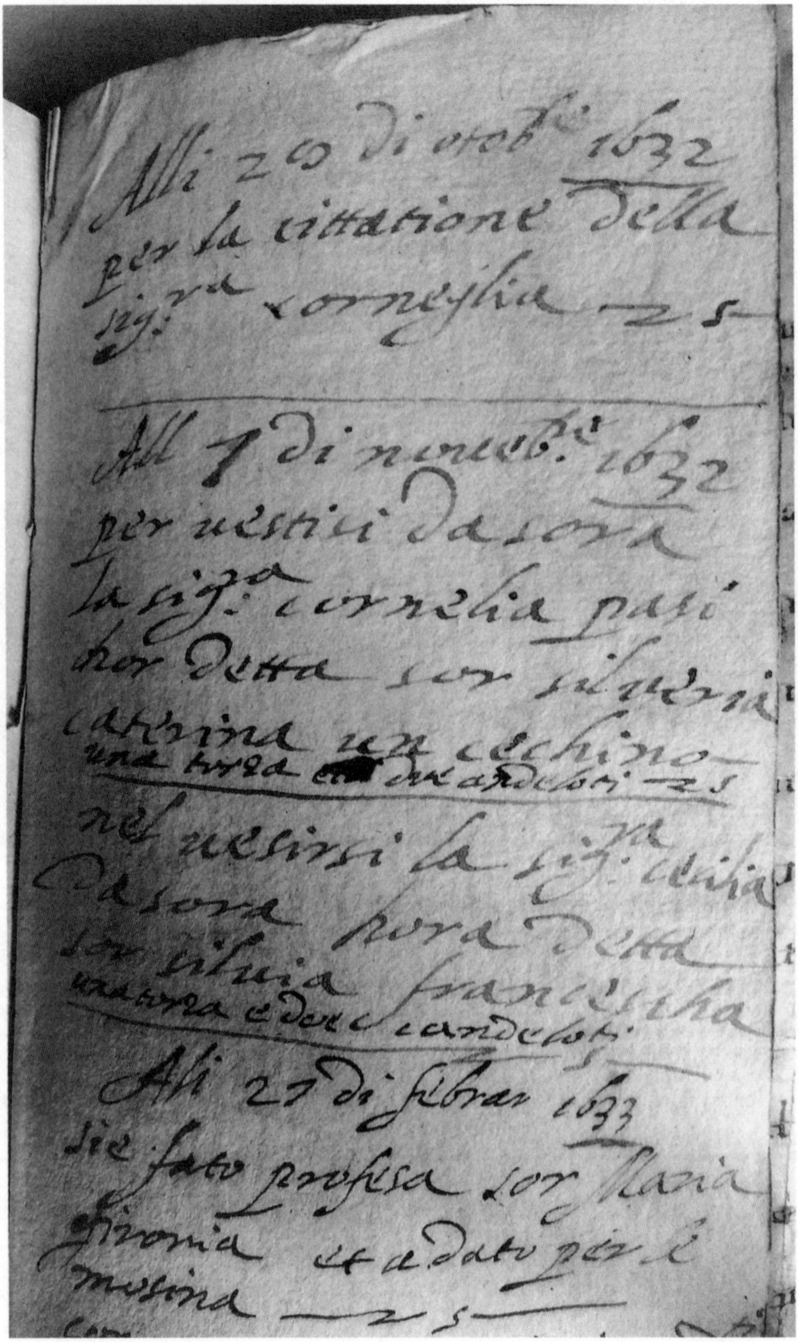

Alli 20 di ottob.re 1632
per la vestitione della
sig.ra Cornelia — 25

Alli 7 di novemb.re 1632
per vestirsi da sora
la sig.ra Cornelia pasi
hor detta sor Silveria
Catterina un cechino
una torta e dui candeloti — 25
nel vestirsi la sig.ra Cecilia
da sora hora detta
sor Silvia Francescha
una torta e dui candeloti

Ali 27 di febrar 1633
si e fato professa sor Maria
Gironima et a dato per le
mesina — 25

daughters: an arrangement of great concern to the ecclesiastical hierarchy, ever mindful of prostitutes' predisposition to corrupt their offspring.

Although such premature arrivals at the Convertite often remained there for life, Suor Silveria Catterina was determined that her daughter should enter a more respectable house. When Catterina reached the requisite age of twelve, Suor Silveria enrolled her among the Lateran Canonesses of San Lorenzo. Shortly before Christmas in 1643, in anticipation of her daughter's eventual profession, Suor Silveria sent her all the furnishings required for comfortable convent living.[31] After the events of April 1, 1644, clerical investigators suspected that this convent trousseau was part of the fugitive mother's plan to leave nothing behind when she made her escape. Perhaps they were right.

We know hardly anything of Suor Silveria Catterina's convent life during the late 1630s. The apothecary Generoni stopped by now and again, perhaps smelling of nutmeg, cloves, or almond oil, to share light repasts in the parlatorio. He continued to offer the occasional lavish gift that raised eyebrows within the cloister. Apart from her servant Eufrasia, Suor Silveria made few friends on the inside. Except, that is, for Suor Angela Ginevra Gnocchi. "She was a good girl, La Gnocchia was, but then she became friends with Suor Silveria, who was her undoing." (Or at least that was how the bursar remembered things with the benefit of mid-1640s hindsight.)[32]

Suor Angela may not have needed much "undoing." A soldier named Francesco Gonzino had known Suor Angela (carnally, all agreed) before she entered the Convertite in 1631. He habitually visited over the years, and by the late 1630s he started arriving with Carlo Possenti, who paired off with Suor Silveria Catterina. In convent lore, recollections of the soon inseparable sisters, the enamored soldier, and the disreputable priest, plotting together in the parlatorio, became act 1 to 1644's act 2 in a morality play that had yet to play itself out. It seems that the restless Suor Silveria had been plotting her escape for years. ("Oh, it's been so many years that even if I wanted to tell you how many I couldn't!" exclaimed the bursar.)

But an assassin ambushed Gonzino. He lingered a week on his deathbed, long enough to send a Capuchin monk to exhort the pair of convertite to learn from his example: Angela and Silveria should be good nuns "and no

FIGURE 12 (*opposite page*). ASB, Corporazioni religiose soppresse, 9/6828. Sacristan's record of Cornelia Pasi's acceptance and clothing ceremony at the Convertite (1632). Reproduced with permission of the Ministero per i Beni e le Attività Culturali, Bologna (no. 1102, October 9, 2014).

longer have that heart's desire to flee." In retrospect one sister claimed, "Some said that if Gonzino hadn't died, Suor Angela and Suor Silveria her companion would have fled the convent together with Gonzino and Possenti, his companion." A disconsolate Suor Angela Ginevra followed Gonzino not long thereafter, her once-imperiled soul presumably secure and on its way to a better life. But Suor Silveria Catterina remained deaf to Gonzino's exhortations, already plotting the next act (or so some nuns later imagined).[33]

Gentile Regi entered the convent scene in 1641, filling the void left by Suor Angela. A search for Gentile Regi in the convent archive creates the uneasy feeling that when she fled, she managed to expunge virtually all archival traces of herself. Suor Laura Vittoria Regi appears in none of those parlatorio roll calls where Silveria Catterina turns up. After Silveria and Laura's flight, investigators dispatched a notary to SS. Filippo e Giacomo, where the convent's lay administrator handed over an impressive volume bound in tooled leather highlighted in gold. The notary copied the record of Gentile's profession: on February 18, 1642, Gentile made her monastic profession in the hands of Bolognese nuns' vicar Monsignor Ascanio Rinaldi and took the name Suor Laura Vittoria. That same nuns' vicar would be among the first to hear of her flight barely two years later.

That imposing volume has vanished, probably into some bibliophile's collection, but the far less pretentious sacristan's vacchetta for 1640–42 escaped such pilferers. In November 1641 the sacristan initially recorded in a crude, barely legible scrawl, "I Suor Vicenza Felice, the same week, we accepted Signora Gitile [*sic*] as a nun; she gave one double ducat as a charity offering to the sacristy" (fig. 13). Laura Vittoria made a grand convent entrance. Her sister Giustina was on hand on via del Rondone to watch when the carters' gate swung open to admit an impressive cartload of furniture, testimony to La Rossa's success in the world she was leaving behind. "In that convent there was nobody who had stuff like what my daughter had," her mother proudly recalled.[34]

Suor Silveria Catterina assumed the role of Laura's "maestra" right away, to teach her the ins and outs of convent life. Although Laura did spend the requisite three months on probation, there is no record of a full novice year, only a cryptic note in the notary's copy of her profession from the vanished volume, "having been exempted from that." In mid-February 1642, the sacristan dutifully reopened her little vacchetta to record, "The same week, Signora Gintille was made a nun and a professed nun; she gave two double ducats as a charitable offering to the sacristy." That is the last record of Suor Laura Vittoria's convent existence.[35]

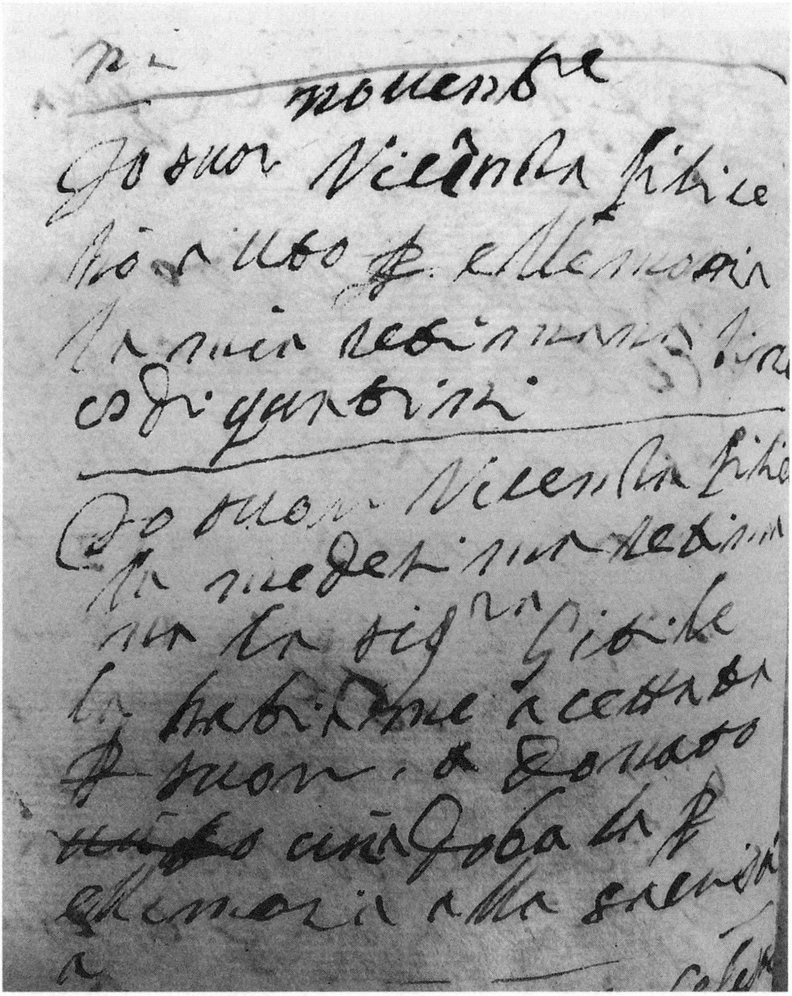

FIGURE 13. ASB, Corporazioni religiose soppresse, 9/6828. Sacristan's record of Gentile Regi's acceptance at the Convertite (1641). Reproduced with permission of the Ministero per i Beni e le Attività Culturali, Bologna (no. 1102, October 9, 2014).

It was not long before nuns began to notice that Laura Vittoria was becoming the new Angela Ginevra. "Those two sisters were always inseparable," according to one nun, "and lived their lives constantly together—whether eating, or drinking, or sleeping, as if connected. They couldn't have been more closely joined." Disapproval of their exclusive ways also resonated within the wider community. "Those two sisters were the type to show off how much they always had going on at the grates, parlatorio, and the gate. And they were standoffish compared with some sisters here in the convent, though they'd order many of them about. But they wouldn't chat with anyone in a way that ever let them figure out what they were up to."[36]

"TOO MUCH FREEDOM AT THE GATE AND THE GRILLES . . . AS IF THIS WERE NOT A SACRED PLACE!"

Then, far from such hints of intramural disharmony, fiercer male quarrels between the Barberini papacy and Odoardo Farnese, Duke of Parma, flared into the War of Castro. With soldiers streaming into town by Christmas 1642, not only Bologna's women of the world had their hands full. There were many more mouths to feed, thirsts to slake, weary or drunken bodies to bed down, and, naturally, piles of dirty linen to bleach and starch. SS. Filippo e Giacomo felt the invasion's disruptive effects more than most of Bologna's convents.

All Bologna's nuns performed some sort of "manual labor." The most refined monastic hands created artificial roses with a natural look and odor (at Santa Margarita) or confected sugar candies shaped like fish (at San Giovanni Battista). Lesser institutions kept busy with appropriately ruder tasks. Dealing with dirty laundry fell to Bologna's reformed prostitutes. Not just any laundry, however. As an eighteenth-century Bolognese poetaster put it in the caption to a watercolor showing a convertita hard at work (fig. 14), "They starch fine sleeves, they starch fine collars / For prelates, priests, and for lay scholars."[37] But had he been writing during the War of Castro, this poet might well have concluded "For *soldiers*, priests, and for lay scholars."

To more pious convertite, it may have seemed that Commander Cornelio Malvasia was launching military assaults against Borgo del Rondone rather than against the Duke of Parma. One venerable elder later proclaimed, "There's been too much freedom, with so many sorts of people coming here, which easily caused this sorry episode. And in future it will be necessary to address this, as I mightily desire!" Another senior sister chimed in to deplore

FIGURE 14. BCB, MS B 3574. A Bolognese convertita ironing linens (seventeenth century). Reproduced with permission of the Biblioteca Comunale dell'Archiginnasio, Bologna.

"too much freedom at the gate and at the grilles! Without any respect, as if this were not a sacred place!"[38]

With baskets of laundry streaming in through the gate, many of the sisters (at least after April 1644) held Suor Silveria Catterina and Suor Laura Vittoria responsible. "They were almost always at the grates, and so many gentlemen and foreigners came that sometimes there were ten or twenty people here for them." Or, as one portinara extravagantly put it, "A lot of pages and servants came for them—they were summoned four thousand times a day, so to speak!" So the nuns counterattacked: they informed Bernardino Generoni that Suor Silveria was frequenting the parlatorio. Generoni cut her off without a quattrino.[39]

By then perhaps it no longer mattered. Suor Silveria Catterina seems to have combined business acumen with entrepreneurial spirit to create a thriving laundry business in a time of expanding markets. What her cloistered sisters, ex-boyfriend, and clerical superiors perceived as insufficient modesty we might see as initiative and commitment to good customer service. Sister after sister expressed dismay to hear Silveria and Laura "running frantically" to meet their clients. Perhaps these cloistered businesswomen recognized that even servants and soldiers with money in their purses did not like to be kept waiting. After the burgeoning business required taking on assistants, Suor Eufrasia never spoke to male customers, who were best left to Suor Silveria. Playful affability, particularly when accompanied by a flash of those much-admired teeth, offered more encouragement to repeat business than a frigid display of sanctimony.[40]

As business boomed, the pair elevated Suor Eufrasia to shop foreman in return for a modest cut of the earnings. "'Who wants to work for Cardinal Donghi?' Suor Eufrasia said one day, and I said, 'So give it to me. I'll take it because I've got no work,'" one sister later testified. "So she handed it over. And since then she's always given me collars, sleeves, and handkerchiefs to starch." Little by little, laundry earnings trickled down.[41]

Suor Silveria and Suor Laura also pointed out when certain garments needed to be replaced: they could also help with that. When they expanded their cloister enterprise into the sewing and sale of linens, they also continued to subcontract. They hired less talented sisters to sew up new shirts, handkerchiefs, and collars (for a pittance). Then they themselves added fine lace in the Flemish style on cuffs, collars, and shirt fronts and sold the finished products to local gentlemen and foreign soldiers for several times what they had cost to make. Even if they sometimes entrusted the finer needlework to another sister, they took credit for it themselves. (Good business practice required that their clients assume they were donning the delicate work of Suor Laura Vittoria's fair white hands or of the little lady with the shining eyes and mystic smile, not the work of some convent drudge.)[42]

Their sisters in religion watched in dismay as Suor Silveria and Suor Laura laid up for themselves one earthly treasure after another. Silveria, of course, some whispered, already had a purse full of doubloons when she came through the gate back in 1632. Laura's cartload of furniture had included a very grand armoire painted and polished in imitation of marble, with a cat painted on one side looking as if it might be alive. Suor Silveria had also inherited all of Suor Angela Ginevra's worldly goods (including a diamond ring worth £200, to which she later added a large central diamond worth £300). For years Bernardino Generoni also continued his largesse. (Silveria added still more links to a gold chain he'd once given her: when she wore it, the chain hung halfway down her thighs!)

But there was (much) more. Silveria owned twenty or thirty rings, three gold crosses, and several rosaries—just the coral on one was worth fifteen scudi. Silveria's armoire shimmered with silver, including a pair of large silver plates, fulsomely engraved SSCP (Suor Silveria Catterina Pasi), each worth twenty-five scudi, and numerous other pieces, plus ten silver forks and spoons and as many knives with silver handles. She had "everything you could list" when it came to linens: more than a hundred ladies' blouses and forty pairs of sheets, plus countless elegant towels and tablecloths richly decorated with fine Belgian lace. "In a word, she had more herself than the entire convent," Generoni remarked (thinking especially of his own munificence). One nun spoke for them all: "The fact is, she lived like a princess."[43]

Suor Eufrasia asserted that Suor Laura Vittoria "had little" by comparison. Still, Laura could claim her own piles of fine linens and an ample supply of silver forks and spoons, some silver fruit plates, a ring with a rosette of rubies, and another decorated with a Maltese cross in enamel. Captain Giovanni Francesco Tenerino gave La Rossa a stunning rosary of emeralds and, in 1643, a full Carmelite habit of fine serge. (One suspects that Tenerino's mind was less on her spiritual welfare than on the famously fine white flesh the habit would soon be prickling.)[44]

Thus Suor Silveria and Suor Laura had scraped together precisely the pelfe that Thomas Coryat deplored (although they did so in a new, "respectable" profession). But the censure such unseemly wealth provoked inside SS. Filippo e Giacomo was eclipsed by the schadenfreude incited by the pair's scandalous behavior in the parlatorio with the priest Possenti and the eye-catching Captain Donato Guarnieri, who were so many years younger than the nuns. Possenti had haunted the parlatorio ever since Suor Angela Ginevra Gnocchi's day. When Guarnieri showed up, what did Suor Laura do? The former prioress fumed, "It's public knowledge—and patently obvious—that if the gatekeepers called to Suor Laura Vittoria, 'Captain Donato Guarnieri is here and wants you,' then she immediately went running with Suor Silveria. I'm an old woman of seventy-four years, so my eyesight is not great. But I know that Captain Donato was Suor Laura Vittoria's beloved—that's clear and manifestly known to all the sisters!" Where would it all end? Certainly not in any good place.[45]

Suor Maria Diana Sturoli had seen nothing like it in all her years serving in every office from prioress right on down to convent bursar, the position she filled in spring of 1644. She also knew the protocols of convent security in her sleep: the gatekeeper kept the key to the inside gate in her cell. The key to the outer gate should hang on a nail in the parlatorio, which should be locked up after dark. The parlatorio key (which also worked other interior locks) should be returned to the prioress. That was all well and good, but it made things inconvenient for the bursar attempting to go about her business, which did not simply end at sundown. So it made sense to close up the parlatorio but hide the key in the door curtain. Then Suor Maria Diana, as bursar, could retrieve it when she needed to unlock the pantry late in the evening to fetch the next day's bread.

A little before 10:00 p.m. on March 31, she and her conversa soundlessly went about their business through the Great Silence that filled the hallways, by then darker than dark. By the light of the single lamp that the conversa carried, the bursar, after months of practice, had little trouble discovering the key behind the parlatorio door curtain. She loaded her servant with enough loaves for Friday and retraced her steps to hide the key. After she turned back toward the cloister, something startled Suor Maria Diana: she heard or sensed movement in the deep shadows near the bell by the parlatorio door. "You seem afraid—go stand over there," the bursar firmly commanded the conversa, to mask her own anxiety. At the sound of her voice, disembodied giggles issued from the darkness. Oh, those two—Suor Silveria Catterina and Suor Laura Vittoria: they seemed to be feeling their way along the wall toward the parlatorio without a light. They could frighten some poor older sister to death! Silveria and Laura moved into the fringes of the lamplight, hesitated, then turned back toward the cloister and disappeared into darkness. Suor

Maria Diana did not linger to see if they doubled back after she and the servant went on their way. "Who was that?" the conversa whispered. "Suor Silveria and Suor Laura Vittoria." What business had they got prowling about near the parlatorio without a light in the middle of the night? It was not worth transgressing the Great Silence to find out.[46]

But, of course, before first light the next morning the clanging of the bell would break the Great Silence, announcing Leonardo Ortolano, draped with cast-off Carmelite habits. That peal would initiate the long answer to her question, one that some would prefer to let pass.

3

THE SOLDIER OF MISFORTUNE AND THE TAILOR'S SON

SELLSWORDS

> Mercenaries are useless and dangerous because they are disunited and undisciplined, unfaithful, gallant among their friends, craven among their enemies. They have neither fear of God nor fidelity to men. The reason is this: they have no other love or grounds to hold them on the field but a trifling wage, which is insufficient to render them ready to die for you. They love being your soldiers while you do not make war. But when war comes, they run away.[1]

Niccolò Machiavelli took as dim a view of mercenaries as Thomas Coryat took of courtesans. They were not so different, really. As Antonia explained to Nanna in Pietro Aretino's *Six Days*, "The whore acts like a soldier, who is paid to do ill; her shop peddles that thing she's got to sell."[2] Mercenaries, similarly short on life options, also sold their one ready resource: themselves.

Like Gentile Regi, Donato Guarnieri may have entered his line of work because it ran in the family. He grew up in the Alpine foothills near Bergamo (fig. 4; 45.691101° N, 9.69028° E), 110 miles north of Bologna, in Gorlago (45.673575° N, 9.825666° E). To outsiders the region seemed as alien as distant lands beyond the nearby peaks. Farther down the Italian peninsula, Donato

FIGURE 15. Gorlago, the Castello, home of the Guarnieri family, with the sixteenth-century double loggia they added.

needed only to open his mouth to mark himself as a foreigner and something of a yokel, whose singular speech seemed less an Italian dialect than a foreign tongue. Thomas Hoby, glossing Castiglione's derision of a "Bergamask Cowherd" and his "Countrie speache of Lumbardye," put it bluntly: "the woorst speach in all Italy."[3]

The Guarnieri were not cowherds. They had taken over Gorlago's late medieval hilltop castle after the former ruling clan was driven out, and in the early 1500s they enlarged it in elegant Renaissance style (fig. 15). Donato may have spent the raw winters of his childhood playing in the shelter of its delicate double loggia or roaming the finely frescoed, vaulted chambers of the principal floor. In warmer seasons, perhaps he explored the surrounding lushly wooded hillsides, always alert for prowling members of rival families.

It is unclear if Donato followed his older brother Alessandro off to school in Parma, where Alessandro, at least, mixed with schoolboys from some of northern Italy's elite families. Both brothers acquired enough education to read and write fluently. Beyond that, Alessandro may never have fulfilled his teachers' expectations. He ended up as a bandit and petty *condottiero*, hiring out a rough force of relatives and other locals under his command to whoever needed muscle and steel and had the money to pay for them.

That included Odoardo Farnese, Duke of Parma. The brothers almost certainly accompanied the duke south in 1642 to teach Urban VIII a lesson. The Guarnieri band would have passed the gates of Bologna during Farnese's rout of papal forces that September, returning to camp sooty and smelling of smoke after torching Barberini abbeys near the city. Then they may have joined in the free-for-all scramble for booty at the cry "havoc" farther south at Città di Pieve (42.956699° N, 12.0079° E) in early October. Whether the Guarnieri boys quietly slipped away (just as Machiavelli predicted) at the threat of Cardinal Antonio's advancing army or reluctantly withdrew when the duke sounded retreat is unclear. Donato Guarnieri later claimed they left their liege lord in disgust.[4]

The Guarnieri brothers could not simply go home to Gorlago: authorities in Bergamo and Venice had banished the pair for breaking jail after having been locked up for murder. Young Donato claimed no part in the business: it was Alessandro who had orchestrated the woodland ambush of a Bergamasque gentleman. Fortunately the Duke of Parma's papal foe was still recruiting in 1643. That summer Alessandro rode south with Donato, two cousins, and eighteen horsemen; Cardinal Antonio judged them a worthy addition to the cause of Saint Peter. Alessandro signed on as a colonel and Donato as captain of a company of *corazze* (soldiers in armor).[5]

After postings in Castelfranco (44.596401° N, 11.0519° E) and Rimini (44.056702° N, 12.5454° E), at Christmas 1643 Captain Donato received his final assignment to Ravenna (fig. 4; 44.418301° N, 12.1864° E). His company remained there more or less continuously until ordered back to Bologna in May 1644, when peace came and the army disbanded.[6]

Colonel Alessandro Guarnieri brought his wife, Laura, from Bergamo to Bologna, to an apartment behind the college of canons of Santa Maria Maggiore on via Galliera (44.498030° N, 11.342040° E), a few minutes' walk north of Piazza Maggiore. For five months this became the center of the Guarnieri entourage of relatives, servants (all from home—no need to hire nosy locals), and military hangers-on, with Colonel Alessandro as *padrone*. Members of Bologna's Bergamasque expatriate community, including the apothecary Bernardino Generoni (whom we know as La Generona's former keeper), soon found their way to the apartment.

The gratifying appearance of Count Francesco Pepoli's wife marked a social arrival of sorts for Laura Guarnieri. (Count Francesco remembered

Colonel Alessandro from school in Parma.) The count also brought along his cousin, young Count Alessandro Maria Pepoli, who became Alessandro Guarnieri's fast friend—quite remarkable (and cause for disapproving comment among the Bolognese elite) given their markedly different places in the aristocratic pecking order. The Guarnieri family moved a few blocks east the following spring to an area behind the cathedral of San Pietro, in via del Monte (fig. 5, O; 44.496275° N, 11.344026° E). The busy social circle tagged along.[7]

Donato Guarnieri remained at the edge of this lively circle. For the younger brother, not much past twenty, Colonel Alessandro, nearing forty, had become as much a father as a brother. An intimidating figure (big and heavy, as Guarnieri men and women tended to be, swarthy, with black hair that covered his forehead and sporting a little beard), the colonel could be moody and prone to emotional instability, which some described as fits of madness. He kept close tabs on his younger sibling, who was, after all, still in the midst of that extended Italian male adolescence called *gioventù*. Twice a week Donato could expect to receive news and instructions from him. That Colonel Alessandro rarely missed a postal delivery during his little brother's posting in Ravenna hints at the strength of their connection.[8]

Colonel Alessandro Guarnieri took fraternal loyalty and obedience for granted. Young Donato never questioned it, demonstrating an old-fashioned steadfastness when his brother ordered him about on military or family business. Nothing suggests that the younger questioned the wisdom of the older, whom Donato referred to as his padrone. The padrone kept Donato at arm's length, beyond the reach of his personal business, and Donato accepted his exclusion without resentment. Both brothers presumably recognized that what you don't know you can't tell (though it can still hurt you). "My brother didn't discuss his business with me because he preferred that I didn't know about it," Donato claimed. "I don't know why, I didn't ask, and I couldn't have cared less."[9]

"Whenever I've wanted lady friends, they've never been lacking," the attractive younger Guarnieri bragged. Donato followed the path typical for young men in the throes of gioventù, possibly taking it for granted that he would marry when he was as old as his brother (if he lived that long). In the meantime he was content to pay for pleasure with no strings attached. His first taste of Bologna was La Bevarina (the Little Bavarian). Next, for something a shade more exotic, he tried La Turchetta (the Dusky Little Pigeon, with a liking for red shoes). But Giulia Ragazzi, called La Fratina (the Little

Friaress, because she always dressed in homespun beige monk's cloth) became his favorite, or at least the most handily accessible: she got down to business near Santa Maria Maggiore, just to the right of Colonel Alessandro's front door.[10]

La Bevarina, La Turchetta, and La Fratina probably took their money and counted it an easy wage, content in anticipation of repeat business: Captain Donato was very presentable, tall (about six feet) but rawboned, on the scrawny side for a Guarnieri. The gangling lad was surprisingly pallid for all his time in the field, barely able to sprout a wispy mustache but always in need of a shave. He parted his flaxen-tinged hair on one side and let it fall over the opposite ear. The reticent youth looked too young to be a captain, with large, pale eyes that we today might call crazy blue, which some nuns found appealing and others found menacing (particularly in retrospect).[11]

Also catching a lady's eye may have been the fine figure he cut, *alla franzese*. Bologna's tailors received him as happily and as often as did the city's women of the world. More of his pay probably went to his tailor than ended up atop the credenzas or in purses hidden in the bosoms of La Fratina and her colleagues. After finishing an initial pair of dark serge breeches with wide laces and a doublet of white leather, both trimmed in gold, sewn up within days of the young captain's first pay packet, his tailor delivered another half-dozen suits of clothes before Christmas, culminating in an arresting complete outfit (jacket, breeches, and riding cloak) in scarlet with silver trim and silver laces.[12]

To finish off these sartorial masterworks, the captain required the appropriate linen. His sister-in-law shepherded him to the convent of SS. Filippo e Giacomo, to which family servants had begun transporting the Guarnieri laundry on the recommendation of Donna Laura's genteel lady friends. Donato dropped a full month's salary for a dozen shirts of finest linen, with flourishes of Flanders lace on collars, sleeves, and shirtfronts, which bloomed with refined needlework.

It was the work, he learned, of a Suor Silveria Catterina and her protégée, Suor Laura Vittoria. Laura Guarnieri was expanding the family circle to include this inseparable pair of cloistered nuns, to the limited extent that monastic enclosure permitted. Soon the hang-about convent servants began carrying messages and parcels to and from Casa Guarnieri. Laura Guarnieri even contributed her own harpsichord for one of Suor Laura Vittoria's superior parlatorio entertainments. Colonel Alessandro, too, did occasional reconnaissance of the parlatorio, perhaps because reports of his younger brother's frequent visits there were causing concern.[13]

During Donato Guarnieri's extended furloughs at Christmas 1643 and during carnival 1644 and subsequent absences from Ravenna (with or without leave), the lanky, elegantly clad captain caught the eye of the convent gatekeepers often enough that they imagined he was constantly in Bologna. Even when the parlatorio teemed with other visitors, from a purported ten or twenty a day to "a thousand an hour" (as one gossipy porteress put it),[14] the tall, fair-haired young soldier in scarlet was hard to miss. Many nuns knew him only by his burgeoning reputation for frequenting the convent, based chiefly on what the gatekeepers eagerly shared or what Suor Laura began to say about him. How much of all this was true? How much was Suor Laura imagining or making up? Was she perhaps toying with the cloistered vicarious thrill seekers, ready to be titillated? The spirit of critical inquiry never hampered the cloister rumor mill, which ground slowly and small-mindedly, fed by what a few sisters saw, others thought they saw, or many imagined, then eagerly shared over their washtubs.

Given monastic enclosure, there really was not much to see apart from endless tête-à-têtes between the attractive soldier and the striking nun, almost a decade his senior, separated by the parlatorio grilles. There was also not much to hear except Suor Laura hurrying from upstairs to answer Captain Donato's summons. Between their meetings, the servants carried letters and messages in and out—at least some of them for Captain Donato, or so the servant Leonora claimed.[15]

In retrospect, the nuns may have thought they recognized many more significant signals of the impending outcome, although their meaning proved to be ambiguous, depending on the narrator. At carnival time, for example, several nuns claimed to have seen Suor Laura Vittoria send a cartload of her finest furniture to the Guarnieri household, explaining that it was "for her Donato," as one nun put it.[16]

Young Donato's reciprocal gifts to Suor Laura revealed a rustic generosity that might have tempered any sister's righteous indignation in the face of such parlatorio shenanigans. The Bergamasque army captain once surprised Suor Laura with a string of partridges, fresh and ready for plucking. Some sisters may have recognized the notoriously fertile birds as symbols of true love, but just as many would have called them lascivious and satanic.[17] On one occasion Captain Donato sounded the bell, called for Suor Laura, and asked that the gate be opened. When Laura appeared, with half the convent probably watching from above the cloister loggia, her returning hero offered his spoils of war: a pair of cows. They wandered around the convent's east meadow, fertilizing the grass and keeping it down, until the novelty wore off. Then Suor Laura Vittoria sent for a butcher and sold them.[18]

The most provocative cause for speculation was Suor Laura's carnival appearance in a stunning scarlet outfit identical to Captain Donato's. One nun claimed Laura "freely stated that Captain Guarnieri had a suit of men's clothes made for her that was scarlet and all covered with silver." But another told a different story, "Suor Laura said, 'Have a peek at how well Captain Donato's outfit fits me.' And it did fit her, in fact, except that the collar pulled a bit because she was big and tall."[19] The vicaria had no doubts about who looked better in the red suit. "That red outfit tricked out in silver fit her so well that one seemed to behold that same Captain Donato in terms of size—though she was beautiful and well built, whereas he was lean with a thin, small face and wide, pale eyes."[20]

"For the whole of carnival Suor Laura Vittoria wore Captain Donato's clothes, which he'd left in her keeping," the exasperated prioress Lucina Conti recalled. "Suor Laura Vittoria wasn't content simply to dress like a man inside the convent; she also insisted on visiting the parlatorio to flaunt herself in her men's clothes. Well, I threatened her in no uncertain terms that such behavior would not be tolerated. Nevertheless, once during carnival she went to the parlatorio anyway to show herself off to Captain Donato, her sweetheart, or so I believe—since she had no other lover that I know of. I exposed this misconduct when I discovered her in the parlatorio with some other sisters—hiding under a bench so that I wouldn't see her!"[21]

Religious observers never got beyond the image of this transgressive woman dressed as a man—a former prostitute turned nun to boot. The prospect of prostitutes or nuns in drag remained an abiding source of clerical anxiety and prompted regular prohibitions of such cross-dressing, particularly during carnival. That so many convertite seem not to have forgotten Laura and Donato's dress-up games of matching outfits or shared clothing makes one wonder if there was more to it than audacious and immodest self-display. Given the rigors of post-Tridentine monastic enclosure, what passed for convent romance was much more limited than what went on in Pietro Aretino's *Six Days* or what still goes on in the public imagination when the subject comes up.[22] Walls and grates were formidable barriers to close familiarity. But nuns were past mistresses at discovering ways around the barriers that hedged them in.

Perhaps the independent-minded Laura recognized in the captain's left property a clandestine means to bridge the barrier between them. To appear publicly as striking mirror images of one another proclaimed a kind of union. When Suor Laura Vittoria donned Captain Donato's clothing, such frivolous parlatorio display perhaps also disguised subtle intimacies of secondhand scent savored in private, a "sensuousness" that her vigilant superiors would have been right to fret over (if such a thing had even crossed their minds). When Donato returned safe from the fray, perhaps Sister Laura returned his garments as she had worn them, fragrant with sensual traces of her own. Perhaps he noticed. Or perhaps Donato simply dropped them off at his sister-in-law's before heading out the door in search of La Fratina.

With the end of carnival in February 1644, Captain Donato appeared less frequently at SS. Filippo e Giacomo than the sisters later remembered. After the fateful April 1 when Silveria and Laura disappeared, even the sisters had no recollection of having seen him for two weeks. The innkeeper at the Sign of the Two Keys in Ravenna where Donato was billeted paid little attention to the captain's comings and goings, which were difficult to follow since he always disappeared at night. (Donato's servants explained that he traveled after dark to outwit his enemies.) The innkeeper thought he might have disappeared four or five times during Lent and after Easter, when his servants claimed he was visiting Colonel Alessandro Guarnieri in Bologna. (The inn's proprietor was careful never to pry, lest the captain's page happen to comment to his lord on the innkeeper's nosiness.)[23]

WAR GAMES

With the beginning of Lent 1644 Donato Guarnieri returned from carnival's romantic diversions to wartime's mundane realities: long stretches of idleness and boredom punctuated by brief bursts of uproar that often ended anticlimactically. Then came the debacle at the Fortezza Lagoscuro on March 17. Sergeant Major Benedetto Machiavelli, newly appointed governor of the Fortezza Lagoscuro, commanded Guarnieri and his company of corazze to join a host of others in a march to Ferrara (fig. 4).[24]

For two weeks Guarnieri and his men stumbled into and over hundreds of other soldiers billeted in the cloisters of Ferrara's monastery of San Cristoforo (44.844115° N, 11.625354° E), but Sergeant Major Machiavelli found a room he was content to share with Captain Donato. The military crowds roaming the streets passed their time in idleness or at the Inn of the Torretta on the central piazza. Gentlemen with money as well as time to waste sought out the gaming table in the antechamber of the papal legation.[25]

But on a dark night early in Holy Week, a general alarm startled Donato Guarnieri and the sergeant major from their bed: Venetian forces were massing along the Po a dozen miles northeast of Ferrara.[26] Guarnieri rousted out his men to join more than a thousand horses and as many soldiers in the piazza, where by smoky torchlight they formed up into companies from throughout the northern Papal States: corazze, carbineers, dragoons.

More refined participants also mustered amid the chaos of the piazza, on the sidelines for diversion and entertainment. Lieutenant General Cornelio Malvasia invited Count Ferdinando Ranuzzi, an amusing twenty-two-year-old relation of dubious parentage (aristocratic father, very ordinary mother) to come along. Ranuzzi's friend Chaplain General Carlo Possenti—looking unclerical in high boots and spurs, cape, sword, and a pair of pistols—had to call to the young count from the darkened street below his bedroom window, lest he miss this chance to demonstrate the soldierly side of his *virtù*, the defining qualities of noble masculinity.[27]

The force headed out into thick late-winter fog about dawn. The column moved as noiselessly as it could through the impenetrable haze.[28] At last, after midmorning, the misty blanket began to lift over the uniformly flat, waterlogged expanse of empty landscape, disrupted by sporadic tall, leafless poplars, dark cypresses, and black silhouettes of low farm buildings, abandoned to the mercy of passing forces of whichever side. Just the possibility of seeing what lay ahead eased tensions; conversations resumed. Five hours into the lumbering tramp, Sergeant Major Machiavelli appeared at Donato Guarnieri's side. Riding stirrup to stirrup, the pair shared the lunch they had packed in Ferrara.[29] It was dusk by the time the army finally trudged into sight of the enormous palace at Copparo (fig. 4; 44.895256° N, 11.827559° E), looming above the flat, open countryside.

Captain Donato led his company through a lofty vaulted gate guarded by a crenellated tower rising several stories above the massive encircling wall. The entire army slowly filed inside through a great front quadrangle with tall, square pepperbox towers anchoring its corners (fig. 16). Various companies were ordered to different parts of a less lofty but equally expansive service area at the back, whose surrounding cloisterlike arcade could shelter the thousand horses and men. Officers and gentlemen would seek shelter in less public quarters to the front.

After settling his men out back, Guarnieri tagged along after Sergeant Major Machiavelli through the frescoed loggia and opulent front apartments. He was somewhat out of place amid a dozen of Commander Malvasia's senior

FIGURE 16. Copparo, Delizia Estense. The sole surviving tower from the front quadrangle, where Possenti, Guarnieri, Ranuzzi, and the papal army bivouacked during Holy Week 1644. Photo: Luca Salvucci, Bologna.

officers and intimate familiars, who headed toward a hall upstairs where simple fare brought along from Ferrara awaited. Donato followed Machiavelli to seats comfortably close to a hearth at the near end of the hall, allowing his superior the warmer place. Malvasia and his elite companions continued toward preeminent, if chillier places at the far end of the room, where they dined informally, standing around a table laid for them. It was the simplest sort of repast: meatballs or small veal rolls, stuffed with fennel and basil and roasted, plus bread and wine. Pleading lack of appetite after their earlier picnic in the saddle, Guarnieri and Machiavelli soon left the comfort of the fireplace and returned to their men below.

Donato moved among scattered fires that had sprung up in the darkened courtyard until he spotted his own company through the pungent haze. They had pulled off their boots, and legs surrounded the fire like so many spokes, their soles perilously close to the flames to dry and warm their feet. He supervised the distribution of both hay and bread, plus a little cheese for as long as it lasted. Then he sat among them in the warmth of the fire, because the night was overcast and dank, and listened for an hour or so.

Sergeant Major Machiavelli moved out of the gloom into the firelight. Guarnieri's men looked up—the sergeant major himself had come looking for Captain Donato. Guarnieri followed his superior between pools of firelight back across the quadrangle, into the quieter front courtyard, and up the stairs. They navigated a long string of dark connecting rooms to find one that remained unoccupied. Donato shed his boots, crawled into bed fully clothed, and huddled beneath his cloak. He shifted unobtrusively, nestling into the mattress as if that might force some warmth up from the straw inside. As he waited for his body heat to gain ground against the invading cold, he quietly eased his back into Machiavelli's warmth. The dozing sergeant major reflexively settled in around him. (When winter temperatures lingered in unheated interiors, soldiers grasped whatever warmth they could.) From outside the shuttered window, Guarnieri perhaps caught a few voices sounding faintly and gradually dwindling as soldiers retreated from the thickening smoke of their dying fires to sleep with the horses in the cold comfort of the surrounding arcade. Guarnieri knew that come morning his joints would ache from hours of immobility, resisting the impassable perimeter of cold that hemmed in his unprotected front.[30]

A courtyard trumpet roused Donato at first light. He and Machiavelli descended to roust out any dawdlers. There would be no climactic confrontation: the Venetian opposition had decided to give Copparo a pass and had retreated back across the Po, if indeed they had ever crossed the river at all. With no enemy to fight, Malvasia ordered an early retreat. Free of yesterday's anxiety, with discipline relaxed during the march back, the force did not spare the countryside or the empty farmhouses they had passed on the way forward.

Captain Donato idled about the city through the rest of Holy Week.[31] Shortly after Easter, he was ordered back to quarters. Guarnieri observed Easter Monday or Tuesday on horseback with his company on the fifty-mile trek back to Ravenna. By then peace negotiations were already concluding in Venice. After that, he and his company had little reason to stir until early May (or so he later claimed). Then orders came to march back to Bologna, where Cardinal Barberini proclaimed the peace. After settling accounts, in early June the decommissioned Captain Donato passed through Porta San Felice and struck off toward Bergamo and home.[32]

"THAT MASTER OF THIS WORLD"

> If we accidentally meet with any one whom we never saw before, without considering what degree of respect he may really deserve, for fear of saying too little, we usually allow him something more than he can justly claim; and because he is well-dressed, call him, perhaps, "your Honour," or "your Lordship," though, probably, he may afterwards prove to be nothing more than a barber or a taylor.[33]

Within a year of war's end, Don Carlo Possenti—"that master of this world," as Suor Laura Vittoria's sister once called him, canon of Santa Maria Maggiore and chaplain general of Marchese Cornelio Malvasia's papal forces—would rise even to the rank of vice duke of the duchy of Segni and be counted among the members of Rome's renowned Accademia degli Humoristi.[34] Yet he was nothing more than a tailor's son.

Possenti must have embraced the old maxim "Generositas virtus, non sanguis" (Nobility is virtù, not blood).[35] He got as far as he did by recognizing early on that a clever tailor's son needed influential patrons to notice his virtù if he cherished any hope of rising above the barbers and the tailors. And Carlo Possenti longed to be a gentleman.

By Carlo's birth in 1613, his father Lorenzo Possenti was sufficiently prosperous to be attracting other tailors to work under him and soon owned a substantial property on via Mascarella (44.498904° N, 11.349692° E), a little over ten minutes' walk north of Piazza Maggiore. Carlo managed to evade a demeaning life in trade, however. His uncle, Giovanni Battista Possenti, canon of the venerable collegiate church of Santa Maria Maggiore, probably first noticed his nephew's precocious intellectual inclinations. Perhaps it was Uncle Giovanni Battista who rescued him from the dead end of the tailor shop and nudged him in the more promising direction of holy orders. There is not the slightest evidence, however, that Carlo Possenti ever felt any spiritual calling. Quite the opposite. He was smart enough to recognize that the church had as much room for the ambitious as for the religious. The former were much more likely to rise to the top.[36]

Giovanni Battista Possenti died in 1623, however, with little chance to smooth his nephew's path toward clerical preferment. Five years later, fifteen-year-old Carlo donated £150 to the canons of Santa Maria Maggiore to open the door to a canonry at his late uncle's institution. He retained that position until Cardinal Barberini elevated him to Vice Duke of Segni in 1645. In the meantime he garnered a few benefices; their earnings were modest, certainly not enough to support him in any style he would have preferred. But by the 1640s, thanks to his new army chaplain's salary, he could manage, provided he continued to live at home, did not gamble, and wheedled extra funds from his father. Lorenzo Possenti was bedridden by then, so there was a good chance that Don Carlo might soon come into a tidy inheritance.[37]

In advancing his clerical career, Carlo Possenti probably spent less time reading the Bible or the church fathers than manuals on gentlemanly virtù such as Castiglione's *The Courtier* or Giovanni Della Casa's *Il Galateo* (*A Treatise on Politeness and Delicacy of Manners*). He certainly had little time for his missal or breviary. Once he got around to ordination a decade after acquiring his canonry, he never gave much thought to saying the Holy Office or daily mass. One Bolognese urban legend captured perceptions of the secularity of this secular priest. Some said that as chaplain general Possenti neglected to read the last rites over dying soldiers. Instead he comforted them and sent them off to paradise with selections from Giovanni Battista Guarini's *Il pastor fido*.[38]

Poetry, not piety, served the ends of this complete gentleman. Possenti began to haunt Carlo Manolesi's bookshop near the voltone dei Caccianemici, "as men of talent do" (as the bookseller put it).[39] There he could demonstrate literary refinement and hobnob with gentlemen such as Count Ferdinando Ranuzzi, another regular at Manolesi's establishment. Some, in fact, ascribed Possenti's social success to his cultivation of poetry. Girolamo Colonna had no sooner become archbishop of Bologna than Carlo Possenti, barely twenty by then, dedicated his *L'architettura* (1633) to him. There is no evidence that Archbishop Colonna took much notice.

By then Possenti was also a member of Bologna's Seconda Accademia dei Confusi and affected the nickname "Accademico Confuso." In 1632 he joined dozens of colleagues in contributing to the academy's *Lodi al Signor Guido Reni*. Further testimony to Possenti's literary and social success appeared that same year: *Il sogno d'Armindo solitario idillio per lo ratto d'Helena di Guido* (The solitary Armindo's dream: Idyll on the rape of Helen by Guido). Bartolomeo Cavalieri dedicated this poetic discourse on Guido Reni's painting to "the most illustrious and most reverend lord, Signor Carlo Possenti." Cavalieri exclaimed, "I'd like to show the World that Virtue has the power in me to accomplish all that it wishes if a maligning star would not make the results discordant with my desires." Possenti may have winced, recognizing how closely Cavalieri's sentiments matched the discord between his own social aspirations and his ill-starred birth. A dozen years later Cavalieri may have blushed at his own prescience in dedicating a poem about the rape of Helen of Troy to the alleged perpetrator of the "rape" of two nuns from the convent of the Convertite.[40]

Possenti aimed high in his search for a dedicatee for *L'amicizia di Venere con Diana* (Venus's friendship with Diana, 1638; fig. 17): the distinguished Marchese Giovanni Niccolò Tanari, Bolognese senator and sometime governor of Rimini. In October 1639 Possenti's star rose dramatically: he cowrote the poetry for a spectacular opera cum tournament on horseback, performed by select Bolognese cavalieri in Piazza Maggiore to honor the papal legate. *I furori di Venere* (Venus's frenzies) was all directed by the figure who would become Possenti's patron, Marchese Cornelio Malvasia, eminent man-at-arms, Bolognese public servant, and prominent intellectual.[41]

Possenti's final publication, inspired by the War of Castro, takes the form of an "ode," dedicated to Marchese Malvasia, "bidding him leave the softness of the Villa at Sasso for his accustomed martial undertakings." "To arms, Cornelio, to arms!" Possenti exclaims. "Where hides the warlike spirit that dwells so famously in you?" The prelate also proclaims a martial spirit of his own, "Cornelio, hardy custom of fierce valor shall thrust you now into battle—I, too, hear that warlike call in my heart, though this flowing robe binds my foot." Possenti's pesky cassock did indeed pose an impediment to his vaunted aspirations.[42]

FIGURE 17. Carlo Possenti, *L'amicizia di Venere con Diana* (Bologna, 1638). Reproduced with permission of the Biblioteca Comunale dell'Archiginnasio, Bologna.

Don Carlo captured a place in Marchese Cornelio's inner circle as chaplain general to his military force: an ideal way to combine the noble profession of arms with the unfortunate restrictions of Possenti's clerical calling. Cardinal Barberini confirmed Possenti's commission when his army from the south met forces from the north in October 1642. "When it was time to return to Bologna, His Eminence commanded me to follow him, as I have always done at his expense," Possenti later recalled.[43]

A single poem, surviving unpublished in a manuscript compendium of War of Castro documents, reveals that the army's new chaplain general still found a little time for poetry. In "On a Most Beautiful and Passionate Youth from Ferrara," Carlo Possenti (styling himself an "academician of the night," probably a reference to Bologna's Accademia della Notte) offers twenty-two quatrains to a young Ferrarese "ruler of hearts": "Beneath your lash sweats your steaming / Neapolitan destrier [warhorse], who loves your bit [in his mouth]. / And to serve the Sun whom he has on his back, / he nailed down the moon under his feet. / . . . Follow the course of your regal river [the Po], / which describes to you imitable examples: / If it laps its banks with the tongue of love, / it is answering with kisses, the one who embraces it." The identity of this "most beautiful youth" remains a mystery. Could it possibly be La Generona in her suit of Spanish yellow, sword, and spurs during her visit to Ferrara? (Probably not.) Even in our age of literal-mindedness, possible polyvalent readings of Possenti's text (which finds no equivalent in the priest's published work) would be hard to miss.[44]

Carlo Possenti began to appear regularly in Lieutenant General Malvasia's entourage at Palazzo Malvasia, where he often ate and sometimes slept. Don Carlo and Marchese Cornelio could be seen promenading together in the piazza, visiting the marchese's relatives at the convent of San Lorenzo and otherwise moving socially and militarily within the elite.[45]

By 1643 Carlo Possenti thus offered living proof of what a tailor's son could do if he recognized the social realities that Castiglione aptly summarized: "Given two gentlemen of the court, as soon as it is discovered that one of them was well born and the other not, the latter will be respected far less than the former, and only after a great deal of time and effort will he win the good opinion that the other acquires instantly, merely because of his nobility."[46] Time and effort could never entirely compensate for lack of good breeding, however. Carlo Possenti's elevated circle would have recognized that nature had not implanted the noblest seed in him.

His superiors may well have smiled at how fervently the tailor's son seemed to espouse *Vestis virum facit* (Clothes make the man). The War of Castro allowed this man of the cloth to remake himself in military style. He traded long clerical garb for a cream-colored linen doublet and breeches with a black velvet cloak reaching to mid-thigh, together with riding boots and spurs. Whenever possible he added a sword and firearms.[47]

Beneath the fancy clothes many observed a patent effort that clouded Possenti's carefully constructed virtù. Cardinal Antonio's secretary, Giovanni Braccesi, who confronted a stream of self-promoters at the Palazzo del Legato, claimed to find Don Carlo's attempts to win introductions to friends of powerful friends particularly vexing. More telling was the cleric's apparent lack of self-control. Possenti showed little sign of an ability to moderate his passions that should have come with age: the ambitious priest seemed mired in perennial gioventù. He was quick to fall out with friends and even quicker than young nobles to take offense and to act on it. "When one sees those sorts of people, it muddies one's blood," he was heard to say about his supposed enemies.[48]

Few also failed to notice how the canon and chaplain general would sneak off to the convent of the Convertite to loiter in the parlatorio with a nun almost ten years his senior. He tried to time such visits to when his mother wasn't looking. If she found out and chastised him for behavior both illicit and unbecoming of the clergy, he shot back with the classic teenager's response, "You can't prove it. If others go there, why can't I?"[49]

No one was more scandalized by Possenti's behavior at the convent than the nuns. Several sisters had overheard Don Carlo's passionate declarations of love to Suor Silveria Catterina in the parlatorio. Possenti also sent one of his father's assistants to the Convertite to take her measurements and make her an elegant scarlet ensemble that matched La Rossa's.[50]

Evidence suggests that this infatuation was not entirely mutual, that the relationship was more complicated, even dangerous. The abandoned letters in Suor Silveria's cell suggest an on-again, off-again character to the relationship and La Generona's ambivalence about the passionate young clergyman. There is no evidence that Possenti was in Rome in February and March 1644, when the letters were signed there. Perhaps Suor Silveria retained some attachment to another admirer less than a month before she abandoned his letters.

Of course, everybody in the convent knew about the priest's explosive confrontation in the parlatorio with the foreigner Ximenez. It would be tempting to ascribe the nuns' descriptions of such immoderate passion to cloistered imaginations were it not that Carlo Possenti had a history of violence. A chapter meeting at Santa Maria Maggiore in February 1636 described the absent Carlo Possenti as "imprisoned in the Torrone of Bologna." He and his brother Jacopo were locked up there for seven months after taking potshots at Francesco Maria dall'Aglio with their harquebuses when Possenti's long-standing friendship with the victim went bad. The court banished the Possenti brothers from Bologna, but they managed to return to the city after only a short period in exile.[51]

Barely two years later, the Possenti brothers were back in the Torrone. They had teamed up with three of Bologna's most notorious criminals to hoodwink a current Possenti lady friend, a prostitute living on via Fondazza. After sweet-talking her out of her keys, in February 1640 the cleric and his crew broke in and stole cash and other possessions, sold the objects, then divided up the spoils. Carlo and Jacopo were banished to Ferrara. Thanks to administrative changes at the papal legation, the lucky Possenti boys had their banishment lifted within a few months, in time for Carlo to capture the position of chaplain general in the papal army.[52]

Possenti's demons reemerged barely two weeks before the nuns disappeared. On March 12, Count Ferdinando Ranuzzi arrived late at a tavern, expecting to dine with friends he had invited for a meal. The count discovered that a common soldier named Galeazzo Mariani, rather than awaiting his arrival, could not resist helping himself to fresh oysters. Then he left, taking a visiting Ranuzzi friend with him. The count suggested that Mariani needed to be taught his place and left in a huff. About 1:00 a.m. the luckless Mariani crossed paths with Ranuzzi and Carlo Possenti, who appeared out of the darkness with a lantern near Piazza San Domenico. As Mariani greeted them, Ranuzzi made an obscene gesture, while Possenti, with an upward twist of his sword, laid Mariani's face open and knocked out all his front teeth.

Two weeks later, as Bologna buzzed with talk of the fugitive convertite, Mariani lay near death in the Ospedale della Morte. When he could leave the hospital, the left side of his face was so disfigured by the sfregio Possenti had given him on Ranuzzi's behalf that he was reluctant to appear in public for months. "When Don Carlo Possenti saw me from time to time after he'd wounded me, he laughed in my face and pointed me out to those walking with him as if to say 'the sfregio that guy's got on his face—that came from my blow.'"[53]

Then after April 1 everybody was talking about the sfregio to Carlo Possenti's virtù: his implication in the nuns' abduction. This went beyond uncontrolled passion—as one observer put it, "that was gallows business."[54] Shortly thereafter Marchese Cornelio Malvasia dropped Don Carlo. According to Cardinal Antonio Barberini's personal assistant, Giovanni Braccesi, the rift occurred "as a result of certain works of poetry." Marchese Cornelio had discussed rumors with Cardinal Antonio concerning Possenti's participation in the convent misadventure, however. Malvasia may have decided that the war's end provided a convenient opportunity to break with this talented young clergyman, whose defect of inferior birth was beginning to show.[55]

In spring 1644 Don Carlo started to haunt Cardinal Antonio Barberini's antechamber and to cultivate the legate's right-hand man, Giovanni Braccesi, on Cornelio Malvasia's recommendation. In light of the intercession of the priest's noble acquaintances, Cardinal Antonio came to feel that Possenti deserved some future consideration. When Cardinal Antonio prepared to return to Rome, an influential acquaintance reminded him that Possenti would be pleased to follow him to Rome to receive the position previously promised him.[56]

In late July 1644, when Giovanni Braccesi came out to board a carriage to Rome, he discovered Carlo Possenti standing there holding a little suitcase. What could he do? Courtesy required that Braccesi and his party share the carriage with him, although it meant that Braccesi had to leave his servant behind for lack of space. On their arrival in Rome, Possenti stuck to Braccesi like a limpet for the rest of the summer. When Braccesi moved to rooms of his own at Palazzo Barberini in the fall, Possenti continued to dog him. But when Braccesi accompanied Cardinal Barberini to Monterotondo for the Christmas season, there was no place for Possenti in the carriage. Fortunately, Possenti's old friend Count Ferdinando Ranuzzi had recently appeared in Rome too. So the wandering priest showed up on his doorstep near Piazza di Spagna (41.905935° N, 12.481908° E) and began to live under his roof and share his table.[57]

Finally, in March 1645 word went out that Don Carlo was going to Segni, in the mountains south of Rome (fig. 4; 41.6883° N, 13.0163° E), as vice duke. He left Rome to assume a high office that many in Bologna would never have imagined just a year earlier. As Carlo Possenti explained with studied courtly modesty, "I allowed myself to be ruled by His Eminence and never questioned his commands. Since he deemed it appropriate to involve me in government, I accepted in order to obey him."[58]

4

A GRAVE MISTAKE

As Carlo Possenti, the new Vice Duke of Segni, was settling in south of Rome, life in Bologna was returning to normal. Isabella Machiavelli recognized the change even from outside the city wall as she approached Porta Santo Stefano (fig. 5, N; 44.484804° N, 11.35616° E) on the road from Florence. The gate no longer bristled with guards, who had brought traffic to a standstill when she left Bologna almost two years earlier during the turmoil of war.

In August 1643 Isabella had resolved to move to the city on the Arno to join her son, Francesco Maria dall'Aglio, who had sought refuge there after a harquebus fusillade nearly killed him. That had nothing to do with the War of Castro, however: enemies in an old feud had ambushed him. By May 1645 Isabella Machiavelli was ready to return to her empty nest: a house three minutes' walk down via Santo Stefano from the city gate that marked her departure and return. The property stood amid a stretch of nondescript arcaded buildings, almost directly opposite the voltone del Baraccano (fig. 5, M; 44.4861° N, 11.3543° E). This lofty vaulted passageway still marks the way from via Santo Stefano (fig. 5, K) to the venerable church of Santa Maria del Baraccano and the location of Bologna's erstwhile Conservatorio del Baraccano for girls at risk.[1]

The minimal rent that Donna Isabella received during her Florentine sojourn hardly compensated for the vexations waiting on her return. In April 1644 Isabella's brother, Dionisio Tomassini, maggiordomo to young Count Alessandro Maria Pepoli, rented his sister's place to the count's closest friend, Colonel Alessandro Guarnieri. Once the war ended, the colonel decamped without returning the keys. Isabella arrived with her household staff (just one thirteen-year-old foreigner named Giovanni Tedesco, "Johann the German"). They discovered that the doors were locked up tight and the keys were nowhere to be found. Isabella had no choice but to contact authorities at the Torrone, hire a notary to handle the legal requirements, then find someone to break into her own house.[2]

The shuttered exterior along via Santo Stefano was indistinguishable from its neighbors, but from the back the house had become a drag on the neighborhood. A once well-tended garden, bordering open land that stretched to the back wall of the convent of Santa Cristina to the north, had grown into a tangled wilderness. The shutters on the rear windows stood open. Neighbors claimed that for months they offered a gaping invitation to thieves or anybody else looking to get inside, particularly since the sills were not very high above the ground.

Isabella discovered that the water in her well had risen ominously, its slimy surface fouled with foamy scum; clouds of mosquitoes rose to plague Madonna Isabella and young Giovanni during early summer evenings. The German sweated to clean the well out properly. As the level dropped after he emptied a stream of buckets, his rope began to snag something. In the shifting disk of mirrored sky at the bottom he could make out an object breaking the surface. With some patient fishing he managed to drag up a spade. Donna Isabella claimed it wasn't hers; the lack of corrosion on its blade suggested it had not been down there long.

The mysterious shovel and the open rear windows offered the only exterior testimony to recent habitation. A busybody across the wall asserted that ever since the brother, Dionisio, hauled away furniture for safekeeping in spring 1644, neighbors hadn't seen a soul arrive or leave. The neighbor claimed to have heard the clatter of a carriage at least once, however: late one night, long after she had gone to bed. She couldn't say exactly when and couldn't tell if it had stopped outside or passed along to someplace farther up the block.[3]

Clearly someone had been living there. A bed of ash and charred logs covered the hearth and spilled out onto the floor. Firewood still filled a room to the right of the staircase. Upstairs, somebody had dragged a small bed from the dark passageway where it belonged into a brighter butler's pantry, lit by windows facing the back garden.

Machiavelli and her servant set to work reclaiming the principal floor and making the whole place more habitable as late spring turned to summer. They ignored the wine cellar on the ground floor, to the right of the main entrance, as they busied themselves with an endless series of more urgent tasks in May and early June. But by the summer solstice, June 21, the wine cellar could no longer be ignored. As temperatures and humidity rose and the building's south-facing exterior soaked up the sun for minutes longer every day, Giovanni may have hoped the facade's arcaded walkway, shading the ground floor, might at least keep the unopened wine cellar from turning into an oven. Foul odors filtering from inside suggested that no one had entered in an age. It was no wonder Donna Isabella sent him and other boys recruited from the neighborhood to deal with it while she went back upstairs.

Giovanni manhandled the groaning door ajar. He batted at a sticky pall of cobwebs that clung to his cheeks and hair as he pushed through into the darkness. The stench of a stifling wall of fetid air slapped him full in the face as he apprehensively shuffled his feet onto what felt like a rough brick floor. He waited for his eyes to adjust to the dim light filtering through the half-open doorway. He could make out very little except bundles of wood in the deepest shadows along the wall to his left, spread haphazardly across the pavement. A dead rat must be squashed somewhere in that pile.

The youth realized he was taking shallow breaths to keep the foul air from his lungs. He retreated to the comparative coolness of the entryway where the air was fresher and went in search of his mistress, leaving the door open as wide as possible. Isabella sent him back to move the wood to a shed behind the house.

Despite their mounting disgust, Giovanni and some other boys reentered the fetid gloom and struggled to shift the heavy bundles. Giovanni staggered as his foot slipped from brick into soft earth: the pavement beneath the wood seemed fractured. The dirt also looked disturbed and slightly mounded. Uncovering the earth released a suffocating putrid odor—not even a plague of squashed rats could produce such a stink. Giovanni felt his gorge rise and tried to hold his breath as the stench clogged his throat. But youthful curiosity overcame revulsion. Flies drawn in through the door buzzed around the boy's face as he knelt and began to scoop the loose soil aside with his bare hands. The dirt grew ranker by the handful. He stumbled out into the light and air to catch his breath, then hurried back upstairs to call his mistress.

Isabella Machiavelli did not pass beyond the entrance to the darkened cellar before hurrying off to find a neighbor. When he responded to the banging on his door, he found her babbling incoherently (or so it seemed to him). He too hardly needed to cross the cellar threshold. The woman was useless in her present state; he commanded Giovanni Tedesco to accompany him downtown to inform the authorities.

It took barely twenty minutes to reach the Torrone prison (44.495° N, 11.3411° E), at a rear corner of the Palazzo del Legato (fig. 5, H). The teenager, not the neighbor, found himself standing before the auditor of the Torrone. "I've come before your most illustrious lordship to report that today my mistress was having some bundles removed from the wine cellar at our house opposite the Baraccano on via Santo Stefano, where I was also helping. I smelled a stink—such a stench that I got curious and started digging. It looks like someone dug a grave."[4] The auditor ordered his second-in-command, trailed by the inevitable notary, to accompany the informants and a pair of sbirri back to the scene of the apparent crime. As they passed the church of San Biagio (suppressed; 44.489953° N, 11.340348° E) the assistant auditor paused long enough to command two idle workmen, haplessly loitering outside (in the wrong place at the wrong time), to join his party. Someone would have to do any dirty work and heavy lifting. The pair knew better than to object. They would long speak of that afternoon as it continued to cloud their daydreams and darken their nights.

With a few swift kicks, the sbirri cleared a path through a crowd of curiosity seekers under the portico outside Isabella Machiavelli's door, craning their necks for a look inside. The cellar door to the right stood open, just as Giovanni Tedesco had left it, although by now the putrid stench had seeped out into the entry hall. A faint hum inside the dark recess heralded a plague of flies that had swelled to biblical proportions. The servant spotted his mistress waiting in a far corner of the passage, rubbing her forearms distractedly: a helpless woman alone.[5]

The assistant auditor approached Isabella to begin his investigation by the book: "Do you know or could you imagine what brings these men and me to your house?"[6] (His nose alone should have hinted at the answer.) He did not advance beyond the cellar door before sight, sound, and stench literally gave him pause. He ordered lights brought in, provided the impressed laborers with spades, and set them to work. Removing the remaining bundles of wood revealed a patch of broken pavement roughly seven feet by five. Dust from the digging rapidly clouded the suffocating atmosphere, so that work proceeded slowly, with frequent breaks, as the auditor waited impatiently outside. Long before the diggers reached the one-foot level, they could no longer avoid stepping down into the foul-smelling pit. They were standing nearly waist deep when they first called out to their superiors. The reddish soil was turning white: they had hit quicklime. The lime dust added to the choking haze stung the eyes, made breathing nearly impossible, and turned the dim lamplight ghostly pale. Work slowed to a crawl.

A few inches into the lime, the workmen called out sharply to the auditor. Covering his nose with a handkerchief, he edged his way toward the pit. A body lay half buried in lime: face-up, naked, but surprisingly intact, with feet toward the street. As the diggers cautiously cleared dirt and lime from around the corpse, they recognized that the eerily preserved body was female.

Squeezed awkwardly against the pit walls, the men worked carefully to drag the cadaver from its resting place. As they lifted it clumsily to the surface it became apparent that although flesh had fallen from the bones in some places, the body would likely come out whole. When they laid it gently on the pavement, light penetrating the grave revealed the outlines of a second corpse right under their feet. The auditor called for more lights. This cadaver also lay face-up, but in the opposite direction, head toward the street.

The workmen struggled out of the grave and carried the first body out into the entryway, trailing cascades of dirt and lime. They deposited it on a makeshift table, then returned to its companion while their superior attended to the initial discovery. Once again the workmen slid down the sides of the pit and worked to free the second corpse from the confining soil and lime. Then, alone in the cellar, they paused a moment to stare into the grave, less in respect than in queasy fascination. The grave's lower occupant must be a full head taller than the companion who had lain atop it. "I'd say when she were alive she were one big lady!" a workman exclaimed.[7]

Despite the corpse's imposing stature, taller than most graveside observers, there could be no question that she was very much a woman. Although bones with shreds of desiccated flesh adhering poked through where the blackened skin had burst at her sides, the front of the body, where the lime was thickest, remained amazingly uncorrupted. Even in death, at the bottom of the pit, this cadaver remained statuesque, with an ample bosom, well-proportioned limbs, and long-fingered hands that must have been beautiful before the skin withered and turned black. Against the white lime in the flickering light, her head seemed ablaze with a halo of bright red hair. An arm's length farther down the naked body, another fiery patch flared through the lime from the cleft where belly met legs.[8]

The workmen repeated the careful extraction and transferred the body to another waiting table. At the auditor's command, they proceeded to measure the remains. A workman called out specifics and the notary duly noted them down: "two and a third ells, less one digit, Bolognese measurement" (the smaller woman—a little under five feet); "two and a half ells plus four digits" (her taller companion—an inch or so under six feet).[9]

In the meantime, the auditor had dispatched the bargello to fetch the Torrone's staff physician and two barber surgeons. For years these case-hardened professionals had attended to the ailments of unfortunates and the afflictions they suffered at jailers' hands or during enhanced interrogations. The medical trio fought their way through the burgeoning, increasingly boisterous crowd outside the door at Casa Machiavelli and took charge of the postmortem examination. To that end, one workman found a broom and vigorously swept away dirt and lime still collected in bodily crevices or cavities.

Then, with self-conscious professionalism, the medical team set to work on this welcome change from the usual abrasions, contusions, and dislocations. They gently poked and prodded, conferring sotto voce, largely to demonstrate their individual powers of observation. They too marveled at the remains' singular state of preservation. "Since they were buried in a cellar where air couldn't enter and the soil was fresh but not damp, and they were enveloped in lime, which attracts moisture, they could be excellently preserved in the condition that I see here," one barber surgeon remarked. His colleagues agreed that the lime must have drawn off bodily fluids, encouraging something akin to mummification.[10] Anterior portions, especially the face and most intimate ventral area where lime easily collected, were dry and wizened but intact; posterior regions suffered greater corruption. The dorsal area of the redheaded body, which had been laid out on bare earth before lime was shoveled into the grave, showed more bare bone.

Apart from her superior state of preservation, the shorter cadaver seemed rather nondescript. Her breasts were unquestionably female but betrayed signs of middle age. Instead of bright red, her hair was a dark chestnut. Although both women's hair was long in front and at the temples, from the crown of the head on back it was cropped very close—resembling the tonsure monastic women received when they took their vows.

The smaller woman's withered lips had contracted in a grimace that revealed a full set of remarkably beautiful, even teeth. Nobody failed to notice their incongruously white sheen, which stood out against the wrinkled, tobacco-colored skin of her face. In life, a smile from this little woman might have brightened a room as effectively as her companion's more flamboyant features.

The auditor commanded that the corpses be turned and manipulated in every direction, and the workmen responded so diligently that some might have winced at the indignity of it all. With the bodies facedown, the medical examiners spotted a cord knotted at the back of each neck, drawn so tight that they were hidden in the creased skin of their throats. But where the cords pulled away stiffly from the vertebrae at the knots, they were impossible to miss. On the auditor's orders, a barber surgeon found scissors, delicately snipped one cord at the knot, and extracted it from where it cut deeply into the redhead's throat. The grisly reality of how the unfortunates had died was irrefutable.

A few hours of daylight remained on a summer solstice that everyone near the tables (except perhaps the barber surgeons) wished would end. But they could not leave until Isabella Machiavelli, Giovanni Tedesco, the neighbor, the laborers from San Biagio, the medics from the Torrone, and any other witnesses had all been properly deposed. Only then could the party leave the bodies under the watchful eyes of a pair of sbirri guarding the door. Judging by the number of people who later boasted of having inspected the corpses, the opportunistic policemen may have been quick to supplement their notoriously meager earnings by charging admission.[11]

By late afternoon, word of the sensational discovery had spread as far as the duomo, where a subordinate hurried to inform his superiors. Admitted into the presence of Monsignor Domenico Oddofreddi (who had assumed the position of vicar general a year earlier), he announced the shocking discovery. "People are saying they could be those two convertite who fled the convent last year. I wished to inform you so that, should it prove true, you can take action for justice against the guilty."[12]

The vicar general summoned his archiepiscopal auditor in criminal matters: none other than Monsignor Alfonso Arnaldi. Oddofreddi sent him off in haste with the inevitable notary, together with the necessary witnesses. Monsignor Arnaldi's entourage parted curious bystanders outside Casa Machiavelli and demanded admittance. In the deserted entry hall, he finally caught up with the fugitives who had eluded him fourteen months earlier—or at least with two plain closed wooden boxes to which their remains had been transferred before secular authorities departed at the end of their very busy day. Arnaldi raised the lids and hastily noted the cadavers' sex, size, hair style and color, state of preservation, and the cords around their throats. (With the bodies confined to their boxes, we might wonder how he managed to spot the cords, particularly on the redhead—a barber surgeon had snipped hers away by then.) His witnesses were duly sworn and hastily testified in similarly perfunctory, virtually identical fashion to what they had "very clearly seen" (which included the garrote that was no longer there). For the archiepiscopal curia, it seems to have been business as usual.[13] As he made his way from the Baraccano back downtown, one wonders if Monsignor Arnaldi perhaps regretted that he had left undone those things which he ought to have done back in April 1644. He presumably realized that now they would be coming back to haunt him.

Perhaps as Alfonso Arnaldi was in transit to or from the duomo, the Torrone's busy bargello reappeared before his superior. "It's widely believed that they could be those two nuns from the Convertite. They might have ended up at that house, where they were strangled and suffocated. Or else they were brought there after their murder. They say the mother of the one called La Rossa and her sister are now in Bologna—I'm going to find out. And I've heard that in Bologna there's also a certain apothecary from the Generoni family who was intimate with that Suor Silveria before she entered the convent. One could discover if these bodies are in fact the nuns by bringing those three to identify them. I wanted to inform your lordship, and I will carry out whatever orders it may please you to give me in pursuit of justice."[14]

When sbirri came pounding on their door and took them into custody, it may have seemed to Lucrezia and Giustina Regi that they were caught in a replay of April 1644. As officers once again hustled them into the Torrone, they surely wondered how long it would be this time before they would see the sun again. The bargello brought Lucrezia into the presence of the auditor himself. Her interrogation began predictably enough.

"Do you know or might you guess the reason for your present interrogation?"

Lucrezia pleaded ignorance. Her interrogator continued down a leisurely path toward his eventual objective.

"What persons make up your family?"

"I have nobody else in this world but my one daughter Giustina, who lives with me. And I've got a kitchen maid who waits on us both."

"Did you have other children?"

"I had two sons and two other daughters. The boys died at about sixteen to eighteen months. Camilla died at about twenty to twenty-four months, and another girl named Gentile entered the Convertite about four years ago and took the name Suor Laura Vittoria."

"What is the present situation with this Gentile, known as Suor Laura Vittoria?"

"Last year, 1644, after Easter, I received word that my daughter had been taken from the convent with her maestra, Suor Silveria. After that I never saw her again; I heard around town a while ago that the two had been murdered and buried someplace or other, so people said. But that's all I ever knew."

The auditor asked about the missing daughter's appearance and any distinguishing features, which Lucrezia enumerated in detail.

"Would you recognize your daughter Gentile if you saw her—or her corpse?"

"Yes, my lord, I'd recognize my own daughter Gentile, even if I saw her corpse—she was my daughter, after all. I'd know her even from her bones!"[15]

The auditor left it to his notary to interrogate Giustina Regi. "When and where did you last see Gentile after she became a nun?"

"On the feast of San Giuseppe last year—1644—it was March 19. She called me to the convent to lend her six double ducats for some convent business. After that I never saw her again."

"Do you know anything about Gentile's whereabouts and if she is still among the living?"

"I'll freely tell you exactly what I know: after she disappeared not only was she never seen again, as far as I know, but it's commonly believed she was murdered."

"Do you know, or have you heard, who took her away?"

"There's no way, my lord, I could possibly know if this person or that one removed my sister Suor Laura Vittoria, much less who killed her or had her killed."

Giustina also spoke at length of her sister's appearance. The notary probably took no notice of hints of pride and affection that colored Giustina's view of her older sister's commanding physical presence.

"My sister Gentile was very tall—she stood taller than me by a good bit," Giustina observed, raising her hand high above her head. "She was one of the big girls around here, one of the tallest I ever saw. And she had hair much redder than I've got."

“Would you recognize Gentile if you saw her—or her corpse?”

“There’s absolutely no doubt that I could recognize my sister Gentile—alive or dead. She was my sister, after all, who I spent many, many years with. Of course, I’d know her!”[16]

The Regi women must have experienced a mix of surprise and relief, then a sense of grim inevitability when the auditor consigned them not to a jailer, but to the assistant auditor and his constable attendants, in company with a notary and even the prison’s barber surgeons. They all made their way out of the Torrone and headed eastward. They passed Santo Stefano, San Biagio, and eventually stopped before what the women recognized as the voltone del Baraccano. But their guards took them in through a door across the street, as a group of bystanders stared and whispered.

Taking places somewhat apart, auditor and notary assume the role of dispassionate observers to the human drama playing out in the entryway at Casa Machiavelli. The corpses no longer repose neatly in last evening’s caskets but once again lie extended for easy access on the tables, this time strategically separated. Only mother and daughter are new to this scene; for some returning here for a second time, they are by now more interesting than the pair in nonspeaking roles, ostensibly the stars of the show.

The diffident women, firmly directed first toward the diminutive cadaver, watch with revulsion as the surgeons put the remains through a repetition of yesterday’s postmortem gymnastics, to make sure the witnesses are spared nothing. “No—even though I’ve inspected it carefully, I don’t recognize her,” Lucrezia claims, “though her hair is cropped close like a nun’s.” “In truth, I can’t say to your lordship that I know her. She’s been buried a good while, after all,” Giustina adds.[17]

Officers closely herd Lucrezia and Giustina toward the other table, preceded by the determinedly efficient barber surgeons. As the medical team reveals the long-limbed, red-haired cadaver, the mother reflexively clutches her belly, then faints dead away. In the same moment an attentive policeman notices Giustina’s ginger complexion turning ashen and steps forward to break her fall. The zealous medical men, vinegar flasks at the ready, kneel beside the women and apply their arts to bring them around. Giustina refuses to open her eyes at first. Lucrezia in the meantime affirms, “At my very first glance I knew that this is the body of Gentile, my daughter.” Giustina quietly echoes her, “I no sooner set eyes on her than I recognized that fair colossus and the imposing stature of Gentile, my sister.”[18]

With mounting animation, mother and sister recall all the familiar features: the impressive, finely proportioned physique, the singular red hair, the beautiful hands. But the women take their observers by surprise when they single out a scar under the left ear. The skeptical surgeons move in quickly for a closer look, tut-tutting dubiously. Even the auditor abandons his post near the wall: in her excitement, Giustina impertinently urges him to come closer as they point out the mark. The surgeons jostle about the corpse to reclaim their territory, brows furrowed, earnestly comparing notes as if nobody else were there. They call for a candle, light it, then hold it near the jaw, below the ear, peering at the putative scar as closely as their noses will permit. They scrape and pick at the spot with a penknife until they tease up what they finally agree is scar tissue.

"It is certainly true that in our other inspection the scar was overlooked. Since the flesh on the face is dried out and almost roasted, so to say, with many wrinkles that look more ridgelike than the scar itself, it would be impossible to see the scar if these women had not pointed it out, because it is so well healed. Thanks to the diligence of the surgeon who treated it, only the tiniest scar remains: approximately the length of a finger. Though it might have been longer, but the skin under the jawbone is gone."

After this climax, ferment subsided into the predictable formality of depositions, recorded on the spot both from the bereaved relatives and from the defensive medics. ("Your lordship observed yourself that in order to be absolutely sure we had to light a candle. . . .")[19]

"In truth, I tell your lordship that after such close intimacy with my sister Gentile for the many, many years that we were together—I can say that, truly, this is the body of my sister."

"As for my poor daughter," Lucrezia added, "I clearly recognize her, for all her blackened flesh, so dried out and shriveled. Your lordship never beheld how that beautiful figure, bigger than a man, looked in life." Lucrezia contemplated what her daughter had become, laid out before her on the makeshift table. "There aren't many as grand as she was, and that is the truth."[20]

Downtown at the Torrone, the bargello brought in the apothecary Bernardino Generoni. Generoni testified that he had continued faithfully to assist Suor Silveria Catterina "with her every need" for a decade after she took the veil. But he had stopped visiting her eighteen months earlier (which would have been during the eventful carnival of 1644). "I didn't go speak to her any longer because I didn't like hearing that she was spending so much time at the grates and in the parlatorio: I wanted her to retire from the world, as suits a nun."[21] Generoni made the journey up via Santo Stefano, where he confirmed Suor Silveria's identity with little apparent fuss, but he could offer only an educated guess about Suor Laura Vittoria's identity.

Although each body now had been independently identified, due diligence required further confirmation. The fugitive Silveria's servant Leonora would have been an obvious choice, but by then she had passed to a better life. Authorities had never managed to collar Suor Laura Vittoria's errand boy Galeazzo (Monchino); besides, word on the street was that he had been murdered shortly after the nuns' disappearance.[22] That left the sisters of SS. Filippo e Giacomo. Professed nuns could not join the pilgrimage to Casa Machiavelli, of course, and the high drama of a parlatorio viewing was out of the question. But a conversa was not bound by the rule of monastic enclosure, since she did not take solemn vows. The responsibility fell to a veteran conversa who had been completely absent from the earlier proceedings and to another old-timer who had in fact first broken the news to Suor Eufrasia in the early hours of April 1, 1644. At the temporary morgue on via Santo Stefano they played their parts efficiently and decorously, with a minimum of fuss. But we are left to imagine the scene that played out when the pair returned home to the corner of via delle Lame and via del Rondone.[23]

Suor Silveria Catterina and Suor Laura Vittoria lay in Casa Machiavelli for another full day, until after sunset on Friday, June 23. Auditors, barber surgeons, and notaries left them alone, though they certainly were not left in peace. The number of gawkers who wheedled their way past the door in via Santo Stefano so clogged the vestibule that sbirri transferred the bodies to the garden behind the house, where "everybody from Bologna" trooped past, robbing La Generona and La Rossa of any possible dignity and repose.[24] After nightfall on the third day, they were taken away and reburied. We do not know where.

Were it not for their murderers' trust in received scientific wisdom, Silveria and Laura might still lie unnoticed beneath the cellar floor of a house opposite the voltone del Baraccano in Bologna (where who knows how many other forgotten corpses may still lie buried). From early modern times to the present, quicklime has remained the chemical agent of choice when inconvenient corpses await quick disposal, as writers of crime fiction regularly confirm. In fact, quicklime can do quite the opposite: it can preserve. But if a murderer turned undertaker in Donna Isabella's dark cellar reassured his mates, "This should do the trick" as they began to shovel lime over La Generona and La Rossa in 1644, it was an honest mistake.

Relating the remarkable preservation and eventual discovery of Laura's and Silveria's cadavers sixty years after the fact, Bologna's enthusiastic chronicler Antonio Francesco Ghiselli would attempt to turn their murderers into early modern equivalents of that regular butt of late-night talk show humor, the stupid criminal: "Instead of lime, they covered them with plaster, which preserves and does not destroy. The plaster worked prodigiously in conserving the two cadavers, which were otherwise all decayed, except for those parts."[25] Ghiselli apparently placed as much faith in the efficacy of quicklime (as opposed to plaster) to promote decomposition as the criminals he disparaged. In fact, the Torrone's medical team seems to have got it right. Everybody who testified stipulated lime (*calx/calcis* [Latin] or *calcina* [Italian]), not plaster (*gypsum* [Latin] or *gesso* [Italian]). Lime may burn the surface of the skin ("roasting" it, as one barber surgeon described it), but it also desiccates rather than destroys the flesh, thereby tending to preserve it looking rather like jerky.

In the weeks after that eventful Wednesday in June, Isabella Machiavelli, too, wistfully pondered the misdeeds and apparent mistakes of stupid criminals. As the first to have entered this scene, perhaps she should have the last word as well.

> I'm amazed that those who murdered the sisters didn't just bury them out back in the garden—either that or throw them down into the big sluice that runs right under my house. It's the end of a great stream that flows out from underneath all of Bologna. Then the corpses would have been much harder to find. And then I would never have had to suffer all the damage and all the disruption I went through because those bodies turned up at my house.[26]

5

PAS DEVANT LES DOMESTIQUES

No sooner were La Rossa and La Generona laid to rest again, out of sight, than for some they once more passed out of mind. The Bolognese vicar general and other local clergy had a more immediate preoccupation. On June 24, 1645, a new archbishop left Rome, bound for the second city of the Papal States. Bologna's native son Niccolò Albergati-Ludovisi made his triumphal entry through Porta Santo Stefano on July 1.[1]

In the meantime Cardinal Lelio Falconieri, the papal legate, had been less distracted than local diocesan clergy. As early as June 25, Falconieri wrote to Innocent X's young cardinal nephew, Camillo Francesco Pamphili, about the grisly discoveries opposite the Baraccano. "We are undertaking an investigation with all possible diligence," he hastened to report, but that would require the archiepiscopal court's transcript from 1644. "I therefore thought it wise to request that Your Eminence obtain His Holiness's order to the archbishop to provide this legation with a copy, without throwing up any ecclesiastical embargoes. Besides, that ecclesiastical tribunal cannot appropriately punish such an atrocious offense."[2]

Two days later, without waiting for word from Rome, the Torrone's assistant auditor picked up where he had left off on June 22. Heeding gossip roiling around Bologna's arcades and piazzas, he dispatched sbirri to fetch a widowed serving woman and part-time silk weaver named Taddea Bertolotti.

"What do you know about any recent evil doings in Bologna?"

"Nothing except that last Sunday at the church of San Martino where I went to Mass I heard that authorities discovered two cadavers buried in Madonna Isabella dall'Aglio Machiavelli's wine cellar. They say they're those two convertite, La Rossa and her companion."

"Do you know how the nuns were removed from the convent, where they were taken, and who took them?"

"My lord, I can only tell you what I know about where they were taken. Your lordship may be aware that I'm the daughter of the late Anna Bertolotti, wet nurse to the late Count Alessandro Maria Pepoli." Perhaps Donna Taddea paused to allow her interrogator to take in this impressive fact. "I used to visit the count's house frequently to look after him or the others whenever they got sick. Last year, before the feast of Our Lady of Borgo di San Pietro (which we celebrate two weeks after Easter), something new happened.

"During that time everybody around Bologna was talking about La Rossa and her companion. Diana Tomassini, maggiordomo Dionisio Tomassini's daughter, constantly asked me what people in town were saying about those convertite. One day when Count Alessandro Maria Pepoli overheard us he said, half laughing, 'There's no longer any danger of those nuns being found.' After I heard that, I began to suspect that the count might have been involved or informed about where the nuns were taken. But I didn't say anything to anybody.

"Then one night last July or August, Giulia Santi said she strongly suspected that those two convertite might be buried somewhere in the palace. She also told me she knew for sure that those two nuns had been brought to Count Alessandro Maria's house on the feast of Our Lady of Borgo di San Pietro.

"And that's all I know. Giulia Santi and I always suspected that those nuns were buried in the palace somewhere, after what I'd heard the count say, together with what Diana, who was always asking about this business, said."

"Who else knows about this?" the auditor inquired.

"The conversation was strictly between Giulia and me. Diana Tomassini would know if the nuns were in the house, because she had the key. So would Messere Dionisio Tomassini, her father, especially because Dionisio had the keys to the house where I heard the bodies turned up."[3]

When the legate's letter reached Rome, Cardinal Pamphili responded in terms unlikely to please Cardinal Falconieri. "His Holiness has determined that since the investigation of the nuns' escape began in the archiepiscopal court, justice should proceed from there. He desires that you provide that tribunal with all the assistance it requires to ferret out the guilty."[4]

Pamphili followed up with a perhaps equally unwelcome letter to Bologna's novice archbishop, Niccolò Albergati-Ludovisi. "The enormous crime committed last year cannot be unknown to Your Eminence, which is to say, the flight from the Convertite of the two sisters whose cadavers were lately discovered, displaying manifest evidence of violent death. His Holiness commands that you issue uncompromising imperatives to your ministers to proceed as diligently as possible with the investigation previously undertaken by that tribunal, in order to discover the criminals."[5]

By July 16 sbirri had tracked down Giulia Santi. Authorities brought the middle-aged spinster not to the archiepiscopal court, as one might expect given Cardinal Pamphili's orders, but to face the assistant auditor at the Torrone.

"Did you know Count Alessandro Maria Pepoli?"

"I knew him very well, indeed," Donna Giulia answered, probably with a hint of pride, "throughout the time when he was the premier cavalier of this city. For three years before his death I was the woman in charge of his household."

"Where did the count and his family live?"

"Count Alessandro Maria had his home in the palace of the Lords Pepoli on strada Castiglione. His whole family lived in rooms near Count Roderigo and Count Francesco Pepoli."[6]

Half a dozen branches of the Pepoli clan shared the massive edifice on strada Castiglione (fig. 5, E; fig. 18; 44.492541° N, 11.346336° E). Since the early 1300s, when the family effectively ruled Bologna, the palace had expanded to include a hodgepodge of large courtyards and more modest *corticelle*, a maze of passageways, grand staircases and narrow spiral ones, and eventually more than two hundred bedrooms. A four-story crenellated wall imposed an external uniformity that masked the less orderly interior. Rows of pointed gothic windows and a few gateways, framed in fine Bolognese terra-cotta work, scarcely diminished the fortress-like impression of looming masonry. At its most expansive, the palace ran along a 145-yard stretch of strada Castiglione, from modern-day via Sampieri to via Pepoli. In Giulia Santi's day, it covered roughly the northern seventy-five yards. Complete with a moat-like canal that lapped against the facade's narrow sidewalk, the palace looked

more like a fortified castle than an aristocratic urban residence. Today a row of finely wrought serpentine hooks protruding from the wall, perhaps for tying up watercraft, offers the only hint of the canal, which was covered over within twenty years of this story.[7]

Giulia Santi continued without prodding to describe the mysterious eviction of some servants from a few ground-floor palace rooms. "The count's maggiordomo, Messere Dionisio Tomassini, said that he didn't want men fit only for dogs' company to stay in those rooms and muck everything up. So his daughter Diana and the servants tidied up the rooms and closed them off, including the window shutters facing the padrone's courtyard. Then ten days later the windows were reopened. In the meantime nobody from the household ever entered."

"Why were the rooms sealed like that?"

"I'll tell your lordship everything I know. It's this." Donna Giulia paused, took a breath, and launched into her story. "On the morning of the feast of Our Lady of Borgo di San Pietro, after Count Alessandro Maria's lunch, he told me he wanted to go lie down for a while. But he said Colonel Alessandro Guarnieri (who often came to visit his lordship, because he was his dear friend) might come looking to have a word with him later on. If he came, I was to fetch the count immediately."

A little before vespers, Colonel Alessandro Guarnieri did appear at one of the gates. Giulia called to him from a window that her master would be down shortly, then went to inform the count, who was still napping. As the count hurried downstairs to meet the colonel, he had no idea that Giulia had gone to watch from a window overlooking the palace quadrangle. She said she saw Colonel Guarnieri appear under the vaulted passageway running between the palace courtyard and the carters' gate facing strada Castiglione. In this dim passageway Giulia also spotted two women, hand in hand. They scurried along the passage and disappeared through a different doorway into a corridor that led toward the recently shuttered ground-floor rooms.

"As they passed through the passageway from the carters' gate they were directly facing me, and I clearly saw that one of them was taller than the other, large in stature—a young woman, nice-looking, with a fair complexion. The other one was a little older, dressed all in black, with a shawl over her head. When I saw the women go in through the door, I figured those rooms had

FIGURE 18 (*opposite page*). Bologna, Palazzo Pepoli Vecchio, La Generona and La Rossa's second hideout.

been tidied as a place to keep them. And after they entered the rooms, I never saw them again. That's all I know."

"Do you know who the women were?"

"From discussions in the house, with the count himself and with Diana, who was continually asking everybody what people were saying about the nuns who'd fled, and if they'd been found, I'm sure that these two were the missing convertite."

"Do you know what happened to them?"

"I'd have no way of knowing," Giulia insisted, with a slight shake of her head. "Several days after the women entered the house, I clearly heard Diana say, 'God knows where the bones of those poor nuns are,' and that they'd been in several places, without saying exactly where. I remarked that it would have been better if they'd been taken back to the convent. She replied that they didn't want to go back. If they'd wanted to, Count Alessandro Maria would have had them brought back there and would have arranged everything with their superiors so that this business was hushed up. Then, recently, when word went around that they'd been found buried in the wine cellar of the sister of somebody named 'Dionisio,' I got very suspicious that our Dionisio had a hand in the business."

"Do you know how long the women stayed at the count's?"

"When the window shutters were reopened, I figure they'd left. What's more, during that time the count twice went out at night—he never went out at night otherwise (for fear of being murdered). After the rooms were completely reopened, they were never closed again during the time I remained in the count's service."[8]

Only after Giulia Santi's interrogation did the investigation shift from the Torrone to the archiepiscopal court, as the pope had commanded. Or so Bologna's neophyte archbishop dutifully indicated to Pamphili on July 19. "I was of course already well apprised of the crime committed in this city in the matter of the convertite. The city supposes that a certain Dionisio Tomassini, former servant of Count Alessandro Maria Pepoli, ought to be very well informed about this business, since the cadavers were discovered in his sister's wine cellar. Which is as much as I can tell Your Eminence for now."[9]

This often-mentioned Dionisio Tomassini and his two daughters, Diana and Domenica, were probably just names to the archiepiscopal newcomer, but they were no strangers to his competitors at the Torrone or to his subordinates. After Count Alessandro Maria Pepoli's sensational demise the previous September, as we are about to see, lurid details of what had been going on for years behind the palace wall along strada Castiglione spiced the conversation of scandalmongers in the piazza right up to the moment when the grisly discoveries in Isabella Machiavelli's cellar eclipsed them.

In his chronicle of Bologna's first families, *Cronologia delle famiglie nobili di Bologna* (1670), Pompeo Scipione Dolfi discreetly chose never to mention Count Alessandro Maria Pepoli, whom Giulia Santi dubbed "the premier cavalier of this city." Several decades later the family's self-appointed chronicler said of Count Alessandro Maria's branch, "These were from an infected line."[10]

When it came to Count Alessandro Maria Pepoli, his relatives, peers, and servants would likely have agreed with Baldassare Castiglione: "Another thing seems to me greatly to damage or enhance a man's reputation: choice of really intimate friends. A man who associates with the ignorant or wicked is taken to be ignorant or wicked."[11] Count Roderigo Pepoli, Alessandro Maria Pepoli's uncle, did not hide his disapproval of the company his nephew kept. Count Roderigo's maggiordomo recalled that "a close friendship, indeed, the very closest, existed between Colonel Alessandro Guarnieri and Count Alessandro Maria. They were together quite often, almost all the time, in fact. I heard their close friendship discussed in Count Roderigo Pepoli's house. He didn't like his nephew keeping company with Guarnieri, because he said he wasn't of equal birth to Count Alessandro Maria."[12]

Somewhat ironically, Dionisio Tomassini, Count Alessandro Maria Pepoli's own maggiordomo, expressed similar disapproval of his master's companion, Colonel Alessandro Guarnieri. "It would have been better if Count Alessandro Maria hadn't become his friend," Dionisio later observed. "At first Count Alessandro Maria was a fine gentleman. But after he began to keep company with Colonel Guarnieri he started to pick up his vices of cursing or showing little reverence at Mass, for example."[13] But Dionisio Tomassini was hardly one to be casting aspersions on his employer. By the summer of 1645 the Tomassini family's affiliation with their master had caused far wider comment than Colonel Alessandro Guarnieri's.

SISTER ACT

How eighteenth-century opera librettist Lorenzo Da Ponte would have delighted in the tangled relationships of Count Alessandro Maria Pepoli and his household servants, the Tomassini family! Had he ever heard of them, we might have another opera in the manner of Mozart's *Marriage of Figaro*, mixed with Pergolesi's *La serva padrona*.

Dionisio Tomassini entered the service of Count Alessandro Maria's father, Count Romeo Pepoli, in the mid-1620s, when Alessandro Maria was a luckless boy of about eight. (His mother had died when he was still a baby and his paternal grandmother died before he turned five.) Tomassini brought with him a wife and two daughters. The elder, Diana, must have been about Alessandro Maria's age, while Domenica would have been not much beyond babyhood. Alessandro Maria may have been drawn into this socially inferior family circle for want of any proper alternative.[14]

By the late 1630s, after Count Alessandro Maria succeeded his father as padrone, little Domenica Tomassini, the prettier of the two sisters according to the servants, was blossoming into womanhood.[15] The servants could not fail to notice changes among the children. "A thousand times I saw Count Alessandro teasing her, joking with her, touching her, and kissing her," Taddea Bertolotti recalled. "I saw him hug and embrace her, throw her on the bed, or on the chests, or on the floor. And I observed her even sitting on the count's bed when he was undressed and putting her hands on him under the covers and fondling him."[16]

After five years or so, the count also developed a taste for the more mature charms of Diana. "We other servants all recognized that the count only wanted to keep company with those sisters—it's absolutely true that he was mad about those women," the count's manservant affirmed. "At night I saw the sisters go to the count's bed, this time one, another time the other, and sometimes even both at once!" according to another servant. (Domenica Tomassini admitted to Giulia Santi that the count slept between the two of them.)[17]

It did not take long for the consequences of such shameless behavior to become obvious: baby bumps blossomed. The births began in January 1640, when Domenica (still a minor) bore twin girls. Count Alessandro Maria handed them over to Taddea Bertolotti when the time came to drop them off at the foundling hospital. Diana eventually entered the competition as well: in March 1643 she produced a girl. At the time of La Rossa and La Generona's disappearance in April 1644, the two sisters were both pregnant. They scandalized Pepoli family and staff by delivering their offspring in the count's own bed within two weeks of each other later that summer.

By then Count Alessandro Maria had come down with what Donna Taddea described as a throat ailment. It was serious enough that he (and the Tomassini) turned their thoughts to putting his house in order. When a notary arrived at the count's bedside to draft a will on August 7, 1644, the Tomassini sisters took pride of place: two thousand scudi awaited each of them, in recognition of their years of "faithful service." The count also acknowledged paternity of Diana's two daughters and named little Antonia and Margarita the sole heirs to his considerable fortune.[18]

There was not a word about Cesare Pepoli, the count's bastard half-brother, whom he really should have legitimized. Fifteen-year-old Cesare stormed into his brother's bedroom, stamping and ranting, "You left something to Dionisio's big-gutted daughters and you've left nothing to me, your own brother? You'd better consider giving me what's due me or you might regret it!"[19]

In the face of domestic unrest and his own deteriorating condition, Count Alessandro Maria withdrew with the Tomassini to a rented country house, bringing along a few other servants, drafted into a motley excuse for a security force. Cesare Pepoli was not so easily eluded. After sunset on September 28, 1644, he and his henchmen blasted their way into the count's hideaway. Dionisio Tomassini successfully hid under a bed. Diana saved herself by leaping out a window amid a hail of harquebus fire. Domenica barely survived a stab wound to the chest and fled to a convent.

Count Alessandro Maria foolishly emerged from his barricaded bedroom on reassurances that he would not be harmed, but then he began to haughtily berate young Cesare. Unsurprisingly, his half-brother and his *bravi* set on him with swords and stilettos. The count pleaded for time, at least, to confess. "Here's your confession!" Cesare shouted as he pointed his pistol at his face and pulled the trigger. So ended the ignoble, perhaps best forgotten life of Giulia Santi's "premier cavalier of this city," dead at age twenty-seven.[20]

Dionisio Tomassini fled to Florence. Less easily cowed, Diana Tomassini got herself appointed as her daughters' guardian, with permission to inventory the late count's estate. Count Roderigo Pepoli, Alessandro Maria's uncle and rightful heir, promptly instituted an investigation of his nephew's incestuous ménage. Unintimidated, Diana and the Tomassini alleged that Count Roderigo had duped the bastard Cesare and masterminded the fatal assault on Count Alessandro Maria's country villa. On June 22, 1645 (the day after the grisly discoveries up via Santo Stefano), Count Roderigo Pepoli learned that the auditor of the Torrone had condemned him to be beheaded for complicity in his nephew's murder. The count skipped town for Padua. But since the case pitted a noble from one of Bologna's premier families against a crew of household servants, many surely suspected that the auditor's judgment might prove both precipitous and imprudent.[21]

Diana Tomassini's reputation therefore preceded her when the archbishop's sbirri took her into custody just a month later, on July 25, in the matter of the murdered convertite. Possibly recognizing that this was no ordinary housemaid, the bargello imprisoned her atop the soaring Torre Prendiparte, eleven stories above the ground. She shared this diocesan prison with a growing crowd of witnesses down below, waiting to testify, plus a few prostitutes who had run afoul of holy mother church.[22] (These days, since the tower's transformation into a boutique bed-and-breakfast, well-heeled bridal couples pay 350 euros a night for remodeled prison cells.)

When Diana Tomassini first faced interrogation on July 27, her declaration of her place in the Pepoli household may have provoked an exchange of looks between auditor and notary: "For the space of twenty years I lived continuously in Count Alessandro Maria's house. He had secretly married me four years ago in the presence of a solitary priest." (This was a textbook example of why, eighty years before, the Council of Trent had done its best to ban clandestine marriages.)

As the auditor took his time getting to the point, the closer he got to Palazzo Pepoli and its mysteriously shuttered downstairs rooms, the more evasive Diana became. She echoed the story of the scruffy servants' eviction but pleaded ignorance about who replaced them. "I suspected there might be someone in there, but I never saw anybody. I only started going over there when it got hot and the rooms were reopened."

The interrogator gradually pinned her down. "Do you know anything about the two nuns?"

"I knew they fled the convent because people were talking about it all over the house. And the count spoke of it."

"What did you hear?"

"That they went away with Captain Guarnieri and Possenti. The count was discussing it at the dinner table. We women certainly may have spoken about it, too. (We talk about lots of things.) We discussed their disappearance and God knows where their bones might be. I heard they'd turned up in Count Francesco Pepoli's house, and then somebody said they were kept at Count Alessandro Maria's. And I pitied them when I heard that they'd run away from the convent, that they'd been murdered and other things I can't remember."[23]

Diana later claimed that because of her terrifying imprisonment atop the tower she could not think straight. When reassured that there was no danger in telling the truth, she resolved straightaway to reveal whatever she knew.[24] "To tell you the honest truth, as if I were standing before God, I know that those nuns were at Count Alessandro Maria's because he told me so. But did I see them? I never saw the slightest trace of them."

From then on Diana's chief concern was to concoct testimony that kept her as far as possible from harm's way. Her version does not entirely agree with Giulia Santi's, but it rings true enough to suggest a plausible reconstruction of the scenario. On Saturday before the Feast of Our Lady of Borgo di San Pietro, Count Alessandro Maria first revealed his entanglement in this sticky business: "Diana, you should know that Colonel Alessandro Guarnieri is sorely vexed because he's holding on to those two convertite who ran off. They're someplace where they're just waiting to be discovered. So he wants to get them out of there and wants me to do him the favor of keeping them here, in a room where they can stay secretly." Diana's confusion about the dating of events obscures what may have happened next. Like Giulia Santi, she described Colonel Guarnieri's after-lunch visit, but not as being to deliver the fugitives. "The colonel came to arrange the way to bring in the sisters. They agreed to bring them in at night." (This makes more sense: the count and the colonel would not have shepherded La Rossa and La Generona through town in broad daylight.) "I saw them inspect the side street and test the gates for noise." (This would have been a gated side entrance in modern-day via Sampieri, 44.493079° N, 11.346788° E.)[25]

Late Sunday night seems the most likely time for the transfer. By 10:00 or 11:00 the household had gone to bed: Diana heard them climbing the stairs to their rooms. After 2:00 a.m. (once the sbirri were unlikely to be out on patrol), Diana left her own bed and went to the count's bedroom. He had undressed and was lying awake. She dressed him and he quietly went downstairs, explaining only that he would be taking delivery of the nuns. Shortly thereafter she heard Colonel Guarnieri arrive with several men. "From the sound of their footsteps, I imagine there might have been four or five. But I remained sitting on the count's bed. I think Possenti was there, but I don't know for sure."[26]

Diana claimed the nuns slipped in through a front entrance. But of course she had not actually seen anything herself. "The count told me they came in through the large courtyard, through the little wooden entry out front" (possibly the little door still visible in the larger wooden door at via Castiglione 6). "I caught the sound of their footsteps because I knew they'd be coming in."[27]

Count Alessandro Maria took the nuns to hide out in a downstairs reception room close by, where they remained the next day. But that could only be temporary: the room was much too accessible. La Rossa and La Generona were shifted to the more isolated, shuttered rooms formerly occupied by the male servants. (Perhaps this was when Giulia Santi saw them creeping in and out of doorways in the courtyard. She too confessed some confusion about the specific day.)

Diana also spoke vaguely of the nuns' initial hideout. "There were two small children there who might give them away. Count Alessandro Maria said that one sister left to be with Possenti and the other went to be with Guarnieri; that is, La Rossa left for Guarnieri. But La Rossa didn't see Guarnieri because at that time he wasn't in Bologna."[28]

In subsequent days, Count Alessandro Maria struggled to maintain secrecy about his clandestine guests: a futile effort, judging by all the palace speculation about the shuttered rooms. "The staff didn't provide them with meals or anything at all. The count went to a pantry where we always kept prepared things, picked out some, and brought it to them: hard-boiled eggs, salami, cheese, bread, and wine. The count always went to fetch it with his very own hands because he didn't trust anybody." Diana's apparent amazement at the count's behaving like a servant, of course, underlined her lack of direct involvement. Not that her interrogators were quick to believe it.

"Given everything you appear to know, your intimacy with the count, and your access to the keys, it seems highly implausible that you never set eyes on those sisters."

"Although I did have the keys and the count did take me into his confidence, I absolutely never saw them," Diana insisted, then carefully explained. "The count didn't want me going down that spiral staircase to the rooms because I was carrying his child—I gave birth on August 1. I had previously miscarried after tumbling down those very stairs."[29]

A week passed. La Generona and La Rossa showed no sign of leaving. After nine days the count started complaining that he needed to visit his country villa at Durazzo (44.58105° N, 11.679557° E) but, as he put it, "I can't go because I've still got those devils, the sisters, in the house."[30] After more than a week locked up in semidarkness, the fugitives started to have misgivings about Count Alessandro Maria and Colonel Alessandro Guarnieri.

When their keepers suggested it was time to move them again, they balked. "They didn't want to leave the house if they hadn't received a letter from Captain Donato Guarnieri," Diana recalled. "I remember the count told me that during the time the sisters were at the house, Donato Guarnieri wasn't in Bologna. Or else they wanted a letter from Possenti."

On Thursday, April 21, a letter conveniently appeared. "It arrived from Possenti. (The count showed it to me before the nuns saw it.) It said that the sisters should go with the ones who would come to fetch them at night. Soon they would all be together. They would all enjoy good times and be happy. After the count let me read it, he took it down to show the nuns."[31] So La Rossa and La Generona took Possenti at his word and agreed to go.

The nuns disappeared late on Friday night, April 22. (Diana was certain it was Friday because she had eaten nothing but a meager meatless supper that day.) Once again she was with the count in his bedroom: Alessandro Maria undressed and got into bed as usual, without a word about the nuns' imminent departure. Then around midnight, he roused himself and announced that he was going to hand them over. Nobody knocked, called out, or whistled. When he disappeared down the dark staircase, lit only by the solitary candle he was carrying, Diana listened awhile at the top of the stairs. All she heard was the faint scraping of the gate as it opened and closed.[32] Half an hour later the count returned. After another day or two the shutters down below once again stood open.

"Maybe two or three days after the nuns were no longer there, I asked what had happened to the sisters and where they were now. The count said the colonel had 'iced them' or 'had them put down' or some such words. I took that to mean they were dead. And that's all I know: what the count said."

"What do you know about how they were killed?"

"I don't know anything, because that's all the count told me. I responded, 'Oh, those poor souls! God knows where they ended up. God knows what sins they'd committed out in the world to get themselves killed.' And the count replied, 'I can assure you that La Rossa committed no sins at all.' That was because Captain Donato Guarnieri, who had got her to flee, was still not in Bologna at that time. As for the other sister, the one who'd left to be with Possenti, the count didn't say that she'd done nothing at all. Only that La Rossa hadn't committed the slightest sin.

"Then he added that Colonel Alessandro Guarnieri had them killed so that La Rossa wouldn't end up in the hands of his brother. Captain Donato came to Bologna—he arrived shortly after the nuns left the house—I remember that the count told me so. Count Alessandro Maria also said that Colonel Guarnieri was alarmed because his brother Donato was going around asking about those sisters and especially La Rossa. He didn't want to tell him they were dead, so he just said they were someplace where they'd be fine and his brother shouldn't give it another thought.

"So I asked Count Alessandro Maria once again, 'But why did he have to kill the second one, if he just wanted to keep La Rossa from ending up with his brother?' He said that Colonel Guarnieri had them both done in because anybody who found the one would also have found out what happened to the other. So La Generona posed a threat."

The count summed it all up with a chuckle and perhaps a wink: "My friend Colonel Guarnieri was very conscientious about doing a job right!"[33]

6

NOVUS HOMO

The Pepoli-Tomassini investigation was barely under way before the curia set off in pursuit of another lead. The former archiepiscopal bargello had been heard around town claiming to have spotted La Rossa in late spring 1644.[1] On July 18, 1645, that constable, who fifteen months earlier was strong-arming witnesses to testify, found himself compelled to give evidence. And he responded to his interrogator's predictable opening question with the predictable answer: "No, my lord, I don't know why your lordship wants to interrogate me."

Without much prodding, the bargello embarked on his story: A sergeant came up to him in the piazza claiming, "I think I've found the nuns, because one of them is scarred." When the bargello informed Monsignor Pier Donato Cesi, the vice legate, he scoffed: a scar crawling up a whore's cheek was hardly compelling evidence. La Bruna, pulled off a bark to Ferrara in a futile waste of time, had been misidentified as La Rossa thanks to just such a scar. So the bargello went off on his own to find the sergeant, who led him to a house near the voltone dei Caccianemici (fig. 5, F; fig. 7; 44.492236° N, 11.345210° E). "As the sergeant was leaving that house, I saw a woman approach the window. I clearly recognized her as La Rossa, because before she became a nun I was acquainted with her, and she had red hair. So I referred the whole matter to

Monsignor Cesi. A Gandolfi lives in that house; I believe he's called Bonaventura."

"Do you know anybody else who visited there?"

"Nobody except Don Carlo Possenti. I saw him come and go many times."

The vicar general hurriedly dispatched sbirri to apprehend Bonaventura Gandolfi, but they returned empty-handed: Gandolfi had moved to Rome six months earlier.[2]

The next day Archbishop Albergati-Ludovisi added a personal postscript to his letter to Cardinal Pamphili in Rome: "I know you will have been informed that a certain Gandolfi (in whose house one of the two nuns was spotted) is living in Rome. He's only got one eye, and all the Bolognese there know him. If one laid hands on Gandolfi and Dionisio Tomassini, one assumes that everything would be cleared up."[3]

It took most of the week to track down Gandolfi's former Bolognese housekeeper. She testified on July 23 that for years her former master had rented out rooms to visiting gentlemen from Cardinal Antonio Barberini's entourage.

"Apart from those who lived there, did other gentlemen visit Gandolfi's?"

"I heard that a Signor Giovanni Braccesi came often, and Possenti, who's a big-shot priest. I saw him arrive frequently."

"Did any of those gentlemen ever keep someone in their own apartment, especially last year after Easter?"

"Once I'm sure I heard that. There was some foreigner, a soldier, who came into the kitchen and exclaimed, 'They're saying that one of those convertite who were abducted could have been here, in this house!' I just overheard him speaking to the other servants in the kitchen when I was fixing something to eat. The servants just laughed and said they didn't know anything about any nuns in the house."[4]

Two days later, on July 25, the convertite in Borgo del Rondone discovered they had visitors. For the first time in fifteen months, an archiepiscopal investigator found his way back to SS. Filippo e Giacomo; this time nuns' vicar Ascanio Rinaldi himself showed up. It seemed a curiously perfunctory visit: only three sisters were called to the grates. The first witness had nothing much to offer. When witness number two brought up only Possenti and Guarnieri, Monsignor Rinaldi inquired if the pair ever brought along any companions. "Signor Giovanni Braccesi sometimes came for Suor Silveria—but he didn't come often," she replied. "Sometimes I saw him with Possenti, and sometimes with Guarnieri, and also with both of them, but infrequently."

The nuns' vicar began to fold Braccesi into the mix. "After the nuns' flight, did Guarnieri, Possenti, and Braccesi visit the convent?"

"We never again saw any of those you named come here."

The last witness, former prioress Lucina Conti, could be counted on to respond forthrightly. Still, the nuns' vicar tried to point her gently in the right direction. "Do you know or have you heard if any others came to the convent more frequently than Possenti and Guarnieri?"

"There was no shortage of people who came here, as I believe the whole world knows," Suor Lucina responded with her customary bluntness.

"Did you ever hear anybody mention *Giovanni Braccesi*?" (Perhaps Rinaldi was growing impatient with his own beating around the bush.)

"Yes, my lord, I heard Braccesi mentioned. They said he sometimes came for Suor Silveria. But I never saw him, and he didn't come as often as all those others. Since the day they fled we haven't seen Possenti, Guarnieri, Braccesi, and the others at the convent."[5]

A name uttered only twice during the investigation back in April 1644 was now being mentioned in the same breath with the two prime suspects: Giovanni Braccesi.

Once his advance man had laid the groundwork, Vicar General Domenico Oddofreddi appeared in the parlatorio a week later. A numbing succession of forty nuns filed hurriedly through on that August 1. Most had nothing to say, but a few named names.

The reliable former prioress Lucina Conti offered a new take on the name the nuns' vicar had fed to her on July 25. "There's talk about Braccesi because he was in love with Suor Silveria Catterina. I don't know personally, I just heard talk about it." This new name now turned up on the tongue of half of those with anything relevant to say.

"The opinion here in the convent is that Possenti, Guarnieri, Braccesi, and also Lord Cardinal Antonio Barberini's man Castrodini are guilty of this crime" (Suor Lodovica Bertolasia). "There was too much visiting at the grates by Possenti, Captain Guarnieri, by a certain Tenerino (who's a captain), by Braccesi (who was auditor at the Fortezza), and some others" (Suor Alessandra Mattea Cerni). "It's the common opinion that those guilty of this crime could only be the priest Possenti, Guarnieri, and Braccesi, who came to the convent and who were always here" (Suor Isabetta Serafina Alberti). "Possenti, Captain Guarnieri, and Braccesi also came, and a Tenerino too. But most of all Possenti and Captain Guarnieri and Braccesi. Throughout the convent the belief has always been that they arranged and carried out the nuns' flight" (Suor Paola Lorenza Cantari).[6]

Even as the nuns whispered Giovanni Braccesi's name in the corridors, chapel, and refectory at the Convertite, Innocent X had passed judgment and moved to act. About 8:00 p.m. on July 25, Rome's lieutenant governor followed a small army of heavily armed sbirri (variously reported as between a hundred and three hundred) and some twenty-five Corsican soldiers up the Quirinal Hill to surround Palazzo Barberini (41.902979° N, 12.488916° E). Once all the entrances had been secured the lieutenant governor and several constables dressed as priests invaded the palace, where a Vatican infiltrator waited. The spy led them not to Giovanni Braccesi's own rooms on an upper floor, but to Cardinal Antonio Barberini's private quarters. There they discovered that the door to a room adjoining the cardinal's bedchamber was locked. The spy softly knocked, "My lord, I've come about a brief." "This is not the time for briefs" was the feeble reply from within.

While cassocked policemen stood guard outside the door, the lieutenant governor made his way to the palace dining room, where Cardinal Antonio Barberini and an intimate familiar or two were in the middle of dinner. Once a steward announced him, the governor declared that he had come on Innocent X's orders to arrest Giovanni Braccesi. "I'll see if he's in my room," Barberini replied. "You can take him once I've summoned him."

"I've already got him under guard, don't you know," answered the judge. (Those at table may well have exchanged looks at this impertinent breach of protocol.)

"Well, then, execute His Holiness's commands," Cardinal Antonio responded.

When the door was unlocked, the judge and his pseudo-priests beheld Giovanni Braccesi in his nightshirt, weakly attempting to aim a long-barreled carbine in their general direction. He had just risen from his sickbed, in the throes of a bout of catarrhal fever. Once he learned their papal business, however, he relinquished his firearm and offered no further resistance as he was bound with chains, manacled, and hustled to a carriage in the courtyard.

"Away with you, then, Braccesi!" Cardinal Antonio exclaimed with strained heartiness as the carriage slowly rolled toward the gate. "Go along cheerfully and accept a few days in jail for love of me." As crowds gaped, the small papal army conveyed the shackled Braccesi from the opulence of Palazzo Barberini to the oppressive dungeons of the papal prison of Tor di Nona (41.900984° N,

12.467661° E) beside the Tiber, for what the cardinal promised him would be but "a few days in jail."[7]

Within hours, Braccesi's sensational arrest and the outrageous invasion of Palazzo Barberini (a confounding disrespect for the cardinalate that stunned the college of cardinals) became the talk of Rome. A report sent home on July 29 by Venice's ambassador captures one lurid, carefully spun view of the event. It is worth quoting for its firsthand revelations about Innocent X's presentation of the matter.

> Cardinal Albergati-Ludovisi has turned his hand to the case of those two nuns abducted from a convent in that city and entertained in the house of Cardinal Antonio's personal attendants, then cruelly murdered and buried in a private house, where they thought the crime would also be buried in eternal oblivion. But someone smelled an intolerable stench there in the recent heat. In a wine cellar they discovered two heads—the nuns'—completely intact, though the rest of their corpses had rotted away.
>
> The pope tells me he is pressing this case tirelessly, not just for himself, but also to satisfy the world's outcry against whoever either ordered such wicked and lewd acts to satisfy his own appetites and sensuality or tolerated and consented to them to please his intimate familiars, who dared to commit the most wicked, detestable villainies within his shadow.
>
> So the other night, to shed light on the crime, a certain Braccesi was taken prisoner in Cardinal Antonio's own palace, encircled by a large force of sbirri and Corsican soldiers. Braccesi is a young man of humble birth, but raised up to excellent circumstances solely because of Antonio's favor. This Braccesi already stands convicted, even if he has yet to confess that he had a hand in it—indeed, that he might have been the prime mover behind the nuns' escape. And in the end he may have barbarously ordered their deaths and burial.[8]

"I ALWAYS HAD A DESIRE TO SUCCEED AT THE COURT OF ROME"

Giovanni Braccesi, who has remained invisible in this story until now and whose fortunes had drastically turned overnight, was neither as common nor as ordinary as this Venetian aristocrat assumed. Describing Braccesi's arrest in a letter written the same day, the Florentine ambassador ascribed his exemplary rise less to Cardinal Antonio Barberini than to Braccesi's "lively intelligence and his assiduous application of extraordinary talents to the rigors of important enterprises. Not only did he retain absolute control of His Eminence's household, but he executed his most important business on his own authority."[9]

Seventeen years earlier, in 1628, the teenage Giovanni Braccesi had left home in Pisa, where his was among the city's three dozen most prominent families. The ambitious youth was determined to join the "new men" who relied more on intellectual ability and resourcefulness than on illustrious family background to rise within Rome's clerical aristocracy and bureaucracy. "I always had a desire to succeed at the court of Rome," he later confessed.[10]

Young Braccesi intended to settle in with his father's brother, a lawyer then making his way in Rome. But the death of the boy's father compelled his uncle to return to Pisa as the new head of the family. Giovanni fell back on a maternal uncle, Annibale Luparini, much to the consternation of his father's brother. Luparini had garnered substantial wealth, to be sure, but he was "a very ordinary sort of person" (as his nephew once put it). He earned all that money in a local bakery, helping his father-in-law provide bread for Roman jails. Young Giovanni moved into Casa Luparini on Piazza Capranica (41.899965° N, 12.477899° E), two minutes' walk from the Pantheon.

Braccesi embarked on a long program of study, first under the tutelage of a local humanist "professor." When he was properly groomed, he moved on to the Jesuit Collegio Romano (41.897859° N, 12.480085° E), where he joined some two thousand other ambitious young men preparing for careers in the Eternal City and similarly exalted venues. Giovanni devoted himself to the humanities and nurtured a particular enthusiasm for the fine arts, which might enable him to fulfill the role of "virtuoso of taste" within the entourage of some prince of the church.[11]

After several years of study, Braccesi grasped an opportunity to see a bit of Italy. This was also an inoffensive way to extricate himself from Uncle Annibale's influence and thus to mollify the padrone back in Pisa. Giovanni shared his ambitions with a Roman bureaucrat, Dottore Martino Tondi, who proposed that the young man accompany him on his travels on important Vatican business. Months ran to years as Giovanni Braccesi shadowed the busy Dottore Tondi from Nettuno south of Rome (41.460300° N, 12.6582° E) to Mantua in the north (45.1492° N, 10.7737° E). When Tondi eventually moved on to Ferrara (44.811501° N, 11.872° E) as commissary, Braccesi went along too.[12]

Braccesi's life changed decisively when he caught the attention of Cardinal Stefano Durazzo (1594–1667), who arrived in Ferrara as papal legate in 1634.

FIGURE 19. Bologna, Palazzo del Legato, Camera degli Cavaglieri, where Braccesi presided, 1640–44.

The cardinal called Braccesi to his service as commissary of the legation and subsequently as secretary of briefs. Durazzo—blind in one eye, somewhat volatile, "not much courted by the nobility and little esteemed at court"[13]—must have challenged Braccesi to hone the interpersonal diplomatic skills and facility in elite practices that were essential to any would-be Vatican bureaucrat. He rose to that challenge.

When the pope named Durazzo Bolognese papal legate in May 1640, the by now indispensable Braccesi naturally followed in his accustomed role as secretary of briefs. Before long he added auditor of the Fortezza Urbana in Castelfranco to his administrative responsibilities. Amid the looming hostilities of the War of Castro in 1642, as Braccesi's star continued to rise, Durazzo's declined. By autumn the Barberini had removed him from power in Bologna. Cardinal Durazzo returned to Genoa as archbishop, but Braccesi stayed behind. When Antonio Barberini reached Bologna, he found Giovanni Braccesi efficiently at work and named him vice commissary general of the papal army. Braccesi came to be recognized as Cardinal Antonio's right-hand man, as he presided over the legate's "Camera degli Cavaglieri," where the cardinal's gentlemen stood guard (fig. 19). In the sixteen years since leaving Pisa, Braccesi had thus become in many ways the consummate novus homo.

When not managing Cardinal Barberini's hectic antechamber, Braccesi lived somewhat modestly amid the opulence of Bologna's Palazzo Fava, just a few minutes away (at modern-day via Manzoni 2, fig. 20; 44.496586° N, 11.341821° E). He shared these impressive quarters with sometime vice legate and commissary general Monsignor Alfonso Litta. One would like to imagine Braccesi awakening to the sight of Jason and the Argonauts or Aeneas's founding of Rome, represented by the Carraccis in the palace's fabled frescoed friezes. But by the time Litta spread himself throughout the apartments, all that remained for Braccesi was a solitary sitting room with an antechamber and a room barely large enough for a single bed. His valet had to tuck himself into a large walnut *cassone* (chest) in the antechamber (rather like bedding down in a sarcophagus). Other staff made do with dormitory quarters opposite the church of San Columbano, seventy yards away, where they bunked on army cots amid stored household goods and firewood, in a room devoid of furniture.

It was impossible for Braccesi to receive guests for more than an evening. ("He didn't have the means at home—he had nothing but a single bed for himself," an associate remarked.) But among the gentleman card players in Cardinal Antonio's Camera degli Cavaglieri, Braccesi's hospitality became a legend. "All the gentlemen of the court hung out in his rooms, and he fed them," one military colleague exclaimed. "So many thousands came to Signor Giovanni's apartment that I'd have no way to know who his closest friends were. Those who came to dinner most often were Lord Cardinal Antonio's courtiers, and so many others that I wouldn't know how to name them," according to another.[14]

Such courtly affability and generosity were part of a carefully honed public persona. "He was a man who showed great respect for everyone, without distinction. You saw him in company with great men and with small (that is, those of low degree)," claimed one appreciative military subordinate. Yet Braccesi never lost a gentleman's sensitivity for appearances. ("I never went walking with him because I was ill dressed," his scullery boy recalled.)[15]

A combination of his family inheritance, his patrons' largesse, and a certain frugality enabled Braccesi to accumulate a nest egg running to several thousand scudi. He spent perhaps more than he should have to indulge his budding taste for fine art. By the 1640s he had acquired the beginnings of a

FIGURE 20. Bologna, Palazzo Fava, where Braccesi resided, 1640–44.

very respectable art collection, including a Guercino. This transformed his constrained apartments into a miniature, carefully modulated reflection of Palazzo Fava's grander spaces beyond his door. But he always kept money close to hand, "intending to spend it traveling through the world with others, a notion I've always had in my head," as he put it.[16]

That notion was unrealistic, given the rigors of international travel: Giovanni Braccesi would not have been up to it. A lack of physical robustness accompanied the general impression he gave of constant intellectual preoccupation with weighty matters. A colleague's assertion that "when he went out, he went in a carriage" is not entirely accurate, but it very likely reflects a general impression of his infirmity, echoed in another's remark that "he was someone who entertained at table every day—when he wasn't ill, that is."[17] Braccesi fell seriously ill in August 1643 and was still convalescing the following Eastertime. When Cardinal Antonio hastened to Ferrara in the final days of the war, Braccesi had to come separately by boat because he could not tolerate jolting across the countryside in a carriage.

Four months later, toward the end of July, Giovanni Braccesi followed Cardinal Barberini to Rome. He left Bologna in notable style, with most of the remaining army officers accompanying his carriage out of the city to honor him and wish him a safe journey. He would not have failed to recognize the social and political implications of such a send-off.[18]

Braccesi soon joined Cardinal Antonio at Palazzo Barberini. In October, workmen created Braccesi's new quarters from formerly separate rooms on an upper floor. They enlarged the doorway between them, finished in decorative stucco and plasterwork in imitation of the finer work downstairs. The simple original fireplace was reworked to make a more appropriate statement, with a mantelpiece incorporating additional plaster and stucco decoration. Now he could show off his art collection to better advantage.[19]

But illness stalked Braccesi to Rome and to Palazzo Barberini. In late winter and spring of 1645 he was regularly in and out of bed as his fevers came and went while he nevertheless attempted to go about Cardinal Antonio's business. After he fell ill again in mid-July, Braccesi disregarded the admonitions of his friends and the sterner commands of the cardinal's personal physician, then reluctantly took to his bed and barely stirred for almost a week. The solicitous Cardinal Antonio eventually moved him for safekeeping down from his apartment to the room adjoining the cardinal's bedchamber. Braccesi found himself in surely the most elegant bed he had ever occupied, with an imposing tester and hangings painted in silver blue with all manner of birds and other charming features of the natural world. As he settled himself on the mattress of finest red leather and reclined on a pair of matching bolsters, Braccesi must have wondered at just how far he had come since he first took up residence in Rome as a teenager seventeen years before.[20]

"HE STANDS CONVICTED, EVEN IF HE HAS YET TO CONFESS"

Giovanni Braccesi contemplated a very different reality after sbirri took him from bed and threw him into the dungeons of the Tor di Nona prison on July 25. As Braccesi languished in his cell, Innocent X's investigators in Rome and Bologna worked to strengthen their case against him (and also against his unmentioned powerful superior). On July 27 Bolognese investigators asked Diana Tomassini what she knew of Giovanni Braccesi. "I don't know this Signor Giovanni Braccesi, nor did I ever hear his name mentioned; if he was ever at Count Alessandro Maria's, I never met him," she replied unhelpfully. Two days later a laundress friend of Gandolfi's wife rattled off the names of all Messere Bonaventura's recent tenants, but had nothing at all to say about Giovanni Braccesi.[21]

Immediately after finishing at the Convertite on August 1, Vicar General Oddofreddi began rounding up Braccesi's former colleagues. What they had to say over the next few days notably contrasted with what the handful of nuns had helpfully offered him. "I don't know that Braccesi was ever at any convent. I never saw Signor Giovanni go to the Convertite, nor do I believe he went there, because of his weighty occupation" (Giovanni Pera, Braccesi's former army acquaintance). "I don't remember ever seeing Signor Giovanni Braccesi at any convent, nor do I know that he was friends with any sister. Except that he had his laundry done at the Convertite; I went there to deliver it and pick it up" (Peregrino Turi, Braccesi's page). "I don't know that he was ever at any convent. I heard that he's been imprisoned in connection with this case, but I don't know that he had any part in it. I never saw anything to suggest that" (Tomaso Bentuoli, former coworker from the Fortezza Urbana).[22]

Word on the street in Rome (at least out of earshot of Innocent X) was also shifting. The Venetian ambassador's next dispatch to Venice, dated August 5, told quite a different story from the one of July 29:

> Braccesi, imprisoned in the case of the nuns from Bologna, was not guilty of any complicity in the act, so they say, but only of a simple sharing of what happened with those who committed it. So his incarceration, solemnized

with so much show, with sbirri and Corsican soldiers, and with a thousand other cunning slights, was ordered for no other reason than as an excuse to carry off all the administrative records for all the funds spent in the recent wars (over which he had authority).[23]

Comments in the ambassador's previous communication had also suggested that papal strategies were not entirely (perhaps not even primarily) about Braccesi. "Absolutely nothing is excused at the papal palace that might prejudice and arouse distaste against the reputation of the house of Barberini, with predictions of imminent major proceedings." Another Roman observer's description of the insolent behavior toward Cardinal Antonio during the nocturnal invasion of his palace provided further clarification: "Word is there was an express command from the pope to lay hands on Antonio if they encountered the slightest resistance regarding Braccesi's arrest."[24] Giovanni Braccesi, it seems, was bait on the hook of the latest prelate to fill the shoes of the fisherman.

As the Bolognese curia continued to root around for links between Braccesi and the sinister goings-on near the voltone dei Caccianemici, it also quietly probed for evidence to implicate the more powerful figure "in whose shadow these most wicked, detestable villainies might have been committed," as the Venetian ambassador put it. Had there been a cover-up? Bologna's busy new vicar general turned his attention to the clerical investigators who had preceded him in pursuit of justice back in April 1644. Thus it was that Bernardino Cattania, the previous vicar general, found himself under interrogation about his own handling of things. Cattania did his best to wriggle off the hook.

"The information I gathered was taken only fifteen or sixteen days after the crime, because I couldn't play a part from the start since it fell under the jurisdiction of Monsignor Rinaldi, the nuns' vicar," he was careful to point out. "I learned about it through a letter from the then cardinal archbishop. I remember that subsequently I gathered the information I deemed necessary in the case."

"Did anything indicate where the nuns might have been concealed?"

"The bargello brought someone to my chambers who claimed to have seen one of the nuns in a house by the voltone dei Caccianemici. Straightaway I had Monsignor Cesi, the vice legate, informed. But his illustrious lordship said he didn't believe it. Once he was thoroughly informed, then he would follow up on it, or so the bargello reported to me."

"Did you ever have recourse to your superior in Rome?"

"I did. I believe Lord Cardinal Colonna responded that he could not believe that Monsignor Cesi, a gentleman of such pellucid conscience, would neglect this sort of business."

"Was the trial ever completed?"

"It remained incomplete for want of the authority to lay hands on those who might be guilty."

"Don Carlo Possenti, who was seriously singled out in the investigation—why wasn't he arrested?"

"You would have to ask Monsignor Rinaldi, who was prohibited from arresting him. I lacked the authority to arrest a chaplain in His Holiness's army."[25]

The next day it was not nuns' vicar Rinaldi, but criminal auditor Alfonso Arnaldi who likewise found the investigative tables turned on him.

"I didn't discover any culprits or accomplices, only loud public clamor about Don Carlo Possenti and Guarnieri."

"Did you perform due diligence to arrest the guilty?"

Arnaldi inevitably ducked into the shadow of his superiors. "I left all that to Monsignor Rinaldi, who began the case as nuns' vicar. I also left it to Monsignor Cattania, the vicar general, to whom I am subordinate. I heard there were impediments involving the papal army. Rinaldi and Cattania didn't get what they wanted from Monsignor Cesi, which is to say, to put some of the soldiers in chains. I did everything required of me that I could accomplish within my authority and that I deemed necessary. Clearly, the whole matter involved the army, where our authority did not reach."

"Why didn't you have recourse to secular authorities?"

"That wasn't for me to do, but for Monsignor Rinaldi, who began the case, and Monsignor Cattania, who followed up on it. The two did everything possible, especially to have Possenti arrested. But from what they told me, Monsignor Cesi raised difficulties. It seems to me that they said Possenti was supposed to have been in Ferrara when the nuns escaped, and therefore they couldn't believe he took part in it."[26]

It fell to Innocent X's Roman detectives to oblige him with evidence more to his liking. By early August sbirri in Rome tracked down the young woman Bonaventura Gandolfi had hired as his children's nursemaid and subsequently brought along to Rome in January 1645. Young, simple Domenica offered a wealth of information about the Gandolfi household. She revealed that a day or two after Suor Laura and Suor Silveria's disappearance, Cavalier Girolamo Pazzi, one of the Gandolfi's aristocratic tenants, overheard Gandolfi's wife discussing this scandalous news in the kitchen while she bleached her husband's collars. "Cavalier Pazzi said that a certain gentleman had told him they'd run off and that Signor Giovanni Braccesi had helped them. My mistress asked where Braccesi had taken them, and the gentleman said he thought Braccesi had put them in the house of a relative of his, who lived near Porta San Felice."

The servant claimed that Dorotea Gandolfi had hurried over to the Convertite to share this news with a cloistered cousin. "She confirmed that it was true: Signor Braccesi had helped them get away. And Braccesi had also been at the Convertite on the day right before they ran off." (Several nuns had already indicated, however, that *Possenti* was the alleged visitor to SS. Filippo e Giacomo shortly before the escape, when Braccesi was in fact still in Ferrara.)

"Do you know Giovanni Braccesi?"

"Only by sight. Because he sometimes came to visit Cavalier Pazzi and the other gentlemen, and I heard them call him 'Braccesi.' I saw him come especially before the time when the nuns disappeared. I don't remember seeing him again after they fled."[27]

Young Domenica's minimally reliable revelations were just what investigators hoped to hear and whetted their appetites for Bonaventura Gandolfi's subsequent testimony. Alas, it proved disappointing: he had nothing worth saying about Giovanni Braccesi.[28]

Signora Gandolfi also proved much less helpful than the Gandolfi nursemaid had led interrogators to anticipate. She prattled on with endless irrelevant information. In the end she offered an accusation scarcely more detailed than her husband's: "People in Bologna say publicly that some of Cardinal Antonio Barberini's gentlemen had a hand in arranging their escape. In particular they named Braccesi and Castrodini, who I've never met myself. That's just what I heard around Bologna."[29] Well, at least she mentioned Braccesi.

It was beginning to look as if Giovanni Braccesi's sensational arrest for complicity in the nuns' abduction and murder rested on secondhand kitchen gossip from a servant of dubious credibility and on what a few nuns obligingly claimed to have seen or (more commonly) heard from their limited perspective within convent walls near the edge of town.

Which is not to say that Giovanni Braccesi's fortunes stood much chance of turning once again. His ordeal had scarcely begun. He would "stand convicted, even if he has yet to confess" for as long as papal investigators hoped for further revelations from obliging convertite and from the likes of Gandolfi's nursemaid. And who knows what Braccesi might eventually be constrained to reveal about those he served. So if small fry such as Giovanni Braccesi languished—or perished—in the net while Innocent X trolled for bigger fish, it served a greater good, the *favor fidei* ("the priority of the faith," as the church described the ends that justified its sometimes dubious means).[30]

7

LIGHT AT THE TOP OF THE STAIRS

The Bolognese inquiry lumbered forward through July as investigators concentrated on the nuns' Pepoli hideaway. Where had they taken refuge before they slipped into Palazzo Pepoli? "From what the count told me," Diana Tomassini recalled, "they went to the house of a poor man whose ruination they could be, but he didn't tell me who that poor man was."[1] And for now, nobody else was telling the authorities.

Almost six weeks into the investigation, Archbishop Albergati-Ludovisi informed Cardinal Pamphili that the Bolognese curia might issue an edict of immunity to all who came forward to tell everything they knew.[2] After the decree was posted on August 4, when bailiffs brought in the next key witness, she clearly suspected the reason for her arrest. About Easter 1644 she had stopped to deliver thread to a part-time glove maker named Doralice Pallada, who lived on the top floor of a house along strada Maggiore (fig. 5, B; fig. 22, C; roughly 44.490351° N, 11.356535° E), the city's chief east–west thoroughfare, not far from Porta Maggiore (fig. 5, A; fig. 22, B; 44.49° N, 11.35727° E). The harried servant who came down to admit her grumbled about all her extra work because of "two pretty ladies—very pretty" who were visiting (but secretly: they were staying where nobody could see them). When the witness next visited in early May to help with the laundry, a few exquisite linens and lacy towels surfaced in an otherwise dingy pile. Madonna Doralice revealed that the two mysterious ladies had left them behind, along with some other lovely things, including a man's doublet of scarlet baize and matching breeches, all embellished with gold. Doralice even modeled them for the visiting laundress.[3]

Sbirri promptly went off in search of Doralice Pallada's former servant. Life had proved unkind to Catterina Milani, the heavyset figure with a perpetually discontented expression who confronted investigators the same afternoon. Like many widows, she had fallen on hard times and into sin after her husband's death. Catterina eventually landed at the Opera dei Poveri Mendicanti, for fallen women who could not afford the Convertite's price of admission. Casa Pallada had been her first stop after rehabilitation. She busied herself with endless kitchen and domestic chores and looked after the Palladas' two daughters and the bastard daughter of a family friend, Federico Panzacchi. At night she collapsed on the pallet in the kitchen she shared with her brood.

"Yes, there were two pretty ladies—very pretty!" Catterina confirmed. "One were tall with red hair and a scar under her ear; she were dressed up like a man. The other one were smaller and heavier, with dark eyes, dark hair, and pretty white teeth. She were done up like a man too. They said they were the wives of two merchants and left their husbands to escape their beatings. On their last day I saw both of them in tears. They said their husbands had sent out letters asking after them, so if they didn't want to get caught they had to move on."

"What did Doralice say about them?"

"She never told me nothing at all, just time and again not to tell nobody. She even made me stay inside for five or six days for fear I'd say something to somebody."

Catterina also spoke of a mysterious chest overflowing with fine linens and elegant apparel. A few days after the pretty ladies vanished, a stranger appeared at the door with a giant laundry basket and removed all the fine things; there was so much that she had to make several trips.

"They told me that servant lives on via Mascarella."[4]

Vicar General Oddofreddi had long had his eye on the house of an invalid tailor on via Mascarella, of course. On the morning of August 8 a servant named Bartolomea Galliani from via Mascarella reluctantly faced Monsignor Arnaldi. Naturally she claimed to have no idea why she had been arrested.

"Where do you live?"

"At the house of Lorenzo Possenti."

"Do you know if Carlo Possenti is acquainted with anyone named Pallada?"

"No. At least I don't know anybody by that name."

"Did Don Carlo ever send you to a house on strada Maggiore?"

"No, my lord."

Monsignor Arnaldi signaled the bargello. While Bartolomea fidgeted, he went out, then reentered with Catterina Milani.

"Yes, my lord." Catterina nodded emphatically in Bartolomea's direction. "That were her, the one that come to the Palladas'."

Arnaldi quietly shifted his gaze back toward Bartolomea. "Do you still dare to deny that you know the Palladas, much less that you've been to their house?"

"I don't know anybody named Pallada! I've never been to any house on strada Maggiore!"

Arnaldi shook his head and patiently regarded her with a charitable smile. "Now, Bartolomea, I would urge you to speak the truth. There is really no point in lying when this witness has identified you to your face."

"I don't know her." Bartolomea's eyes shifted from Arnaldi to Catterina. "I was never at the Palladas' on strada Maggiore."

"Yes you were!" Milani interjected indignantly. "You're her that came to pick up them linens. You showed up three times!"

Arnaldi paused, appraising one, then the other, then returned his full attention to Bartolomea. "Think on the remedies that the law provides, Bartolomea, against any who persist in such falsehoods."

"I was never there!"[5]

The auditor abruptly signaled the bailiffs. They brusquely hauled Bartolomea over to where a heavy rope snaked down from a pulley overhead. Arnaldi looked on with an air of detachment as the men stripped the servant down to her shift. She tried to cover herself, but they forced her hands behind her back and tied them. They attached the rope to her wrists as she collapsed in a heap, like so much dirty laundry. Guards pulled her to her feet none too gently and held her tightly by the arms, lifting her off the floor.

"Bartolomea, will you now speak the truth?" Arnaldi paused, eyebrows arched, but only for a moment before nodding theatrically toward the bailiff.

"I'll tell the truth, my lord!" Bartolomea cried out. "It's true! I was once at the Palladas' on strada Maggiore to fetch some linen!"

"Won't you freely tell the truth, Bartolomea? We've already heard that you were there several times."

"Only once!"

The auditor gestured and the slackened rope slowly drew tighter.

"I'll tell, my lord—I was there twice!"

"Bartolomea, do you still insist on hiding the whole truth?" Arnaldi's pace quickened, and his benevolent tone slipped away. "To suffer in torment—is that what you want? When another woman has testified to your many visits?"

Immediately the rope jerked tighter, as if unbidden. The guards began to let her drop.

"It's true, it's true, my lord—three times!" Bartolomea screamed.

"Did someone send you, or did you go on your own, and why?"

"I already told you! I went three times! To pick up linens! Because Don Carlo Possenti sent me! I took them to Don Carlo's and gave them to him. Later he sent them away."

By then his midday meal was probably waiting. Arnaldi called a halt and had Bartolomea Galliani released. Once a barber surgeon gave her a perfunctory once-over and declared her none the worse for wear, she gathered up her clothes and shambled off to a cell somewhere.[6]

She would have much more to say next time, eager to please with whatever she thought they wanted to hear. It was a simple matter of timing, the criminal auditor may have observed over lunch. After preliminary pauses of encouragement, at a certain point one must accelerate unexpectedly, so the reluctant witness imagines she has waited too long and resisted too late, and now there is no escape. With a day or two to reflect and remember, next time Bartolomea would be quite ready to share her store of information.

"Why did you first deny, but later confess that you went to the Palladas'?" Arnaldi asked mildly when Bartolomea reappeared two days later.

"Your lordship can understand that I've been with Carlo Possenti for sixteen years. So I wouldn't want to do him any harm."

"Were you ever at the convent of the Convertite?"

"Yes, my lord. Don Carlo sent me to Suor Silveria Catterina, during the two months before the sisters ran off, to deliver letters from Don Carlo. Suor Silveria, she also gave me letters to bring back. Don Carlo was careful to hide that he was sending me, though, because his mother didn't like it one bit. She'd scold him and then she'd tell me I'd sinned too, because the vicar general outlawed such visiting."

"How did you hear about the nuns' disappearance?"

"On Easter Tuesday afternoon Don Carlo told us he was going to Ferrara, so that his mother would know where he was at. Then the morning after somebody snatched the sisters Count Ercole Bentivoglio showed up at the house asking for Don Carlo. His mother said he wasn't in Bologna because he'd gone to Ferrara. The count replied, 'I'm glad to hear it, because two nuns were abducted from the Convertite and people are saying that he's the one responsible.'"

"How long was Don Carlo in Ferrara?"

"He came back to Bologna after maybe four or five days. He stopped at the house an hour or two after dark with Count Ferdinando Ranuzzi. I remember he knocked on the door and when his mother went to open it she started crying. She said the authorities wanted to lock him up because people said he'd made off with the nuns. But both Don Carlo and Count Ferdinando Ranuzzi assured her that there was no danger because he hadn't committed the crime."

"When and why were you sent to pick up the linens?"

"I don't remember how many days later Don Carlo told me to go to Andrea Pallada's place on strada Maggiore, past via Fondazza. I should ask for Guarnieri's things. So I went three times on a day when Don Carlo's mother wasn't at home. I no sooner managed to get it all back there than Don Carlo showed up and stuck it in a chest. Then that evening he sent it away with some workman from strada Maggiore."

"How do you know he was from strada Maggiore?" Arnaldi interjected.

"The night before I went to get the linens, Don Carlo was at the house with Colonel Alessandro Guarnieri. (Don Carlo lit a lamp for him, so I recognized Guarnieri's face in the light and he called him 'Signor Colonel.' I overheard them while I was in the kitchen, through the doorway.) Don Carlo said, 'I'll send my servant to pick up the linens at Pallada's place.' Then I heard Guarnieri say he'd have one of his workmen from strada Maggiore take the chest away. He came to get it about 10:00 at night, and Don Carlo went with him."[7]

By now other possible accessories before or after the fact had begun to fall into (or through) Albergati-Ludovisi's net. About midnight on August 9, sbirri from both the curia and the Torrone went looking for Count Ferdinando Ranuzzi at Palazzo Ranuzzi-Manzoli (now via Zamboni 14–16; 44.495332° N, 11.34819° E, the Hotel San Donato, much changed). When nobody answered their knock they broke down the door, then wandered through the silent apartment, peering into dark rooms on the first and second floors. Nothing: not a soul seemed to be at home. Not a stick of furniture remained either, apart from a solitary walnut bed, glimmering with gold ornament, and a mattress or two, abandoned in Ranuzzi's bedchamber. Bailiffs eventually rousted out a lone caretaker, who confirmed that the count had left Bologna a year earlier, bound first for Venice, then for Rome. In March or April 1645 he had arranged for a local bookseller to dispose of the contents of his apartments. Clearly Ranuzzi had no intention of returning.[8]

The next morning the archiepiscopal bargello arrested Carlo Manolesi at his bookshop (roughly 44.492446° N, 11.345025° E),[9] not far from the voltone dei Caccianemici. Manolesi revealed that Ferdinando Ranuzzi had first appeared at his shop three years earlier and in spring 1645 had engaged the book dealer to sell off his property.

"Do you know or have you heard the reason for Count Ferdinando's departure?" the interrogator asked.

"I heard from various people in my shop that he left because he was mixed up in the business of the nuns. They said he took part in getting them out of the convent. If it's true or false, I don't really know."

"Why did Count Ferdinando get involved? Did he act alone or with others?"

"I heard absolutely nothing about that."

"Given your close friendship, it is highly implausible that you took no part in these crimes," the interrogator broke in, "either before or after the fact, or that you should be so ignorant of them."

"You lordship is trying to embroil me in something that I never sought after," Manolesi protested. "I never took the slightest interest in all that."

"Do you know a Carlo Possenti?"

"Yes, my lord, for five or six years, because he often spends time in my shop, as men of talent are accustomed to do. The two were friends. I regularly saw them together."

"Who were Ranuzzi's closest friends?"

"As I said, I often saw him with Possenti. And with Negrino Negrini, who also visited my shop."

"Do you know Giovanni Braccesi? Did you ever see him with Count Ferdinando?"

"I know Giovanni Braccesi, but I never saw him with the count. I definitely saw him with Possenti, though. When they went walking together."

"Did you hear anything about Possenti's part in the nuns' escape?"

"Immediately afterward I heard the opinion that Possenti had snatched them."

"Do you know where the nuns were hiding?"

"I heard that they were at Count Alessandro Maria Pepoli's. It was something widely discussed around Bologna."[10]

The name Negrino Negrini would not have escaped the auditor. In late July the vicar general had received an anonymous letter on behalf of a zealous nun at the Convertite whose fervor moved her to contact church authorities. (Despite her purported fervor and the curia's repeated exhortations to come forward, that convent witness's identity remains a mystery.) The nun urged them to arrest one of "the peasants of a certain Negrino Negrini. If you lay hands on him, you'll learn everything, because he was a confidant of the one who did the murders and burial. Then the one named Negrini could more easily be captured."[11]

On August 2 the archbishop informed Rome that sbirri were scouring the countryside for this "most important assassin." He was never captured. In a subsequent letter, the archbishop confidently predicted the imminent arrest of Negrino Negrini by "a renowned sbirro called Zampone [Pig Trotters], who knows everything there is to know on the subject." The expert Zampone may have been famous, but Negrino Negrini eluded him.[12]

On the day after Bartolomea Galliani's second interrogation, the archbishop sent Auditor Arnaldi to ransack Carlo Possenti's rooms on via Mascarella. Meanwhile the busy bargello headed across town to arrest the Palladas. But their apartment was empty: they too had skipped town.[13]

Perhaps the Palladas were less expert than more elusive persons of interest, for it took less than twenty-four hours to track them down. The simple Andrea Pallada claimed disingenuously that his sense of civic duty prompted his return: "I've come to satisfy my obligation, in obedience because I heard there's an edict requiring everyone who knows anything about the two nuns' flight from the Convertite to tell everything they know."

Doralice Pallada (clearly the shrewder half of this partnership) tempered candor with enlightened self-interest. "I heard that everyone who'd helped out the runaway nuns was ending up in jail. So me and my husband left town because we were afraid—though we were innocent. We went to Padua to fulfill a vow we made three years ago when my husband was really sick. But as soon as we learned that the lord cardinal our archbishop fervently desired us to return, we eagerly came to tell the truth and give satisfaction. We did so gladly, in fact, because we'd seen that edict commanding everyone to tell what they knew. (Of course, it hadn't yet appeared when we left Bologna.)"[14]

The Palladas were people of an extremely ordinary sort. For several years Andrea served as a swordsman to Federico Panzacchi, who became his close friend and confidant. In the mid-1640s Andrea Pallada continued to work in security service as a guard at the Palazzo del Legato.

In autumn 1642, Pallada's long acquaintanceship with Carlo Possenti had shifted to a sense of personal obligation. When Andrea's little brother Carlino entangled himself in a crime that was gallows business, Possenti's eloquence convinced authorities to commute the brother's sentence to banishment and military service. (This amounted to capital punishment, briefly postponed: not long thereafter Carlino died in battle at Spoleto.)[15]

At Christmas 1643 Carlo Possenti informed Andrea Pallada that he could soon return the favor. During the following Holy Week the priest approached Pallada in the piazza: he wanted to have a look at Andrea's apartment. Don Carlo paced about with obvious dismay. Could a doorway be cut from a corridor into the most secluded rear chamber, to make it accessible without traipsing through the entire apartment? Pallada reminded Possenti that he was a renter. Where did he get such a curious idea? "After a solemn and long-winded preamble, Don Carlo announced that he would like me to take in two women from Ferrara, to get them out of a bit of bother or hurly-burly that might befall them," Pallada later testified.[16] The fugitives needed to slip in as unobtrusively as possible, without risk of discovery during their stay. The obliging Andrea reassured the priest that nobody but his family would ever see them. Despite his misgivings, Possenti agreed. He further announced that shortly before the women's arrival a chest full of their belongings would appear.

On Easter Monday evening, as Andrea and Doralice sat eating in the kitchen, they heard a knock. The servant Catterina lit a candle and descended the darkened staircase to the street, where she discovered Don Carlo Possenti. "Inform Messere Andrea that Don Carlo Possenti is here and wishes to speak with him." Catterina reverently escorted the impressive priest upstairs, showed him into a dark little gallery, and obligingly left him her candle as she went off in the dark to fetch her master. When Andrea joined him out of earshot, Doralice got up and moved closer to the door. "Don Carlo asked my husband for the key to the building's main entrance because he wanted to bring the two Ferrarese ladies to our house the following Thursday night."[17]

On Thursday night the Palladas should set a lighted candle at the top of the stairs, leave the interior bolt on the entrance unlocked, and withdraw to the inner reaches of the house. Sometime after 2:00 a.m. someone would let the women in through the lower door. Nobody upstairs should go to investigate until after they heard the door close. (Possenti knew the danger of eyewitnesses to these misdeeds and their perpetrators.) Possenti took the key to the lower door and left. "So, who's supposed to pay for the keep of these Ferrarese ladies?" Doralice sniffed rather acidly once the priest had gone. Pallada showed her a doubloon that Possenti had handed over on the stairs to cover any expenses before his return from Ferrara.

On Easter Wednesday a stranger appeared at the Palladas' door, groaning under the weight of a massive wooden crate. "Don Carlo Possenti sent this here chest," he mumbled in an alien brogue. After commanding him to deposit it in the rear chamber, then sending him about his business, the inquisitive Doralice went back for a look: the lid was nailed down tight.[18]

Thursday evening Andrea was off at work, leaving his wife to fret on her own. The servant Catterina tucked the Pallada brood into bed and went off to doze by the fire. Doralice sat alone in the gloom, waiting. Well after midnight she was roused by a faint, hollow scraping of the door below, then heard hesitant footfalls on the stairs. Doralice waited an extra minute before her curiosity got the better of her and she stole toward the staircase in darkness. The candlestick was missing, but she could distinguish its flickering light receding toward the back of the house, along with the soft scuffle of boots. She followed the glow and whispers to the rear bedroom.

"When I saw them it seemed like a bad dream. The smaller one said, 'Oh, lady, what are you doing!' (I didn't recognize her.) 'Don't you remember visiting me three years ago at the Convertite? I'm Suor Silveria Catterina.' But if she hadn't told me who she was, I wouldn't have known her, because she was dressed like a man." While their discomfited hostess took this in, both her guests shed their boots, swords, and other male attire and snuggled under the covers in the larger bed in the unheated room.[19]

But nobody slept. The new arrivals chattered incessantly: they said they had unlocked the carters' gate while they wandered innocently around the convent garden after dusk. "If we didn't leave tonight, then we could never hope to do so ever again."[20]

In the wee hours of April 1, still long before dawn, Andrea Pallada stopped at the house after escorting a departing courier as far as Porta Maggiore.

"Is anybody here?"

"Come in here, then. See for yourself what's happened. Have a look at these 'Ferrarese ladies' who've been dropped at our house!" exclaimed Doralice as she descended upon her husband and led him back to the bedroom, where the nuns were wide awake.

"As soon as he saw them he just about fell over dead," Doralice recalled, "because he recognized one of them as Suor Silveria."

"What kind of business is this?" Pallada exclaimed. "How did they get here? He said there'd be two ladies from Ferrara! What was Don Carlo thinking? What has he done, to bring these women here and put us in this kind of danger? He's out to ruin me!" Suor Silveria did her best to calm him down and explain. "Both she and her companion had left the convent that night and had come to my house on Don Carlo Possenti's orders," Andrea related.[21]

Everyone went silent when they heard the front door open and close. Two shadowy figures, their faces shrouded in their capes like infidel Turks, each holding a lantern, noiselessly appeared in the shadows near the top of the stairs. Andrea signaled Doralice to retreat to a darkened adjoining room, where she slipped behind the bed hangings. The intruders silently entered the back bedroom, nodded to the sisters, and uncovered their faces. "I saw that it was Count Ferdinando Ranuzzi and Negrino Negrini. I definitely knew who they were, though I never hung out with them," Andrea related. He resumed his complaints about Don Carlo's deception. "When they saw how scared I was, they told me to get a grip on myself. They warned me to keep quiet if I knew what was good for me. Because otherwise—well, I ought to know how these things could turn out when cavaliers play a part in them." The men handed over various odds and ends, together with pairs of men's breeches, and left without another word.[22]

"I heard from the two women that those two, Count Ferdinando Ranuzzi and Negrino Negrini, had brought them to the house that night," Doralice later claimed. "First they'd taken them to Count Ferdinando's house (where they said they'd had a drink), then they brought them to our house."[23]

Too distraught by Possenti's duplicity to return to duty, Andrea crawled into bed and curled up beside his wife, wide awake, until the sun came up. When he returned to quarters as sunlight spread across the piazza, he heard that his commanding officer had been abruptly called to a meeting in the Palazzo del Legato. He reappeared shortly to spread the word of the nuns' flight and to emphasize the need for total commitment to their recapture. From his post nearby, Andrea watched as sbirri came and went from postings at every city gate. The jittery Pallada ambled about trying to avoid the endless babble about La Rossa and La Generona's disappearance.

At dinner he told Doralice there was such commotion all over town because of the runaways that he was determined to get out of there. She answered that if he left, she was coming too. Again Suor Silveria attempted to reassure them. "I shouldn't worry about a thing, because when Don Carlo got back, he would sort out everything," Pallada recalled. "Which is how it went, in fact. Once Don Carlo was back, the commotion died down. I didn't notice any further effort to find the nuns."[24]

Andrea began to avoid the apartment, shunning the back bedroom and speaking to the sisters only when he brought them food. The women of the house, on the other hand, settled into an affable if uneasy conviviality. Short, round little Silveria cut a comical figure in her fashionable men's garments tricked out with silver and gold and topped with a floppy two-feathered cap. Since she could never stay warm in the chilly early days of April, she tried to wear her lacy scarlet baize man's doublet and breeches as long underwear beneath her outer garments. Given the extra layers and her full figure, she was bursting out of her doublet and could do up the silver laces on her breeches only partway. Silveria finally complained with a laugh that the pinched waist of men's fashions gave her a stomachache and peeled herself out of the bottom layer. Her attentive hostess lent her a light wool dress of similar Florentine red to replace her man's outfit beneath her top garment. For the rest of her stay Silveria donned the odd combination whenever she felt a chill.[25]

Doralice and the servant Catterina could not help curiously eyeing the great crate hulking in a corner of the bedroom, and the nuns could not resist showing off the contents. Catterina produced an intimidating cleaver with which the sisters attacked the cover. After long chopping sessions that seemed certain to rouse the downstairs landlady, punctuated by long pauses to catch their breath and recover from nervous laughter, they sent Catterina off to burn the splintered remnants of the lid.

Transferring the contents to a walnut cassone of Doralice's provided a chance to display a magical succession of fine, perfectly white matching sheets, pillowcases, towels, and handkerchiefs, mostly trimmed with layers of lace, plus opulent bed hangings, men's shirts and women's blouses, and other garments of silk and other fine fabrics, many with silver or gold buttons and other costly ornamentation. To the *ooh*s and *aah*s, La Rossa and La Generona responded that these things were like slaves' goods compared with the gold and silver treasures they had already sent to Carlo Possenti. As further confirmation, they ate all their meals with magnificent silver forks and spoons and knives with silver handles.[26]

Barely a day after receiving his unwelcome guests, Andrea Pallada protested to his former employer turned confidant, Federico Panzacchi, "This is the fine favor that Possenti, that nuns' aficionado, wanted of me! I'd like you to come see this spectacle for yourself—these two old dearies that this folly was committed for!"

Panzacchi made his way to the apartment on strada Maggiore, ostensibly to look in on his illegitimate daughter. Doralice called him into the back bedroom, where La Rossa and La Generona had been observing him through the crack in the door. They hoped he could ease their melancholy and satisfy their curiosity. What were people saying about them and their flight? "I replied that they were saying it was craziness on their part, that they had committed a grievous sin," Panzacchi reported when it came time for him to testify. "I asked why they had run away from the convent. They told me the old one had left because of Don Carlo Possenti, her beloved. The other one said she had done it because of Captain Donato Guarnieri. And they fretted over Don Carlo's delay in returning from Ferrara."[27]

After an anxious weekend, as Pallada stood guard in the piazza, he caught sight of Possenti, still in his high boots and traveling cloak, coming out of the Palazzo del Legato. Andrea caught his eye and furtively beckoned for the priest to follow him up the steps and into the looming basilica of San Petronio on one side of the piazza (fig. 5, G; 44.492744° N, 11.343025° E). After they quietly crossed to a shadowy side chapel, Andrea immediately began to protest Possenti's callous deception. "Leave your door unbolted tonight," the priest broke in. "I'll be coming over." He turned and hurried back across the deserted nave and out the door.

Possenti waited until about midnight, long after the Pallada children and the servant Catterina were asleep on the kitchen floor, before he let himself into the safe house on strada Maggiore. "But, Don Carlo, this wasn't the favor you asked me for!" Andrea protested as the priest came up the stairs. "These two weren't from Ferrara. This business will ruin me and my family—that's for sure!"

"Look here," Possenti interrupted irritably. "There's absolutely no danger. If the nuns were ever discovered here, you could just say that I brought them in by hoodwinking you," Possenti continued with a hint of mockery. "I didn't tell you they were nuns from the Convertite. You foolishly fell for what I said—that they were two ladies from Ferrara. So quit fussing. I'll get them out of here before anything like that happens."[28]

Possenti strode to the rear of the apartment and entered the back bedroom. He peremptorily showed La Rossa out and shut the door behind him. Through the door, the others heard the faint rattle of the bolt being thrown. Laura Vittoria spent the next two hours in an adjoining room with the Palladas while they all did their best to ignore the muffled sounds from beyond the locked door. When the pair emerged it was too dark and too late for anyone to notice whether Silveria Catterina was blushing.

After this hot and hasty reunion, Silveria Catterina waited several days before "her beloved" showed up again. This time the priest took his time behind the locked door, alone with La Generona for five hours in the chilly back bedroom. The sky was already brightening when Andrea and Doralice awoke to see the priest slink through their darkened bedroom, lantern in hand, and disappear down the stairs. This time Silveria did not come out to see him off. "Now, whether those two crawled into bed together, that I don't know, because I couldn't see whatever it was that they were up to in there," Doralice later testified. "I do know for sure that on the night when he hung around until the sun was coming up, La Rossa had to go and sleep in a bed in our other room." And the next morning La Generona slept late.[29]

During the interludes between Possenti's nocturnal visits, with Andrea regularly away on duty in the piazza, life on strada Maggiore dragged on in anxious limbo, brightened only by Federico Panzacchi's occasional visits. When he inquired about the empty, lidless crate in the nuns' bedroom, Doralice eagerly unlocked her cassone and brought out its contents for him to admire. Silveria pulled out a pair of red silk breeches and another of turquoise, which she offered to Doralice. Even the servant Catterina received more modest gifts of two linen blouses. When her hostess called in her daughters and dressed them up in this unaccustomed finery, Silveria rummaged around for further presents: a pair of delicate pink taffeta ties with large gold fasteners, a purse of red Persian silk covered with golden mesh that might even be real, and a precious rosary of coral with a golden crucifix for Doralice. She presented the younger daughter with a silver ampoule for perfume, with gold filigree, on a delicate beaded chain. The wide-eyed older girl received an unusual little *agnus dei*, resembling an oversized communion wafer impressed with the image of the Lamb of God on one side and the Madonna on the other. It was not the ordinary kind contrived from flour paste or wax but was made of silver. Silveria showed the girl how a relic could be hidden inside. Perhaps thoughts of her own daughter Catterina prompted Silveria's extravagant generosity. Catterina was waiting to take the veil at San Lorenzo someday—if that day ever came.[30]

For more than a week Carlo Possenti must have chafed at what he saw as Pallada's craven sniveling about the risks Possenti's ruse had brought down on his family. Abject fear, it seemed, could vanquish any sense of obligation in such a man, who repaid magnanimity with ingratitude and impertinence. Finally, when the two crossed paths on Sunday, April 10, Possenti announced that Colonel Alessandro Guarnieri would get the nuns out that night.

Doralice was resting in her bedroom after her weekly excursion to Mass with the servant Catterina, followed by a rare feast day dinner of veal and pigeons, when she heard Possenti let himself in after sunset. He summoned the nuns to the front room, but she declined to rouse herself to greet the man she now called "that vile priest." While the more obliging Andrea lit a lamp and went down to the cellar to fetch wine for his guest, Possenti ordered Silveria and Laura to be ready to leave in a few hours. "Where are we going?" Silveria asked. "Will you be coming to get us?"

"It won't be me. You're going to another house. You'll be fine there. Be sure to remember to bring everything of yours."

"We won't forget."[31]

"Put on the same things you wore when you left the convent to come here. Leave a light at the top of the stairs. But don't move from up here until you hear the front door open and someone come inside. Then go down in the dark. Don't bring a light."[32] (Possenti had not forgotten the danger of potential eyewitnesses.)

The nuns had nothing much to do to get themselves ready. Silveria decided against trying to squeeze back into her scarlet doublet and breeches. She handed the outfit over to Doralice. "Take these. I may send for them later. But if I don't, they're yours to keep."

They set a candlestick at the top of the stairs. Then there was nothing to do but wait.[33]

It was long past midnight before Andrea, Doralice, and the nuns heard the door open and the scuffle of a small crowd, filtering up toward the lighted candle at the end of the hall. "Keep quiet! Move! Get down here, now!" Silveria and Laura paused long enough to embrace Doralice. "Pray for us!" Silveria whispered. Then the two hurried downstairs into the darkness.[34]

Andrea waited until the door shut, then went down to bolt it. The Palladas picked up the candlestick and wandered back to the empty bedroom. Andrea inspected a curious pile of hair lying on the bed: a hairpiece, rather tatty, that must have been Silveria's, judging by the color. He noticed a shiny object on the wall, glittering faintly in the dim candlelight. Silveria had pinned up a silver pocket watch at the head of her bed. The pretty little thing had stopped. He shook it and tinkered with it. Perhaps Panzacchi would know where to get it repaired. Silveria must have forgotten it. Or perhaps she left it behind as another parting gift, since it was no longer any good to her.

A slim pocket-sized book lay open on a prie-dieu beside the bed, its pages fanning slightly open. On the first page Andrea could make out the Blessed Virgin, floating heavenward, her eyes turned up as if to read a title above her head: "Devotioni alla Santissima Vergine Mater di Dio." Had Silveria forgotten this as well? Andrea slipped the little volume into his pocket. Perhaps it was another parting gift, since it too would be of no more use to her.[35]

At lunchtime a day or two later, Andrea Pallada was halfway home when he ran into Carlo Possenti in Piazza Santo Stefano (fig. 5, D; 44.492323° N, 11.348611° E). Despite Don Carlo's express command, the silly women had managed to leave behind just about everything they needed to take with them when they left. "Bring those things to me at once—meet me inside Santo Stefano—it's always open." Andrea hurried home, where he retrieved two sets of the nuns' finest sheets from Doralice's walnut cassone and the parcels that Ranuzzi and Negrini had dropped off on the night the nuns arrived. He retraced his steps to Santo Stefano, where he found the priest waiting impatiently just inside the ancient church (44.491985° N, 11.34894° E). Possenti hastily inspected the parcels to be sure they still contained the valuable silver cutlery: two four-tined forks, two knives with solid silver handles, and two spoons—the large, expensive sort currently in fashion. Then he stowed everything out of sight under his cloak. "I'll soon be sending someone to pick up all their other things."

"Suit yourself. Send them whenever you want."

Don Carlo turned and left. Pallada watched from the shadows inside the doorway as the priest strode across Piazza Santo Stefano in the direction of Piazza Maggiore or strada Castiglione.[36]

When Andrea returned from guard duty at week's end, all the fine things were gone. Doralice informed him that Possenti's servant Bartolomea had needed several trips and half the day to empty the cassone and carry everything away. On a break halfway through, Doralice could fortify her only with an egg and a little cheese—it was Friday, a fast day, after all.[37]

Another week passed before Pallada next spotted the priest, who collared him in the street. "They say you've still got several of their things at your place."

"Well, I don't know anything about that. Maybe they left some trifles for the children."

Don Carlo's lingering, hard look was a challenge, but he said nothing more and just walked away.

"He knows absolutely everything that's here, and he wants every last thing!" Doralice fumed when her husband described this latest encounter. But Don Carlo never turned up in search of what he imagined the Palladas had filched.[38]

In the waning days of April, Andrea Pallada rarely saw his old friend Possenti, and then only from a distance, which was probably quite all right with him. He heard rumors that La Rossa and La Generona had been hiding out in Palazzo Pepoli. Pallada also heard that the fugitives had briefly hidden out at the house of Squint-Eyed Gandolfi, the one-eyed army man who lived near the voltone dei Caccianemici.[39]

When the freak snowstorm struck on May 9, Doralice anticipated word any day from the perpetually shivering Silveria Catterina, who would need her castoff elegant garments. No word ever came.

After early summer returned, when Andrea Pallada did cross paths with Carlo Possenti, he furtively asked after Silveria Catterina and Laura Vittoria. "Oh, they're very well, indeed. They're doing just fine: somewhere far away, in a place where the devil himself couldn't molest them. They asked to be remembered to you and your dear wife. And Laura Vittoria's servant Galeazzo—Monchino—he's joined them too."

Don Carlo Possenti very likely smiled to himself at the irony of this banter, surely lost on this gullible creature of lesser intellect. But his meaning did not escape Andrea Pallada, who rarely missed anything to be seen or overheard in Piazza Maggiore. "So I figured they must definitely be dead by then," Pallada later recalled. "There were mutterings around Bologna that they'd been murdered and buried somewhere. And word was that the same thing had happened to La Rossa's servant, Monchino, for fear he might reveal who snatched the nuns. From what I heard, he knew everything there was to know and had carried off a good part of the nuns' things from the convent.

"I told my wife what Don Carlo Possenti said: that the nuns were doing fine and sent greetings to me and her. Doralice admitted that she already suspected the poor sisters must be done for. Suor Silveria had told her she'd send for her red doublet and breeches—but she never did, not even when it snowed and stayed so cold for so long. That's why my wife figured her for dead.

"That Suor Silveria—she always did suffer so from the cold."[40]

ROME

8

DRAGNET

CARLO POSSENTI

July 18, the feast of the local patron saint, Bruno of Segni, marked the high point of the year in Segni (41.6883° N, 13.0163° E), perched atop a craggy mountain forty miles south of Rome. It also heralded an administrative challenge for the town's untried vice duke, Carlo Possenti, who had found his way up the mountainside barely two months earlier. There would be the inevitable procession and High Mass on the feast day, with the throng of faithful to be kept in order. For most outside the episcopate, the festival's true highlight happened the day before: the *caccia del toro* (bullbaiting) in the piazza outside the cathedral. The capricious violence of that spectacle could be contagious and spread havoc among the crush of frenzied spectators.

As Don Carlo hurried out of the ducal palace on the morning of July 17 to take his place of honor in the cathedral portico, the local innkeeper, who doubled as postmaster, delivered a letter. The impatient Possenti broke the seal and skipped to the end, "Your most devoted servant, C. R., in Bologna, 8 July 1645." It was from Carlo Raguzzi, presumably with more ill-starred supplications. Possenti had already written that he could do nothing more for him. Instead, the missive contained news:

> These Bolognese gentlemen can't believe that your lordship now holds the position of vice duke and would have me swear to it on the Gospel. . . . I've no news at all about Your Friend—just that a cavalry ensign reported that the colonel is in Piedmont. . . . The latest here is that at Dionisio's sister's place opposite the Baraccano they found two bodies identified as those two convertite. . . . They're accusing a certain Guarnieri, or two Guarnieri, and it so happens that your name was mentioned too. . . . Word was that Dionisio had been murdered, but that proved false. . . . There's no other news, except that I pray you to keep me close in Cardinal Antonio's memory.

Possenti dropped the letter on his desk, left the ducal residence, and set off up the hill through the boisterous throng making its way toward the cathedral square (41.692828° N, 13.023236° E).[1]

A vice duke should arrive by carriage, but carriages could scarcely negotiate the steeply winding tracks that passed for streets in Segni. Even apart from its administrative challenges, the duchy of Segni demanded adjustments from its neophyte governor.

The town had never completely recovered from depredations in 1557, during Pope Paul IV's abortive attempt to drive the Spanish from Italy. The locals were still getting used to their latest overlord, Cardinal Antonio Barberini. Uncle Urban VIII had bestowed the fiefdom on his nephew half a dozen years before, when the current lord of Segni fell on hard times and had to liquidate various assets.

Possenti's Segni commission had finally come through in March. Only then did the novice governor realize what lay ahead. Not only had Cardinal Antonio's new appointee never overseen a duchy, Possenti had never even governed a household. He had lingered in the family nest in Bologna, ignoring for more than a decade the stipulation that canons of Santa Maria Maggiore live in community. His mother was always on hand to keep Casa Possenti running smoothly.

Now his Segni appointment required him to assemble a staff of his own. He fired his first hire from Rome after a month and had to replace him with a rustic local. A Roman friend, anticipating Don Carlo's social responsibilities on San Bruno's Day, dispatched a Florentine cook to the mountainous hinterlands. If he worked out, Possenti intended to keep him on. The arrival of Possenti's little brother Francesco Maria two weeks into his residency at least afforded him some companionship, but in social refinements the youth, fresh from his regiment, was only marginally more sophisticated than Possenti's rough-hewn local servant. This unimpressive cadre constituted the extent of the vice duke's entourage.

On April 9, Palm Sunday, Don Carlo, his servant, and the muleteer who provided the horses had set off from Rome. By late morning they passed into hill country and onward into the valley of the river Sacco, gradually winding their way upward into the mountains. Above them, here and there a few towns and citadels clung to the rocky high ground in fortified isolation. In deepening twilight, a hospitable gentleman opened his house to them, sparing them a twisting ascent up the gorge in darkness. Next morning they continued upward along sheer limestone escarpments. Nothing interrupted the eerie silence except the distant sound of a woodcutter's ax carried through dark expanses of giant oaks, elms, and chestnuts. The party's eventual arrival at olive groves, canebrakes, and flax fields on terraces carved into steeper hillsides heralded a return to civilization.[2]

A final bend in the road disclosed Segni, huddled along a rocky ridge more than two thousand feet higher than Rome, which already seemed a very distant forty miles away. Beyond the city gate, jumbled rows of indistinguishable squat houses scrabbled up the hillside. Unpredictable blotches of black and gray tuff or brick disrupted expanses of rough, timeworn limestone walls. Everything looked cobbled together and aimlessly patched, without symmetry or order. The muddled townscape might have called to mind crumbling blocks of Gorgonzola cheese.

As one who prided himself on his nerve, Carlo Possenti put a good face on what must have seemed a sorry circumstance. This posting to Segni, far from the centers of culture, may have begun to feel like a banishment. How did one negotiate social proprieties in such a place? In Rome and Bologna Possenti was gratified if a superior came out to receive him, perhaps descended the stairs, or even did him the honor of greeting him at the door. Did anyone among the Segnini require the vice duke even to rise from his chair?

The vice duke's obligatory surveys of his immediate territory revealed little to pique his enthusiasm. Various hoary ecclesiastical edifices and the Palazzo Comunale that faced off with the cathedral across the town square were as lacking in architectural distinction as the close-packed houses clustered about them. Judging by the hodgepodge of pale limestone and black tuff, intermittently scarred by ancient arched doors or windows, roughly filled in long ago, the use of stucco to mask architectural irregularities had never penetrated as far as Segni.

Few trees or gardens broke up the gray monotony of the townscape.

Patches of green chiefly derived from cabbages planted on the sheltered side of massive retaining walls and battlements. Pigs roamed the terraces, living on acorns harvested for them from nearby forests. They too blended into the townscape: their mottled black skin seemed to have taken on the town's ashen hues.[3]

But Carlo Possenti could not fail to wonder at one singular feature of the landscape: colossal walls protruding from rugged hillsides to encircle the town. Rising to intimidating heights, these monuments from some distant age had been laid from gigantic limestone blocks, so finely shaped that they fit together without mortar, held in place only by their immense weight. Since men could never have shifted such enormous stones, Cyclopes must have built these walls, or so the locals claimed. And many believed it, too.

Having made his way to the crowded square and up the cathedral steps, Possenti soon recognized that his preeminent station offered prestige, but not a decent view of the violent spectacle below. Those across the way might have a fine view of both him and the bull, tethered to a stake in the middle of the square by a long rope around its horns. But since the church facade faced east, the sun would be in his eyes all morning. Given the escalating carnage below, Possenti may have found it hard to maintain the air of detachment he assumed was appropriate for someone in his position.

So Colonel Alessandro Guarnieri had quit Bologna and headed north. None too soon, apparently. (Even amid the gory spectacle, Possenti could not put Raguzzi's letter out of his mind.) "It so happens that your name was mentioned too." Of course it was. It had been mentioned ever since the nuns disappeared. But he was in Ferrara on April 1, 1644, as Cardinal Antonio himself had affirmed.

As the bull died amid the frenzied dogs below, Possenti noticed his steward edging his way up the cathedral steps. He bent down to catch whatever he was trying to tell him.[4] "A certain commissioner has just arrived from Rome at the palace to sort out some business."

"What sort of business?"

"I don't know, my lord. But he's got a large company of heavily armed sbirri and maybe twenty Corsican soldiers with him."[5]

Don Carlo hesitated; some of his habitual self-assurance seemed to fade. He sidled down the steps, away from his attendant, who watched in confusion as his master threaded his way through the crowd and disappeared behind the bell tower in the middle of the piazza. The servant caught sight of Possenti skirting the Palazzo Comunale, across the square. He seemed to be heading north, toward the upper reaches of the town—*away* from the Roman legation awaiting him below near Porta Maggiore.

Possenti continued his retreat to a point just outside the Portella, a break in the ancient wall that marked the edge of town and the final ascent to the mountaintop. As he paused to catch his breath, he apparently recovered from his uncharacteristic loss of nerve. Flight presented clear proof of culpability. Besides, what chance was there of eluding them down such rugged tracks through that unforgiving wilderness?[6]

Possenti later claimed that his inexperience in protocol had left him in a quandary and prompted his withdrawal. Whose authority took precedence: that of Cardinal Antonio Barberini, lord of Segni and Possenti's direct superior, or that of this commissioner from Rome, encroaching on the cardinal's dominion? It fell to the commander of Segni's constabulary to negotiate between Roman authorities and the vice duke, who descended to the town center but entered the cathedral to await further word from the messenger. Possenti presumably assumed (misguidedly, given Innocent X's resolve in the matter) that the church provided safer ground than a meadow outside the city wall: if necessary he could claim sanctuary. "The major clarified that the lord commissioner was not there in a show of force," Possenti later explained, "but to conclude certain legal matters. When I recognized how courteously he addressed me, I resolved to return and invite him to my home." The commissioner claimed to be pursuing either a miscreant priest or a bandit, according to various reports. Given that Possenti was a cleric who had twice been banished from Bologna, the commissioner's ruse would have matched his prey in either case.[7]

First vespers of the Feast of San Bruno of Segni were sounding by the time Carlo Possenti made his way back down from the cathedral to the ducal palace. As he greeted the commissioner with well-rehearsed gentility and invited him to share a festive meal prepared by his new Florentine chef, the captain of the Roman guard laid hands on Possenti and placed him under arrest. Guards took him in chains to Segni's tavern nearby while other investigators searched his rooms and confiscated potential evidence, including a letter lying on his desk.

At dawn on the Feast of San Bruno the force headed back down the mountain toward Rome's Tor di Nona prison. That was where Carlo Possenti first confronted his accusers three days later. The lieutenant governor of Rome began, unsurprisingly, by asking the cause of his arrest. "I cannot imagine why," Possenti replied.[8]

DONATO GUARNIERI

The Venetian ambassador to the papal court concluded the long, newsy dispatch in which he first described Giovanni Braccesi's nocturnal arrest with word of Possenti's capture as well: "At this moment I've just been informed that a certain Carlo Possenti, Vice Duke of Segni, a fiefdom owned by Cardinal Antonio Barberini, has been imprisoned on charges regarding the flight and death of the two nuns. In short, they are sparing no effort to bring to light whoever committed the crime."

The Venetian ambassador's wealth of information about the case was meant to buttress another objective, however: Innocent X's desire to enlist the Serene Republic's aid in those efforts. That was in fact the primary reason the ambassador wrote in the first place:

> The pope told me that because they say Captain Donato Guarnieri could be from Bergamo and hence a Venetian subject, His Holiness fervently wishes to entreat the Serene Republic kindly to oblige him by vigilantly determining, in utmost secrecy, where he might be. And should he be within its jurisdiction, to secure his person. This Guarnieri is young and cuts a handsome figure, well turned out. He formerly served Cardinal Antonio in the recent wars as a captain of corazze and was naturally disposed toward inclinations common among those of little conscience and shameful habits.[9]

Little did the Venetians know how easy it would be to flush this prey, oblivious to impending danger, in their own backyard.

After he was discharged in late May 1644, Donato Guarnieri had waited another two weeks before he took leave of his brother Alessandro and returned home. Bergamo and Venice had rescinded Donato's banishment during his two years away at war, so he was free to return to Gorlago, where his family celebrated his homecoming a few days later.

Colonel Alessandro Guarnieri's banishment, on the other hand, remained in force. In less than a week Donato dutifully set out for Venice to sue for remission of the decree. For more than a month he shuttled from Venice to Bologna and back, fruitlessly negotiating. On July 13 Donato's head began to throb, followed by backache, chills, and fever. He reluctantly took to his bed and then discovered he was incapable of leaving it. For a month he lay in Venice, caught in the ague's grinding rhythm of lassitude yielding to shivering and fevers. Toward mid-August he had improved enough to hire a litter borne by mules to carry him home to Gorlago. He had no sooner arrived, however, than the ague struck again with such virulence that his hair fell out. It was the second week of October before Captain Donato could once again stand on his own.[10]

Meanwhile Alessandro Guarnieri dallied in Bologna as his fortunes slipped into decline. After the smooth-cheeked bastard Cesare Pepoli slaughtered Count Alessandro Maria Pepoli in late September, Guarnieri lamented to his barber, "I no longer have a single friend and patron left here in Bologna." Guarnieri sent his wife off to Gorlago while he tried to dispose of everything they had accumulated. Although a local innkeeper was taken with a painted armoire that glowed like polished marble, he rejected the rest. Guarnieri's temper flared ominously, and the innkeeper noticed three or four thugs blocking the door. The goods began to look more appealing. "I figured that if I wasn't content to buy the stuff, he'd be happy to force me to," the innkeeper later recalled.[11]

Colonel Alessandro's nefarious ways followed him out of town. He and his men could not resist teaching a lesson to a luckless French jeweler imprudent enough to wander the byways between Bologna and Modena unprotected: they relieved him of his valuable stock-in-trade. Bolognese authorities fruitlessly issued a decree of banishment against the fugitive colonel. "They say in Bologna that he left a bad stink behind him," a military colleague later remarked.[12] (He was not referring to the corpses by then buried in Isabella Machiavelli's wine cellar.)

During Lent 1645 Donato Guarnieri heard that his brother's felonious past had caught up with him. Authorities had raided his house at San Martino dall'Argine (45.103° N, 10.5224° E), seventy miles southeast of Bergamo: Colonel Alessandro, his visiting youngest brother, and most of his men had been captured and imprisoned in the unassailable fortress at Bozzolo (45.1034° N, 10.485° E), three miles away. Donato saddled up and rode south. At Bozzolo he confronted massive ramparts rising from the level plain, substantial enough to withstand cannons. A moat would keep besiegers' scaling ladders at a safe distance and make sitting ducks of any foolhardy enough to take to the water.

Security at the fortress had grown lax, however. Donato talked his way inside and discovered his brother held on a very light tether, at large within the fortress. Colonel Alessandro, of course, offered no explanation for his incarceration, and Donato characteristically did not ask for any. The colonel divulged that he intended to break out after nightfall. Donato should gather his brother's horses and wait at the house for word that he and his men were free, then bring the mounts to a bridge at the border of the territory. Whoever got there first should await the other's arrival.

Nobody guarding the fortress saw or heard anything as the colonel's men broke out a window grate and shinnied down a rope. Nor did they hear the double splash when Alessandro and his youngest brother leaped from the battlements into the moat and waded ashore through fortunately shallow water. In a quarter of an hour the entire company was heading toward the rendezvous.

Donato collected the horses and ran them across flat, open countryside to the bridge on the river Oglio to await the fugitives. No one was in sight, but as he reined in at the crossing, Colonel Alessandro and the others emerged from beneath the bridge and scrambled up the riverbank. They rode to a hideout a safe distance from the border. After five or six days Alessandro Guarnieri and his company headed north toward Piedmont, leaving Donato to shepherd his younger brother back from this escapade (his first time away from home) and to smooth things over with their mother in Gorlago.[13]

In May 1645 a letter from Alessandro Guarnieri found its way to Donato in Bergamo. He claimed to have gone to the port city of Genoa, trolling for some military commission. Spain, where conflicts with Portugal, France, and Catalonia dragged on, or Malta, given the permanent Ottoman threat, seemed most promising. The matter of Alessandro's Venetian exile was still unresolved, however, because of Donato's prolonged bouts of ague. The younger Guarnieri should resume negotiations where they had been suspended a year earlier.[14]

In late June Captain Donato once again set out for Venice. A week earlier, of course, the Bolognese papal legate had broken the news of the grisly discoveries in the Machiavelli wine cellar and had named a single culprit: Donato Guarnieri.[15] During July, investigators focused chiefly on suspects who served Innocent X's broader agenda: those they could connect to Antonio Barberini. In the meantime Donato Guarnieri resumed his unrewarding quest on his brother's behalf in Venice. Were it not for his singular fraternal loyalty, together with a soldier's habit of following orders without question, he might have gone home before Innocent X summoned the Venetian ambassador and asked for a particular favor. Guarnieri had been pursuing his quest for a month when the ambassador dispatched his letter to his Venetian superiors on July 29. The letter reached Venice within the week. The sbirri who arrested Donato on August 4, within hours of the letter's arrival, knew exactly where to look for him.

Word of Donato's capture reached Gorlago in no time. On August 7 Niccolò Guarnieri set off to come to his son's defense, bringing along Donato's cousin, an inexperienced youth named Ottavio Agosti from nearby Grumello (45.634102° N, 9.87802° E). While they waited for the boat from Padua to Venice, word arrived that Niccolò Guarnieri's youngest son had been ambushed in an ongoing family feud back home. Niccolò handed over all the cash he could spare and sent his nephew off toward the lagoon on his own.

For a month Ottavio Agosti lingered in anxious frustration on the quay beside the doge's palace or on the bridge across the Rio di Palazzo (45.43364° N, 12.34094° E), studying the prison as if that might yield something useful. His attempts at discovery yielded old legends and horror stories, eagerly whispered in a garbled accent by loiterers outside, or dubious advice from self-proclaimed legal experts, eager to assist the smooth-faced youth and separate him from Uncle Niccolò's money.

As he sat alone after midnight in a shop that sold aquavit, Ottavio resolved to send Donato a note. Perhaps he could pay a jailer to deliver it. "Keep your spirits up. I've come to do everything possible to demonstrate your innocence." Even he was unconvinced. And even if a coin in the hand made a guard agree to pass the message along, what chance was there that he would actually do so? Ottavio crumpled the paper and tossed it into the canal.[16]

It would be wrong, however, to underestimate the naive teenager from the Bergamasque hill country. An Agosti relation put him in touch with an advocate willing to advise him and go through the legal motions, however futile (for a considerable fee, of course). Ottavio also made his way to the prison, where he paid the vice captain of the guard what was already owed for Donato's two weeks of room and board. (In Venice, as elsewhere in Italy, only impoverished prisoners escaped paying their own way.) Young Agosti quickly fell into the habit of tipping whoever he imagined might provide his cousin with a better bedsheet or a larger portion of bread. Beyond the £200 that the vice captain demanded for a month's prison living expenses, Ottavio Agosti handed over another £70 in bribes.[17]

By the time Ottavio reached Venice, Innocent X's negotiations with the doge and the Senate for Guarnieri's extradition were under way, delicately mediated by the nuncio of Venice, the legate of Ferrara, and the archbishop of Bologna. The nuncio most certainly reframed Cardinal Pamphili's "order" for Guarnieri's extradition as a "humble request." (This was no time for papal imperiousness.) Thanks to young Ottavio Agosti's efforts, Bergamo raised strong objections, arguing that it was unprecedented to extradite a subject for punishment of crimes committed beyond a governor's own borders. Indeed, a Roman observer recorded at the end of August, "Here many believe that the Republic of Venice may not turn him over because he is its subject."[18]

It seems that in the meantime Colonel Alessandro Guarnieri had not sailed to Spain or Malta. Word from Bergamo put him possibly in France, Geneva, or Flanders. A particularly reliable source informed the nuncio in Venice, however, that the colonel was soldiering in France or Bavaria. When he learned of Donato's arrest, with little thought for family crises Alessandro switched allegiances and joined the Swedish army. He presumably hoped the avenging arm of the Lord's representative on earth would be too short to reach him amid Protestant Swedes, even if his ear was not too dull to discover what he was up to.[19]

As August ended, another flurry of letters landed on the nuncio's desk, urging him to press the case with the doge, inquiring if he had done so, and asking about the result. By then the nuncio had already pleaded before the doge and senators, who, as he reported, "set the satisfaction of the Supreme Pontiff above every other concern," including Bergamo's strong objections and the sticky issue of Guarnieri's Venetian citizenship. "For that reason the resolution was passed in absolute secrecy, and likewise the protocol for handing him over."[20]

Neither side wanted any slipups, prompting a further epistolary blizzard amid tight security. It was almost midnight on September 2 when the Venetian secretary for Roman affairs appeared at the nuncio's door with the senators' specific stipulations. Guarnieri would be taken by boat up the river Po to Polesella (fig. 4; 44.9608° N, 11.7494° E), which marked the boundary of Venetian and Ferrarese territories, to rendezvous there on a day specified by Cardinal Donghi. Donghi wrote back that it should be Saturday, September 9, at about 4:00 p.m.[21]

For all the secrecy shrouding Donato Guarnieri's extradition, his cousin Ottavio Agosti was in the crowd outside the prison at dawn on Friday morning, September 8. After more than a month, he finally set eyes on his cousin when guards hustled him in chains from prison to pier. "Sir! Captain Donato!" Ottavio called out cheerfully. Guarnieri was oblivious: his head and upper body were completely shrouded in a cloak (the customary Venetian method for transferring prisoners). Agosti sidled over to a guard he knew to be from Bergamo, who divulged that the Venetians were taking the prisoner on an overnight journey to Polesella. (So much for tight security.) "Would you tell him to keep his spirits up and not to worry about anything? That

I'm coming to Ferrara and Bologna to help him?" The Bergamasco furtively nodded, then shifted away after the youth pressed a gold coin into his palm.

Soldiers clumsily manhandled Guarnieri aboard and settled him next to the captain of the guard and the nuncio's agent, while twenty heavily armed guards surrounded him. Ottavio pushed his way along the quay, through the curiosity seekers, over to a boatman preparing to board. He, too, hurriedly agreed to convey words of encouragement when he spied the coin in the young man's outstretched hand.

The boatman jumped aboard as the vessel glided heavily out into the lagoon. A second bark, packed with perhaps another thirty guards, took up a position in its wake.

Clearly the Venetians were taking no chances.[22]

9

CAT AND MOUSE GAMES

Andrea: "Ah, let's go see the German Cemetery, the Vatican Obelisk, Saint Peter's, the Pine Cone Fountain, the via dei Banchi, the Tor di Nona."
Maco: "Does the Tor di Nona ever ring vespers?"
Andrea: "Yes, with quick jerks of the strappado."
Maco: "What! God forbid!"

PIETRO ARETINO, *LA CORTIGIANA* (VENICE, 1534), ACT 2, SCENE 3

In Aretino's satirical drama, the naive, sickly Maco de' Coe has left Tuscany for the Caput Mundi to make his way at the papal court (just as Giovanni Braccesi would do a century later). His host ushers him around the top tourist attractions, including, strangely enough, the Eternal City's notorious jail, cited in the same breath as Saint Peter's Basilica. Since the early 1400s the medieval Tor di Nona (41.900984° N, 12.467661° E) had served as one of the pope's prisons.[1] By the time Carlo Possenti and Giovanni Braccesi landed there in July 1645, it was a tower in name only: just three stories tall, with the Tiber lapping at the lower level. (Rome's modern thoroughfare, the Lungotevere Tor di Nona runs about three stories above the river.) Within a decade Innocent X would order the construction of a new model papal jail a few blocks south. Shortly thereafter the ancient prison was replaced, quite incongruously, by an opera house.

Sbirri hustled Possenti and Braccesi in through the facade's solitary gateway, across the river from Castel Sant'Angelo (41.901056° N, 12.470542° E; another prison for those who ran afoul of the papacy). The Tiber flowed close by, quietly undermining the prison's crumbling foundations, minimally protected by a slapdash embankment, no match for floods that periodically inundated the cells of the jail's lower level. No one rang for the gatekeeper: the busy portal never closed because there was so much traffic in and out. Before wardens moved Possenti and Braccesi through an interior pair of heavy wooden portcullises to their places of detention, they stopped to record their names in the prison log. Any possessions were confiscated, enumerated in a separate logbook, and deposited in a locked casket. Rumor said that Possenti was carrying a stunning five hundred scudi in gold. (In fact, he had only twenty-seven scudi on him, which probably never found its way into the prison strongbox: sbirri supplemented their meager salaries by whatever means they could.)[2]

The more fortunate prisoners landed on the prison's upper level, a lighter, more open, public area for debtors, petty criminals, and those who had already been interrogated, with a chapel and even a tax-free wine bar (thanks to Pope Pius V). It was not for the likes of Possenti and Braccesi, however. As a cleric, Possenti might have expected to be taken to an adjoining building reserved for clergy. Given his illness, Braccesi should have been confined in the infirmary on the upper level. But instead, both were committed to the infamous maximum security area called Le Segrete.[3]

In these dank, airless cells, solitary prisoners' human contacts consisted of brief moments when they received a measure of wine at midday and evening, together with bread (presumably from the ovens of Braccesi's uncle). Despite such efforts at isolation, shortly after Possenti's arrest, Roman observers reported the capture of a malefactor on a nearby rooftop, attempting to communicate with Don Carlo through a window.[4]

An avviso also reported that "Monsignor the governor of Rome has been excluded from this case because of his dependencies upon the Barberini. Giovanni Domenico de Rossi and the treasurer of Rome are exclusively to conduct the entire trial."[5] It is not surprising that Innocent X declined to entrust this matter to Governor Giovanni Girolamo Lomellini: as Bolognese vice legate, Lomellini had shared Palazzo Fava with Giovanni Braccesi. Rumor had it that the governor dragged his feet for a week rather than invade Palazzo Barberini to arrest Cardinal Antonio's valued assistant.[6]

In contrast, Lomellini's lieutenant, Giandomenico Rossi, by age forty-eight had earned a reputation for determination and notably audacious prosecutions. One Bolognese chronicler remembered Rossi as "a criminal investigator, both notorious and cruel," who resorted to methods of "absolute barbarity."[7] Today he calls to mind his operatic equivalent, Baron Scarpia, the merciless Roman chief of police in Puccini's *Tosca*. In short, Rossi was the perfect man for Innocent X's purposes.

CARLO POSSENTI

Giandomenico Rossi first matched wits with Carlo Possenti on Friday morning, July 21. Don Carlo still wore his vice ducal finery, with an elegant linen shirt lavishly garnished with lace, by now soiled and stained with sweat. Possenti probably betrayed little hint of intimidation as he met his opponent's eyes, and Rossi probably took his stare for studied impudence: Don Carlo's reputation as "very bold" and "of fierce temperament" preceded him.[8] The prosecutor may have recognized in Possenti a type too intent on the impression he was making to recognize his interrogator's wider purposes. Securing Possenti's confession was the objective, but the prosecutor had orders to snare more significant prey, within whose shadows the pope believed such detestable villainies had been committed. With feline patience, Rossi would toy with this one, unhurriedly batting him from one line of inquiry to another until confusion set in and the quarry failed to anticipate the hunter.

When Rossi promptly set out to link Don Carlo intimately to Antonio Barberini, Possenti seemed too self-absorbed to spot his agenda. His self-aggrandizing half-truths suited the prosecutor's purpose nicely. "Cardinal Antonio received me at Viterbo [in autumn 1642]. When it came time to return to Bologna His Eminence ordered me to follow him, as I've always done, at his expense, with the salary and honors appropriate to my modest talents. . . . Cardinal Antonio, who took me under his protection, commanded me to move to Rome. I came with other gentlemen who followed His Eminence as I did. . . . I always stayed at Cardinal Antonio's, at His Eminence's expense, and I associated with the cardinal's courtiers: Signor Braccesi and all the others."[9]

When Rossi drifted toward the telltale letter confiscated at Possenti's arrest, Don Carlo claimed that, apart from his mother, "Nobody else from Bologna wrote me, and I don't remember writing to anybody. You see, more than a year has passed since I left there."

Possenti was lying glibly, as Rossi well knew, so he gently cornered him. "Around the *time of your arrest* had you received any letters?"

"I remember that when they took me they looked in my desk and removed three or four; I think one was from Bologna. I don't remember what was in it; I opened it and saw that it was signed only with capital letters. I left it on the desk unread because I didn't recognize the author and I was in a hurry to see the bullbaiting."

Of course, this feeble attempt to mislead probably fooled no one, but Rossi let it drop for then and turned to Possenti's criminal history.

"I was once in jail in Bologna and then banished to Ferrara with my late brother," Possenti reported. "From what I could figure out, some spiteful people said my brother shot a harquebus at somebody named Francesco Maria dall'Aglio. Otherwise I've never been in jail or tried for any crime."

This was a bold-faced lie. Rossi chose that moment to break off this session. The notary handed Possenti the transcript so he could affirm the truth of his string of half-truths. Guards returned him to his cell to ponder over bread and wine what had been going on that morning. Why not a word about La Generona and La Rossa?

Only when Rossi and Possenti faced off that afternoon did the prosecutor begin to nudge his captive in that direction. "Who were your particular friends in Bologna?"

"I wouldn't know what to tell your lordship," Possenti responded with studied affability, "because I was always friends with everybody. During the war years I didn't have much time to mix with anyone except Cardinal Antonio's officials and courtiers," he added, perhaps with a certain air of hauteur.

Eventually Rossi herded him toward a corner. "Tell me about the monasteries of monks and the convents of nuns in Bologna."

"There are lots of them. These are the ones I can remember. . . ." Possenti rattled off half a dozen male monasteries and convents, including the Convertite. "I've often called at Sant'Agnese because I know a friend of my mother there; the Convertite, because I knew a nun named Suor Silveria Pasi; and Santa Maria Maddalena because my sister is there." (A marginal note signals Possenti's first acknowledged link to the murdered Suor Silveria. Rossi would also not have missed Possenti's telltale shift to past tense in mentioning her.)

Possenti could not have missed the patent disingenuousness of Rossi's quick follow-up. "Your sister is still in Santa Maria Maddalena, I take it? And the other one, is she still at the Convertite?"

Don Carlo had probably been rehearsing this answer since the nuns disappeared. "All are in their convents except the disgraced Suor Silveria, who fled the Convertite last year with another nun." Without further encouragement, he carefully volunteered, "I know they fled because it was widely proclaimed as common knowledge and public talk in Ferrara. The news arrived there while I was serving Cardinal Antonio, my master. The vice legate of Bologna sent word to Cardinal Antonio in Ferrara to give him the news." With his alibi established, he presumably felt confident enough to volunteer, "I was friendly with that nun called Suor Silveria for six or seven years."

Rossi showed not the slightest interest. Instead, he signaled the notary to show Possenti that anonymous letter from Segni. "Do you recognize this letter?"

"If your lordship doesn't let me read it, it's hard for me to figure out who might have written it," Don Carlo responded smartly. "But I'd say it's the same one that they took from me, which, as I said, I hadn't yet read."

The notary handed over a sheet of cheap paper, covered on both sides in an untutored scrawl (fig. 21). Possenti made a show of studying it. "From the contents, I can't imagine that this was written by anybody but my friend Carlo Raguzzi from Bologna."[10]

Rossi seemed to take little notice. He rose abruptly, terminated the interview, and sent Possenti back to his cell to wonder just where things were headed. He would have ten days to brood about it before he next set eyes on Giandomenico Rossi.

GIOVANNI BRACCESI

From the moment of Carlo Possenti's capture, watchful eyes outside Palazzo Barberini remained on the lookout for Giovanni Braccesi, known to be holed up inside. As word of Possenti's capture spread, Braccesi was nowhere to be seen. Then on Tuesday morning, July 25, a carriage was spotted leaving the palace with Braccesi inside. The carriage stopped awhile at the residence of a Barberini ally from the college of cardinals but eventually made its way back to Palazzo Barberini by midday. Innocent X and Camillo Pamphili recognized how easy it would have been for the carriage to slip innocently out of town. That night papal forces undertook their nocturnal invasion of the Barberini palace.[11]

Within hours of his capture, it was Giovanni Braccesi's turn to face Giandomenico Rossi. After ten days' illness and a night in Le Segrete, Braccesi's sorry condition might have suggested an easier adversary, but Rossi's familiarity with Braccesi's years of industriously navigating the risky milieu of clerical princes suggested otherwise. Braccesi's studied self-control made him

FIGURE 21. Processo, fol. 281. Carlo Raguzzi's incriminating letter, discovered in Possenti's desk in Segni. "I have no news of Your Friend" appears 9–10 lines up from the bottom; the discovery of the bodies, 6–7 lines up; the accusations against Possenti, 3 lines up. Courtesy of the Ministero dei Beni e delle Attività Culturali e del Turismo, Rome, ASRM 64/2014 (further reproduction prohibited).

less likely than Possenti to trip over his own ego. But the extent of his commitment to a gentleman's code of loyalty (whether to equals, superiors, or inferiors)—that remained untested.

Rossi's initial questions yielded nothing to merit even a single marginal note in the transcript. Before long Rossi stopped beating around the bush. "Do you know someone named Don Carlo Possenti? What can you tell me about him?"

"I know Don Carlo Possenti very well. I got to know him when he came to my house with Cornelio Malvasia, who asked me to recommend Possenti to Cardinal Antonio: he might wish to honor him with some position when the job of chaplain major of the cavalry was pending. His Eminence told me that since that position would be appropriate for Possenti, he would provide it." Potential guilt by association must have been on Braccesi's mind, however. His answers ran on for pages to deflect and control the direction of other questions, sketching a relationship that was all about business, not friendship. According to Braccesi, at war's end Barberini promised Don Carlo a position in government, which explained why Braccesi had to bring him along to Rome.

"When did you learn about Don Carlo's imprisonment, and who told you about it?"

"It seems to me that it was on Wednesday of last week [July 19]. Many people brought it up. Signor Matteo Nardini, the cardinal's auditor, might have been the first to tell me that Don Carlo had been arrested in Segni."[12]

Rossi already had his eye on Nardini, auditor general of the Bolognese legation during Antonio Barberini's time there. Within days Nardini was arrested. "They hope to discover from Nardini whatever secret orders Antonio gave him in Bologna when he committed the nuns' case to him," an observer reported. "It would surely be unthinkable to harm Antonio except through this means: that he hindered the pursuit of justice in these wicked crimes. They can't argue that he was guilty of the crimes, only that he used such stratagems to cover them up."[13]

"Why was Don Carlo imprisoned?" Rossi asked innocently enough.

"I don't know. Especially because on the Saturday before news of his imprisonment [July 15] I found myself ill." Braccesi launched into the details of his ailment, but Rossi would not be diverted. "Well, nevertheless, can you suggest the reason Possenti was jailed?"

"I couldn't imagine why, because he was not at liberty to press that sort of familiarity upon me and to share his personal concerns in ways that might enable me to fathom why he was jailed."

The prosecutor was getting nowhere. "Did aberrant events or shameful crimes often occur in Bologna?" At last Rossi shifted Braccesi toward the Convertite.

"A surfeit of crime happened in that town," Braccesi responded. "I don't believe I've seen any city where there's greater criminality than in Bologna."

When Rossi asked for specifics, Braccesi cited a few aristocratic assassinations. With studied disingenuousness, the prosecutor pinned him down, "So, were they all *male*, all these murder victims?"

"All those that I can remember happening when I was in Bologna involved men; I don't remember any women getting murdered then."

Then, as if embarrassed by his feeble ruse, Braccesi relented, volunteering a stream of unsolicited information: he had nothing to hide. He described the recent discovery of two bodies in a house on via Santo Stefano. "These cadavers were identified as the two convertite who escaped from their convent during Cardinal Antonio's time. Despite our best efforts, it was never possible to discover how."

Now marginalia begin to litter the transcript. Braccesi worked to evade Rossi, spinning more unsolicited information into his replies to control the direction: any connection he had with the convertite (like everything in his life) was strictly business.

"Do you know those nuns' names? What sort of connection did you have with them?"

"One was called La Generona. I knew La Generona personally—or rather, she did my laundry. After Cardinal Durazzo came to town, La Generona began doing lots of our laundry, because he encouraged all his entourage to avail ourselves of her services." (Braccesi was only heeding a superior's command.)

"What do you know about the nuns' flight and deaths?"

"I don't know anything, because, although we made our best efforts regarding their flight [as Braccesi kept insisting], it was impossible to discover how they fled. I first learned about it from Cardinal Antonio: he told me either in Ferrara or on the way back from Ferrara to Bologna."

"Did you customarily visit the Convertite because of your friendship with La Generona?"

"When I first came to Bologna I did," Braccesi admitted. "After La Generona told my servants to invite me, I went to the convent three or four times to speak with her. After that I wasn't there for years and years: I can't remember ever returning after those early days."

"Did you ever go to the convent with Don Carlo Possenti?" (Rossi knew the convertite's allegations in that regard.)

"No, my lord. I don't remember ever seeing Don Carlo at the convent."

That was enough for one morning. Giovanni Braccesi signed his testimony and was returned to Le Segrete.

Giandomenico Rossi resumed Braccesi's interrogation three days later, on July 29. "Did you discuss Possenti's arrest with anyone else?"

"Yes, my lord, with the many others who came to visit me when I was ill. Everyone regretted Possenti's misfortune, assuming he was innocent. But if he were in fact guilty of some crime, nobody would desire his punishment more than I, who took him into my home when he arrived in Rome. And I said that it seemed to me that any good, worthy man, if he happened to be tarnished somehow, ought nevertheless to be respected for the time being. I would wish to speak not ill but well of him until I knew if he were guilty or innocent. We had such discussions while I lay sick in bed in my rooms at Cardinal Antonio's palace."[14]

Amid such platitudes, there was no point in sowing hints of criminal immunity in return for helpful testimony. Further interrogation about palace reactions to Possenti's arrest proved equally unhelpful, particularly after the prosecutor chose to question Braccesi's illness. In Rossi's view, Braccesi promptly assumed the role of malade imaginaire. After several minutes of symptoms and their day-to-day progress, of visits by His Eminence's personal physician, of treatments, of excursions to a nearby pharmacy for syrups, of schedules for their ingestion, Rossi seems to have lost patience. He terminated another disappointingly unproductive session.

CARLO POSSENTI

Since Giandomenico Rossi may still have considered Braccesi the potentially exploitable link in the chain of evidence that he hoped would lead to Antonio Barberini, he summoned Braccesi for a third session on Tuesday, August 1. When that match also ended in a draw, Rossi opted to give Possenti another try the next morning, after a ten-day hiatus. Prolonged solitary confinement had not tempered Don Carlo's impudence: "You're making quite a career out of this," he quipped.[15]

"Do you know Giovanni Braccesi, and for how long?"

"I know him because he came to Bologna with Cardinal Durazzo. When he was Cardinal Durazzo's gentleman I didn't have much to do with him, except to say hello. But after he became an army official I often visited his place and spoke with him."

"Do you know who did his laundry?"

"My Lord, Signor Braccesi was one among so many others who had his laundry done by the Convertite. That Suor Silveria, the one I previously mentioned, she did his wash."

"In arranging for his laundry, did Signor Giovanni become friends with Suor Silveria?"

"I wouldn't know what to tell your lordship," Possenti replied smoothly, "because that nun was friends with half of Bologna, and especially with foreigners and laymen. I do know that I sometimes saw Signor Giovanni speaking with Suor Silveria when I went to the convent."

Rossi did not miss this contradiction with Braccesi's prior testimony. "When exactly did you see Giovanni with Suor Silveria?"

"Oh, so infrequently that I couldn't tell your lordship when or how often. Besides, for two or three years, when the military was in Bologna, I rarely visited the convent because Suor Silveria had made friends with lots of soldiers and other mongrel rogues from the army."

"Well, did you see Braccesi speaking with the nun last year?"

"Absolutely not. I am certain of it, because I know Signor Giovanni had lots of army business to attend to."

Rather than Braccesi's high-minded moralizing, the prosecutor had to contend with Possenti's guileful vagueness.

"Why did the two of you go to the convent to speak to that nun?"

"We both went about our laundry."

"There must have been *other* reasons," Rossi broke in, scoffing. "The very idea that two fine gentlemen delivered and picked up their own linen is as silly as it is implausible."

"I don't know the details of his business. I quit going there after the army arrived and I didn't go as often."

Neither Possenti nor Braccesi was ready to turn witness for the prosecution. Rossi was well aware by now of the convertite's views of Possenti's relationship with Suor Silveria; he opted to see where Don Carlo would run with that. "Let's turn to your assertion that you stopped visiting the convent so often after you saw Silveria becoming overly familiar with soldiers and other reprobates."

"Before the soldiers came Suor Silveria lived a reasonably modest life, so I freely got to know her. Since I found her properly humble, I was partial to her conversation. But when she took that other road and started getting friendly with soldiers, then I stopped visiting her so often, because I detested the whorish life she chose, and the dissolute practices she pursued with the lot of them."

"Did you communicate your displeasure to Suor Silveria and try to correct her wayward lifestyle?"

"From time to time I sympathetically admonished her to leave off such behavior. I remember that when I tried to correct her, she responded angrily, 'I choose to do things my own way! You're nothing to me! Leave me be!' She would be friends with whoever she liked. Faced with such impertinence, I called her a trollop—she didn't deserve the help of a gentleman, but only of men fit for a dog's company. Although my annoyance eventually passed, I no longer cared that she went astray in her own way."

"So who were all these military men," Rossi broke in, "and the others Suor Silveria set her eye on?"

"There were so many soldiers that I wouldn't even know where to start. She carried on with an ensign named Filippo Ximenez, for example. He hung around the grates with her more than anybody else."

Possenti's clash with Filippo Ximenez was the stuff of convent legend. Since Possenti had played the Ximenez card, the prosecutor followed suit. "What do you know about this Filippo Ximenez?"

"Several nuns told me all about him. And sometimes I also caught Ximenez speaking with Suor Silveria. I never became indignant about it except once, when Ximenez tried to pretend he wasn't speaking with Suor Silveria. 'What sort of behavior is this?' I exclaimed. But he blustered with excuses and tried to deny what was going on. So I complained about his trying such deceptions with me and urged him to go about his business because his conduct was leading Suor Silveria into occasions for sin. That was certainly true: I knew for a fact that Ximenez had Suor Silveria's portrait painted and was carrying it on his person, and Suor Silveria was also carrying Ximenez's portrait." (Now there was a detail the nuns had somehow overlooked.) "When he realized he'd been found out, he blushed, didn't dare say another word, and went about his business."

"What did Suor Silveria say when she heard all this?"

"She started screaming at me that she'd do as she liked. I answered, 'So be it.'"

"Did you ever learn what happened to Suor Silveria and the other nun after their convent escape?"

"I never heard a thing, though last year there was lots of gossip that they'd been found dead in one place or another. Then recently—in that letter your lordship had me read—I also learned that they were found dead in the house of Dionisio's sister."

"Do you know this Dionisio's sister?"

"No. But I certainly know Dionisio." Possenti's eyes narrowed and his voice hardened. "It's common knowledge that he was present at the death of my brother Jacopo, who was struck by harquebus fire. This Dionisio is the uncle of my enemy Francesco Maria dall'Aglio and worked for Count Alessandro Maria Pepoli, that gentleman who got himself killed."

"Do you know the Guarnieri whom Carlo Raguzzi accused of the nuns' murder in his letter?"

"I know they are two brothers," Possenti replied with a shrug. "We spent little time together. I was always wary of them because they were close friends of that Count Alessandro Maria Pepoli who had a hand in the harquebus attack on my brother."

Giandomenico Rossi waited until August 4 to make a final run at Possenti. What a wretched figure he cut by then, the prosecutor may have observed, after three weeks of solitary confinement. He was doing his best to ignore the state of his frilled shirt, even filthier and by now certainly infested with vermin.

Rossi returned to Possenti's well-rehearsed alibi. The prosecutor's sharp ear probably picked up Don Carlo's uncharacteristically clear recollection of the days around Easter 1644. "I stayed in Ferrara until Good Friday and then returned to Bologna to celebrate Easter at home. I was delighted when Signor Malvasia (who was also home for Easter), subsequently decided to return to Ferrara right away, so I accompanied him back to Ferrara: I left Bologna on Easter Tuesday [March 29] of last year. I don't remember exactly what day the news of the nuns' escape arrived in Ferrara, but it could well have been Friday of that same week [April 1]. I was in Cardinal Antonio's antechamber."

"How did you return to Ferrara the last time?"

"I went on the packet boat with Count Giovanni Francesco Isolani, Signor Malvasia, Signor Lorenzo Grimaldi from Bologna, Signor Malvasia's valet, and many others I can't remember, who left from the Porto Navile about 4:00 p.m."

Rossi quickly exploited this display of recollective powers, "Where were you earlier on the day when you went back to Ferrara after Easter?"

Possenti suffered sudden memory loss. "It's been so long that I really can't remember what I did or where I went before I left Bologna on that Easter Tuesday."

Rossi posed a final question, innocently enough: "On the day you left Bologna, did you go anywhere on horseback?"

(Don Carlo had said nothing about horses in any of his earlier testimony.) "I don't remember if I went out on horseback that day." (His memory apparently continued to weaken.) "No, I'm certain I did not, because I went to catch the boat on foot."[16]

Don Carlo returned to Le Segrete with a touch more anxiety than when he had left, or so Rossi hoped.

GIOVANNI BRACCESI

Giovanni Braccesi faced Giandomenico Rossi for a final time on August 6. Despite Matteo Nardini's speedy release after his recent unproductive arrest, Rossi continued to pick at speculations in Cardinal Barberini's circle about Possenti's imprisonment. "Did you tell anybody else what Nardini revealed to you?"

"I really don't remember. But I would have discussed it with many others. People in my rooms were talking of nothing else, because Don Carlo was the cardinal's minister. Everyone was speculating about why, and some mentioned the business of the nuns, because earlier in the year there was talk that he might have been named in the investigation."

Two weeks into the interrogation, Braccesi finally offered the first allusion to Possenti's implication in the crime. "Did authorities in Bologna indicate that Possenti was named in the investigation, as you suggest?" Rossi asked.

"While I was in Bologna in the cardinal's entourage, word was going around that Possenti might have been named, a notion that also made the rounds among the common people."

"Did Possenti make a practice of visiting the Convertite?"

"When I first arrived in Bologna, I heard that he did, but I wasn't really in a position to know for certain myself. Especially because before the discovery of the nuns' escape he had no dealings with me apart from those related to his cavalry chaplaincy."

"In your previous testimony you said you did not know and could not imagine the reason for Possenti's incarceration, but now you are saying it was because of the nuns' flight."

"What I said earlier I repeat now: I do not know the reason, nor can I imagine why he was arrested. What I said just now may reflect *some other's* opinions, described earlier: everybody was arguing animatedly about Possenti's arrest and hazarding reasons for it. I took little note of those possibilities because such speculations often have little foundation. I would also suggest that what I say to you *now* I would also have said to all of them *then*: I do not know, nor can I imagine, the reason for his arrest."

Rossi probably recognized that Braccesi would not be easily tripped up as long as his eloquence and frankness might disguise the truth. The prosecutor took aim at a possible flaw in Braccesi's prior testimony. "Did you ever see Possenti at the Convertite?"

"Never that I can remember. Because, as I said, I went there a few times only in the beginning, when I first arrived in Bologna. I didn't know Carlo Possenti then."

Finally, Rossi pounced. "The testimony of previous witnesses calls these assertions into question. I caution you to tell me precisely whether you ever went with Possenti to the convent."

"I say that I absolutely do not remember seeing Don Carlo at the convent. I went there only during a very brief period, more than five years ago, a few times after I first came to Bologna, but from then on I never remember going back. Furthermore, I daresay that after the war started, for about three years, I never visited the convent. Nor could my friendship with Don Carlo offer an opportunity to know his business. As all of Bologna knows, the character of our associations precluded him from sufficient familiarity to speak about his concerns with me unless it involved providing him with some sort of position."

Faced with such unflappable intransigence, the prosecutor landed somewhere entirely new and unexpected. "Do you know someone called Bonaventura Gandolfi?"

"Yes, my lord, because he was employed at the Fortezza Urbana, which required him to confer with me." (With Braccesi, everything was business, always business.)

"Would you know if this Bonaventura owned a house in Bologna?"

"Yes, my lord, in a place called the voltone dei Caccianemici."

Two weeks into his interrogations, Rossi at last focused on the allegations that first linked Braccesi to the nuns' disappearance. "Did you ever spend time at Bonaventura's when Cavalier Pazzi lived there?"

"Once in a while. And one evening I went to dinner when they entertained ten or twelve Bolognese gentlemen. But otherwise, never."

Rossi may have tried to lodge a sting in his final queries. "Do you now, or did you ever, have any relatives in Bologna?"

"No, I've no relations in Bologna, nor have I ever had any," Braccesi replied, perhaps with a perplexed look.

"Are you familiar with a place called 'Porta Felice' or 'San Felice'?" (Ross watched closely for any telltale signs of deception: a Gandolfi servant claimed that Braccesi had hidden the nuns near there.)

"There's a city gate called 'Porta San Felice,' the one that leads to Castelfranco."

"Do any of your friends live nearby?"

"Yes, my lord, for example the Grimaldi, the engineer from the Fortezza Urbana, and some others I don't remember."[17] (Braccesi betrayed nothing except, perhaps, a further hint of bewilderment.)

Rossi rose as the notary passed the transcript to Giovanni Braccesi for his fourth signature since July 26, and the bailiff returned the prisoner to Le Segrete. It would be more than a month before he and Giandomenico Rossi matched wits again. Then it would be not in Rome's Tor di Nona, but in the Torrone in Bologna, back at the scene of the crime.

10

HOME COURT ADVANTAGE

"The word is that Possenti has confessed in such a way that the immunity already offered him will definitely not be honored," an avviso reported on August 2. "They also say that Braccesi has clearly revealed his involvement with the nuns, and now they're badgering him to discover if he participated in their abduction and the thefts of their property. They will also be pursuing the matter of his wartime embezzlements in Bologna, after confiscating his papers to this end."[1]

A flurry of such reports, more or (often) less accurate, quickly found their way into ambassadorial dispatches. The Florentine ambassador offered a particularly intriguing one as early as July 23. "I know from a person worth believing that, in his own defense, Possenti wrote something rather like a manifesto. (Cardinal Colonna has the original.) In it he confessed to his former friendship with the nuns but claimed that for a long while he had nothing to do with them because of the intimate attachments they formed with Benedetto Machiavelli [Donato Guarnieri's military patron in Ferrara], Giacomo Reggi [a close Barberini associate], a Bergamasque colonel [Alessandro—*not* Donato—Guarnieri], Giovanni Braccesi from Pisa [mentioned even before Braccesi's arrest], the castrato Malagigi [Antonio Barberini's highly favored singer], and even with lowly soldiers." Two weeks later the ambassador added,

"They say, though I don't think it's true, that for revealing these things, Possenti secretly asked for immunity, provoking a certain indecisiveness among these experts in crime about granting it to him—although they could always be intending to delude him."[2]

Such accounts agree only marginally with surviving evidence from behind the bars of Tor di Nona prison, although they offer a sense of the range of accusations roiling around on the outside. When he wrote to Cardinal Albergati-Ludovisi on July 26 (three days after the Florentine account), Camillo Pamphili, the pope's cardinal nephew, had indeed proposed a strategy that must have been on many minds. "To get at the truth in this business, it will be very useful to offer immunity to one of the accomplices so that he will reveal exactly what happened."[3] But the trial record offers no hints of immunity or of Possenti's having named names from Barberini's circle. If some decision had been made by early August to deny Possenti immunity, it more likely resulted from his obfuscation, not from any "confession." The avvisi's suggested revelations regarding Braccesi's convent involvement had gone no further than talk of his laundry and a few convent têtes-à-têtes that both Braccesi and Possenti insisted were ancient history.

At that moment, however, Roman gossip revolved less around the nuns' abduction and murder than around alleged discoveries among Possenti's and Braccesi's personal papers. These purportedly included scurrilous texts attacking Innocent X, his unpopular sister-in-law Olimpia Maidalchini, and her son, Camillo Pamphili. Even before the pope's election, witty attacks on Donna Olimpia, particularly her relationship with her brother-in-law, began to appear on Pasquino, Rome's famous "talking statue," around the corner from Piazza Navona. They did not stop with Giovanni Battista Pamphili's election as pope. A French dispatch from the month before Possenti's and Braccesi's arrests describes a similar example. The description used cipher (printed here in italics) for the more sensitive details.

> [Innocent X] thinks no further than *to enrich his own relatives* and especially *Donna Olimpia, about whom, therefore,* one hears *a lot of filthy rubbish,* which assures that the fine *wits have reason* to keep busy *and that the Pasquinisti* get no sleep. Although he was not *indisposed, His Holiness* did not go to the *service* at *San Giovanni in Laterano.* That night someone *attached* a wonderful conceit *on the obelisk* in *the piazza outside the palace* [in Piazza San Giovanni in Laterano], to be seen the next morning. It *said in large letters, "Non licet tibi habere uxorem fratris tui"* [It is unlawful for

you to have your brother's wife (Mark 6:18)]. This suggests that *His Holiness* did *not* want *to participate in that service* because he feared that *Saint John the Baptist* would say the same thing to him that he said *to Herod*, as the *office hour* says, in *the readings proper* [to the day].[4]

As for investigations of Possenti's (or less likely Braccesi's) purported attempts at similar displays of wit, not a trace turns up in the trial record, but local gossip was full of them. The Florentine ambassador reported in cipher (here, in italics), "*Donna Olimpia is enraged* because *some writings against her* are going *around* and they say that *one* of them has been seen *titled 'L'Olimpiade' about the governing of Pope Innocent X*." Another offered further detail about the same work. "Sources clearly state that remarkable texts were discovered in Possenti's and Braccesi's possession, above all, one titled 'L'Olimpiade' and one remaking of the poem that begins 'Tocca Musa il Colascione,' which viciously disparages Donna Olimpia and Cardinal Pamphili. And they would take them for works by that same Possenti."[5] Given Don Carlo's enthusiastic, self-serving poetizing, the idea seemed plausible enough. The same reporter further described the song "that wounds Donna Olimpia to the quick" as "Prendi Musa la Mia Piva ò Prendi Musa il Colascione" ("Take up, O muse, my bagpipe" or "Take up, O muse, the colascione").

Nor could French correspondents resist these delicious revelations, which provide a sense of the papal party's obsessive concern with such dubious verses. "It's believed that Braccesi and Possenti were also arrested because together they concocted a text that shamefully affronts Donna Olimpia, titled 'L'Olimpiade.' Some believe it was found on Possenti's person, because when a gentleman commented to Prince Niccolò Ludovisi [Donna Olimpia's son-in-law] that they should search Possenti's house and seize all his papers, the prince responded, 'That's unnecessary because they'll find what they're looking for on his person.'"[6]

Alas, the song that provoked such a stir has never come to light. But even the often-quoted offending line reveals that it was not only scurrilous but also salacious. The bagpipe, with its phallic blowpipe and scrotum-like wind bag, commonly stood in for "a man's privy members" (as John Florio put it in *Queen Anne's New World of Words* of 1611). The look of the colascione (a three-stringed lute-like instrument) was similarly suggestive: a six-foot neck, carefully fingered by the player, attached to a bulbous body. In the full text, did Innocent X, or perhaps even Donna Olimpia's son, exhort her to grab hold of his metaphorical bagpipe?

Variations on this indecent theme continued to come to light. A letter sent off to France on August 7 related not only the alleged discovery in Braccesi's apartment of his autograph copy of "L'Olimpiade," but also an autograph "in terza rima or quaternaries that runs 'Tocca musa il colascione,' which is later reprised as 'Sporca musa il colascione'"— "Befoul, O muse, the colascione." In another French correspondent's description of "another especially vile text against these two" (Innocent X and Donna Olimpia), the original "Tocca musa il colascione" becomes "Tocca musa *al cu*lascione." The pope thus exhorts Donna Olimpia to "Touch, O muse, the big bad ass."[7] No wonder the papal family was livid and bent on revenge.

Back in Bologna, Archbishop Albergati-Ludovisi anxiously awaited clarification of a possible change of venue for the trial. When Pamphili informed him of Rossi's recent accomplishments, he continued, "I must reverently remind you that this case requires a top criminal investigator to prosecute it. It would be prudent in future to communicate everything that is being done there in Bologna until such time as another decision is reached regarding how and where to continue the case."[8]

Albergati-Ludovisi could not fail to catch the implicit criticism in Pamphili's allusion to a top criminal investigator. In his reply of August 2, after passionate reassurances about the local curia's prosecution of the case, he acknowledged that "if, however, Your Eminence deems it appropriate to send us a prosecutor more to your own taste, I could not but esteem him. You are already aware that when the suggestion to send such a person was first put to me, I acknowledged that it would better satisfy His Holiness and Your Eminence—and be the greatest relief to me."[9]

The person Innocent X deemed just the man for the job was a foregone conclusion. By the time Camillo Pamphili informed Albergati-Ludovisi on August 12, the news had already been leaked in Rome for a good three days: "Giovanni Domenico de Rossi, judge in the case, will go to Bologna with the broadest possible authority to pursue the trial, because many who are well informed about the matter are imprisoned there, and they can clear up this important affair." The same source added a few days later that "Rossi will bring Possenti and Braccesi with him, because the punishment ought to follow at the place where the crime was committed." He concluded, most revealingly, "At the papal palace they believe the infection could even spread to those who think themselves most immune."[10] French dispatches offered one further revelation that would not come out for months in Italian sources: "His Holiness has promised to make Rossi the supreme head of the Torrone in Bologna after the termination of the case, which presupposes that he will do his worst to deserve it."[11]

Giandomenico Rossi therefore knelt to kiss Innocent X's feet on August 12, received from Cardinal Pamphili's hand the commission granting him unparalleled powers and authority, and solemnly swore to prosecute the case with due diligence. In describing the event, the Florentine ambassador added, "Rossi alone reported having found on Possenti a letter by Braccesi, but without any signature, which urged him to flee. And among Braccesi's papers were many letters from cavaliers from Bologna, which informed Cardinal Antonio of the discovery and disinterment of the nuns' cadavers."[12] The supposed Braccesi letter sounds remarkably like Carlo Raguzzi's, signed with initials, which sbirri confiscated from Possenti's desk. The transcript of the investigation makes no mention of the putative letters to Antonio Barberini.

Rossi did not hustle his prisoners from Rome to Bologna with indecorous haste. The journey was as much a work of pontifical propaganda as a pursuit of papal justice. It would take ten days for the 350-mile progress to reach the second city of the Papal States. Innocent X would dig deep into his private purse for five hundred scudi in gold to pay for it.[13] Nevertheless, Rossi opted for a discreet nocturnal departure from Rome on August 16 rather than risk running the gauntlet of unruly Roman crowds in daylight. Possenti and Braccesi, still heavily manacled and shackled, passed through the portcullis and emerged from the Tor di Nona into thick darkness—the last-quarter moon was waning.[14] A few smoking firebrands dimly illuminated a waiting coach and a force of perhaps twenty armed guards on horseback. Possenti probably made his way to the carriage with as much swagger as permitted by his chains and the warders who hustled him along. The frail Braccesi may have relied on his jailers' support to negotiate the walk to the coach.

If subsequent reports can be believed, when Possenti and Braccesi entered the carriage, they discovered they were not alone. Even in the gloom, thanks to his missing eye, Bonaventura "Guercio" Gandolfi from the voltone dei Caccianemici was unmistakable. Another figure allegedly sitting back in the shadows would remain an enigmatic, ominous presence, for he wore a mask.

The mysterious masked man became the focus of wide speculation. According to the Modenese ambassador, "Various chatter is going around about the masked man taken with Possenti and Braccesi; he's somebody knowledgeable about the whole nun business who is coming to Bologna to offer a very detailed account, after being assured of immunity." A French source described him as Cardinal Antonio Barberini's unnamed former maggiordomo from Bologna, returning to the scene of the crime.[15] But to compound the mystery, the trial transcript contains absolutely no trace of Barberini's sometime maggiordomo or of anybody else likely to have been the elusive star witness in the mask. Perhaps he was a spy, placed in the carriage to eavesdrop during the journey. Or perhaps he never existed at all.

Once the company cleared Rome's Porta del Popolo, heading north, it took the rest of the night and most of the next day to cover the sixty miles along the ancient Roman via Flaminia to Terni (42.5602° N, 12.6468° E). The next morning Rossi and company set off into the Apennines, toward Spoleto (42.7453° N, 12.7384° E), where the local governor awaited the prosecutor for lunch. The governor was not the only one expecting them. As the coach wended its way up the hill to the governor's residence within the walled medieval fortress that loomed over the city, the entire population turned out to watch them pass. The ashen Braccesi, listlessly staring at the ground and "looking more like a corpse than a man alive," may scarcely have noticed. But Possenti appeared merry, even brazen, talking animatedly and joking, "like a bridegroom led to his wedding."[16]

On Saturday, August 19, Rossi led his party northeast through the mountains and down the eastern slopes toward the coast. Rossi slackened his pace on Sunday afternoon when the company reached Loreto (43.4403° N, 13.6074° E), overlooking the Adriatic, site of the Basilica of the Holy House of Loreto, one of Roman Catholicism's most popular pilgrimage sites. Rossi postponed departure on Monday until after lunch to allow time for spiritual tourism, confession, and Mass. The extent of the prisoners' participation is unknown, though the presence of their closely guarded carriage must have distracted many in the pious throngs as, amid their prayers, they whispered its story from one to another.

Rossi hurried the group onward on Monday, August 21, to Ancona (43.6333° N, 13.5° E), on the Adriatic. For the next two days an ocean vista opened through the windows to the right as the coach skirted the coastline on route to Rimini. On Wednesday, August 23, they rendezvoused at Rimini (44.059° N, 12.5632° E) with a waiting guard of twenty-four from Romagna and headed inland on the final straight stretch toward Bologna. By the time they reached Faenza (44.2862° N, 11.8835° E) toward evening on August 24, just thirty-five miles short of their goal, the escort had swelled to the size of a very large platoon.

As Rossi's party made its way toward Faenza, a stunning rumor reached Rome: Braccesi was dead! Cardinal Antonio's gentlemen claimed that puny

FIGURE 22. Pio Panfili, *Veduta di strada Maggiore* (1784). A, Palazzo Bargellini; B, Porta Maggiore; C, the nuns' first hideout; D, strada Maggiore. Reproduced with permission of the Biblioteca Comunale dell'Archiginnasio, Bologna.

Signor Giovanni had succumbed to the rigors of the journey and his harsh treatment. Outside Palazzo Barberini more sinister suspicions quickly began to circulate. The cardinal's courtiers "neglected to mention the assumption their news provoked: to bury the evidence that Braccesi could reveal against his patron, poison finished him off."[17]

Another letter sent off to Rome the following day, however, reported Giovanni Braccesi still very much alive, though unwell, when the coach turned up in Bologna on Friday, August 25. By the time the prisoners' carriage rolled through Bologna's Porta Maggiore (fig. 5, A; fig. 22, B), the original double circle of twenty horsemen had swelled to a company of more than seventy-five. Many times more curiosity seekers waited under the arcades along strada Maggiore to witness it (fig. 22, D). "There was such a crush of the populace and of the nobility that the pope himself might have been there!" one reporter exclaimed.[18]

Between the horsemen clogging the street and the clouds of dust they kicked up, it would have been nearly impossible to tell prisoner from pope.

Much to the crowd's frustration, the guards staunchly followed orders, continuing to encircle the coach, stirrup to stirrup and nose to tail, as they conveyed their captives "as secretly as possible" along strada Maggiore. Probably no one who was actually there to witness the spectacle recognized the irony as Possenti and Braccesi passed right by the top-floor apartment where La Generona and La Rossa had hidden out for more than a week right after their escape (fig. 22, C). (By now, virtually anybody informed about the matter was languishing in jail, had fled the city, or was dead.)

Once the procession skirted Piazza Maggiore and reached the Torrone (fig. 23; 44.495° N, 11.3411° E), guards quickly hustled the prisoners inside and locked them in separate cells, each in the custody of a full-time guard. They accomplished the task so smoothly that some local chroniclers believed the prisoners had been dropped off for safekeeping at Palazzo Bargellini, halfway along strada Maggiore (fig. 5, C; fig. 22, A; 44.49226° N, 11.35187° E).[19]

According to reports, Possenti continued to maintain "an impudent look" as he rode past the throngs in the street. As for Giovanni Braccesi, "they have brought him to rock bottom." Just a year before, many among the flower of Bologna's nobility and leaders of the papal army had done Braccesi the honor of escorting his carriage to the city gate and even beyond, to bid him farewell as he returned to Rome. Many of them must also have been there to witness his sorry return. "How strange it must be for Braccesi to show himself in such misery and in chains," a chronicler remarked, "in the very place where formerly he held sway with infinite polish and incredible arrogance."[20]

FIGURE 23 (*opposite page*). Pio Panfili, *Carceri di Bologna*. The Torrone, on the right, as it appeared in the eighteenth century. Reproduced with permission of the Biblioteca Comunale dell'Archiginnasio, Bologna.

4
3
5
6
2

BOLOGNA

11

"*IN THIS TOWN THEY'RE ALL MALICIOUS LIARS!*"

Bologna's Torrone, at the intersection of present-day via Ugo Bassi and via Giacomo Venezian, at the northwest corner of the Palazzo Comunale (fig. 5, H), seems less intimidating today than when sbirri hustled Carlo Possenti and Giovanni Braccesi inside. Over the years, additions atop adjacent walls have risen to the summit of the tower so that now it resembles a stubby pepper pot (fig. 24; 44.495° N, 11.3411° E). In 1645, when it still appeared taller, large grated windows pierced the walls of its second and third floors, illuminating cells reserved for prisoners "at large." Outside, friends standing on steps or clinging to iron rungs mortared into the masonry below the second-floor grating passed information to inmates clustered around the windows above. Minimum security detention like theirs would not do for Possenti and Braccesi. Once again they found themselves in isolation on the lower levels of the Torrone's "Le Segrete." Jailers made no move to unlock the manacles and shackles they had worn for more than a month. Although specially assigned guards kept constant watch on the pair, Possenti and Braccesi remained perpetually chained to the wall, even when trying to sleep on their pallets.[1]

It would be a week before Giandomenico Rossi next confronted them. He had bureaucratic tasks to fulfill: letters from Cardinal Pamphili and the

FIGURE 24. Bologna, the Torrone, where Possenti, Guarnieri, and Braccesi were imprisoned, interrogated, and tortured. Photo: Luca Salvucci, Bologna.

governor of Rome to present to the papal legate, Cardinal Falconieri, and to Archbishop Albergati-Ludovisi. Amid the polite show, no one had any doubt who would call the tune from now on. Cardinal Pamphili had written to legate and archbishop to ensure unhesitating cooperation. There would be no clerical immunity. Rossi would come and go wherever he pleased, detaining and confronting whomever he pleased. The archbishop would guarantee that issues of ecclesiastical jurisdiction and rival clerical authority posed no impediments of the sort that had shielded Possenti the previous year. In an implicit show of no confidence, Rossi brought along ten sbirri of his own. Cardinal Pamphili commanded Legate Falconieri to fire an equivalent number of the least competent locals to save a few scudi. (No wonder that barely a week after Rossi's arrival, Albergati-Ludovisi needed to recuperate with a few days of rest and fresh air in the countryside.)[2]

Rossi left introductions with the present auditor of the Torrone for last. Perhaps the incumbent had heard rumors that he was receiving his eventual replacement. Their encounter must have been tense. (Roman reports claimed the auditor was detained and called to explain his inaction right after the nuns' flight. Within three days that rumor proved false, but then as now, discredited hearsay could take on a life of its own.)[3] The auditor put the best face on it and, as if acknowledging the inevitable, invited Rossi to lodge at the auditor's residence.

The next day Rossi began his search for his own accommodation. He selected the massive, rather severe Palazzo Bargellini, still under reconstruction at strada Maggiore 44 (fig. 5, C; fig. 22, A; 44.49226° N, 11.35187° E).[4] The palace became both a residence and a place to interrogate lesser persons of interest who need not be confined at the Torrone or archiepiscopal prison, which by now had few vacancies thanks to this case.

Rossi's busy round of interrogations began on Friday, September 1. The prosecutor filled the time between questioning Possenti and Braccesi with the crowd of witnesses whose preliminary testimony was familiar from the transcript of previous Bolognese efforts. Some detainees had been sitting in jail for weeks, awaiting the prosecutor's arrival. Rossi's carriage became a familiar sight, seven days a week, as it rolled from the Torrone, to the archiepiscopal prison, to Palazzo Bargellini with the indispensable notary visible inside, seated opposite him. It could occasionally be spotted near the edge of town, outside the Convertite, during Rossi's sporadic visits to prepare the nuns for confronting the culprits face-to-face.

Rossi chose to begin with someone having nothing good to say about Carlo Possenti. The horribly disfigured Galeazzo Mariani, missing all his front teeth, with a livid scar running up his left cheek from chin to eye socket, perhaps provoked momentary curiosity, followed by unfeigned indifference, when Rossi first set eyes on him at Palazzo Bargellini. As he sat through Galeazzo's eager description of the night when he received the sfregio at Possenti's hands, Rossi would have recognized how the brutal act established a gentleman's obligation between Don Carlo and Count Ferdinando Ranuzzi. Possenti's aristocratic friend repaid him for the March 12 attack on Mariani by spiriting Laura and Silveria away in the early hours of April 1, 1644.

The prosecutor took note of Mariani's assertion that when he finally ventured out in public, he spotted Possenti with one of Ranuzzi's men on via Santo Stefano. They were lounging against a column in the shade of the arcade opposite the Baraccano: outside Isabella Machiavelli's townhouse, where the bodies were discovered thirteen months later. It was right before the parish Corpus Christi procession (May 19, 1644), just a few days after La Rossa had last been seen near the voltone dei Caccianemici.[5]

After lunch, Rossi moved to the archiepiscopal prison, where Dionisio Tomassini had been waiting since August 8 "in a cell; so now he's telling everything" (as Albergati-Ludovisi had assured Rome). Tomassini claimed that during the eventful days at Palazzo Pepoli in April 1644 he had been nursing the ague, confined to his chair at home, dosing himself with syrups. Dionisio's employer had told him nothing about the mysterious guests in the shuttered downstairs rooms, Tomassini insisted. "He never confided in me or in others—because he knew that whenever I knew any little thing I couldn't keep it to myself."[6]

Tomassini proved more helpful when it came to Carlo Possenti. "I spotted that priest Possenti, Count Alessandro Maria Pepoli, and Colonel Alessandro Guarnieri together all over Bologna. I also once saw Possenti come to Count Alessandro Maria's place after those nuns ran off. A long time afterward I heard that the nuns had been at Count Francesco Pepoli's and Count Alessandro Maria's. I started to believe it because of his dealings with Colonel Alessandro Guarnieri and also because the count had started hanging around with the priest Possenti, who he hadn't mixed with before. Last year, especially after the nuns fled the convent, I saw Count Francesco Pepoli, Colonel Guarnieri, Count Alessandro Maria, and Don Carlo Possenti walking about the city together."

Such eyewitness testimony to guilt by association sounded too good to be true. (After all, Tomassini was supposed to be laid up at home with the ague, not watching the world go by in the piazza.) In the end, Rossi made little direct use of it. He released Tomassini on bond. Five weeks after entering the archiepiscopal prison, he walked free in the sunlight and fresh air, without ever coming face-to-face with the accused.[7]

We cannot know Carlo Possenti's thoughts during the month since he last confronted Rossi on August 4, or what might have passed between him and Braccesi as their carriage trundled through the mountains and along the coast from Rome to Bologna. But when Rossi and Possenti next faced one another at the Torrone on September 2, Don Carlo, who in Rome proclaimed "I'm generally a friend to everybody," now trusted nobody. "In this town they're all malicious liars!" became his refrain.[8]

All those liars were also out to get him. There were any number of other possible perpetrators of these crimes too, Possenti implied. Given Suor Silveria Catterina's wanton convent lifestyle, he contended, any of her many visitors might have spirited her away. He, on the other hand, was regularly out of town, particularly at the time of the nuns' flight. "How can you be so convinced of my constant hanging around the convent if during wartime I was hardly ever in Bologna? And I can prove it!" he insisted. Possenti again raised the amorous specter of Filippo Ximenez as a prime candidate: Suor Laura Vittoria let Don Carlo know that "Suor Silveria had fallen in love with Ximenez. I never saw Ximenez at the convent after we had words." (Of course not: Don Carlo was purportedly out on military patrol somewhere.) "But Suor Laura Vittoria told me he visited secretly, both night and day."[9]

There were other plausible suspects too. "It's certainly true that Captain Giovanni Francesco Tenerino was accustomed to go to the convent, and so did Captain Fava." In case authorities had interviewed Tenerino, Possenti did his best to undermine his credibility. "Tenerino was my friend at first. But after Signor Cornelio Malvasia threw him out of his palace, he always hated the rest of us and went around speaking ill of me especially. What he might have said, I don't know, but he's a scandalmonger, that one."

Nor were the convertite to be trusted. "It's really unnecessary to believe these nuns, who perhaps testified about that business of me and Ximenez, because they're silly women. If your lordship wants to believe the nuns' tittle-tattle, you should know that not one of them was there when I yelled at Ximenez, except for Suor Eufrasia and Suor Silveria." Possenti suspected that Suor Eufrasia, too, might have something to say in his disfavor. "Since she wanted to keep Suor Silveria mixed up with so many different lovers, Suor

Eufrasia always had it in for me. That Suor Eufrasia is nicknamed 'La Birana' because she's a certain Francesco Birani's thing—he hates me to death."

When Rossi brought up Suor Laura Vittoria's family, Possenti wasted no time in defaming them too. "Suor Laura Vittoria had a mother; if I'm not mistaken, she's called Lucrezia, but she's an old common whore. And a sister whose name I don't even know, who's a whore too."

"Why would you volunteer that they're prostitutes?" Rossi raised his eyebrows at Possenti. "That wasn't my question. . . ."

"So that you'll be clear about their distinguishing features. It's a well-known fact."

"Perhaps you had other motives. . . ."

"I called Suor Laura Vittoria's mother and sister whores because that's what they are!"[10]

Don Carlo also claimed to have kept his distance from the Guarnieri brothers. "I saw that they hung out at Count Alessandro Maria Pepoli's palace. He's my mortal enemy because he was there, at the attack on my brother, who was killed by seven shots from Francesco Maria dall'Aglio, his uncle Dionisio Tomassini, and others among Count Alessandro Maria's men," Possenti explained. "I'd need a very strong stomach to hang out with Count Alessandro Maria."[11] (Dionisio Tomassini testified quite the opposite, of course, as did others.)

Don Carlo was quick to put as much distance as possible between himself and Count Ferdinando Ranuzzi, particularly around the time of the nuns' escape. "I spoke with nobody except Marchese Bentivoglio in the piazza on the afternoon when I returned from Ferrara, and then I went home and entered the house alone. No friend came to visit me that night either." (From the transcript, Rossi already knew that at least two eyewitnesses told a different story.) "I never spoke with Count Ferdinando at all about the nuns' flight, not in Bologna, not in Rome. I had no reason to."[12] (In that case Possenti would have been the only person in town who was not discussing the errant nuns.)

"Did you see Count Ferdinando anywhere when you returned from Ferrara after Easter?"

"No, not before, not after Easter."

Rossi's incredulous look carried a warning. "Be careful what you say, because if it turns out you've been lying it will go badly for you."

"I'm not afraid of being caught out in a lie, because I never spoke to Count Ferdinando Ranuzzi, not before, not after Easter of last year! After the last time I came back to Bologna, when Cardinal Antonio returned, it was more than eight days before I set eyes on Ranuzzi."

"Why do you offer up such falsehoods when your own mother has testified that Count Ferdinando came with you to the house and later left with you?"

"That's just not true! If my mother said so, she was all muddled. Women get things wrong." Possenti managed a smile. "She's getting old, and her memory can't be trusted."

Rossi remained stone-faced. "There's no point in lying when there were others who also saw the count there that night."

"If you've got other witnesses who say that, I'm telling you they're all liars!"[13]

Throughout Possenti's early September interrogations, Andrea Pallada's name crossed no one's lips. A few minutes away at the archiepiscopal prison, however, the Palladas, their servant, and their friend Federico Panzacchi were offering Rossi a stream of damning testimony. On September 9, Rossi began shifting his questions in their direction. "Did you ever intercede with Cardinal Antonio for the release of anybody imprisoned in Bologna?"

"No, my Lord, never." (Strictly speaking, this was true: Barberini had not been involved when Possenti spoke up for Andrea Pallada's brother.)

At first, Rossi pushed back gently. "I would urge you to try to remember clearly."

"No, my Lord, I never got anybody freed from jail." But then, Possenti paused to reconsider. "One time in Cardinal Antonio's absence I did request his assistant to stay the execution of somebody named Carlo Pallada from Bologna." Rossi could not fail to notice how smoothly Possenti segued into an assault on Andrea Pallada's character. "Signor Federico Panzacchi requested that I disregard my aversion for Carlo's brother, so I said, 'Let's see what can be done.' I decided to help even though Carlo's brother didn't deserve my aid."[14]

To Possenti's considerable satisfaction, Rossi seemed to rise to the bait. "What is the name of this brother of Carlo's, and what caused your falling-out?"

"If I remember rightly, Carlo Pallada's brother is called Andrea. But we loathe each other, because that Andrea has always been a common whoremaster." Perhaps the corners of Rossi's mouth hinted at a smile as Possenti proceeded to implicate Andrea Pallada in a different convent breakout, but one that sounded remarkably like La Generona and La Rossa's. When a local aristocrat fell for the tender charms of a prostitute in Pallada's supposed stable of whores, the youth's family arranged to have her locked away at the Convertite. But, according to Possenti, Pallada conspired to extricate her from the convent, then informed the young gentleman's family that she had fled to Milan. "But then Andrea started to fret that the boy's relatives would get him killed and asked me to intervene with the relatives. Pallada thought I didn't do enough to calm them down, so things got ugly between us. Unfortunate words were spoken, and we came to blows. I punched Andrea in the mustache, he tried to grapple with me, but I got away and acted like I was pulling out a pistol. So he turned tail and that was that."[15]

The last part sounded credible enough, given the personal satisfaction Possenti seemed to take in such violence. The prosecutor continued with a mix of disingenuousness and sarcasm, "How is it that you were so curious about this Giovanna's alleged abduction, yet you took no interest at all in the flight of your own friend, Suor Silveria?"

"I was curious about Giovanna because Suor Silveria imposed on me to find out: she suspected the young man's relatives thought she had a hand in it, since she had custody of Giovanna."[16]

To hear Possenti tell it, he and Pallada were regularly at each other's throats. In 1642 "we had words and came to blows, but Pallada backed off because I had a knife." They were at it again "one day during Lent last year, opposite the church of San Domenico. I let him have it in the head with the cane I was carrying."[17] (Rossi may have noted the similarity of this last dustup to Possenti's run-in with the unfortunate Galeazzo Mariani: same time, same place, only the weapon had changed.)

Rossi finally finished toying with him. "Did you ever seek a favor from Andrea Pallada?"

"No, my lord, never."

"When you returned from Ferrara after Easter did you speak with Andrea Pallada?"

"No, my lord, never."

"I must warn you: the truth will come out about your visits to Andrea Pallada's, both after Easter and after the nuns' abduction, and then it could go badly for you."

"I'm not afraid of being caught in a lie! Because I was never at Andrea Pallada's last year on any sort of business."[18]

Rossi continued with a stream of revelations posed as questions, followed by Possenti's denials. "Do you know that the nuns went to Count Alessandro Maria Pepoli's after they left the convent? Do you know that the nuns later ended up in the hands of Colonel Alessandro Guarnieri? Did you ever write a letter to the nuns after their escape? Do you know who killed them or how their bodies ended up in the Dall'Aglio house?"[19]

Still Possenti remained unabashed.

"Tell the whole truth of your involvement in this case," Rossi insisted, "because the curia knows that in your absence, your friends Count Ferdinando Ranuzzi and Negrino Negrini abducted the nuns and took them to Andrea Pallada's house, which you later visited to satisfy your lust with one of them and to lay hands on their belongings, which you kept for yourself and for your use."

"I am innocent of all this! I had no part in it!"

"The curia knows far more about your complicity in the nuns' abduction and the abominable sacrilege you committed with one of them. What is more, there is proof that you and Colonel Alessandro Guarnieri subsequently murdered them and buried them in the house of Isabella dall'Aglio Machiavelli, where, as God would have it, their bodies were discovered."

"None of this is true! These are all lies by those out to get me! Because after the nuns ran off, I never set eyes on them again!"[20]

With understated theatricality Rossi signaled to a guard, who slipped from the room. Moments later he returned leading Andrea Pallada, who, hand on heart, swore to speak the truth.

"Last year Don Carlo Possenti sought me out because he wanted me to take two Ferrarese ladies into my house. But instead, he had Count Ferdinando Ranuzzi and Negrino Negrini bring in two convertite, one named Suor Silveria and the other called La Rossa. He also had a chest of the nuns' linens delivered there, as I testified in detail in my interrogations."

The notary dispassionately read out page after page of Pallada's earlier testimony.

"Is this the evidence that you gave, and do you swear to it in the face of the accused?" Rossi intoned.

"I have clearly recognized it as my testimony. What I said about Don Carlo Possenti is true, and I hereby affirm it to his face."

Pausing, Rossi looked toward Possenti, who could scarcely contain himself. "I, too, heard what Andrea Pallada alleges against me, and I say that it's false! How can you believe such a fraud!"

"I was telling the truth!" Pallada shot back. "I'm not base like he says! I'm an upstanding man, I told the truth!"

"He's notorious, that one, don't believe him! Not least because what he testified is dubious at best!" Possenti interjected, curling his lip. "Why would I tell him that I was bringing over two Ferrarese women and then bring the two nuns, when I knew that he knew Suor Silveria?" He paused rhetorically, holding Pallada's eye. "And why didn't you tell the authorities you were holding the nuns if they were trying so hard to find them, as you say?"

"Because Count Ferdinando Ranuzzi told me to keep my mouth shut." Pallada ignored Possenti, eager for Rossi to understand. "And he said to say I'd heard nothing about it around Bologna and leave it at that."

"Enough questions. But I repeat: he's my enemy, and vile. Nobody should ever believe him!"

"Never have I been your enemy, Don Carlo!" Pallada called back as a guard ushered him from the room.[21]

The guard returned with Doralice Pallada. Possenti shrugged and claimed not to recognize her. Once the notary had read monotonously from the transcript, she affirmed her testimony.

"Nothing she's said is true!" Possenti shouted.

"Yes, sir, it's true, all of it, just as I said." Both her face and her tone proclaimed Doralice's aversion to the priest.

"I tell you, she's lying through her teeth! And besides, she's the wife of one of my enemies and the sister of another. And she's a woman who mixes with whores and is a common whore herself!"[22] (The faintest smile perhaps crossed Rossi's lips: Don Carlo's fiddle, it seemed, had only two strings.)

Rossi sent Possenti back down to his cell to ponder his deteriorating situation. The prosecutor waited until September 14 to recall him. "Well, now are you disposed to speak the whole truth about the abduction and murder of the convertite?" (From then on, everything would be out in the open.)

"I never knew anything about any of that."

Once again Rossi gestured to a guard, who disappeared out the door, then returned with Andrea Pallada's longtime friend Federico Panzacchi, one of the few Possenti acquaintances he had not attempted to vilify. Panzacchi listened as the notary read through all his earlier testimony, then duly affirmed it: how he had seen and visited with La Generona and La Rossa at the Palladas'; how he had admired their belongings; how he had encountered Possenti's servant, Bartolomea, when she came for their things. And what mattered most, "I asked why they'd left the convent and they told me that one of them, the older one, had left because of Don Carlo Possenti, her beloved."

"This is foul treachery!" Don Carlo erupted. "He must have conspired with

Pallada and fell into this blunder at his insistence: Pallada made him say what he wanted him to say. I know nothing about any of this!"

"If it weren't the truth, I wouldn't have said it," Panzacchi replied, drawing himself up before he turned to leave.[23]

By then it should have dawned on Possenti that the swelling crowd of eyewitnesses had exceeded the pair required as credible proof in the matter of the nuns' abduction.

The next day Rossi seemed to head into new territory. "After your return from Ferrara after Easter of last year, did you ever revisit that city?"

"No, my lord . . ." (This was probably not what Don Carlo anticipated.) "I never again went back there. . . ."

"Do you know an inn in Ferrara called the Torretta?"

"Yes. I was there a few times five or six years ago, when I was banished to Ferrara. Then I was there again last year. Not for very long, not more than half an hour—Cornelio Malvasia's secretary, Ascanio, who was having it off with the innkeeper's wife at the time, invited me to go for a drink." Possenti smirked expectantly as he shared this gratuitous detail, but the impassive Rossi refused to play along. "I was there with Count Isolani, Signor Guidalotti, and Sergeant Major Navarra, plus two or three others I don't remember, but I think they were from Signor Cornelio Malvasia's."

"Did you take any women with you to the inn?"

"No, my lord—never."

"Do you know the innkeeper of the Torretta?"

"I wouldn't know him and I don't know his name."[24]

Rossi once again summoned a guard, conferred briefly with him, then sent him out. The guard returned with two strangers of about Carlo Possenti's height. "Get in line with these two," the prosecutor ordered the priest. "Take whichever position you want." Possenti moved over to stand between the newcomers. The guard waited until all was in order, then escorted another stranger into the room.

"Do you recognize the man who appeared at your inn with the group you mentioned in your testimony?" Rossi asked him. "If so, touch him."

"One of these men was in the group that came to my inn with those two women. He's the one in the middle." (The innkeeper touched Don Carlo.) "He was one of them."

Again the notary read ad infinitum from the transcript. The innkeeper duly affirmed his testimony, in the face of Possenti's rising discomposure.

"What a great falsehood! It's a foul lie that I was at his tavern with two women! I can prove that after I returned from Ferrara with Cardinal Antonio I never again left Bologna. I've got a hundred thousand witnesses to confirm it, and I'll call them when your lordship lets me mount my defense."

"I told the truth," the innkeeper responded with an air of wounded respectability. "I've got absolutely no interest in any of this, and I've suffered considerable loss and plenty of inconvenience from having to come over to Bologna twice about it."

"So, when did I supposedly come to your inn with those women?"

"At the beginning of May of last year, or at the end of April."

"How did you happen to see me?"

"I observed you eating some fennel as I passed by the table. When I saw those two women dressed as men I said, 'Oh, what pretty little page boys!' One of those with you asked if I liked them. But I knew for sure they were women, because they had no beards and from the way they talked and walked."

"Enough! This man is contemptible and shameful!" Possenti blustered. "And that wife of his is a common whore, which all of Ferrara knows!"

"I am an honorable man," the innkeeper insisted as Rossi excused him and he left the room.[25]

By an interesting coincidence, the next day a lawyer appeared at the Torrone to petition the court on Possenti's behalf: his first documented attempt at a defense. "Neither the nuns' abductors nor those who received them were his friends; on the contrary, they were his mortal enemies, just as they are today. As for those who testified against him, some are also his mortal enemies, while others are vile, poor criminals, of unstable moral character, deceitful perjurers." The lawyer also dutifully asserted Possenti's primary (although increasingly thin) defense: "At the time of their abduction from the Convertite, he was not in Bologna, but in Ferrara. He neither knew about nor participated in their removal, and he never stayed with them anywhere."[26]

Perhaps in response, Rossi planned a special courtroom drama for Possenti's next appearance that same morning: he brought back the much maligned Andrea Pallada to confront the priest a second time.

"You have already confirmed your testimony under oath in the face of Carlo Possenti," Rossi announced. "But would you now be prepared to demonstrate your truthfulness even under torture?"

Rigorosum examen (the seventeenth-century euphemism for its twenty-first-century equivalent, "enhanced interrogation techniques") was most commonly invoked to encourage full disclosure from a reluctant accused. But it also served less frequently as a means to corroborate a witness's controversial testimony or accusations that an accused vehemently denied. Torture thus could serve as a sort of rite of passage to demonstrate witness credibility.[27]

"Yes, my lord, I am ready to confirm it, even on the strappado, if need be." Pallada showed more determination than apprehension. "Because everything I said was true."

On Rossi's signal, guards moved Andrea to where a rope snaked down from a pulley dangling from the ceiling vault. They undressed him, tied his wrists behind his back, and attached the rope above his wrists. As they drew the rope taut, he instinctively bent forward until his arms, extended behind him, and his upper body paralleled the floor.

"Do you speak the truth, in the fear of God?"

"I spoke the truth. Had it not been true, I would not have spoken." Pallada cranes his neck to catch and hold Rossi's eye. "Now I also stand ready to affirm it on the strappado, or wherever may be necessary."

The rope tightens and the pulley squeaks faintly as it begins to bear Pallada's weight. His body lists forward, and he unconsciously goes up on tiptoes. Guards at his sides lift him slightly from the floor, the rope pulls taut, then the guards release him almost gently (fig. 25). "Jesus!" It is more a grunt than a cry. Pallada tries to pull his knees up toward his chest, sways almost imperceptibly and rotates erratically. Pallada's face and hands have turned a livid red. In the tense moment there is no sound except his shallow gasps. "It's all true, my lord!" he blurts out, "what I testified about Don Carlo! He had Count Ferdinando Ranuzzi and Negrino Negrini bring the two nuns to my house and had me keep them there for as long as I said in my testimony. Under torture, I confirm all of it! Because it's the truth!"[28]

"He's lying through his teeth!" Possenti exclaims, with as much outrage but perhaps a shade less certainty. "It's not true, anything he said!"

"I am telling the truth! This confirms it!" Pallada pants. "Yes, lord! Yes, lord!"

Rossi remained unusually still, quietly waiting as the notary, scarcely looking up, continued to write down every detail. When the faint pen scratching finally faded, the prosecutor signaled the guards, who efficiently let Pallada down and lightly steadied him. They untied his hands, waited while the barber surgeon adjusted his arms, then helped him into his clothes and tried to spare his arms as they half led and half supported him from the room. Sbirri escorted Pallada out of the Torrone, not without a certain admiration: Would they have done as well? There they let him go. He need not return to a cell

FIGURE 25. Domenico Beccafumi, *Inquisition Scene*. The strappado, inflicted on Possenti, Guarnieri, and Pallada. © RMN-Grand Palais/Art Resource, NY.

at the archiepiscopal prison: Rossi had authorized his immediate release on bond.[29]

The prosecutor had made his point with minimal, calculated risk: Pallada was a simple, sturdy sort, patently aggrieved at Possenti's duplicity, which violated some coarse fraternal code. Pallada would never cave and recant. Besides, Rossi's judicial experience probably reassured him that the ruder sort of witness such as Pallada frequently managed to resist the ruder forms of torture such as the strappado: a little pain would not have compelled him to change his testimony. As important, this spectacle, involving no stranger, but an erstwhile friend, was useful for Possenti to witness up close (although with Possenti's type, a lusty display of anguish might have served better than Pallada's fortitude and grim determination). But let the memory of it work on the priest, with a thought to the future.

In coming days, Rossi left Possenti to ruminate in the dank solitude of his cell. He summoned Don Carlo infrequently for a few more confrontations that seemed inconclusive, almost perfunctory, after what had gone before. Possenti may even have begun to imagine he had weathered the worst of it.

By then, garbled accounts of the secret proceedings at the Torrone had begun to filter back to Rome. According to one commentator, "They say that Possenti may not be persuaded to own up." (That much was certainly true.) "And that it will be necessary to employ torture to get him to confess. But in that case, the evidence against him will easily go up in smoke, because he's the type who'll dauntlessly maintain his denials without fear of any of their tactics, however cruel."[30]

On Tuesday, September 26, at the end of a very busy day, Giandomenico Rossi called for Carlo Possenti. "Well, have you considered owning up to the truth about the rape and murder of the convertite?"

"I've already told you the truth, my lord."

Rossi dispatched the guard. Possenti must have wondered who it would be this time. Some of the others lately seemed inconsequential: chiefly talk of Suor Silveria and Suor Laura, with scarcely a word to implicate him directly.

Bartolomea Galliani, Possenti's old servant, hesitantly entered the room, paused momentarily at the sight of him, then reluctantly took her appointed place. Possenti showed nothing as the notary read from the transcript, describing how it had taken threats of torture to compel Bartolomea to implicate him. Nothing softened Possenti's look of betrayal when the notary read out her final words, "If I lied at my first interrogation, it was because of the affection I feel for Don Carlo's household."[31]

"It's not true, none of it!" Possenti shouted. "She hates me. And I know that in her heart she knows none of it is true!"

"It's the truth. Yes, my lord, it's true."

Possenti reassumed the role of advocate for the defense.

"Bartolomea, do you remember what happened after you visited Giovanni from your village, when I'd forbidden you to: that I gave you a thrashing?"

"It's true, my lord, that he beat me." Bartolomea's gaze wandered to where Rossi was sitting.

"Do you remember how I also beat up your brother?"

"No sir, I forgot that, just like I forgot the way you beat me. I never gave it a thought, and I always forgave you for it."

"When did Count Ferdinando Ranuzzi come to my house (or so you say) on the night I returned from Ferrara?"

"It was two hours after sunset."

"What does Colonel Alessandro Guarnieri look like?"

"He's a big man with a shock of dark hair and a beard. He's swarthy, with black hair."

When Possenti shrugged dismissively and declared, “No more questions,” Rossi briefly turned the tables. “Where were you when you beat Bartolomea? Was anyone else present?”

“I beat her at home. I don’t remember anybody else being there.”

“How long ago was that, and after her beatings did Bartolomea continue faithfully to serve you?”

“I beat her four or five years ago, and she’s served me ever since.”

“I never hated you, Don Carlo. I’ve always thought of you like a brother.” For a moment, Bartolomea looked into Possenti’s face, then turned and walked unsteadily from the room.[32]

Rossi eyed the prisoner coldly, with a studied hint of distaste, until he heard the door close.

“Take him away.”

As the notary shuffled his pages, gathered them into a sheaf and knocked blotting sand from them, Rossi rose and called for his carriage.

Perhaps he would remove Catterina Possenti, Don Carlo’s mother, from impending witness confrontations. There was really no need for her testimony and the pain it would cause her.

12

"I DON'T KNOW THIS SUOR LAURA VITTORIA!"

Sunrise seemed to smite Donato Guarnieri like an open hand when a guard finally removed the cloak from his head. He had stumbled blindly as sbirri manhandled him along the quay, propelled him over the gunwale to his seat, and chained him to a mast. The boat had set off across the lagoon, into the sun. As it yawed to starboard, guards still blocked Donato's view, but he could tell they were headed not landward, toward Padua, but out to sea. His ears told him that the security-minded Venetians insisted on a journey to Polesella entirely by water, to discourage any would-be liberators foolhardy enough to contemplate ambushing fifty guards armed to the teeth.

The little convoy sailed south the length of the lagoon, as far as Chioggia, then turned out into the Adriatic. The boat pitched and rolled as it skirted a stretch of coastline, then slipped back inside a sheltering outer bank and eventually found its way to the river Po. There they turned inland.

After nightfall, the journey became a curious descent into limbo. Guarnieri could make out nothing in the darkness beyond the gunwales and lost much sense of time or place. Then, not long after midnight, the moon rose nearly full, revealing shadowy riverbanks hulking on either side in the silvery gloom. Treacherous island sandbars surfaced silently from the flood, signaled only by spectral vegetation that had taken root there.[1]

About the hour of the wolf, a quiet voice near his ear roused Donato from fitful sleep. "Your cousin says to keep your spirits up and not to worry. He's coming to help prove your innocence." Donato started awake as someone brushed past him. The voice was gone.

At dawn the dark barriers hemming in the flow resolved into brakes of trees and tall bushes clustering at water's edge. They continued to block the view from Guarnieri's seat amidships, screening almost everything but an occasional disembodied rooftop above tangled treetops. He could be anywhere. Tension spiked at every passing bark, as his guards suspiciously scanned its gawking crew.

A subdued surge in activity toward midafternoon first hinted that Polesella (44.9608° N, 11.7494° E) must be nearby. A pair of longboats, bristling with armaments, came into sight along the southern bank. After hanging back for cautious mutual inspection, the two parties converged and documents were passed back and forth. Suddenly the cloak again enveloped Guarnieri's head. He felt himself hustled roughly through anonymous hands into the boat alongside.

Donato's new captors lost no time in covering the remaining dozen miles to Ferrara. His wardens busied themselves officiously as the boat approached the dock toward dusk on September 9. They paraded the prisoner past a few curious bystanders congregating here and there along the street to the Palazzo del Legato: the case of the convertite was nearly the cause célèbre in Ferrara that it was in Bologna. Cardinal Donghi promptly dispatched a courier to inform Archbishop Albergati-Ludovisi. Donghi also hastened to apprise Cardinal Pamphili of Guarnieri's safe arrival: everything had gone according to plan. Better still, Venice insisted on paying for the first leg of Guarnieri's journey.

Ottavio Agosti had watched helplessly from the quay near the doge's palace as the boats disappeared across the lagoon into the sun's glare.[2] He wasted little time attempting to follow their progress: he had much to do to make good on his promise. Yesterday he had already crossed to the island of San Giorgio Maggiore (45.429508° N, 12.342530° E), just across the lagoon, where the venerable Benedictine monastery rises bright and serene. Bearing an extravagant gift of fresh fish and other delicacies, he sought out the abbot, to whom he related the family's predicament. The benevolent cleric heard him out, offered whatever encouragement he could, and provided young Ottavio with a letter of introduction to his counterpart at Bologna's monastery of San Procolo.

By midafternoon on the day of Donato's departure, Ottavio was ready to follow him. Of the £1,200 Uncle Niccolò had entrusted to him a month before, less than £400 remained. The youth hired a gondola to ferry him to the station in time to catch a packet boat to Padua before suppertime. After a damp night beneath the full moon, he reached Padua in time for breakfast before departing for Ferrara. By the time Ottavio arrived there on September 10, any excitement surrounding his cousin's arrival had subsided. Donato had been safely tucked into a prison cell the previous afternoon, but talk on the street told young Ottavio just how close he was behind him.

Donato Guarnieri sat in his cell in Ferrara for three days, oblivious to his cousin plying the street outside. In the meantime messengers passed back and forth along the thirty-five miles to and from Bologna to arrange the last leg of his passage. On September 11 a courier delivered Rossi's final orders to Cardinal Donghi. The following morning Donghi's forces escorted Donato to the border, where they transferred him to Rossi's police, seconded by a substantial military force. They conducted the prisoner directly to the Torrone, "very well guarded, this very night," as Albergati-Ludovisi breathlessly informed Cardinal Pamphili on September 13. The Bolognese archbishop, fresh from his country rest and recreation, must have been confused. Guarnieri had arrived less dramatically and in broad daylight on Tuesday, September 12, allowing time for Rossi to begin interrogating him later that afternoon.[3]

Pamphili certainly failed to notice the mistake, and a disappointing revelation was yet to come. For weeks the cardinal nephew had been writing to Albergati-Ludovisi, Donghi, and the papal nuncio in Venice to expedite the extradition of "Colonel Donato Guarnieri." On September 6 the Bolognese archbishop, hurrying to catch his carriage to the countryside, paused long enough to offer Pamphili the good news that "the nuncio of Venice has obtained Colonel Guarnieri from the Senate." In the aftermath of Guarnieri's successful transfer, the nuncio set the record straight: "Since in various letters Your Eminence has written 'Colonel Donato Guarnieri,' I feel that I should inform you that I would suppose with considerable assurance that this one in custody is not the colonel, but the captain, as he is called. His *brother* is the colonel, who they say is fighting in Germany."[4] The big fish (Colonel Alessandro Guarnieri) got away; the papal net had snagged only small fry (the colonel's little brother, Donato).

Ottavio Agosti did not linger in Ferrara. By a stroke of luck, he crossed paths with a Roman gentleman escorting a lady friend back to Naples, and the generous fellow travelers invited Ottavio to share their carriage. When they reached Bologna late on September 11, Agosti tagged along in search of lodgings. For three days he shared their company and several meals at the fine Osteria del Pellegrino in via Vetturini (modern-day via Ugo Bassi 7, 44.495273° N, 11.340299° E; fourteen-year-old Mozart would stop there 125 years later, and his father described it as "the best inn in the city").[5] Ottavio soon sought more modest accommodation at a boardinghouse across town, a good ten minutes' walk from the Torrone but only a stone's throw from the monastery of San Procolo (fig. 5, I; 44.489735° N, 11.340883° E). The earnest Ottavio wasted no time in presenting himself to the Benedictines on September 12. The abbot immediately put him in touch with legal counsel. Ottavio spent the rest of the day (and more than 10 percent of his remaining cash on hand) conferring with lawyers.

On Wednesday Agosti first made his way to the Torrone. Weeks of hanging around the prison in Venice had steeled him for the Torrone's daunting exterior and the sour smell of sweat, mold, and urine exuding from the walls inside. After momentary loss of nerve, he approached a sbirro idling near the door, slipped him a coin, and asked to be taken to the man in charge. The size of the tip momentarily distracted the bailiff from what the obviously inexperienced spendthrift was trying to say. He grimaced to make sense of the young foreigner's brogue (although the tip spoke clearly enough), fixed him with an appraising eye, then slouched off toward a large grated opening. "Oy, Silvano!" he barked. Ottavio, trailing after him, scanned groups of prisoners congregating beyond the bars while Silvano Guardiano (Silvano the Warder, as he was known) approached, sizing him up. Again Agosti's hand went into his purse and slipped encouragement to the warder as he explained his business and urged him to look out for his cousin. "You need to talk to Captain Giovanni Battista Prigioniero [Giovanni Battista the Jailer]. He were the one you're wanting. He'll do right by you. But not today. Come back tomorrow."

Before Ottavio returned on September 14, he arranged for a demijohn of wine to be delivered to the Torrone. He also brought along linen, fresh shirts, and sheets. A bit surer of himself now, the youth paused to chat up Silvano Guardiano at the grate, then penetrated farther into the prison's recesses until he encountered Captain Giovanni Battista Prigioniero, the head jailer. "Oh, he were in good hands, your cousin. I pegged him for a gentleman of quality. So I already picked him out a fine mattress and one of my better sheets." The captain nodded repeatedly and grinned reassurance as he pocketed his tip. "So don't you worry about nothing. I'll see to him." There was also the matter of Donato's keep: they settled on £4 a day, with a week payable in advance. Ottavio's shrinking assets took another hit.

Silvano Guardiano and Giovanni Battista Prigioniero sent him off with a reassuring wave. Agosti perhaps breathed a little easier as he went in search of his lawyer. As Silvano and Giovanni Battista watched him go, they snickered. Guarnieri, the kid's relative, would see none of it.[6]

On Tuesday, September 12, Giandomenico Rossi had the day's witnesses shifted to the Torrone to save time: Donato Guarnieri was due that afternoon. By midafternoon Federico Panzacchi was suggesting, tellingly, "There has never been any rift between Pallada and Possenti, or any dislike that I know about. On the contrary, they were friends."[7] Then the prosecutor abruptly broke off the interview: Guarnieri had arrived.

What, Rossi must have wondered, did he stand to gain from this lesser of the Guarnieri brothers, whose extradition had become a major diplomatic exercise? Donato Guarnieri might be a source of indignant speculation at the Convertite, but beyond the convent walls, other players overshadowed him. Once his extradition was settled, Roman commentators on the case forgot him. His name disappeared entirely from dispatches to Venice, Modena, Florence, and Paris. The world no longer cared about this nobody from Bergamo.

Even at the Convertite, talk was often of "the Guarnieri," "the colonel," or "Signora Laura" (Colonel Alessandro Guarnieri's wife). The morning of Donato Guarnieri's arrival, Dionisio Tomassini claimed not even to know who Donato was. Federico Panzacchi seconded him a few hours later: "I don't believe I know Captain Donato Guarnieri; I certainly know the colonel, his brother, by sight." The previous week, Diana Tomassini had asserted, "I only caught a glimpse of Donato Guarnieri sometimes in the large courtyards of Palazzo Pepoli, and I wouldn't know who he might be." Perusing the transcript of earlier Bolognese interrogations, Rossi discovered more of the same. A Pepoli servant had observed only Colonel Alessandro Guarnieri visiting Count Alessandro Maria Pepoli, never Captain Donato Guarnieri. Similarly, a Braccesi servant was familiar with Colonel Guarnieri but didn't even know he had a brother.[8]

Ever since the day the nuns disappeared, allegations against Donato Guarnieri had been based overwhelmingly on hearsay, with certain confusion and hints of mistaken identity involving his brother mixed in. About all that could be said was that some hearsay originated near a principal in the case. Doralice Pallada and Federico Panzacchi both claimed to have heard directly from

Suor Laura Vittoria that she had left the convent for love of Donato. Diana Tomassini heard from Count Alessandro Maria that the nuns had left to be with Possenti and Captain Donato. On the other hand, the count also told Diana Tomassini that by the time the nuns left Palazzo Pepoli, when they had already been on the run for three weeks, Donato Guarnieri had yet to appear in Bologna. And because of Donato's prolonged absence, Count Alessandro Maria had assured Diana that La Rossa's rehabilitated virtue remained intact.[9] Clearly, Donato Guarnieri himself must be the one to confess the true extent and nature of his crimes.

Rossi fixed Captain Donato with a cold, appraising eye. The convertite who once found this figure dashing would turn up their noses at him after his forty days in a dungeon. The sorry state of his once fine jerkin of Spanish leather, tricked out in gold, proclaimed the depth of his decline. His dark, gold-trimmed serge breeches by now were threadbare and well past filthy. A film of sooty prison dirt and a sparse, scruffy beard coated a complexion turned cadaverous after weeks in darkness. The long, fair hair, known to turn the occasional nun's head, now looked ashen and patchy, cropped unfashionably short. The prosecutor leaned back slightly, wrinkling his nose. He saw no reason to hide his distaste.

"Why do you suppose you're a prisoner, conveyed to this prison?"

"I don't know, and I can't imagine why, because I've done nothing wrong."

Gaucheness, not intentional insolence, probably explained the lack of deference in this answer, the prosecutor may have assumed. Rossi let him run on about how life took him from a Bergamasque jail to service under the Duke of Parma, to enlistment in the papal army, and finally to his postings at Rimini and Ravenna.

"Did you ever return to Bologna from Rimini?"

"Only once, when I came to spend Christmas with my brother and his wife." After a moment's hesitation, Guarnieri continued, "Now, come to think of it, I returned for carnival and stayed five or six days, then went to Ravenna." Guarnieri rattled on with a barrage of unsolicited information. In Rossi's experience, such displays were often diversions from more hazardous ground. "Then I returned to Bologna in May of last year. I wasn't here more than five or six days before my company was demobilized, and after that I went back home to Bergamo."[10]

Just an ordinary year of an ordinary mercenary's life in wartime. "So, during your time in Ravenna you never once returned to Bologna?" Perhaps Rossi smiled faintly, arching an eyebrow with a hint of mockery, at this point still more amiable than threatening. (The nuns gave the impression that young Donato scarcely left the convent grates.)

"No, I never went anywhere." After a pause and a flutter of the eyes, "except for two weeks before Easter, when Sergeant Major Benedetto Machiavelli ordered me to Ferrara. I stayed there for ten or twelve days, then returned to Ravenna."

Another feint, the prosecutor observed, to divert attention from Bologna. Perhaps the young man didn't recognize that Ferrara too posed dangers. Rossi followed his lead. "During that time, did you ever leave Ferrara?" Only twice, Guarnieri claimed: once to stand night watch at Lagoscuro bridge with Machiavelli and once when the army marched to Copparo. There, as Guarnieri seemed at pains to point out, he was under the solicitous eye of the attentive Sergeant Major Machiavelli. (Was this perhaps the captain's attempt to claim a sympathetic witness in high places? He would not have known that Roman gossip had previously linked Benedetto Machiavelli to the convertite. To hear the nuns tell it, Donato Guarnieri also went absent without leave when the sergeant major wasn't looking, to visit La Rossa on Palm Sunday.)

Rossi shifted abruptly. "Are you friends with Don Carlo Possenti?"

"Not except to say hello in Bologna and when we were stationed in Castelfranco."

"Were you ever at his house?"

"No, my lord—never." (Possenti's servant had said otherwise just a few hours earlier.)

"Was Carlo Possenti sometimes at your house?"

Again, telltale volubility to deflect guilt by association. "Yes, my lord. Carlo Possenti came to our house sometime around Christmas the year I came to Bologna, to speak with my brother the colonel. But I don't know what they talked about because they'd always go stand apart. I never saw him there except at Christmas because, as I said, I wasn't in Bologna much."

Ah, as you keep insisting, Rossi perhaps said to himself. "When you returned from Ravenna, before you were discharged, *then* did you spend time with Possenti?"

"No, my lord." Another lie, then, another feint. "He was sick at that time—that's what my brother, Colonel Alessandro, heard, in conversation with somebody—I can't remember who—who mentioned that Don Carlo was sick, so my brother said."[11]

Rossi sent Guarnieri off to his cell. This pale spirit of perpetual negation had learned a prisoner's first commandment on his way upriver: admit nothing, deny everything. Breaking down this Lombard hill country bumpkin could prove a tedious slog, possibly to nowhere. Unless, with encouragement, this nobody had useful things to say about those who were somebody.

September 13 was entirely Donato Guarnieri's day. The notary scrambled to keep up with his overabundant, useless information demonstrating his absence from Bologna from Lent 1644 until his company was recalled to Bologna in May. When the prosecutor inquired about matters of the heart, Donato responded enthusiastically. Was he trying to suggest that his dalliance with women of easy virtue kept him too busy to think about their retired counterparts at the Convertite? Captain Donato's list of conquests rivaled the catalog aria from *Don Giovanni*: La Catterina, La Turchetta, La Frattina, La Bevarina. . . . The prosecutor took note. A sweep of local red-light districts landed some of them briefly in stir. With nothing useful to contradict Guarnieri's claims, La Turchetta and La Frattina were out on bond, back on the street, and down to business within seventy-two hours.[12]

Rossi allowed the interrogation to ramble awhile. Then from out of nowhere, "Who did your laundry in Bologna?"

"We had our laundry done by Bologna's convertite—for me, my brother, and the whole family." After the slightest hesitation, "Just as much as mine, my sister-in-law had them do her husband's and the rest of the family's." Guarnieri falters. Feeling the weight of the prosecutor's gaze, his eyes flick toward the bench, then look away. Rossi has paused and is studying him.

At the innocuous mention of the convertite, Donato Guarnieri blushes. . . .[13]

Prosecutor and notary perhaps exchanged a fleeting look as the notary resumed his work.

"What were the names of these convertite?"

"I don't know. There are way too many of them to remember," Donato mumbled with a shrug. "But she was old."

"How do you know all this: that there are lots of them and what they're like?"

"Because I went there. . . ."

After another affected pause, Rossi continued, "When? What for?"

"Five or six times at Christmas, to have some shirts made. I brought along a mercer and the nuns bought the fabric and lace for me, enough for twelve or fourteen shirts, which they made in installments."

"Who were these nuns?"

Donato appeared momentarily at a loss. "The one who took the fabric was called . . . Suor Silveria. But I don't know if she made the shirts or if some other nuns did."

Rossi fixed him with another incredulous look. "It seems implausible that you wouldn't know the identity of their maker since you had to pay her for them."

"I've no idea. I left it to my sister-in-law to handle that. She didn't tell me, and I never asked."

"Do you know the names of any other nuns besides this Suor Silveria?"

"No, because, as I said, I was only there a few times—I certainly heard the others called names like Catterina, Agnese, and so on."

Perhaps hoping to scare up another telltale blush, Rossi pulled up sharply, "Do you know if there was another nun at the convent named Suor Laura Vittoria?"

Donato's pallor remained unchanged. "I believe so. Sometimes I heard them call a nun by that name. I think maybe I might have met that Suor Laura Vittoria, but I'm not sure who she could be."

"Don't be so vague. Answer me precisely." Rossi's voice was low but nevertheless sharp. "Did you know this Suor Laura Vittoria?"

"Lots of different nuns that live there came to chat when I visited," Guarnieri answered feebly.

"Answer explicitly—did you or did you not know Suor Laura Vittoria, alias La Rossa, a nun at the convent of the Convertite in Bologna?"

During this exchange Donato increasingly stiffened, intermittently scowling at his accuser. He glanced away impertinently. "Maybe I knew this Suor Laura Vittoria alias La Rossa, maybe I didn't. I can't remember."

"It is incredible that you cannot. You may compel this tribunal to invoke other appropriate and effective means to constrain you to answer precisely."

"You can do whatever you want," Guarnieri answers quietly, but with an edge to his voice, "because I don't remember if I knew this Suor Laura Vittoria, alias La Rossa, but it could be—or maybe not."

Rossi nods to the guards, whose accustomed impassivity has faded. They brusquely propel Guarnieri toward the strappado, undress him, and secure him to the rope with palpable relish: this kid in his fancy jerkin needs taking down a peg. There is nothing tentative about the way they draw the rope tight this time. Like dogs on point, they await Rossi's signal.

"Are you prepared to answer the question? *Did you or did you not know Suor Laura Vittoria*?"

"I've said what I've got to say!"

The chief constable commits Guarnieri to the air with gusto.

"O Holy Mother of God, help me!"

Rossi looks about for an hourglass, turns it over, and pauses. "Answer my question precisely to avoid further suffering."

"I've said what I have to say!"

Rossi eases back into his chair, glancing occasionally at the hourglass as minutes drag past.

Finally, a dull "I didn't know her, Suor Laura Vittoria." Donato had been hanging for fifteen minutes by then. His mulishness was gone.

"Since the prisoner has answered precisely," Rossi proclaimed to no one in particular, "he may be taken down."[14]

There was no consideration in their manner as guards hustled Guarnieri away. Guarnieri lied, of course. (No surprise there.) Truth was not the objective; it was compelling him to answer. And in the end, answer he did. Pain had not hardened his defiance: no streams of vulgar, unimaginative invective, hissed at the prosecutor, as sometimes happened. Justification for the strappado had been thin, but it suited the circumstances and was well within Rossi's authority: a useful pretext to begin breaking Guarnieri down, to demonstrate his powerlessness and isolation, past hope and help. Above all, to make him realize that now he was nothing but Rossi's creature.

Prosecutor and prisoner faced off again the next day. The session on the strappado, it seemed, had little impact: the youth remained unyielding. Before long Rossi resumed his warnings to tell the truth. To no avail.

"Do you know what became of the nuns after their escape?" Just how far would Donato take these pleas of ignorance?

"No, because I never tried to find out: not about how they did it, not about who they were, not about what happened to them. I never had the slightest interest in anything about them."

The prosecutor jettisoned any remaining subtlety. "Do you know who Suor Laura Vittoria was, the other one who ran away? What about the suit of clothes that you had specially made for her? Answer truthfully."

"My lord, I never knew this Laura Vittoria and was never her friend. I never even spoke to her. I've no idea who she might be. I don't know her!"[15]

Perhaps face-to-face confrontations would shake Guarnieri's determination. There was plenty of time for that.

Rossi's mood cannot have improved the next day, when a lawyer appeared before the tribunal, come to plead for "one Ottavio Agosti, a relative," on Guarnieri's behalf and to offer the usual boilerplate legal objections and petitions. "First and foremost, due consideration that the prisoner's present circumstances be concordant with his noble origins: a youth, legally under age, born of noble stock"—this petty hoodlum, born into a noble lineage of hoodlums! "Someone should be permitted to see to his care, if he be prepared to tender all necessary funds to that end. The same Donato should be set free and restored to pristine liberty until someone can see the documents against him and prepare his defense"—so lawyers all say! "Furthermore, he ought not to be subjected to enhanced interrogation techniques, given that his right to a defense, according to civil, canon, and natural law, cannot be set aside." Well, the advocate showed up a bit late for that. Without much thought, Rossi added the petition to the growing pile of documents in the case.[16]

It would not do, however, for Guarnieri to get wind of this. It could only fortify his vexing intransigence. And this Ottavio Agosti needed looking into. Petitions regarding enhanced interrogation were pro forma, but might he already have learned of Rossi's prior persuasive methods?

Rossi ignored Guarnieri for several days while he orchestrated Possenti's confrontations with the Palladas and the Ferrarese innkeeper. On Thursday, September 21, the time came for Donato Guarnieri's first encounters with those who told alternative truths. Rossi began with someone whose evidence seemed irrefutable, the tailor Giulio Cesare Boschino, who had made no fewer than eight suits of clothes for Captain Donato in 1643–44.

The prosecutor first sent for the prisoner alone, while the tailor waited outside. "Did you ever have Boschino, the tailor, make any other garments apart from those mentioned in your previous testimony?"

"No, my lord."

The prosecutor sought Donato's eye and with affected solicitude, continued, "Wouldn't it be better to tell the truth? How you had Boschino make garments for Suor Laura Vittoria alias La Rossa?"

"No, my lord, I never had apparel of any sort made for La Rossa. I never arranged with anybody to make clothes for that nun."[17]

Rossi signaled. Boschino entered.

"Do you know the prisoner?"

"I recognize Captain Donato Guarnieri."

"Do you know the witness?"

"It's Boschino, the tailor. I mentioned him in my interrogations."

The prescribed routine continued.

"One day Captain Donato Guarnieri came to my shop and told me to go to the Convertite and ask for Suor Laura Vittoria, because she needed some apparel made. When I got there to take Suor Laura Vittoria's measurements, I knocked at the gate and the doorkeeper opened it. (She had to be present when I was measuring her.) So I sewed the outfit: a pair of breeches of Florentine red baize and a matching shirt, with gold or silver buttons, depending on what trimmings were on hand. When I brought her the finished garments, I handed them over to her at the gate, and she gave me the money, as stipulated in my bill.[18]

"I also sewed various outfits for Captain Donato, and during Lent last year I made one of light gray Holland wool, tricked out with gold or silver. If I'm not mistaken, I made it about a month before the nuns ran away." (That would have been around the beginning of March, Rossi noted, when Donato claimed to have been hunkered down in Ravenna.) "I delivered it myself to his brother, Colonel Alessandro Guarnieri's house, and personally helped Captain Donato try it on."[19]

The eyewitness thus confirmed Donato's role in the creation of La Rossa's fabled red outfit, and also handily caught him in another lie regarding his whereabouts during Lent. When the prosecutor turned to Guarnieri, his look may have been less a question than a challenge.

"It's not true! I never sent him to La Rossa to make her that suit of clothes! He's a liar if he says so!"

With studied incredulity, Rossi continued, "If you wish to question the witness, do so now, because the lord governor of Rome bars witnesses' recall for subsequent cross-examination."

"So what do you want me to ask him?" Donato responded bitterly. "He's a liar and a slanderer if he says these things. Someone who has it in for me must have made him say it!" (Now the captain was ringing changes on Possenti's tune.) "I've nothing more to say to him."[20]

Rossi dismissed the tailor before resuming his own assault. "I warn—I exhort—you to abandon such obstinacy and freely speak the truth about your intimate friendship with Suor Laura Vittoria. Otherwise you can expect more of the same from further witnesses. Do you know or have you heard if Laura Vittoria and Suor Silveria can still be found among the living or have ended their earthly days?" Perhaps the scrawny youth's emotions would once again betray him.

"They could be alive or dead for all I know. I've heard nothing about them!"

"Isn't it time to stop all this wrongheadedness and freely confess the truth about the extent of your relationship with Suor Laura Vittoria? But also about the removal of all her possessions to your house? Because extensive evidence makes it patently clear that you were her friend and her lover, but also that beforehand you conspired with Carlo Possenti and with others in the nuns' abduction, to satisfy your lust with them and to steal their belongings."

"Absolutely none of this is true! I had no part in this villainous act! I was never mixed up in that business, not with Don Carlo Possenti or anybody else, and I never laid hands on any of their belongings."

Rossi's voice hardened. "You were complicit not only in their abduction and the theft of their belongings, but subsequently also in their murder at the hands of Colonel Alessandro Guarnieri, your brother."

No sign of astonishment, feigned or genuine. "I know absolutely nothing—nothing at all—about the murder of these nuns. If my brother did it, why lay the guilt on me? My brother never said a word to me about any of these things!"[21] Donato Guarnieri's determination rivaled Possenti's, although the priest at least put up some defense, something for Rossi to work with. This rustic simpleton only ducked his head and denied everything. The prosecutor sent him back to his cell.

Rossi may have decided his only recourse was to wear Guarnieri down, to overwhelm him with accumulated testimony. Over the next eighteen days, Donato faced off with more than twenty witnesses. On September 24 Doralice Pallada affirmed, "La Rossa told me that she had fled at the urging of Captain Donato Guarnieri." Federico Panzacchi's testimony repeated Doralice's words almost exactly. Donato could only reply, "If that nun said she left at my insistence, she was nothing but a scoundrel, because I never made her leave. I was never mixed up in any of this business. And I've never wanted for women!"[22]

As witnesses came and went and the notary droned on, Guarnieri might have realized how rarely his name even came up. After most witnesses, he stuck to a single mantra: "I heard what this person said, and I don't know what they're talking about." Even Rossi would have had to grudgingly acknowledge that, since his name was scarcely mentioned, his assertion did not sound so implausible.[23]

Two eyewitnesses caught Captain Donato in another lie, however. After her initial reluctance, Possenti's servant, Bartolomea Galliani turned out to be a star prosecution witness. Before he trotted her out this time, Rossi sent a guard to find a pair of Guarnieri look-alikes among the other prisoners. "Get into line with them," he ordered. "Pick your spot." Donato stepped in between them. Guards escorted Bartolomea into the room. "Do you recognize either of the Guarnieri brothers you testified about? If so, touch him."

"The one in the middle, he's called Captain Guarnieri." She approached Donato and tentatively touched him on the shoulder. "I saw him come to Don Carlo Possenti's two or three times. I clearly recognize him as the one called Captain Guarnieri."[24]

Donato listened to the reading of Bartolomea's testimony. "Two or three days after I removed the linens from the Palladas', Captain Guarnieri came to the house. He came into the room with Don Carlo, and they stood talking together for a while, but I don't know what they said." Rossi eyed Guarnieri—Bartolomea's testimony put him in Bologna in late April, whatever he might say. "I remember that Captain Guarnieri was also at our house at other times. He came to visit Don Carlo when he was sick last summer, and I heard him called Signor Captain Guarnieri."[25]

"I've never seen this woman," Donato snapped. "She's lying, because I was never at Carlo Possenti's house and don't even know where it is."

"Indeed you were, sir. I saw you two or three times when you came to see Don Carlo when he was sick, and also before he got sick, just as I said."

"She's confusing me with my brother."

"Yes, your brother was there too at Don Carlo's. But so were you."[26]

Interrogations and confrontations had been under way for almost a month before Rossi finally tracked down another important witness: Possenti's former page, Pietro Caccini. Two days later Captain Donato heard his allegations.

"Do you know Captain Donato Guarnieri?"

"Yes, my lord, I know Colonel Guarnieri's brother, I seen him often around Bologna."

"Is he a friend of Carlo Possenti's?"

"Yes, my lord. I often seen them together here and there. Both the Guarnieri brothers were friends with Don Carlo."

"Were the Guarnieri brothers ever at Don Carlo's house?"

"Yes, my lord. The colonel came to visit him two or three times when he were sick last year around summer. I also remember that Captain Donato came there once. I remember because I stayed downstairs, outside the Possenti's door, to play with the captain's page. The two of us were tossing coins."[27]

Donato Guarnieri presumably knew enough to recognize that Rossi had now produced the requisite pair of eyewitnesses to put him in company with the prime suspect. The realization did not produce Rossi's hoped-for reaction, however. "He's not telling the truth! Because I was never at Don Carlo Possenti's house and don't even know where it is. He's mixing me up with my brother."[28]

Giandomenico Rossi still had more judicial stagecraft up his sleeve and a fresh cast of players: nuns at the convent of SS. Filippo e Giacomo. But all in good time.

In the meantime there was the matter of Guarnieri's meddlesome relative. For a week Ottavio Agosti made himself scarce. Then he reappeared at the grates of the Torrone on September 20, looking for Giovanni Battista Prigioniero: another week's prison living expenses were due. The next day, young Agosti also invaded the prosecutor's precincts, lawyer in tow. (To what end is unclear.)[29]

Rossi waited a week to respond: he dispatched sbirri to Agosti's boardinghouse, where they ransacked his room. The only things worth confiscating were his lists of expenses. Sbirri also took young Ottavio into custody. He came face-to-face with Giandomenico Rossi later the same day, but not at the Torrone. That the prosecutor chose to interrogate him in Palazzo Bargellini suggests he was not taking him too seriously. He very likely rolled his eyes, however, at Agosti's response to the customary opening question.

"I don't know why I am in custody of the authorities."

From subsequent, less disingenuous responses, Rossi may have sized him up as a reasonably credible witness. He offered detailed answers: to the point, without his cousin's tendency to volunteer irrelevancies. He also freely admitted his missions to the prison and his meetings with Giovanni Battista Prigioniero and Silvano Guardiano and the generous tips he had offered them.

Rossi had a guard pass him his confiscated papers.

"Yes, these are in my handwriting and contain the expenses I've paid out during this trip."

"Did you try to slip any messages to the prisoner or receive any from him?" Rossi sought and held Agosti's eye.

"No, my lord, I never tried to have messages passed to him and didn't receive any in his name." Perhaps something about the prosecutor's gaze or Agosti's recollections from the confiscated documents made him cautious. "I did ask the guards in Venice to tell him I was there to help him. But otherwise I never transmitted letters or any sort of written notes in Venice or anywhere else."

Rossi frowned stonily. "Answer forthrightly: your expense memos suggest otherwise. How do you explain what you have written here: 'A tip to Silvano

Guardiano' in one list and in the other, 'Item: to pass a note to Signor Donato, one time a Hungarian ducat and another, a half ducat'?"

"Once in Venice I did write a note, late at night in a bar. But I never sent the note because I had no faith in it and tried to get the guard to tell him instead. I gave him a Hungarian ducat and the boatman a half ducat. My lord, you'll find it recorded in one of those lists." He gestured toward the papers on Rossi's table. "Although I did say 'to pass a note to Signor Donato,' nevertheless I didn't have it passed to him. This I swear to you, as a man of honor."[30]

Perhaps the corners of Rossi's mouth twitched at the fresh-faced "man of honor's" earnest affirmation. This waterfly posed no real problems. Two days later the prosecutor allowed Ottavio to post bond and return to his boardinghouse. Young Ottavio swore to appear whenever Rossi commanded.[31] Such an order probably never came; at least no evidence suggests the youth was ever recalled—which does not mean the faithful Agosti was ready to abandon his cousin.

More than a month later, on November 6, Ottavio Agosti's lawyer reappeared at the Torrone to lodge what was as much a protest as a petition. The prison warden should be required to reveal whether Donato Guarnieri had ever received the linens Ottavio Agosti had provided for him. "Since he has not received the soiled ones in return, for washing, one might suspect the new ones were not delivered to the captain." Guarnieri should at least be allowed to wash and tend to his dirty abrasions (of unspecified origin). With winter at hand, he should also be allowed warmer clothing.

Most intriguing is his concluding remark on the subject of torture: "Furthermore, they should not proceed to enhanced interrogation techniques on the pretext, perhaps, of insisting on a precise answer." Had Ottavio Agosti learned of Rossi's extreme measures during Guarnieri's second interrogation? Donato's own testimony hints at possible other breaches in the Torrone's security: "The sbirri in Ferrara and Bologna told me that Don Carlo was brought as a prisoner from Rome to Bologna. I haven't heard the reason. The same bailiffs also told me that Braccesi was brought here with him."[32] Perhaps wardens at the Torrone could not resist giving the generous young Agosti an earful, too. One or more of them may eventually have been moved by Agosti's request to carry messages, since an irresistible reward would likely have accompanied it. Perhaps the encouraging words, "Keep your spirits up," finally penetrated to Captain Donato's cell, offering inspiration to hold out as long as he could.

Captain Donato could not have imagined just how long that would be.

13

"SE SARÀ FATTO PAMPHILIO / I BARBERINI ANDRANO IN ESILIO"

> After Braccesi's imprisonment and because of other subsequent arrests, with scant regard for a cardinal's dignity, Cardinal Antonio's natural melancholy has greatly increased. Not only does he look so run down that he resembles a corpse, but his doctors agree that he might survive but a few months, because they deem what ails him incurable. Especially since his illness is compounded by the ingratitude of his most trusted attendants, who at the sight of the forsaken cardinal's declining fortunes, deserted him. This after he had rewarded them far beyond their quality and merit.[1]

A hint of schadenfreude probably tinges this dispatch, sent off to Mazarin a month after Giovanni Braccesi's notorious arrest. Any who did not exult in the Barberini brothers' decline in the year since Urban VIII's death might have agreed, nonetheless, that it was well earned.

Even before Antonio Barberini, as papal chamberlain, declared his uncle dead on July 29, 1644, and crushed the papal seal and Urban's golden "ring of the Fisherman," anti-Barberini sentiment had begun to erupt around the city. As the pope lay in extremis, a populace that had long suffered from one new papal tax after another, thanks to the ill-fated War of Castro, could be heard shouting insults at Cardinal Francesco Barberini's carriage so insistently that he closed the blinds. When bells finally tolled the pontiff's passing, guards at the Campidoglio kept the mobs at bay to protect Bernini's statue of the Barberini pope.[2]

Rome's late summer heat remained so intense that the stench of death hung over the papal corpse from the first day of its exposure in Saint Peter's on July 31, as the curious shuffled past for a final glimpse or to kiss the pontiff's feet. Stifling temperatures continued on August 9, as cardinals shuffled into conclave to elect Urban's successor. The Barberini nephews suggested the customary venue, the Vatican, despite physicians' warnings of "miasmas and the risk of infection" lurking there.[3]

Francesco Barberini voiced his resolve to see Cardinal Giulio Cesare Sacchetti elected or die trying. Indeed, he allegedly even drew up his will before entering the conclave. Antonio Barberini also backed Sacchetti, as a candidate acceptable to the French crown, which the younger Barberini served as cardinal protector of France. From the beginning, however, the Spanish faction opposed Sacchetti as pro-French, and their leader proclaimed his exclusion on Spain's behalf. When the votes were tallied in late August, Sacchetti received fewer than a third of the number required for election.[4]

The spotlight shifted to Cardinal Giovanni Battista Pamphili. Pamphili was quite acceptable to Spain; he had also been Francesco Barberini's supposed second choice since the beginning, even though Pamphili was widely perceived as no friend to the Barberini. Indeed, among the numerous satirical comments about the conclave attached to Pasquino, Rome's "talking statue," one couplet proclaimed, "Se sarà fatto Pamphilio / I Barberini andrano in esilio" (If they elect Pamphili, the Barberini will go into exile).

France, however, opposed Pamphili as vehemently as the Spanish opposed Sacchetti. But Cardinal Protector Antonio resisted proclaiming Pamphili's exclusion. In an equivocating memorandum to France's Roman ambassador a week into the conclave, Barberini proclaimed Sacchetti a lost cause and hinted that Pamphili deserved a close look as the only alternative. "In all truth, a while ago it became clear to me that the suspicions I sometimes entertained about this person regarding myself were vain, and the work of some hoping to benefit from them. More important, I discovered that on various occasions Cardinal Pamphili acted with high regard and very good sense toward His Majesty's affairs."[5]

The chief concern of Urban's nephews was, of course, the welfare of the Barberini family. In retrospect, some wondered if Francesco Barberini's initial promotion of Sacchetti was a ruse, designed to achieve Pamphili's eventual election, which the new pope would have to recognize as the Barberini cardinals' work.[6] A strategic marriage between the Barberini and Pamphili families could further ensure papal favor and a rosy future for the Barberini clan. Taddeo Barberini conveniently had eligible offspring on offer. Sixteen-year-old Lucrezia Barberini could be matched with Camillo Francesco Pamphili, Olimpia Maidalchini's only son and Cardinal Pamphili's nephew; fourteen-year-old Carlo Barberini would do for Olimpia's younger daughter, Costanza. Cardinal Antonio shared these prospects with the French ambassador: "It is very easy to recognize that this alliance of the new papal family with our own is a sign of future good relations with France."[7]

The French ambassador, however, stood firm: Cardinal Antonio should tell the French faction to support Pamphili's exclusion. As for any possible marriages, he wrote, "Permit me to point out that the chief advantage you might find in this business is based on a marriage prospect that is dubious at best." He concluded prophetically, "Once Pamphili finds himself elected pope, everyone will ask him to give them justice for the wrongs they claim to have received from your family."[8]

By then the Vatican's "miasmas and risk of infection" had begun to take their toll. As early as August 13 the first ailing cardinal abandoned the conclave, followed two days later by another, who promptly died. A further casualty departed the morning of September 10, followed by another later that afternoon. An onslaught of "bilious humors," severe stomach cramps, and vomiting suggested that Francesco Barberini might indeed expire before the election of his preferred candidate, as he had resolved. Instead, he too deserted the conclave, leaving his younger brother in charge.[9] Cardinal Francesco quietly continued to pull strings while allowing Cardinal Antonio, now the self-styled pope maker, enough rope to hang himself if things went wrong.

In balancing his duty to France with conclave realities and family benefits, Cardinal Antonio proved amenable to compromise. The unhappy state of his colleagues, growing impatient or dropping like flies, made concluding the conclave imperative. Cardinal Pamphili's election offered the only way out, with French opposition as the sole obstacle. Time had run out, Barberini claimed: France's equivocating supporters could wait no longer for Cardinal Mazarin's further directives. When the votes were scrutinized on September 15, forty-eight had chosen Pamphili, with only six against. Pamphili was crowned Innocent X on October 4. Five days later, the heat finally broke.

Barberini schemes began to unravel almost immediately. As the pope was carried up the steps at Saint Peter's following his coronation, Cardinal Antonio descended, arms outstretched, and made obeisance. Innocent was observed to raise his right hand as if in blessing, but then he merely stroked his chin.[10]

The following week Mazarin dispatched a courier with instructions on how to proceed with France's disobedient cardinal protector. It fell to the French ambassador's son to deliver a letter to Palazzo Barberini. After frigid pleasantries, Cardinal Antonio asked him his business. The ambassador's son proffered the letter to Giovanni Braccesi, who passed it along unopened. Barberini broke the ambassador's seal, then visibly blanched: he was no longer cardinal protector of France. The king further commanded that the French coat of arms be removed from Palazzo Barberini. The cardinal turned his back and left. The next day, the royal arms of France had disappeared.[11]

The letter to the French ambassador quickly found its way into print so that the world might know the extent of Cardinal Antonio's failings and so that responsibility for French opposition to Pamphili's election could be laid on his shoulders:

> Cardinal Antonio's long-standing objective has been to arouse the Crown's suspicion against the present pope's person. I desired to please Cardinal Antonio, who claimed to have singularly offended my cousin, Cardinal Pamphili, both in his own person and in the person of one of his nephews. That was the chief reason that, after placing inordinate faith in the cardinal's reports, I felt constrained to consent that the French cardinals follow Cardinal Antonio's initial lead. Cardinal Antonio thereby deprived me of the glory and satisfaction of exalting someone preeminently worthy to sit upon the throne of Saint Peter.
>
> I desire the satisfaction never again to be exposed to such failings, and I therefore decline any and all dealings with Cardinal Antonio, whose own actions are already sufficiently infamous to afford him adequate punishment. For he will live in the world without esteem and without respect.[12]

Many shared the Crown's view that some old offense involving a Pamphili nephew would soon move the pope to open reprisals. "It is well known that when Cardinal Pamphili's nephew, Gualtiero Gualtieri, who was serving as Cardinal Antonio's gentleman of the bedchamber, was killed, the cardinal was blamed," seventeenth-century historian Girolamo Brusoni explained. "Because it seemed he wished to punish that young gentleman for an unbounded youthful transgression, insufficiently reverent, even for a youth's vanity, to the person of his lord."[13]

The only testimony to the nature of Gualtiero Gualtieri's youthful indiscretion turns up in the memoirs of Nicolas Goulas, gentleman of the bedchamber to the duc d'Orléans. "Once when his lord sent for him while he was gambling, the young Pamphili [nephew], who served Antonio, responded shamelessly and falsely, 'I have him in my ass all night, can't he leave me in peace during the day!' When the wicked remark was reported to Pope Urban, he took it literally and almost sacrificed both servant and master. So Antonio banished Pamphili [i.e., Gualtieri] not only from the house but also from Rome."[14]

Young Gualtieri took himself and his dishonor off to Milan, where in the summer of 1634 he joined Spanish forces. After the bloody Battle of Nördlingen that September, reports claimed that Gualtieri's body, pierced by a musket ball, lay among the Catholic dead. Many at the papal court whispered that Cardinal Antonio had arranged his death.[15]

More concrete signs of souring Barberini-papal relations appeared scarcely a week after Pamphili snubbed Cardinal Antonio on the Vatican steps: Innocent made Camillo Pamphili, Lucrezia Barberini's supposed fiancé-to-be, a cardinal and named him cardinal nephew. By then Costanza Pamphili was already betrothed not to Carlo Barberini, but to the noted hispanophile Prince Niccolò Ludovisi. The prince's relatives, diarist Gigli observed, "seem to have no greater thought than to see the Barberini brought low."[16] Thus it was that Cardinal Antonio, faithfully accompanied by Giovanni Braccesi, left Rome under a dark cloud to celebrate Christmas 1644 at Monterotondo.

"Councils at the papal palace these days turn around three bits of business," the Venetian ambassador reported in late January 1645; one of them was "to cast down headlong the fortunes of the Barberini." Innocent moved overtly toward that objective in early March, when he created eight new cardinals. As the ambassador put it, "they are all uniformly avowed enemies of the house of Barberini."[17]

In June Innocent planted "a sharp dagger that wounded the heart of the Barberini" (as an antagonistic enemy subsequently characterized it). He ordered a formal audit of the accounts of the Apostolic Chamber from the last years of Urban VIII's reign, as related to the War of Castro. But the offensive stalled: the Barberini brothers appeared untouchable. "The pope told me that he can find nothing that can be made to stick to the Barberini," the Florentine envoy reported to his duke, "because they fixed the books. He said that shortly before Pope Urban died, when he went to kiss his feet, His Holiness exclaimed, 'Lord Cardinal, we have been murdered by our nephews, who made us fight this war and so lose life and reputation.' But the present pope says they smoothed things over and fortified themselves with briefs, bulls, and decrees. So nothing can be done in the cause of justice."[18]

Just when Innocent's attempts to clean house in Rome yielded little but frustration, Isabella Machiavelli's housecleaning on via Santo Stefano in Bologna unearthed the wine cellar's unspeakable bounty. Possenti's and Braccesi's subsequent showcase arrests were only the most sensational among several that enlivened dispatches to various courts and demonstrated a more productive side to the pope's pursuit of vengeance disguised as justice. Immediately after Possenti's arrest, a French correspondent passed along a rumor, which the Florentine ambassador had already mentioned, that "Malagigi" (Cardinal Antonio's cherished and lavishly rewarded castrato singer, Marcantonio Pasqualini) was implicated in the crime, and he spoke of more than twenty invasions of Barberini palaces in search of evidence or culprits. Pasqualini was exonerated shortly thereafter, though the rumors against Cardinal Antonio's probable lover offered a further affront to the prelate's honor. A dispatch to France the following week suggested, in a show of wit, that the neglect of crimes against the papal treasury was only temporary. "Although until now the case of the nuns in Bologna is all they talk about, everybody believes they also intend to geld the Barberini smartly in the *borsa* [the pocketbook, but also the balls]."[19]

Long before Giandomenico Rossi's arrival in Bologna with his prisoners, word about Cardinal Antonio's implication in the whole sordid business was filtering back to Rome, where it often blossomed extravagantly. An August 21 dispatch to Paris offered a mélange of half-truths and outright fantasy: "It's strongly believed that Cardinal Antonio will end up entangled in the investigation of the nuns in no small way. Captain Donato Guarnieri's page, locked up in Bologna, accepted immunity and confessed to everything that happened, because he brought the men's clothes to the convent at the time of the nuns' flight." (Nothing of the sort appears in the trial transcript.) "Among other things, he confessed that, immediately after the nuns left the convent, the cardinal used them carnally." (An impossibility, since Cardinal Antonio was thirty miles away in Ferrara at the time.) "Such a revelation, together with the cardinal's order to Monsignor Rinaldi, nuns' vicar of Bologna, not to proceed with the case, and the silence he imposed on him (as the monsignor testified) could easily embroil the cardinal in such a way as to result in major punishment for him." The Florentine ambassador, on the other hand, told quite a different story. "If they want to believe Monsignor Cesi, Bolognese vice legate at that time, they will find that it's far from true that His Eminence impeded the investigation. When Cesi wrote him in Ferrara that he suspected it would come to the arrest of some relation of his, Cardinal Antonio answered that in that case he should arrest him."[20]

More ominously, in early September a French dispatch reported the arrest of Cardinal Antonio's former manservant. "It's believed with absolute certainty that he was implicated in Gualtiero Gualtieri's murder, which the perpetrator confided to him. They say these witnesses were in fact arrested and required to come here from Germany or Flanders with immunity." The reporter continued with details that turn up nowhere else. "Gualtieri was murdered neither in Germany nor in Flanders but, as I well know, on the street at Viterbo. In order to mislead, the rumor was spread around at the time that he ended up dead in the military campaign."[21]

Amid such troubles, Cardinal Antonio often tried to chase his cares away in the company of Nina Barcarola, one of Rome's celebrated courtesans, particularly renowned for her singing. ("His Eminence makes use of that talent as a cover for his assignations," one avviso claimed.) Shortly after he left her one late September evening, sbirri raided Nina's apartment and carted her off to the Tor di Nona prison. Papal sleuths then spent five hours ransacking the place. Her writings, books, and music allegedly ended up in the hands of the pope and his cardinal nephew, who hoped to discover a copy of the infamous song against Donna Olimpia, "Prendi Musa il Colascione." (A rival courtesan claimed to have heard it wafting from Nina's window.) Rumor further claimed she had somehow received letters from Giovanni Braccesi, even after his arrest. "There were certainly passionate love letters that her ardent lovers had written to her, but not the sort of thing they were searching for," according to one commentator.[22]

Innocent's objective in the raid was, of course, to heap further humiliation on Antonio Barberini. "The sbirri went to Nina Barcarola's with the sole objective of discovering Antonio," the Modenese ambassador declared, "of treating him roughly and of reviling him. They perhaps also intended to tie him up and take him prisoner because he was undressed, without his clerical garb, and therefore incognito." The police, however, seem to have respected the cardinal more than they revered the pope: many suggested that in deference to Antonio, sbirri carefully waited in the shadows until they were sure he had left before swooping down on the courtesan.[23]

First Malagigi, now Barcarola: Cardinal Antonio surely took the arrest and detention of this second musical and sexual favorite as a further injury to his honor.[24] "There are a thousand traps being laid for the Barberini," one observer remarked. "He was well aware that they were making countless attempts to entangle him in the case of the nuns." Cardinal Antonio began to complain of the need for a little rest and recuperation. When he requested papal permission to go on pilgrimage to the Holy House of Loreto and to call on his aunt at the court of Savoy, Innocent X refused. What with the investigation of War of Castro expenditures, it would be most inconvenient for him to be out of reach. On September 27, however, the pope beneficently agreed to a more practical proposal: a few days' hunting in the fresh air at Monterotondo (42.0517° N, 12.6167° E), less than twenty miles northeast of town.[25]

A carriage set off from Palazzo Barberini a little after noon the same day, bound for Monterotondo with only Cardinal Antonio's butler inside. In the meantime Barberini was heading not northeast, but northwest toward the coast, astride a very ordinary mount that usually transported coal, not a prince of the church. South of Civitavecchia (42.0912° N, 11.7968° E), a light frigate from Genoa waited. Barberini, barely distinguishable from the valet accompanying him, hastily went aboard later that afternoon, and the boat set sail. The weather began to deteriorate almost immediately. By the time the crew had fought its way up the coast more than halfway to Genoa, violent swells threatened to swamp the boat or drive it onto the rocky shore. They put in at the port in Livorno (43.5519° N, 10.308° E), where Barberini lay low for a day, in constant fear of discovery. (The Medici, at present no friends to the Barberini family, controlled the city.) Anyone observing from atop the red brick bastions of the fortress looming at water's edge might well have wondered why an unremarkable figure dressed like a barrel maker was reclining on deck while others deferred to him. In Rome the pope still assumed Antonio was roaming the countryside at Monterotondo in pursuit of game.[26]

Several hours after dark on October 1 the boat finally reached Genoa (44.4025° N, 8.93129° E), where receptions appropriate to a cardinal's dignity awaited him. Word of Cardinal Antonio's departure had reached Cardinal Francesco the previous day. He hurried to the papal palace, where he broke the news to the cardinal secretary of state and requested that he deliver Cardinal Antonio's explanatory letter to His Holiness. But the cardinal would not touch it: Cardinal Francesco should seek an audience and deliver it himself. Innocent declined to see him until Monday and then kept him waiting in his antechamber for an hour and a half. He then spurned the letter: "Since the tenor of it must duplicate what has already been conveyed to us, nothing more is required." With great agitation, the pope further asserted that it was inconceivable "that Antonio would have taken a step without his brothers' consent." A few days later the pope requested that the Florentine ambassador ask the grand duke to inform his minister in Paris "that Cardinal Antonio had fled because of the legal business of the nuns in Bologna, in which he should be implicated."[27]

Although Cardinal Francesco denied advance knowledge of Antonio's flight, machinations involving the Barberini family and the French court had been in the works for months. Initially, Barberini equivocation threatened to spoil reconciliation with the Most Christian King, whose requirements included the Barberini family's joining the French faction, purchasing substantial land in France, and sending one of Taddeo Barberini's sons to the French court for safekeeping. Because only Antonio bore the initial brunt of papal vengeance, his older brothers claimed to be so strapped for cash that acquiring property in France was difficult to contemplate.[28]

In the aftermath of Cardinal Antonio's flight and a resultant spike in papal disfavor, the Barberini brothers had reason to reconsider. Special couriers began to traverse the roads between Paris and Rome. On October 6, Taddeo Barberini acknowledged to Mazarin, "Cardinal Antonio's resolve speaks loudly of the circumstances in which the entire house of Barberini finds itself and of the great faith we all must put in the singular beneficence of Your Eminence."[29] On October 14 the matter was finally settled in Rome, with two pro-French cardinals standing in for Louis XIV and Taddeo Barberini representing Cardinal Antonio. The cardinal's brother declared that the family was ready to invest 200,000 scudi in French real estate as expeditiously as possible. The cardinals, in turn, proclaimed that the Most Christian King deigned to receive the house of Barberini under his protection and to honor them "as his good and beloved servants."

On October 15, to thundering drums and blaring trumpets, amid cries of "Viva Francia ed i Barberini," the arms of France ostentatiously rose on the facade of Palazzo Barberini. Before long a parade of carriages was crawling past to confirm the stunning news, "which drew all of Rome to these districts," a Roman agent of Cardinal Mazarin reported to his master. Even the cardinal nephew could not keep away. "I ran into Cardinal Camillo Pamphili at the Quattro Fontane," the agent reported with considerable delight. "He looked more at my horses' backs than at me, with an expression on his face as if he truly had never met me." Cardinal Grimaldi related that the extraordinary applause and festive din outside Palazzo Barberini "was powerful enough to keep the pope indoors for three days."[30]

After his warm reception in Genoa, Cardinal Antonio slowly proceeded toward Paris, delayed by extended political negotiations required to smooth the path, and by the onset of winter. The Christmas holiday was ending by the time he arrived in the French capital on January 6, 1646. In sending home word of his arrival, he claimed rather extravagantly that "I am being caressed by Their Majesties and by Cardinal Mazarin and the rest of these princes and lords in a way I cannot merit."[31]

Many of those same princes and lords would have affirmed only Barberini's final comment. Although Mazarin, four dozen coaches, and a contingent of obliging gentlemen on horseback rode out a respectable five miles to receive Cardinal Antonio and to accompany him to Mazarin's residence, beyond the palace his reception was about as chilly as the season. The aristocracy remained slow to call on this "man of little worth," as Nicolas Goulas described him. Oliver Lefèvre d'Ormesson, master of requests to the Council of State, found Barberini "little, hunchbacked, and ugly," which Goulas maliciously suggested worked to his advantage. "It's amusing that he's made out to be so ugly to all the ladies that there's not one of them who didn't pity the injustice he received." When the clergy stayed away too, His Majesty had to assign the visitor a special clerical detail of an archbishop and three bishops.[32]

Thus, D'Ormesson spoke for many of his countrymen of quality when he observed,

> The pope had him investigated for the death of certain nuns, but actually because, thanks to the emperor, the pope got hold of a man accused of having killed the pope's nephew on the order of Cardinal Antonio and Cardinal Mazarin. It is an act truly worthy of the fickleness of France, thus to receive Cardinal Antonio, from whom the arms of France were ignominiously taken away just months ago, as from a traitor, who despite being protector of the realm, had abandoned its interests.[33]

For the straitly principled (or less pragmatic), royal proclamations, public show, and courtly indulgence could not repair a reputation that the Most Christian King once dubbed "without esteem and without respect."

14

"A FEW DAYS IN JAIL FOR LOVE OF ME"

The cardinal's promised "few days in jail for love of me" stretched to six weeks as Giovanni Braccesi lay on his pallet in the Torrone and the prosecutor tried to figure out how to proceed against him. How could Giandomenico Rossi satisfy Innocent X, given that both the witnesses and their testimony against Braccesi often seemed dubious? Several of Braccesi's servants denied any knowledge of convent visiting. Some claimed never to have seen Braccesi in company with Count Alessandro Maria Pepoli or the Guarnieri brothers.[1] For Rossi, the rational, clear-thinking Giovanni Braccesi was also quite a different adversary than either Carlo Possenti or Donato Guarnieri.

Even before interrogations resumed in Bologna, on August 30 a lawyer appeared to plead for Braccesi (long before there were any such efforts on Possenti's or Guarnieri's behalf). It was the usual boilerplate petition. The lawyer reappeared at the Torrone on September 2 with grievances that should have been harder to ignore: Braccesi's health might further deteriorate in his present confinement. He should receive immediate medical attention and be transferred to a location aboveground.[2] When Giandomenico Rossi confronted Giovanni Braccesi on September 8, his appearance made it hard to dispute his lawyer's admonitions: a cell in Le Segrete was a truly unwholesome setting for an invalid's recuperation.

In Rome, a carefully nurtured disposition for gentlemanly decorum may have induced Braccesi to mask his estimation of Carlo Possenti. By September perhaps he recognized that the Torrone was not Cardinal Antonio Barberini's antechamber and no place for affable courtesy. When Rossi brought up Possenti's self-aggrandizing claim to have lodged under Cardinal Antonio's roof from summer 1644 until his departure for Segni, Braccesi did not disguise his view of Don Carlo's "indiscretion" in freeloading off Braccesi's hosts all summer, then tagging along after him to Palazzo Barberini in the autumn. The exasperated Braccesi had urged Cardinal Antonio to find Possenti a position "at the earliest possible moment, because he had attached himself to me and I wanted to free myself from that bondage." The cardinal's courtiers finally spelled it out to Don Carlo: such imposition would not do. "When he saw that he would not be entirely welcome with me, he took himself off to live at Count Ferdinando Ranuzzi's" in early January 1645.[3]

Rossi eventually objected. "But what would you say to Possenti's assertion that he was at Ranuzzi's only briefly before leaving for Segni?"

"I would respond that Carlo Possenti moved out of my apartment long before going to Segni—absolutely—and then went to Count Ranuzzi's. Weeks before Don Carlo got his commission, Count Ranuzzi started coming to see me repeatedly," Braccesi added, perhaps with a trace of amusement. "He urged me to expedite the matter, since Don Carlo was still dillydallying at his place."[4]

Rossi changed course. "Do you know where Carlo Possenti was at Easter?"

"I don't remember for certain if he was in Ferrara on Easter Sunday, but it seems likely, because most of the cavalry was in town, and he was their chaplain."

Rossi returned to the attack. "You should be able to remember precisely where Possenti was, given the close friendship between the two of you at that time."

Braccesi remained outwardly unperturbed. "Your notion that my friendship with Possenti should assist my memory is unsound, because at that time Don Carlo certainly had no close relationship with me. That began only after peace was declared, when he hoped for some sort of preferment, as I've said before: about the end of April or May 1644, when Signor Cornelio Malvasia very effectively commended him to me."

Braccesi had risen to Rossi's bait. "These attempts to deny your close familiarity with Carlo Possenti only render you more suspect of complicity in these crimes, because a crowd of witnesses has confirmed the close friendship that the two of you maintained in Bologna—from the very beginning."

"I can say with absolute certainty that nobody can claim Carlo Possenti frequented my house; he came only occasionally, sent by Signor Cornelio Malvasia with some query about a job for himself." (How strikingly Braccesi's calm vehemence contrasted with Possenti's bluster in the face of similar offensives!) "As witnesses, I would call particularly Count Onofrio Bevilacqua, Cavalier Scala, Signor Marcantonio Pasigno, Signor Cesare Grassi, and Ludovico Castelbarco, my assistant. They can confirm the truth of my testimony, whatever all of Bologna might say: Don Carlo had no dealings with me except during my final months in Bologna and subsequently in Rome."

"This court has no need of your other witnesses," Rossi shot back—not least because Braccesi's aristocratic witnesses were not as easily cowed as their social inferiors. "There are already plenty of your servants who have testified that ever since you entered Cardinal Barberini's service you were regularly in Possenti's company, eating, drinking, and seeking amusement with him day and night here in Bologna."

Braccesi launched into a flurry of supportive detail. "It is true that there were occasions when Possenti went with me in search of amusement around the city: when I visited the home of Doctor Ponti. . . ." (At the mention of Ponti, Rossi may have gone on the alert.) "I was courting the doctor's lady wife in that amorous way permissible with someone of her rank. Signor Cornelio Malvasia first brought me there, and when he couldn't take me, he ordered Don Carlo to accompany me. So when I wished to visit her, I brought Don Carlo along. That was the chief justification that Don Carlo had for associating with me."[5]

Braccesi's acknowledged dalliance with another man's wife might tarnish the prim image he seemed to polish so carefully, but that was not why Rossi may have sat up and taken note: Doctor Ponti's wife had come to pontifical attention weeks before. The day after Rossi's arrival in Bologna, Archbishop Albergati-Ludovisi wrote to Cardinal Pamphili, "I hear that Doctor Ponti's wife, who separated from Braccesi in the manner that Your Excellency has already heard about, has gone to Modena, perhaps to avoid being harried by Signor Rossi. In order to lay hands on her, it would be good if Your Excellency could write to the Duke of Modena."[6]

This liaison was no secret: Ludovico Castelbarco, Giovanni Braccesi's assistant, confirmed that it had gone on for a good while and lasted right up until

Braccesi left for Rome. "It was public knowledge, because he went there in broad daylight," as Castelbarco put it.[7]

More extravagant Roman gossip (appearing nowhere in the official record) suggests why papal investigators took an interest: Braccesi's reluctant former paramour had the makings of another star prosecution witness. "If necessary, His Holiness will demand of the Count of Novellara one Maddalena Scappi, wife of Doctor Ponti. She could be Braccesi's final ruin," one Roman observer reported. "She was his lover, but when the nuns fled the convent, he jilted her. After the nuns were dead and he returned to his old ways, the aggrieved Maddalena snapped, 'You ended things badly with me and have murdered those poor things. But some day it will all come out, and then you'll be done for!' To which Braccesi answered, 'We are governed in such a way that not even the devil could unravel the web that's been spun.' This clearly reveals how well informed Maddalena Ponti is and that Braccesi is to blame."[8]

Curiously, on the day when Braccesi forthrightly brought up his relationship with Maddalena Ponti ("permissible with someone of her rank," as he put it), Albergati-Ludovisi informed Pamphili that Prosecutor Rossi "does not think it advisable to make any request for Signora Ponti at this time. So I have held on to your letter to the Duke of Modena, in the belief that this will meet with Your Excellency's preferences."[9]

Although papal authorities otherwise expended endless time and resources tracking down persons of interest from Rome to Venice, and possibly as far away as Germany and Flanders, this is the last we hear of Maddalena Ponti. In one of the mysteries of the case, Rossi chose never to play what seemed an ace in the hole. Perhaps undocumented, extrajudicial investigation showed that these allegations could not be true. This infatuation also undermined the credibility of any alleged obsession with La Generona on Braccesi's part, about which the nuns happily fantasized.

The prosecutor passed over Braccesi's adulterous admission without comment. "How long had it been since you spoke to Possenti when you heard about the nuns?"

"I don't remember."

"Well, after you returned from Ferrara to Bologna, did you hear anyone else speaking of the nuns' escape?"

"That was all *anybody* was talking about." (Quite a different response from that of Possenti and Guarnieri, who claimed to have heard little or nothing about Bologna's favorite topic of conversation at that time.) "Officials at both the legation and the archbishopric were doing everything possible to find the nuns. And it seemed incredible that they could have left Bologna when so many soldiers were guarding the walls and the gates. I heard Cardinal Antonio command that every possible effort be expended to find them."

"Did you talk to Possenti about it at that time?"

"No, my lord, I don't remember speaking about it with him until after returning from Ferrara. But it strikes me as unlikely that we wouldn't have talked about it once he later began coming to my place, because in Bologna people were speaking of nothing else."

Braccesi's deceptively forthright, logical responses were no more revealing than Possenti's outright denials. "Leave off all these ploys," Rossi retorted. "Eloquence and frankness cannot disguise the truth. Otherwise your remarks will be taken as an implicit confession of the crimes. Did you or did you not, in fact, discuss the nuns' flight with Possenti after your return from Ferrara? When? Where exactly? And what was said? Answer precisely: this and only this!"

"The absolute truth is that I never had specific discussions with Don Carlo Possenti about details of this nun business. The reason seems to me very compelling: either Don Carlo was *guilty*—in which case the last person he'd mention it to would be me, a high official of Cardinal Antonio's, who was doing everything possible to find out about it. Or else Possenti was *not guilty*—in which case there would be no reason to discuss the matter except superficially, as everybody else in Bologna was doing. And you may rest assured that I do not intend to keep quiet about the truth in this or any other matter." Braccesi drew himself up and sought Rossi's eye. "Because I have neither the inclination nor the motive to excuse Possenti or to cover up such an enormous crime. My discussions about the nun business concerned what an enormous matter it was, that it seemed impossible that they weren't found out, and that I hoped Cardinal Antonio might enjoy the satisfaction of uncovering and punishing the guilty and the nuns themselves."[10]

After this fine upstanding declaration, the prosecutor ended this unproductive session, dismissed Braccesi, and shifted his attentions back to Carlo Possenti, who offered the prospect of greater progress to report to Rome. It would be more than a month before Rossi next tried to build his case against Giovanni Braccesi.

Even before word of Braccesi's interrogations reached Rome, the court of public opinion had begun to render a verdict, influenced by Vatican spin doctors' apparent misinformation. "The common view is that Braccesi's crime consists of having protected the nuns and those who abducted them, and having blocked any proceedings against them, with the help of Cardinal Antonio," one observer reported on September 9. Ten days later (while Braccesi sat in his cell, ignored) the same source reported Rossi's use of "extraordinarily harsh measures" against him: "Braccesi will perish for want of spirit and strength: this is the common view."[11] The prediction was plausible enough, but allegations about Rossi's supposed use of rough treatment at this stage sound implausible.

A week later, at the time of Antonio Barberini's flight, the same observer recounted that the cardinal had recently interceded with Innocent X on Braccesi's behalf, "emphasizing his good service to the Apostolic See in the recent troubles. Innocent replied that it was a case of the worst possible crimes: in good conscience he could not remit them. His Holiness has clearly told many that Possenti is convicted, and that Braccesi is nearing that point."[12]

An early September French dispatch sounds nearer the mark. "The following from Bologna, against Braccesi: nothing at all has been proved, but he is being prosecuted for having known about the crime and not having informed authorities. So they're demanding that he should suffer the same penalty as the murderers."[13]

Only on October 14, after weeks of confrontations between Carlo Possenti, Donato Guarnieri, and their accusers, did Rossi finally recall Giovanni Braccesi. By then Rome was agog at the news of Cardinal Antonio's flight to France. Even as Braccesi's interrogation continued on October 15, the arms of France were rising on Antonio Barberini's palace in Rome: the political landscape was changing.

Perhaps Rossi would have better luck catching Braccesi in a lie with testimony from his servants and colleagues. Rather than employing the direct confrontations that were standard practice with Possenti and Guarnieri, Rossi summarized what witnesses had to say. This, of course, enabled him to ventriloquize their voices to suit his purposes. When Braccesi reiterated his claim to have kept company with Possenti only after war's end, Rossi rebutted him, "Giovanni Torti has testified quite the opposite, in fact: that your friendship began long before Lent 1644."

"Giovanni Torti cannot credibly have contradicted me, for this reason: after he came to my house in March or April [1643], he stayed until the army went on campaign. During that time Carlo Possenti never set foot in my apartment. When Torti returned from the campaign Monsignor Lomellini appointed him overseer of bread in San Giovanni in Persiceto. He stayed there until the termination of his assignment, which, if memory serves, was in March or April 1644. Therefore he could neither have known nor seen if Carlo Possenti had become friendly with me before that time."[14]

"But other witnesses corroborate Torti's testimony," the prosecutor insisted. "What about Pietro Fabbriani? He has testified to Possenti's friendship with you since before last year, 1644," Rossi claimed. He had begun stretching the truth: Fabbriani's earlier testimony precisely confirmed Braccesi's assertion, in fact. (No wonder the prosecutor avoided face-to-face confrontations between Braccesi and witnesses, which would require the literal reading out of testimony.)

Predictably unfazed, Braccesi embarked on another of his obfuscating elucidations. "Now Pietro Fabbriani and all of Bologna, for that matter, could say that one night during carnival, Signor Cornelio Malvasia, Marchese Mario Calcagnini, and I were out masquing together, and Carlo Possenti happened also to be there. But Possenti was masquing neither with me nor in my apartment, but at Cornelio Malvasia's. He'd come along with the others to fetch me at the home of Marianna the actress, where I'd gone masquing alone. During that time, Don Carlo waited upon Signor Cornelio Malvasia and was always with him. So, clearly, he had not yet taken up with me."[15] Again, Rossi was getting nowhere.

On Sunday morning, October 15, Prosecutor Rossi tried shifting his attentions to Braccesi's relationship with the fugitive nuns. Braccesi admitted to having known Suor Laura Vittoria, but only as La Rossa in her days as a woman of the world. "I saw her at festivals and in churches." And in less public places, no doubt, Rossi perhaps thought to himself. For sickly Giovanni Braccesi was turning out to have been quite the ladies' man. The prosecutor had already uncovered his liaison with a married woman. He also knew from another witness's testimony that Braccesi's carnival visit to "Marianna the actress" represented only the tip of the iceberg: he had called on her often, in fact.

There were also Braccesi's many admitted calls on a Bolognese prostitute, Maddalena Fiorentina, back in 1640. A former army colleague further claimed to have walked with Braccesi several times to the apartment of "La Romana, next door to Malvasia." Word from Rome further suggested that Braccesi was among Nina Barcarola's many admirers. But this sin-sodden side to Braccesi's carefully crafted, straitlaced image also suggested that he had more than enough to distract him from any alleged parlatorio dalliance with La Generona, which the nuns alone suggested.[16]

"Is it true that you were not at the Convertite about the time of the nuns' flight?"

"I am absolutely certain that from the time the army began its campaign in May 1643, I was never again at the Convertite. I might say for a considerable time before that as well, but I can't say that for certain." Another careful show of scrupulous honesty gave way to another meticulous substantiation. "Because my last visit was when I went to speak with Angela the actress, who had entered the convent." (Angela? Yet another apparent link in Braccesi's chain of female companions?) "I don't remember whether it was during Lent or Advent, but it was one of those times, before May 1643, because the shutters on the parlatorio grates were closed, as is customary during those penitential seasons."[17] Was there no end to Braccesi's commonsense explanations?

"Do you know or have you heard which gate the nuns used for their escape?"

"I never heard anything about that, only that the two nuns were missing from the convent."

"It is not credible that you knew so little about it when it was public knowledge, even more so since you were a principal official in Bologna, indeed, in the entire province. And particularly since, as you yourself allege," Rossi added, perhaps with a pointed smile, "the authorities made every possible effort to discover the perpetrators of the crime." At last, the prosecutor addressed the issue of Cardinal Antonio's role in the affair, and the alleged cover-up.

"My duties are entirely different from criminal matters such as the business of the nuns," Braccesi carefully explained. "Such matters, addressed to Cardinal Antonio, do not fall to me. Therefore it is not implausible, in fact, that details of the nuns' case did not reach me, since this was exclusively matter for the criminal ministers."

"Carlo Possenti asserts that when you heard the news you proclaimed it to him. Loudly. Is this true? Where exactly did that happen, and what prompted you to mention it to Don Carlo?"

"Carlo Possenti is telling an enormous lie if he alleges that I told him right after I first heard the news from the cardinal, because at that time Carlo Possenti was nowhere in sight. And furthermore, when Carlo Possenti was later at my lodgings I never considered him sufficiently worthy of confidence that I would share anything the cardinal told me with the likes of him."[18]

After this fruitless exercise, Giandomenico Rossi waited another week before next squaring off against Braccesi. By then word had reached Rossi that the entire Barberini family had formally received the protection of the French crown. In the meantime people in Bologna were speculating about some lumber piled inside the basilica of San Petronio. "It's presumed that they must be going to build a stage from which to read the cases against Braccesi, Guarnieri, and Possenti, and also in order to degrade the last of them, who is a priest," reported a Roman observer. "Thus they seem to be nearing the conclusion of the trial."[19] It sounded like another instance of papal optimism: the case was anything but over.

In retrospect, Giovanni Braccesi may have wondered what to make of his meeting with Giandomenico Rossi on October 23. It proved even more perfunctory than their initial Bolognese encounter six weeks earlier. Were he not cut off from the world, he might have wondered if it had anything to do with those shifting Barberini-French-papal relations. Rossi's inquiries regarding Donato Guarnieri provoked the only tension of the morning. "Were you ever at the Convertite with Captain Donato and, if so, when and how often?"

"I was never at the Convertite or in any other place with Captain Donato Guarnieri. On the contrary, I can assuredly say that he spoke to me only twice, about the business of his company."

"Beware of falsehood." When he lapsed into his prosecutorial mode, even Rossi may have set little store by his own assertions. "Because the opposite appears in the record of this investigation: that you sometimes visited the Convertite with Captain Donato Guarnieri."

"Absolutely nobody can maintain, as I said previously, that I was ever at the Convertite with Donato Guarnieri." (Except, of course, for those imaginative sisters at the convent.) "Nor was I ever anywhere else with him. And I can only wonder with amazement that it is possible to find anyone who would dare to testify to such a falsehood—one that can so easily be debunked."[20]

If Rossi had not already recognized how little might be gained from a face-to-face confrontation between the quick-thinking Braccesi and his fantasizing cloistered accusers, perhaps this exchange helped to define that realization. Rossi's efforts over the last ten weeks had yielded virtually nothing. The prosecutor directed Braccesi to sign the transcript, dismissed him for now, and sent him back to Le Segrete. There Giovanni Braccesi virtually disappeared. Months and months would pass before he next set foot outside his cell.

On November 1, the Modenese ambassador reported to his duke, "At the moment, no one has much to say about the case of the nuns, because they clearly recognize where the path to the execution of justice leads. Many are of the opinion that no one stands convicted, and that it will be necessary to proceed to torture to get their confessions. It is surely true that they will be made to suffer in such a way that either they say whatever is desired of them, or else they will lose their lives under those same torments."[21]

15

RETURN TO THE SCENE OF THE CRIME

On October 11, a crowd may once again have gathered across from SS. Filippo e Giacomo. Borgo del Rondone had not witnessed such excitement since La Generona and La Rossa's escape eighteen months earlier. There was not much to see, really. The arrival of a cart loaded with an armoire that looked like marble and other furniture perhaps prompted momentary speculation before it vanished inside the carters' gate. Heads turned and necks craned when carriages eventually rounded via delle Lame and rolled to a stop. As onlookers waited to see who would alight, the carters' gate swung open to let the carriages pass through, then closed behind them. Which prisoners might be inside, who could tell?

The nuns inside stood a better chance of spotting something worth seeing. Above the cloister arcade, the halls were alive with the sound of soft-footed sisters on specious errands, tarrying at upstairs windows for glimpses into the courtyard below. These confrontations would not occur in the safety of the parlatorio. The archbishop had granted Giandomenico Rossi license to invade the nuns' cloister with his prisoners. Sisters summoned to testify would meet the accused beneath the arcade, face-to-face, within arm's length, with no grilles to protect them.[1]

Many nuns must have experienced frissons of anticipation or anxiety at the prospect: Rossi had sent word for more than two dozen to be ready to testify. Servants from palaces uptown, arriving to retrieve their laundry baskets, may have been told to come back another day: right now convent laundresses had the tidiness of their wimples to think about.

For weeks Giandomenico Rossi had been preparing his convent witness list. On rereading the transcript from April 1644, he may have gritted his teeth at local ecclesiastics' missed opportunities, botched arrests, and dereliction of responsibility. The archiepiscopal auditor had summoned only sixteen nuns to testify. Many of his interviews looked perfunctory: often only two or three questions, as if he didn't really want to know or didn't care. Archiepiscopal bunglers had spent inordinate time futilely trying to force sisters to implicate each other. All the while La Rossa and La Generona were hiding out just a few minutes' walk from the archbishop's palace. Investigators seemed more interested in what had happened to the gate keys than what had happened to the escapees who filched them.

Once Archbishop Albergati-Ludovisi assumed command in July 1645, little improved. Ninety sisters had been hastily deposed during marathon sessions shortly before Rossi reached Bologna. With a little advance priming, a handful dropped Giovanni Braccesi's name, which Rossi discovered had otherwise come up only twice back in April 1644—and not as a possible perpetrator of the crime.

Rossi began again with half a dozen convent visits of his own between September 18 and October 6, fitting them in among sessions at the Torrone, archiepiscopal prison, and Palazzo Bargellini and leaving the sisters to speculate between times about the motives behind his questions. The prosecutor recognized that former prioress Lucina Conti, who had handpicked Monsignor Alfonso Arnaldi's original witnesses, had her wits about her. Rossi closely followed her lead, but this time he probed for more telling information. Since he hoped to overwhelm the accused with confrontations, however, he cast his net more widely: half a dozen fresh faces made his final cut. He would turn two of them into stars for the prosecution.

DONATO GUARNIERI

Donato Guarnieri, spirited in through the gate so expeditiously on October 11, was the first to confront the convertite. Beyond the convent wall, little besides pubblica voce e fama clamored loudly against the captain. Most of Rossi's case against him tottered precariously upon nuns' testimony, and convents were notorious sumps of gossip and hearsay. The prosecutor therefore culled his flock for those who could testify about what they had *seen* as well as heard. Several pairs of eyes could be counted on to catch Captain Donato in a few lies. Perhaps they might badger him into the confession crucial for his conviction.

Whispering at the upstairs windows ceased once Guarnieri stood before the makeshift tribunal under the cloister arcade and Rossi began to speak. "Are you ready to tell the truth regarding the excesses about which you have been interrogated?"

"I'm telling the truth," Guarnieri mumbled. "I'm innocent of all this, because I never had anything to do with these nuns."

Rossi's opening "Do you recognize the prisoner?" seemed disingenuous at best. (The possibilities were extremely limited, after all.) One after another, the nuns confidently identified Captain Donato, with the notable exception of Suor Paola Costanza Torosanti. "I can't confidently recognize this man," she reluctantly confessed, "because he's so horribly pale and whiskery; but it could well be that I've seen him off and on." Lest the deck seem stacked against the defendant, Rossi twice went through the motions of conducting a lineup under the arcade. Two sisters picked out Donato Guarnieri without hesitation; perhaps they shuddered as they reached out and touched him on Rossi's command. The prosecutor had made his point.[2]

In 1644 Monsignor Arnaldi had never set eyes on Rossi's first witness, convent vicaria Suor Bianca Ignota. It had taken Giandomenico Rossi to draw Suor Bianca out during a last-minute visit the week before he brought Guarnieri to confront her. Little seemed to have escaped the vigilant vicaria.

"I recognize Captain Donato Guarnieri," she confirmed. Her gaze shifted nervously between prosecutor and defendant as the notary read out her earlier testimony. "He used to come to our convent to visit with Suor Laura Vittoria. Every day (so to speak) I heard Suor Laura Vittoria and Suor Silveria being summoned on behalf of Captain Donato Guarnieri and Don Carlo Possenti. You never heard anybody but Possenti and Guarnieri. One day when I was visiting the parlatorio, two well-dressed pages came asking for Suor Laura Vittoria. A little later Captain Donato Guarnieri himself arrived, clothed in scarlet, garnished all over with silver. He wore a pair of tall riding boots with silver overlay at the tops. Above them, he showed fine-fitting leggings or underhose of sheer linen with handsome lace trimming.

"He ordered the gatekeeper to summon Suor Laura Vittoria. I heard him ask the pages if they'd brought the bologna sausages for Suor Laura, and one replied, 'We have, sir.' Then I left the parlatorio and went to chapel" (perhaps reciting "et ne nos inducas in tentationem," Rossi may well have thought, with amusement at the vicaria's impressive recollective powers when it came to this young man's well-turned thigh.) "I had a long look at Captain Donato's face that day. It struck me that he looked evil. I don't remember exactly when he asked the pages if they'd brought Suor Laura's bologna sausages, but it was during Lent."

Just as important as Suor Bianca's evidence about Guarnieri's relationship with La Rossa, the vicaria confirmed the captain's Lenten visits, despite his claim never to have set foot in Bologna after carnival. Between Guarnieri's tailor and Suor Bianca, Rossi had thus produced the requisite pair of eyewitnesses on that issue. The ever-watchful Suor Bianca had witnessed further revealing encounters between the captain and the convertita. "A while before the nuns fled, Captain Donato gave some of his clothes to Suor Laura Vittoria to hold for him. They were fine looking, too. (I saw them hung up on one of the cloister arcades.) They were of various colors and beautiful, and some were black. I know that he also gave her some doubloons to keep: she herself showed me a bunch of them and said they were 'from my friend, Captain Donato.' I heard the nuns say she gave them back one time when he returned from Ferrara."[3] So much for Guarnieri's denial of having left anything with La Rossa. Suor Bianca also demonstrated that not only Copparo but also Bologna must have figured in the captain's Ferrara itinerary in 1644, despite his persistent claims to the contrary.

"She's not telling the truth!" Donato exclaimed at the conclusion of Suor Bianca's testimony. "I never spoke to that Suor Laura Vittoria like she claims. I was never in Bologna during Lent! I know nothing about this business!"

"Would that this were not the truth—which it is (May God forgive you!)," Suor Bianca shot back with a stinging look, "that you've caused the loss of two souls. And I spoke the truth in everything I said."[4]

Although Rossi's second witness, Suor Clemenza Torti, claimed "to be getting on in years, as your lordship can see," and to be less sure about her powers of recall, she nevertheless promptly confirmed Suor Bianca's testimony. "I certainly saw Captain Donato Guarnieri come often to hang around the convent. And whenever he turned up Suor Laura Vittoria looked delighted and exclaimed, 'Captain Donato has arrived!' I can't say I've seen him here since around Palm Sunday of last year."

Suor Clemenza further claimed to have observed the removal of La Rossa's belongings to Casa Guarnieri shortly before the nuns disappeared. "The servant Angela carried off a large wooden carrier of linens to the Guarnieri's. Suor Laura Vittoria was the one who sent the container to them—I know that because she told me so herself." There was also the matter of Suor Laura's fine furniture that had gone missing. "The furniture that La Rossa sent to the Guarnieri's included two pretty walnut tables inlaid with blond wood. The armoire was large, tall, and beautiful, painted in several colors, including turquoise, so that it looked to me like marble. And there was a little cat painted on it. I remember that Suor Laura Vittoria offered the excuse that Captain Guarnieri was paying her £100 for the armoire, which she said she wanted to use to buy herself a cell of her own. So I asked, 'And if he doesn't pay you—what then?' She answered that she had a handkerchief full of Captain Donato's doubloons. She wasn't really making plans for any cell, however; they were for her own escape."

When Suor Clemenza finished, Guarnieri could only protest, "On Palm Sunday of last year I was in Ferrara."[5]

As the day wore on, witness after witness repeated variations on the same rather meager themes. Eyewitnesses to Donato's Lenten visits continued to proliferate. "I saw Captain Donato Guarnieri here at the convent during Lent, when I went to get flour from the buttery," the convent bursar reported. "I saw him pacing outside the inner gate every day, because to get to the buttery you have to pass by that gate, which often stands open so people can come and go."[6]

As sister after sister came forward to testify, the attending nuns' vicar Monsignor Ascanio Rinaldi probably tut-tutted to himself about all the time they spent idly gazing out cloister windows or dawdling around the gate rather than attending to their prayers in chapel. A surprising number turned out to have been watching when Suor Laura's linens or furniture were spirited away. "Before they fled, the nuns also had a container of cloth goods taken away, covered with a length of taffeta," according to Suor Innocenza Pazienza Serra. "Those sisters had all sorts of fine fabric: red, striped, and in other colors too. Suor Laura sent them to the Guarnieri's house. I myself heard Suor Laura say, 'Take these to the Guarnieri's house,' and she told the servant where they lived." Suor Antonia Romea Stagnoli had no doubt where the furniture was headed: "Suor Laura Vittoria said she was sending it 'to her Donato.'"[7]

La Rossa, it seemed, had also been showing off "her Donato's" doubloons and silver to anybody who would notice. "One time when war was raging," Suor Paola Costanza Torosanti recalled, "I remember that Suor Laura Vittoria showed me and all the other nuns a bunch of double ducats and doubloons. She said they'd been left with her for safekeeping, and she went on to say that

Captain Donato was the one who had left them. If he died in battle, they would all be hers."[8]

Even before midday, Rossi had thus produced more than the requisite number of eyewitnesses to undercut some of Guarnieri's vigorous denials. For his part, Guarnieri seemed to listen helplessly: he retreated into himself and never asked a single question in his own defense. The response, "I don't know anything about any of this," became his feeble refrain.

Halfway through the day's succession of witnesses and the endless ritual of the notary's recitation of prior testimony, Rossi took a different tack. He directed several nuns to examine a large marbleized armoire and a pair of inlaid tables standing under the arcade and to pick through items of fabric, some clothing, and various random objects and bits of jewelry. "After having a good look, I recognize that painted armoire and these two tables with intarsia. They belonged to La Rossa," declared Suor Giovanna Valeria Cortelli. "This coral rosary, this watch, and this red outfit were Suor Silveria's. One of these bed hangings belonged to La Rossa and the other to Suor Silveria. These are the ones I mean," she said as she touched them. "I clearly recognize them from having seen them many times in the fugitives' rooms."[9] Unsurprisingly, other witnesses were similarly confident about almost everything. (The deck was stacked in their favor, of course, since they had honed their identification skills with practice runs during previous interrogations.)

Captain Donato watched it all listlessly, then responded predictably, "I don't know anything, I've never seen this stuff, I don't know this La Rossa—I don't know anything."

Shadows crept across the cloister courtyard by the time Rossi summoned his twenty-third and final witness. There would be no dramatic buildup to the final curtain: the primary revelations had opened the spectacle. The prosecutor remanded Guarnieri to police custody for transport from his respite in the autumn air of Borgo del Rondone back to the dungeons at the Torrone. When the carriages trundled off, the sisters drifted away from upstairs windows and eventually off to chapel. As the Ave Maria sounded from the campanile, many surely continued to wander outside in their hearts, reviewing the day's events as they went through the motions at prayers in the nuns' chapel.

Guarnieri's convent confrontations caught him in a few lies but yielded no prosecutorial coup de théâtre. Young Donato seemed no nearer confession, not so much grimly determined as vacantly insensible to the mounting evidence against him. Rossi had another card to play, however. A further witness in the world soon waited up his sleeve: the Guarnieri brothers' barber.

Young Antonio Zucchini had left his native Piacenza to seek his fortune in Bologna, ninety miles away. He found work in a well-established barbershop under the busy arcade opposite San Petronio, in time to profit from a booming market in personal grooming spurred by the arrival of the papal army. Like the hairdressers, nail technicians, and personal trainers of today, Antonio offered a more or less attentive and, when necessary, sympathetic ear to his clients' small talk as he attended to his delicate business.

Zucchini crossed paths with Giandomenico Rossi only on October 25, after sbirri appeared at his shop and hustled him off to Palazzo Bargellini, where the prosecutor waited. The barber's enthusiastic response to every question presumably convinced Rossi that this witness was unlikely to skip town. Indeed, if called to testify, he would probably arrive early. The prosecutor immediately released Zucchini on bond, with orders to appear at the Torrone the following morning.

The notary may well have recorded the prosecutor's opening question on October 26 before he even asked it. "Are you ready now to tell the truth about the crimes against the nuns?"

"I did not commit the crimes I'm accused of, because they occurred when I was in Ravenna, and I never left there, as I've said before."

"Desist from this obstinacy and freely speak the truth! Otherwise further witnesses will be called to face you."

"I can't say anything but what I've already said."

On Rossi's signal, sbirri ushered Antonio Zucchini into the room. The eager youth probably eyed his bedraggled former client with bald-faced curiosity.

"Do you know the prisoner here present?"

"Yes, I know Captain Donato Guarnieri."

"Do you recognize the witness?"

"I know this young fellow. He's my barber. He took care of me when I was here in Bologna."

The spotlight shifted to the notary, who proceeded to read out the previous day's testimony.

"Do you know Colonel Alessandro Guarnieri from Bergamo and, if so, how?"

"Yes, my lord, I know him, although I didn't know he was called Alessandro. What's more, I know that he has a brother named Captain Donato Guarnieri." The listening Zucchini glanced in Donato's direction. "While they were in Bologna during the war I served as barber to the two brothers for the whole time they stayed here."

"How long was that?"

"Captain Donato was the first to leave. Colonel Alessandro left I'm not sure how long after Count Alessandro Maria Pepoli was murdered. I remember because when I was shaving the colonel he told me he'd lost his only friend and patron here in Bologna—meaning Count Alessandro Maria Pepoli. Colonel Alessandro and also Captain Donato his brother were close friends with him."

"Do you know anything about the disappearance of any nuns from the Convertite?"

"Yes, my lord. People say they were abducted by Carlo Possenti and Captain Donato Guarnieri."

"Was Captain Donato in Bologna at the time you heard that the nuns disappeared?"

"I don't remember. I do remember that Colonel Alessandro asked me what people around Bologna were saying about those nuns. I told him the word was that Captain Donato was the one who arranged their escape. So then Colonel Alessandro said they should know that Captain Donato was in Romagna."

"Did you ever shave Captain Donato Guarnieri after you heard that the nuns had gone missing?"

"Yes, my lord, I don't know how many times."

Rossi stared meaningfully at Donato as the notary continued to read. "How long was it since you shaved Captain Donato that the colonel spoke about the nuns' escape?"

"I don't know because I shaved so many soldiers. I can certainly say that not many days had passed, though. I know I shaved him one or two or maybe three days before the feast of Our Lady of Borgo di San Pietro. I remember that I saw Captain Donato along the procession route on the street coming from the church where the festival was held—there's a fine procession on that day."

"That's not true! I wasn't in Bologna on the Feast of Our Lady of Borgo di San Pietro the way he claims," Guarnieri protested, "because I was in Ravenna at that time, as I keep saying. People can say what they like, but I did no such thing."[10]

None of Rossi's evidence to the contrary could shake Guarnieri from his position. Yet he appeared more curiously helpless than resolute in his intransigence and made such an unchallenging adversary that he more likely provoked irritation in Rossi than any grudging admiration. Thanks to the nuns, Guarnieri's presence at the Convertite and his involvement with La Rossa were now incontrovertible, although Rossi might suspect that the sisters' suggestions about the relationship owed a lot to La Rossa's own romantic imagination. From a legal standpoint, the naively forthcoming barber's testimony, as well as that of Possenti's servant Bartolomea, adequately confirmed that Guarnieri was in Bologna during the time when La Rossa and La Generona were still in hiding. But since some troublesome testimony from Count Alessandro Maria Pepoli's circle suggested that Captain Donato was not in Bologna for much of April, calling the younger Guarnieri's direct involvement in the actual crimes into question, for the time being the outcome of his case remained up in the air.

CARLO POSSENTI

The following Monday, October 30, Possenti faced his cloistered accusers. Such confrontations were less crucial in his case, given other mounting evidence against him. Rossi may have hoped simply to damage the young priest's credibility even further and to expose the depravity lurking behind that brash clerical facade.

The testimony of Suor Bianca Ignota, the vicaria, who first took the stage, contained only perfunctory references to Carlo Possenti. "It was said publicly among us other sisters immediately afterward that Captain Donato and Carlo Possenti arranged the nuns' flight. That's always been the word and still is today."

"I've heard what the mother vicaria said about my character," Possenti intoned once her testimony had been read. (Unlike Guarnieri, he rarely hesitated to rise in his own defense.) "I declare that the rumor that has sprung up against me—or so she claims—is false."

"Everybody's always said it was Don Carlo Possenti and Captain Donato Guarnieri," Suor Bianca retorted. "Because of the way they were always loitering around the convent."

"I would ask her if she herself actually heard here in the convent that I might be guilty of this nun business."

"Yes, sir. They say that you and Captain Donato Guarnieri not only participated in the flight of our nuns, but also had a role in their deaths." Plucky Suor Bianca fixed Possenti with a stern eye. "And I've also heard the same from outsiders when they've come to talk to us at the convent."

"Is her ladyship, the mother vicaria, perhaps aware," Possenti continued with mocking reverence, "that Suor Silveria had doings with other men?"

"I don't know anything about that." The vicaria was not about to yield to this bullying priest. "I do know that lots of people came to speak to her."

"I've no further questions for her," Possenti responded dismissively.[11]

As subsequent eyewitnesses confirmed the vicaria's testimony, Possenti trotted out his standard objection, "She cannot allege such extensive convent visitation, because for the most part I was off with the army." But Suor Clemenza Torti spoke for herself and others. "I saw you visiting the convent more than the others because I was the gatekeeper—I *saw* you."[12]

An equal number undercut Possenti's claim not to have visited the convent a day or two before the nuns escaped. As Suor Maria Giuliana Cocchi put it, "I can certainly say that the week those nuns ran off I saw Carlo Possenti get off his horse at the convent. I remember he was wearing a black fur-trimmed cloak, and he requested that Suor Silveria be summoned. But I didn't see whether Suor Silveria came to talk to him. I can say that whenever somebody called her for Don Carlo, she came running."[13]

Possenti's infamous jealous rages and thuggish behavior had cropped up since day one of the investigation. Rossi arranged for the cleric's pathological volatility to dominate the afternoon confrontations. Suor Giovanna Valeria Cortelli had been among the first to raise the subject at length back in April 1644. "A certain Filippo Ximenez also came to the parlatorio, where Possenti caused an uproar with him. He started yelling at Suor Silveria because he didn't want her mixed up with this Filippo. He began to abuse her and to revile her with shameful, reprehensible, and indecent language. It got so bad that a foreign gentleman who was delivering a letter to me had to turn to Possenti and tell him, 'Calm down, Signor Possenti. One does not use such language with nuns. One should not treat them in such a manner.' Possenti told him to mind his own business, so the gentleman left and advised me to leave the grates, too. Then Possenti took his brawl with Ximenez so far that he even laid a hand on his pistol. Possenti did it for no other reason than jealousy, as far as I can tell, and because of his passion for Suor Silveria."

"As far as the argument I had with Ximenez is concerned," Possenti rebutted, "I had no weapon of any kind when the two of us had words."

"The truth about what you did—it wasn't like you say, Don Carlo," Suor Giovanna Valeria fired back. "I told the whole truth in my interrogations!"[14]

Several other sisters stood solidly behind Suor Giovanna Valeria, more than the law required. Possenti limited his rebuttals to the increasingly feeble, "It's not true that I came to the convent as often as she claims."

Other witnesses revealed that this had not been Possenti's only violent display. Earlier, Possenti had bad-mouthed Suor Eufrasia, as if to undermine any negative testimony: clearly he expected the worst from her. She did not disappoint. "I never spoke with men on Suor Silveria's behalf except during the carnival season at Advent [1643], when I went to the grates to speak with Possenti, who was asking for her," she testified. "Suor Silveria said to tell him that she wasn't dressed and couldn't come right then. (She didn't want to.) When I told Possenti he began to curse God and the Madonna, yelling things like 'God's whore' and similar blasphemies. And he threatened, 'If Silveria doesn't come to me immediately, I'll poison myself!' He surely said that because he was in love with her. When I heard such profanity I went and called the prioress and explained that she was needed. So she went to the parlatorio while I extracted myself from that mess to go to confession."[15]

The intrepid former prioress, Suor Lucina Conti, picked up where Suor Eufrasia left off. "Don Carlo Possenti quarreled as I've described and pointed a pistol at the vault over the grates. He was enraged by the other man Suor Silveria was seeing, by the passion he must have felt for her, and by his jealousy toward someone else. And he was arrogant toward me because I remonstrated with him. Given my office as prioress, I was moved to make certain efforts to correct him. I reminded him that he was a man of the cloth and should set a good example, and that we were likewise poor religious. Therefore he shouldn't come here and cause such scandal. But he became enraged and began to insult me. Then he pointed the firearms he was carrying in my face through the grate and said, 'I don't know what's stopping me from shooting you!'"[16]

The volatile priest remained conspicuously subdued in the face of these attacks. "I've heard what Suor Eufrasia Maria has to say, and I declare that I did not frequent the convent in the way she alleges." Possenti's terse rebuttal to the former prioress also spoke volumes: "I didn't visit the convent as she asserts."[17]

Suor Palma Vittoria Ferri, who had never been called in 1644, offered some of the investigation's most telling revelations. "What I can say is that Don Carlo Possenti always had the most intimate friendship with Suor Silveria Catterina, so much so that he didn't want anybody else even to come near her. And if anybody came he threatened him. He smacked Leonora, Suor Silveria's servant, around because she played the pander for another man.

"Once, when I was in the garden with Suor Silveria, she was called to the grates to meet with Don Carlo. She told me she didn't wish to go, and that she no longer wanted his love and his courtship. She wanted to do what she had a mind to do herself. She claimed he insisted she fulfill some promise she'd made, but she didn't want to. Since she hadn't observed what she'd promised to God, she didn't want to fulfill her promise to him. (But I don't know what she'd promised to him or to God, because she didn't say.)

"She went on to say he had threatened her—to stomp on her belly. He said he wished her no other death except one by his own hand. She exclaimed, 'If he's not coming here through the devil's craft, I don't know how this would be happening!'

"That's why I'm certain he's the one who abducted Suor Silveria Catterina. If he wasn't the one and had it been anybody else, I'm absolutely sure he would have come over here right after it occurred, beside himself with rage, to find out how it happened. So I've no doubt he's the one who's guilty.

"And the reason I know these things is that I heard them from Suor Silveria—from her own lips."[18]

Rossi had to admire Suor Palma Vittoria's indisputable logic. Instead of descending on SS. Filippo e Giacomo in all his fury after the news broke, Possenti had never been seen again.

The usually voluble Possenti had nothing to say in the face of Suor Palma Vittoria's accusations except for his predictable, "As for all the excessive visiting at this convent, it's not true." (Not a word about the rest.)

At the conclusion of business on October 30, Giandomenico Rossi allowed himself forty-eight hours of well-earned repose. (Or perhaps it was the intervening Feast of All Saints and All Souls that compelled him to suspend operations.) Then he continued to tighten the screws on Carlo Possenti. On the same day he had interrogated the Guarnieri brothers' barber the previous week, Rossi had finally come face-to-face with Carlo Raguzzi, author of the incriminating letter taken from Possenti's desk three months earlier (fig. 21). By the time the prosecutor summoned Raguzzi on October 25, the hard-bitten career soldier had already been locked up for two months. "I cannot imagine why I was jailed," Raguzzi avowed. "Nobody in the world could be more amazed!"

This disingenuous remark set the tone to follow. Raguzzi neglected to mention Carlo Possenti among his acquaintances until Rossi specifically brought up the cleric's name. Then Raguzzi claimed to have had little to do with him. Raguzzi rattled on at length about nothing (a telltale sign of someone with something to hide). When Rossi inquired about any exchange of letters, Raguzzi thought he remembered a letter from Possenti asking for news. He described his eventual response in detail, even down to his inclusion of the grisly discoveries opposite the voltone del Baraccano. But Raguzzi forbore to mention that his letter had also cited local accusations against Don Carlo and the Guarnieri brothers.

"What else did that letter contain?"

"I don't remember anything else," he lied glibly.

"Did you sign it?"

"Why yes, my lord, I signed with a C and an R—'Carlo Raguzzi'—the way I usually do." Raguzzi launched into another drawn-out explanation of the reasons for this affectation.

"Did you mention who might have killed the nuns?" Rossi at last nudged the slippery captain into a corner.

"No, I didn't." But in the same breath, Raguzzi seemed to catch on, "though it seems to me I might have written that there was lots of noise about him having done it and then that it might have been the Guarnieri—but I don't really think my letter said that."

"Who was spreading it around that Possenti was guilty of the crime, or the Guarnieri?"

"I heard it first from people passing my house, as I stood in the doorway, and then in the piazza. They were saying it was Possenti, who had already committed a similar crime, and the Guarnieri."

If Rossi caught the captain's reference to Carlo Possenti's conviction for burgling a prostitute's apartment a few years earlier, he let it pass. He signaled a bailiff to hand Raguzzi the incriminating letter. "Do you recognize this?"

"Why yes, this is that same letter I wrote Carlo Possenti, just as I said."

The bailiff promptly reclaimed the letter before Raguzzi could take it all in. Rossi skewered Raguzzi with a piercing look, as if to say, "You're no match for me, you see." "No more questions for now," he declared, then ignored the unsettled captain as sbirri led him away.

Rossi gave Carlo Raguzzi a week's further detention to recognize where his own best interests lay. When Rossi recalled him on November 2, the captain seemed eager to oblige. He went on at even greater length and in tiresome detail about everything: his long friendship with the Guarnieri brothers, his military history back to the 1620s, every letter he had written and received in the past year and every detail of their contents.

Rossi's patience finally ran out. "What prompted you to write 'I've no news of *Your Friend*' in that letter you identified last time?"

"Could you kindly allow me to read what you're referring to?" A hint of anxiety marred Raguzzi's attempt at a smile.

A bailiff showed him the letter, with only the relevant sentence exposed.

"My lord, Don Carlo Possenti wrote me asking if there was news of Colonel Guarnieri." (Raguzzi had neglected to mention that little detail the previous week.) "In responding 'Your Friend' I meant Colonel Guarnieri. I wrote Don Carlo back that I didn't have any news except for the rumor that the colonel was in Piedmont."

"What do you suppose might have prompted Possenti to inquire after Colonel Guarnieri or his whereabouts?"

Raguzzi struggled to read the prosecutor's faintly quizzical expression. "I don't know, although I do know that they were friends, because I saw Possenti and Guarnieri spending time together, not only around Bologna, but also at the colonel's house."

"What were Possenti's words to you when he asked about Guarnieri?"

"Carlo Possenti wrote these words: that I should kindly inform him where Colonel Guarnieri might be."

"Then why didn't you simply write 'Colonel Guarnieri' in your answer instead of using the word Friend?"

"Because when Possenti wrote me for news of Colonel Guarnieri's whereabouts he also added 'my very dear friend and lord.' So I answered that I had 'no news of Your Friend'—because he'd already christened him that way."

"Was there perhaps some other reason why you omitted the colonel's name from your letter?" The prosecutor's voice hardened.

"No." Raguzzi's open-faced affability showed further deterioration. "And I intended no malice in not mentioning the colonel's name. If I had, I would not have named him so freely just now, as I did in fact."[19]

The captain determinedly met Rossi's gaze, which seemed to say, "Then again, a clever fellow like yourself might have finally realized we've been several steps ahead of you all along."

Two days later, on November 5, the captain walked free: Rossi released him on bond. If he chose to recall Raguzzi in his early days of freedom, Rossi may have observed, he would be on his best behavior and disinclined to match wits with him. In this case there was nothing to be gained from an unpredictable confrontation between those two prevaricators, Raguzzi and Possenti: better that Rossi make the best use of Raguzzi's testimony himself.

By his twenty-second encounter with Giandomenico Rossi the next day, Don Carlo had confronted almost thirty witnesses, not counting more than two dozen convertite the previous week. Whom might Rossi still be holding in reserve? The priest had yet to face Dionisio Tomassini or Francesco Tenerino or Galeazzo Mariani. Or Carlo Raguzzi, for that matter. Who else was still waiting?

On November 6, Rossi addressed the issue of Don Carlo's links to those most directly implicated in La Rossa and La Generona's abduction and murder.

"Did you receive any other letters from Carlo Raguzzi during your time as governor of Segni?"

"No, my Lord." That letter had not come up since his earliest interrogations back in Rome, Possenti may have recalled.

"Did you ever write to him, especially during your time as governor of Segni?"

"I remember writing him once to let him know I was governor."

"Did you ask any favor of him in your letter?"

"I don't believe so." Rossi must have spoken to Raguzzi. Had the captain kept his letter?

"What friend was Captain Raguzzi referring to when he said 'I have no news of Your Friend'?"

"I don't know what he meant." Possenti affected an open look.

"In your own letter, did *you* mention any friend Raguzzi might be referring to?"

"I don't believe I asked anything to prompt such a response."

"Well, did you ask for news of *any friend* in your letter?"

"I'm certain that I did not, as far as I remember."

"Did your letter mention Colonel Alessandro Guarnieri?"

"No, I'm quite certain that my letter did not." Possenti's open look stiffened.

"You're lying." The prosecutor's voice remained quiet, but sharp. "Captain Raguzzi has testified to the contrary: that you asked for news of Colonel Guarnieri."

"Raguzzi has got it wrong. I never asked for news of Colonel Guarnieri because I had no reason to ask about him."

"In fact Raguzzi testifies that you not only asked for news of the colonel, but also added 'my friend and dearest lord.'"

"No, my lord!" Possenti blustered, "I never wrote any such thing to Captain Raguzzi. I never wrote anything about Guarnieri to him."[20]

Rossi paused, then signaled offhandedly to the bailiff, who slipped discreetly from the room. Possenti fidgeted, working to recall every detail of their correspondence before the guard brought the captain in to face him. But when the bailiff returned, he was escorting not Captain Carlo Raguzzi, but the pale, disheveled Captain Donato Guarnieri.

"Was your testimony regarding the prisoner here present and his visits to your house the whole truth, and are you ready to confirm it to his face?"

"What I said about Don Carlo, here present, was true. I am ready to confirm it to his face. In substance, I said that Don Carlo was sometimes at our house to speak with Colonel Alessandro, my brother. As I said, they spoke together privately, and then I also spoke with them. I described it better in my testimony."

The notary thumbed through the transcript, searching out the relevant passages, which he read out with his customary detachment, one after another.

"He's mistaken about that," Possenti replied evenly. "He's got it wrong. I was never at Colonel Guarnieri's house, except for the few times that I mentioned, and I never saw Captain Donato there."

"I've told the truth," Donato responded.

"I've no questions for him, except to say that he's made a mistake. He's wrong."[21]

Rossi signaled the bailiff, who removed Guarnieri from the room. After a pause, Don Carlo turned to leave.

"I would urge you to speak the truth about all these crimes. . . ." Possenti hesitated. "Otherwise you can expect more of this sort of confrontation."

"I've told the truth. . . ."

Rossi called over the bailiff to confer in a stage whisper, ignoring Possenti, who shifted uneasily in place. The guard disappeared, then reappeared with a youth in tow: Pietro Caccini, Possenti's former page. Defendant and witness played their parts in the customary protocols. The notary once again shuffled through the transcript to find the relevant testimony.

"Where was Carlo Possenti at the time of your return from Ferrara to Bologna?"

"Don Carlo told me to look for him at Colonel Alessandro Guarnieri's; that were where I found him. I waited a little while for Don Carlo, who came down with one of the colonel's men. The three of us went to the legate's palace. Within half an hour we returned to Colonel Guarnieri's, where Don Carlo didn't stay long. Then him and me came home for a meal. After that we went to Signor Carlo Manolesi's bookshop."

"Did Carlo Possenti return to Colonel Guarnieri's at any other time after returning to Bologna after Easter?"

"Yes, my lord, he went there sometimes. I can't remember how many times, but he used to go to the colonel's often, both night and day."

"Was Possenti friends with Count Ferdinando Ranuzzi?"

"Yes, my lord. I seen the two of them together when we returned from Ferrara after Easter. Don Carlo went two or three times to find Count Ferdinando at home. One time after Easter I also seen the two of them speaking privately in the courtyard of the legate's palace. They talked for a good while."

"Were the Guarnieri brothers ever at Don Carlo's?"

"Yes, my lord. I remember that the colonel went there two or three times to visit Don Carlo when he were sick—close to summertime."[22]

"He's not telling the truth!" Possenti erupted.

"I am too."

"This one robbed me in Rome!" Possenti blustered. "He stole the clothes I had made for him! Then he sneaked off. He left without my leave because he was afraid I'd let him have it when I found out!"

"I never stole no clothing."[23]

Perhaps Rossi caught and held Possenti's eye as the young Caccini left the room, as if to say, "I've got more like him, you know, but by now they hardly seem necessary."

That would have been something of an overstatement. There was a notable slacking off in judicial business during the second week in November. Possenti, Guarnieri, and the neglected Braccesi were left in their cells, still shackled to the walls. Rossi dealt fitfully with a few remaining odds and ends of testimony. Late in the week he dispatched a notary to the Convertite to track down details of La Generona and La Rossa's monastic professions and enter them into the official record.

The next day, November 15, Giandomenico Rossi delivered the entire transcript, carefully wrapped and sewn into canvas, then sealed up with dark red wax, to an official of the postal service, for delivery to the governor of Rome.[24]

The prosecution had not yet rested, however. This was merely a stay in the proceedings.

16

"A GENTLEMAN NEVER TELLS"

After Giandomenico Rossi dispatched the transcript to Rome, the case seemed to stall. The prosecutor called Possenti and Guarnieri only three times over the next two months. He ignored Braccesi. On December 20 the Modenese ambassador offered a rare update on this matter that had once been a weekly cause for comment.

> The case of the Bolognese nuns is evolving with the greatest uncertainty, and now they're seeking evidence as if the investigation were just beginning. Braccesi is hardly culpable, and it looks like he had only a few dealings with the prostitutes turned nuns. Things are getting worse for Possenti, no less regarding his implication in the abduction than in the murder. But he is not convicted, and there are difficulties with implementing the use of torture for him. Because he's a fierce one, they suspect he would bear up under it and that it's going to destroy all the strategies built up until now.

Ten days later the ambassador added, "They say Braccesi may be brought back to Rome, since there's nothing relevant against him in the nuns' case. They may have to proceed against him on other charges."[1]

Perhaps when Antonio Barberini slipped through his fingers, Innocent X's ardor on the Bolognese front began to cool. Recent developments closer to home were clearly offering him more immediate distractions.

IN EXITU ISRAEL

"With tears of blood, I see things going from bad to worse. Words cannot express how it embitters our souls to behold the full extent of the pope's indignation," Cardinal Mazarin wrote in response to accelerating persecutions of the Barberini. In mid-October the diarist Giacinto Gigli reported with considerable understatement that the pope "was not very pleased" by French support for the house of Barberini after Cardinal Antonio's flight and the raising of French arms on his palace. According to Gigli, Innocent X had dredged up "a bull that said if any cardinal accepted the protection of some king, he should be punished." The pope promptly stripped Cardinal Antonio of his offices and divided the spoils among Cardinal Pamphili and other Vatican cronies.[2]

In early November Innocent took the unprecedented step of annulling the protections that Urban VIII had granted to shelter his Barberini nephews. Innocent also ordered a commission to begin auditing the accounts from Urban's declining years. "The pope commanded Cardinal Antonio Barberini to appear in Rome to render accounts," Gigli reported in mid-December, "on pain of a thousand scudi a day penalty; and various servants of his were imprisoned. They're proceeding against Cardinal Francesco Barberini and Don Taddeo Barberini with similar severity." The older Barberini brothers had two weeks to produce their books. When they did, inspectors deemed their records inadequate and full of lacunae. Innocent ordered the sequestration of Barberini accounts, put the brothers under surveillance, and continued to go after their servants. The Venetian ambassador passed along rumors that "rooms were being readied at Castel Sant'Angelo" for Taddeo. Gigli later reported, "They say that on the Feast of the Chair of Saint Peter, January 18, when Cardinal Francesco Barberini would have gone to Saint Peter's as archpriest of the basilica, he was going to be arrested and imprisoned in Castel Sant'Angelo."[3]

On December 22, Cardinal Mazarin dispatched a courier offering the Barberini brothers sanctuary in France and a ship to take them there. On January 16, Cardinal Francesco left a letter at the college of cardinals announcing his departure to escape unjust persecution; he would return when His Holiness was better informed in these matters. After midnight, Cardinal Francesco and Prince Taddeo, disguised as hunters, slipped away from their palaces, together with Taddeo's children, all dressed as pages. They left orders that in the coming days the palace antechambers should remain open, as if it were business as usual. Cardinal Francesco, in the meantime, had also spread the word that he was sick in bed.[4]

To fool papal agents, the Barberini brothers slipped away in different directions. Don Taddeo and his children, with his wife, Anna Colonna, carrying the youngest, went on foot as far as Campo de' Fiori, where carriages and an armed guard from Palazzo Colonna awaited them. Since women did not share blame with their menfolk, Anna Colonna would remain in Rome. She explained to the children that they were all going on an outing to Vigna. "My lady mother, it's the middle of the night," an incredulous young Niccolò Maria Barberini replied. "We're not going to Vigna, we're running away."[5]

The following morning the fugitives reunited along the coast at Ostia (41.732342° N, 12.276370° E). There they hurriedly set sail not on Mazarin's warship, which was mistakenly waiting thirty miles to the north, but aboard a more modest vessel. Wintry blasts began to assault the little boat around midnight, first splitting the yardarm of one of the main sails. They struggled onward through high seas and continuous rain until the wind shredded most of the sails near Genoa. Since violent seas made a landing impossible, the party made for the French coast. But the weather continued to deteriorate; the boat began to take on water, and for eighteen hours it seemed certain to founder. The party knelt before Cardinal Francesco, who heard their confessions as conditions grew dire and time seemed to be running out. He granted group absolution *in articulo mortis*, as at the hour of death. By morning the storm had abated somewhat. Finally, with stores of food and wine exhausted, the crew sighted mountains through the fog and rain: they were approaching the Island of Sainte-Marguerite (43.519264° N, 7.05114° E), opposite Cannes and the Gulf of La Napoule. After landing, Francesco Barberini continued on to Paris, where his notably warm welcome contrasted with his younger brother's previous chilly reception.[6]

DOUBLE CROSS

On January 20, 1646, while the Barberini family struggled in great peril across the Ligurian Sea, Rossi's notary returned to SS. Filippo e Giacomo to follow up on a promising lead. A month before, the Roman governor had forwarded a piece of jewelry that sbirri had taken from Carlo Possenti at his arrest. Ever since the testimony of Possenti's servant Bartolomea and the Palladas had linked him to the fugitive nuns' property, Rossi had been searching for proof that it ended up in the priest's hands after their murder. Various items of jewelry and silver that Don Carlo acknowledged having brought to Rome and Segni seemed to strengthen this possibility. His large spoons in the modern style and four-tined forks sounded suspiciously like the cutlery witnesses had seen in Silveria's and Laura's possession. Possenti claimed, however, that he had bought his from a traveling salesman who had stolen them from an attic in Guia (45.91° N, 12.058° E, north of Treviso and Vicenza) during the military campaign. Possenti had also brought several rings to Rome. The nuns testified that Suor Silveria owned some that sounded similar to Don Carlo's. The priest claimed to have bought two of his from French soldiers and to have taken (not purchased) the others from hapless women fleeing the conflict in Guia. (Spoils of war were apparently an added perk for men of the cloth on campaign, at least those cut from the same cloth as Carlo Possenti.) But apparently sbirri had not confiscated the valuables that Possenti enumerated (or had not turned them over to authorities). It therefore was impossible to confirm that any of them had in fact been La Generona's.[7]

The parcel from Rome finally offered such a possibility. For the fifth time, Suor Jacopa Rossi therefore faced an interrogator across the parlatorio grates, because she recalled seeing La Generona and La Rossa wearing various bits of finery.

"Do you know whether Suor Laura Vittoria and Suor Silveria Catterina had any reliquaries or crosses?"

"A year or two before they left I saw a reliquary cross in the possession of Catterina, Suor Silveria's daughter," Suor Jacopa remembered. "She was going around showing it off to us other nuns. I don't know if they had other reliquaries or crosses because I wasn't close friends with them."

"Could you describe the cross?" the notary asked.

"It was made of red leather tooled with gold lines and may have been a little more than five inches long and two wide. There were various niches to hold relics. I remember that when the girl showed it to me, I took it in my hand and saw that among the things in those niches one relic said 'Saint Thomas.'"

"Would you recognize it if you saw it?"

"Most certainly."

The notary handed her the reliquary cross, recently arrived from Rome.

"This is the same one I saw on Suor Silveria's daughter. Your Lordship can see this niche, right here, below the large one in the middle: there's the name 'Saint Thomas.'"

The notary took a closer look: "S. Tom. Ap. [the Apostle]" appeared on a tiny scrap of parchment.[8]

The vicaria also sent the conversa Prudenza Prosperi along to the parlatorio after she claimed to have something to say about crosses and reliquaries.

"One day I saw Suor Silveria's daughter crying. When I asked what was the matter, she said she'd dropped the cover of a reliquary into the convent sluice, where water flows through the cloister. She was standing looking down into the water, and when I looked I saw the cover of red leather. I paid no attention and went about my business, leaving the girl in tears, because she suspected her mother would come down hard on her when she found out. But I clearly saw it because the water was shallow and clear in that spot. I don't know if they ever got it out."[9]

A convent gardener provided the answer.

"I imagine that Your Lordship wishes to examine me about the cover for a cross of red leather that I fished out of the convent sluice one time two or three years ago. Suor Silveria ordered me to climb down and get it out, so I got it out and gave it to her."

"Would you recognize the cover if you saw it?"

"Yes, my lord. Yes, that's the cover that fell in the sluice, as I said. But I never saw the cross, so I don't recognize it."[10]

Later the same day, back at the Torrone, when Carlo Possenti returned to confront his accusers for the first time since December 16, he may have wondered why Giandomenico Rossi was not in attendance and had handed him off to an assistant.

"Apart from letters, what else was discovered on you at the time of your arrest?" the notary asked.

"They found some money and a little old purse of turquoise and red shaggy plush. Inside there were various relics that my late brother Jacopo of blessed memory used to carry. Since his death I've always carried them. They also found a cross of red leather about five inches long, tooled in gold like a service book. Otherwise, I don't remember anything."

"Is this the one?" The notary held up the reliquary.

"That's the same one that sbirri found on me when they took me prisoner. Signor Cornelio Malvasia gave it to me about four years ago," Possenti hastened to add.

"Why did Signor Malvasia give it to you?"

"I don't know, but we were friends."

"After you received it, did you ever give it to anybody else?"

"No, never. It never left my possession until the sbirri took it. Nobody would have seen it either, except when I used it during the war to bless the wounded."

"Can you be more precise about exactly when Malvasia gave it to you?"

"No, I can't remember. Three or four years ago, as I said."

"Where did Malvasia get it?"

"I don't know. I never asked and he never said."

After a long, skeptical look, the notary sent Possenti back to his cell.[11]

On January 29 the notary went in search of a final witness, this time at the Conservatorio di Santa Croce, a charitable institution for prostitutes' daughters and other girls at risk. Fifteen-year-old Catterina Pasi had been thrown out of the Convent of San Lorenzo once her mother's disappearance left her with no one to pay her dowry. Authorities eventually confined the girl at Santa Croce. If her luck improved, she would remain there for six years and then receive a dowry adequate for a lower-tier convent or an ordinary sort of husband.

"My mother was that unfortunate Suor Silveria Catterina, the nun at the Convertite who fled the convent and then was found dead, as everybody knows. I lived there for about eight years when my mother was alive and left a while before she ran off."

"While you were in the convent, did any reliquaries, crosses, or similar things pass through your hands?"

"I don't remember ever having anything but a cross of red leather with relics inside that my mother sometimes let me wear. I returned it to my mother when I left, and I don't know what she did with it then." Catterina hesitated briefly. "My mother received it as a gift from my father, I think she said. He's now a Capuchin, called Antonio Giovannoni in the world. He lives at the Capuchin monastery in Imola."

"Did your mother ever give it to anybody?"

"I don't know, although I do know that when I left the convent, I left it with her."

"Did it ever come apart and get put back together?"

"It's true that one time I dropped the cover into the sluice, but the convent gardener climbed down and got it, then returned it to my mother."

"Would you know it if you saw it again?"

"Certainly, because I handled it so many times."

The notary handed her the cross and the girl took a moment, gently turning it over in her hands.

"It's the same one—I clearly recognize it."[12]

When the notary extended his hand, perhaps he observed a moment's hesitation as Catterina gave up the precious object. When he dismissed her, Catterina turned and disappeared from sight and from history.

On Friday, February 2, when Carlo Possenti returned for further interrogation, he found that Giandomenico Rossi had also returned and was regarding him stonily.

"Have you anything further to say?" Rossi asked.

"Nothing occurs to me that I haven't already said."

"You had best speak truthfully about how you got the cross you were previously interrogated about."

"I already said that Signor Cornelio Malvasia gave me the cross that the notary over there showed me. He gave it to me here in Bologna, but I don't remember exactly where. I clearly remember that he gave it to me when I became chaplain of the army."

"Abandon these lies! According to several witnesses, the cross belonged to Suor Silveria."

"That's absolutely false! As I said, Signor Cornelio Malvasia gave it to me. It was the year after Castro was taken, the year when the Duke of Parma passed through these parts [1642], when I was made chaplain. He said it would be a good thing if I carried something sacred to use with the dying. I always kept it on me, and when the occasion arose, I always blessed the dying with that cross. And any witnesses who say that it was Suor Silveria's are telling a thousand lies!"

"Once again I warn you to speak the truth, not only about the present matter," Rossi said quietly, with a look of patent disbelief, "but also about all the facts of the case, which is to say, the other excesses charged against you. Your obstinacy has continued as long as it can."

"I've spoken the truth and can say nothing else. I had nothing to do with the crimes charged against me."[13]

Rossi launched into a catalog of what the evidence had shown. How one nun after another confirmed not only the priest's constant presence at the convent, but also his unruly passion for Suor Silveria, which led inexorably to her abduction to satisfy his lust. How witnesses established that he conspired with Count Ferdinando Ranuzzi and Captain Donato Guarnieri in Ferrara and Copparo, then abandoned his post to complete preparations with

Ranuzzi and Andrea Pallada in Bologna. He flamboyantly turned up at the convent, broadcasting his return to Ferrara, to establish an alibi. He displayed an uncharacteristic and implausible apathy about La Generona's abduction and then, when he later encountered Giustina Regi, turned red and pale by turns at the mention of La Rossa.[14]

"It's not true that I was so in love with Suor Silveria," Possenti shouted, "even if I did seek her out at the convent now and then." One by one, he denied the other charges. "Giustina Regi and Suor Laura's mother can say whatever they want about me, because they're both whores. But I am innocent in all this nun business!"[15]

"Do you dare to claim innocence when so much evidence unequivocally establishes your guilt?" Rossi shot back. He glanced down at the page before him and continued his inventory of Possenti's crimes. "You met with Andrea Pallada to arrange to harbor the nuns in his apartment, on the pretext that they were from Ferrara. You schemed with Count Ferdinando Ranuzzi and Negrino Negrini to abduct them on the night of March 31, 1644, having previously contrived the transfer of their goods to Pallada's apartment. In all likelihood you had carnal knowledge with Suor Silveria, your lover, alone with her at the Palladas', behind a locked door. After the nuns left, you had your servant Bartolomea take their belongings to your house. That the two nuns told witnesses Count Ferdinando Ranuzzi and Negrino Negrini removed Suor Silveria at your insistence and the other nun at Captain Donato Guarnieri's further condemns you.

"More telling still is your intimate friendship with Colonel Alessandro Guarnieri, your partner in crime, which the investigation has clearly proved. You deny this, however, citing enmity with Count Alessandro Maria Pepoli, provoked by your hatred for Francesco Maria dall'Aglio. But your frequent visits to Colonel Guarnieri's house after your return from Ferrara, after the nuns' abduction, and your many private conversations with him catch you in this lie.

"At Pallada's insistence, you eventually had Colonel Guarnieri transfer the nuns to the palace of your friend Count Alessandro Maria Pepoli. The nuns were persuaded to leave there only by showing them a letter from you. It must have been in your hand, since they promptly agreed to go, having likely recognized your handwriting, given Silveria's ready familiarity with it from your previous correspondence. Your writing of this letter clearly implicates you in subsequent crimes against the nuns, which Colonel Alessandro Guarnieri committed with your probable participation, at the house of your acknowledged enemy, Francesco Maria dall'Aglio. This was obviously an act of revenge against him. Otherwise you might have buried their bodies in the garden or thrown them into the canal running beneath the house. Although you deny any familiarity with the house, you must have frequently visited there during your two-year friendship with dall'Aglio before falling out with him.

"On top of all this must be added your vile character. You were banished to Ferrara for attempted murder and another time condemned for theft after conspiring with some of Bologna's most notorious criminals. Furthermore, as a priest and military chaplain you interceded inappropriately for those suspected or convicted of atrocious crimes. And you even ignored your priestly obligation to say daily mass.

"Surely it can be no accident that when you, the author of the miserable nuns' death, came face-to-face with Giustina, Suor Laura Vittoria's sister, you trembled and turned pale at the abhorrent sight of a countenance that shared the selfsame blood.

"And finally, what demonstrates your guilt above all else is the web of lies in which you have entangled yourself throughout the investigation, when everything in the transcript patently proclaims the truth."[16]

"Pallada and any others who testified against me can say whatever they want," Possenti stammered, red-faced and trembling. "But none of it is true! I did not have any part in the abduction of those nuns or in their deaths! I took no part in the theft of their property! I don't know anything about any of these things!"[17]

RIGOROSUM EXAMEN

The next day, February 3, just ten days short of Ash Wednesday, papal legate Lelio Falconieri authorized Bolognese carnival celebrations, much to the public's delight. "But should Your Eminence deign to inform me that His Holiness is of the opposite opinion," he wrote Cardinal Pamphili, "I shall order that they be discontinued." Since the legate could not expect an answer for almost two weeks, his timing ensured that life in Bologna could briefly be turned upside down right through Shrove Tuesday.[18]

The incoming post also brought Giandomenico Rossi a long-awaited communication. On January 26 (within days of the Barberini family's flight from Rome), a special congregation had convened before the Roman governor to consider Possenti's fate. After allowing the advocate for the poor his obligatory say on behalf of the accused, the prelates agreed that Prosecutor Rossi could proceed to torture "to arrive at the truth regarding the abduction of Suor Laura Vittoria and Suor Silveria Catterina and regarding Possenti's subsequent copulation with Suor Silveria Catterina." The priest's alleged complicity in the nuns' murder goes unmentioned: presumably the panel deemed the evidence insufficiently compelling. The congregation also rejected any defense on Possenti's behalf.[19]

Rossi wasted no time. When Carlo Possenti confronted him on February 3, the priest very likely had some sense of what awaited, if not its full extent.

"Will you finally recognize that it would be better to speak the whole truth in these matters, which is to say, about the abduction of the convertite, Laura Vittoria and Silveria Catterina, and about your subsequent sexual intercourse with Suor Silveria?"

"I have told the truth. I can say no more."

"Abandon your obstinacy and freely speak the truth!" Rossi paused. "Lest we proceed to the appropriate legal remedies against you."

"I can't say anything more than I've already said," Possenti replied dully. "Do what suits your lordship about the rest."

At Rossi's signal, guards propelled Don Carlo over to the strappado, undressed him, tied his wrists behind his back, attached the rope, and waited, seemingly indifferent, as Rossi intoned his gentle, pro forma exhortations to speak the truth while there was still time.

"I have spoken the truth. Saint Anthony of Padua will help me!"

Rossi nodded. The bargello grabbed Possenti around the thighs and lifted him clumsily off the floor. Guards immediately yanked the rope taut. Then the bargello released him. "Help, Saint Anthony of Padua! Queen of Heaven, help me! You know my remorse! Saint Nicholas of Bari, defend me!" After that initial outburst, Possenti said nothing more.

"Freely speak the truth about your role in the abduction and sexual congress with the nuns, to avoid further torment!"

"I've done nothing!" Possenti cried. "Go ahead, give me everything you've got, by the presence of Diana!" (Was that the best the self-styled poet could do? Rossi had heard the same hackneyed blasphemy so many times before.) "Saint Anthony will help me, you'll see! Saint Anthony, comfort me!"

Perhaps the saints listened as the priest repeated his anguished litany, but they ignored his pleas. His flushed face dripped with sweat despite the winter chill. "Will you leave me hanging like this?" Possenti groaned.

"You need only leave off your hardheadedness! Won't you forthrightly speak the truth? I hear how you are suffering, truly I do!"

"Quit yammering in my ear!" Possenti muttered between clenched teeth. "Because I'll say no more than I've said already!"

At Rossi's signal, the guards twitched the rope.

"Saint Anthony of Padua, you know my remorse!" Possenti pleaded. "And you, Most Holy Queen of Heaven, comfort me as you've done before!"

The priest's harrowing invocations continued, interrupted only by sighs and ragged breathing. When his eyes closed momentarily and failed to reopen, a guard promptly splashed a little vinegar in his face to forestall any fainting fit. Possenti revived with a start, gasping at the pain his jerking brought.

The prosecutor, watching impassively, knew soon enough that this was going nowhere. Rome permitted a full hour, but he left Possenti hanging only until the hourglass registered forty-five minutes.[20] Then at last he signaled. The guards let the priest down and freed his wrists. The barber surgeon expertly wrenched his arms back into place. Rossi sent the priest back to his cell to contemplate what might come next, a prospect that did not bear thinking about.

In nearby Piazza Maggiore carnival revelries continued late into the night. The lowering walls of the Torrone, around the corner, kept such unruly frivolities at bay. Two hours after dark the next day (Sunday, February 4), Rossi began again. "Perhaps now you are disposed to speak the whole truth about the abduction of Suor Laura Vittoria and Suor Silveria Catterina, and about your subsequent sexual intercourse with Suor Silveria."

"I wish I could say more." Possenti's bluster had lost its edge. "I know nothing beyond what I've said already."

"If you do not stop your subterfuge and obstinacy and do not at last speak the truth about your complicity in the abduction of the nuns and the carnal knowledge you had with Suor Silveria, then you lead us to additional torment in its other varieties." Rossi waited. "Which is to say, the vigil."

The dreaded vigil (*veglia*) was horrific enough for Gregory XIII to ban its use in the late 1500s, but Paul V reinstituted it within prescribed limits in 1612. This torment, directed more subtly at the nervous system than other more overtly brutal methods of enhanced interrogation, derived its name from an original emphasis on sleep deprivation: slaps on the head kept a prisoner awake whenever he nodded off over the course of forty hours. With the substitution of more refined techniques of physical torment to prevent rest or sleep, the duration shrank to a standard ten hours within the Papal States, sometimes expanded to twelve hours of suffering. Although many successfully endured the blunt force of the strappado, few withstood the vigil's refinements.

"Believe me, my lord, I don't know anything else," Possenti responded. "I can't say anything further. My lord, do what you will."[21]

Rossi signals the guards, who lead Possenti into a much smaller, claustrophobic cell, bare except for the usual table and two chairs and a rude pallet on the floor. As the guards remove his clothes, the priest notices a curious bulky, three-legged trestle, as tall as a man, topped with a sort of pyramid, hulking in a corner. Rossi enters, a heavy book in hand. (This will be a long process.) He takes his seat at the table.

Possenti now sits naked on the pallet, with jailers standing over him. The prosecutor reiterates his familiar exhortations, to no avail. On Rossi's signal, the Torrone's barber surgeon proceeds to shave all the hair from Possenti's body. (Given the vigil's inherent risks, body hair must not obscure any physical changes to the sufferer.) The shaming nature of the process just might induce a salutary sense of helplessness, prompting an immediate confession. But not this time.

Guards spread Possenti's legs apart and attach his ankles to a heavy wooden crossbar while the bargello ties his wrists behind his back. They carefully place a wide leather strap around his torso, just below his armpits, cinching it up firmly while still allowing room for the bargello to insert his hand inside at the back. (The slight looseness will accommodate swelling of the upper body during the coming ordeal.)

Possenti feels himself lifted awkwardly several feet into the air. Guards quickly connect the leg crosspiece to a rope tied to a ring high on the wall in front of him, while others string up his hands to a pulley overhead, in the manner of the strappado. Finally, they connect ropes from the side walls to the strap around his chest. The barber surgeon directs a guard to move the menacing pointed trestle, the so-called "chair of Judas," to a position beneath Possenti's body. The barber carefully positions the point of the pyramid (sharp enough to cause irresistible pain, but dull enough not to pierce skin and flesh) so that it will dig into the base of the prisoner's spine. After a few painstaking adjustments, guards slowly release Possenti's body, which balances on the painful fulcrum beneath his spine (fig. 26). Any physical relaxation on his part or slackening of his restraints will further force the point into his back. Should he slip from the pyramid, weight shifted to his wrists will likely dislocate his shoulders.

The barber surgeon and guards leave him rigid and teetering in agony on

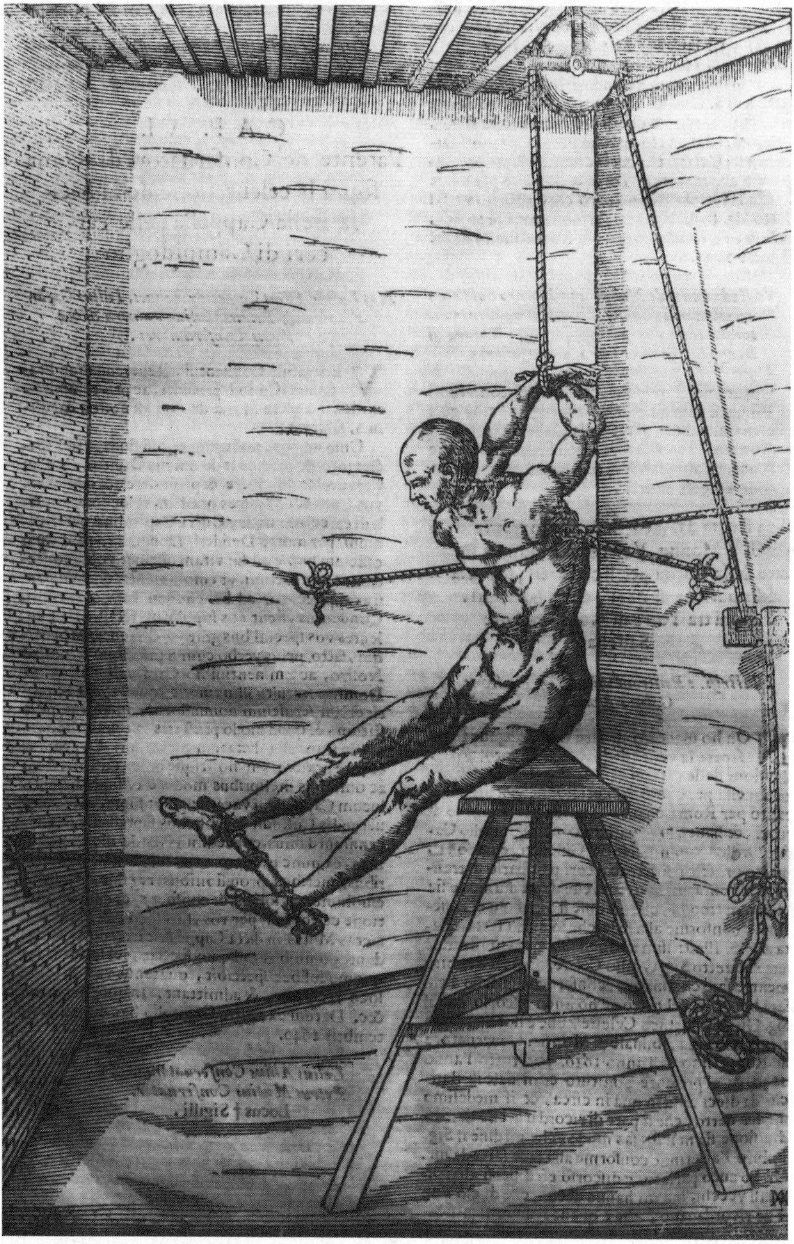

FIGURE 26. Giovanni Battista Scanaroli, *De visitatione carceratorum* (1675). The *veglia* (vigil), inflicted on Possenti. Reproduced with permission of the Biblioteca Comunale dell'Archiginnasio, Bologna.

the point. They close the door behind them. Rossi and the notary are seated at the table, dimly illuminated by a pair of candles. Any windows are shut tight.

"Speak the truth about the abduction and fornication."

Possenti eyes Giandomenico Rossi with a feral look, between fear and defiance. "I don't know what else to say."

With stagey deliberation, the prosecutor turns over a large hourglass sitting prominently on the table, settles into his chair, opens his book, and occasionally turns a page. The notary fidgets: he is there as a witness and to record Possenti's every word. The first hour passes.[22]

"I feel better than I'd ever have thought," Possenti declares during the second hour, with a forced jauntiness that belies his sorry state. By now his body is swelling slightly; it trembles from the chill in the room and from relentless tension as he struggles to resist sagging farther onto the pointed trestle. Looking over his book, Rossi observes him closely. The vigil's early hours are the hardest to bear, when a prisoner's senses remain acute. Despite the cold, Possenti's shaved head and forehead are suffused with sweat, which trickles down to collect beneath his nose. He tries repeatedly to clear it with short, upward puffs of breath, but the maddening drops inexorably regather.

"I won't air my doings in the Piazza. . . ." The priest has lost none of his resolve at the third hour.

"A gentleman never tells his business. . . ." Rossi looks up from his book: at the fourth hour most men are flagging and involuntarily purge themselves, gaining a little relief. Without such evacuation, few survive.

"Keep an eye on the hourglass. . . ." At the fifth hour perhaps the priest's anxiety is rising: a promising sign.

"Oh, what a business this is!" Possenti groans loudly at the sixth hour. Rossi waits patiently, turning his pages.

"What time is it now?" Clearly, the priest is flagging at the seventh hour. By now he should have received a mouthful or two of bread soaked in tepid wine and been allowed to relieve himself. Instead, at the eighth hour Rossi assails his weakness.

"So, will you now speak the truth?"

Possenti's gaze drifts toward Rossi and fixes on his face. "Once you adjust Cipriano's restraints," Possenti mutters (Cipriano is one of the guards who tied him), "then we'll talk about it." The priest still has some fight left in him, it seems.

"Signor Giovanni Domenico, you've been reading *Il mercurio*," Possenti exclaims at the ninth hour. Rossi looks up, startled by the priest's persistent impudence. The prosecutor had recently acquired *Il mercurio overo historia de' correnti tempi*. Vittorio Siri's 850-page insider's history of European events up to 1640 had been available for not much more than a year. (Rossi, Possenti, Braccesi, Guarnieri, La Generona, and La Rossa would all find their way into the next volume of *Il mercurio*, when Siri soon turned his attentions to recent events.)

"What a fine-looking book you've got in front of you, Signor Giovanni Domenico," Possenti quips determinedly but almost inaudibly at the tenth hour, still struggling to resist.

Outside the door, guards and the barber surgeon may begin to wonder where this will end. The barber expected a call to check the prisoner's pulse at his temples. They also know that ten hours is the vigil's standard duration within the Papal States. Possenti surely knows it too.

But inside the door Rossi, turning the pages of *Il mercurio*, makes no move to terminate the proceedings. Another hour passes. From Possenti they hear nothing but quick, ragged breathing.

"Oh, how cold my head feels!" the priest calls out with a loud voice at the twelfth hour. His shallow panting continues, with signs of mounting, if feeble, agitation.

"Signor Notary, how many hours has it been?" Perhaps Don Carlo senses the brightening morning sky through a window above.[23]

At the thirteenth hour the sand has run out. Prosecutor Rossi looks up from *Il mercurio*, picks up the hourglass very deliberately and, as Possenti watches listlessly, inverts it. A fresh cone of sand noiselessly begins to form.

Almost at once Possenti's drooping lids close, his head slumps heavily forward, and urine and feces trickle down the chair of Judas. When the priest starts to writhe and heave, Rossi shouts for the barber and the bargello, who burst through the door and clumsily support Possenti's weight as they loosen the ropes and the cinch around his torso, by now grotesquely swollen. The priest's face is already cadaverous, his throat unnaturally bloated, and his chest, arms, and fingernails are turning gray.

"Take him down!" Rossi barks.

As the barber surgeon and bargello hastily move Possenti to the pallet, his limbs, glistening with cold sweat, drag inertly on the floor. The barber splashes his face with vinegar; they wrap him in a warmed blanket, chafe his limbs, and try to force warm watered wine and a little chicken broth between his foaming lips.

No one thinks to call a priest.

Possenti coughs, his eyelids flutter: he still lives. His body tenses slightly and his lips move, as if to speak. The notary strains to hear.

But then he convulses, retching bile. In a few moments life goes out of him.

Rossi shifts behind the table and rises from his chair, book in hand. "Find somewhere to bury him." The prosecutor leaves them to it.[24]

Carlo Possenti could have been laid to rest with his family in their vault at Santa Maria Maggiore, a few hundred yards north of the Torrone. Instead, that evening carnival revelers would scarcely have noticed a few sbirri hurriedly lugging a heavy sack through the side streets in the opposite direction, toward the monastery of San Giovanni Battista Celestini (fig. 5, P; 44.492266° N, 11.341461° E). Possenti was hastily buried there that night.[25]

Lent was beginning by the time word of Possenti's death began to spread around Rome. When the Modenese ambassador reported the sorry news to his duke on February 17, he probably spoke for many. "With deepest sorrow, everyone received word of Carlo Possenti's death, resulting from the beastliness of the judge, who, strictly speaking, murdered him. One supposes that Innocent X could on no account have known about the judge's proceedings, because if he knew, it would be impossible not to have the judge hanged as an example of villains who administer justice in order to appear flint-hearted, more beasts than men. They say Rossi will be named auditor of the Torrone. But perhaps it's no wonder that he is rewarded when he should be most severely punished."[26]

Within days of Possenti's death, Cardinal Pamphili wrote to inform Giandomenico Rossi of his appointment as supreme head of the Torrone in Bologna, where Rossi formally announced his promotion on February 12.[27] As a French observer predicted back in August 1645, Rossi had indeed "done his worst to deserve it."

17

UNFINISHED BUSINESS

Within days of Rossi's lethal doings at the Torrone, the case briefly found its way back into dispatches and diaries. "One of those being tried in Bologna in the case of those nuns has died during his torments," the Venetian ambassador reported, "without ever voluntarily confessing anything at all against Cardinal Antonio, as desired in order to add new crimes against him." The Modenese ambassador proved more specific. "From a good source one hears that Giovanni Domenico Rossi made every possible effort to entangle Cardinal Antonio in the abduction and other business about the nuns, because the pope infallibly believes that he was the overseer in these outrageous crimes, and that His Eminence fled more for this reason than because of the other charges previously bandied about." He went on to confirm speculations about the prosecutor's just reward. "It's absolutely true that Giovanni Domenico Rossi has been sent the papal brief appointing him auditor of the Torrone, this after he caused Possenti's death during the vigil."[1]

Other conspiracy theorists would spin it somewhat differently. According to one Bolognese diarist, "It fell to the judge to tidy up the room, and he surely aired the dirty linen. It's taken for a certainty that the nuns were abducted for Cardinal Antonio Barberini's sake, that Possenti was the middleman, and that Commissar Rossi let him die under torture, lest he have more to do with the cardinal."[2]

As for Braccesi, the Modenese ambassador concluded, "Word is that they're going to apply the same torture, the vigil, to Braccesi. Because of his frail constitution, either he'll immediately confess what they want to hear or he'll perish in a few hours."[3]

A month later the Roman governor reconvened his committee. On March 10 he informed Giandomenico Rossi,

> In the matter of the abduction, it is resolved that you proceed with the strappado against Captain Donato Guarnieri, imprisoned there, for the full time allowed, but without repetition. And Colonel Alessandro Guarnieri, Count Ferdinando Ranuzzi, and Negrino Negrini are sentenced in absentia: against the latter two, for the nuns' abduction, we impose the customary penalty; and against the colonel, for the treacherous murder of the two nuns, the customary penalty for treachery.

The governor and his council made no mention whatever of Giovanni Braccesi.

On March 23 Rossi published the condemnation of Alessandro Guarnieri, Ferdinando Ranuzzi, and Negrino Negrini in a printed broadside, slapped up on walls around Bologna. Thanks to Ranuzzi's noble status, his "customary penalty" would be a dignified beheading. An ordinary gallows awaited the less illustrious Negrini. For his egregious role in the crimes, Colonel Guarnieri should be hanged, then dismembered. The miscreants were to appear within a matter of days to answer charges.[4]

To no one's surprise, none of the culprits showed up. Negrini had vanished even before anybody went looking for him. Alessandro Guarnieri had last been seen fighting in the Swedish army the previous autumn. Ferdinando Ranuzzi continued to be spotted here and there, always one step ahead of papal police.

The Bolognese Senate, already up in arms about "this style of Rome" in Rossi's manner of handling the Torrone's business, learned of his latest action only after the proclamation appeared around the city. Outraged by perceived violations of local prerogatives, especially regarding confiscation of family property if the accused failed to appear, the Senate demanded the decree's removal and correction. As negotiations dragged on for weeks, both the governor of Rome and the pope rebuffed senatorial demands, although in the politest possible way: they intimated orally, if not in writing, that Ranuzzi family property in Bologna would remain untouched.[5]

But once again, weightier matters in the wider world eclipsed the case of the convertite. Innocent X was understandably vexed by the latest Barberini hegira. Taddeo Barberini's decision to spirit his children to safety caused the pope particular offense: Was he, then, some latter-day Herod the Great? "They've sequestered all the income of the three Barberini brothers," the diarist Gigli reported. "On February 20 a bull was published that ordered all cardinals who aren't prevented by residence in their bishoprics to come to Rome within four months on pain of losing their church incomes."[6]

In France, while the bull circulated from hand to hand, the Crown prohibited its formal publication, amid threats of disobedience to the pope and even another schism. Papal relations with the Most Christian King continued to decline through the spring. French warships ostentatiously prepared to advance toward Tuscany if need be. In late April, with little difficulty, the fleet landed and seized control of fortresses at Talamone (42.553879° N, 11.13496° E) and Porto Santo Stefano (42.43734° N, 11.11784° E) along the Tuscan coast. Mazarin informed his minister in Rome, "Rest assured that if news reached this court that the house of Barberini has been saved from shipwreck and restored to its pristine state, and that the pope has given the king reasonable satisfaction, it would be received with greater pleasure than news of some great victory over the Spanish."[7] Then, after besieging Orbetello (42.443298° N, 11.2232° E), the French fleet sailed south toward Civitavecchia (42.089901° N, 11.7961° E), on the pope's doorstep.

"THE WICKEDEST MAN ON THIS EARTH"

By then ten months had passed since Cardinal Antonio uttered his encouraging "accept a few days in jail for love of me" in the courtyard of Palazzo Barberini. On May 21, 1646, for the first time since October, guards came for Giovanni Braccesi. Nothing indicates that he knew about recent events on the outside: the Barberini exodus, deteriorating papal-French relations, the gruesome proceedings in the Torrone's torture chamber three months earlier.

Braccesi would have immediately recognized something amiss: jailers did not take him to the usual place of interrogation. After climbing what seemed like several flights, he came face-to-face with Giandomenico Rossi in more refined surroundings. From his years at the Palazzo del Legato, perhaps Braccesi recognized them as the apartments of the auditor of the Torrone.

If Braccesi at first felt heartened by this change of venue, the prosecutor's icy demeanor warned against making much of it: merely a day or two might have passed since their last encounter, not the better part of a year. As for Braccesi, for every month, he had aged at least a year.

"Have you anything to add to your testimony regarding the abduction of the two convertite?" Rossi's protocol remained unchanged.

Braccesi offered an inconsequential refinement or two before Rossi resumed his prosecutorial mode. "Abandon your obstinacy. Speak the truth about your continual familiarity with Suor Silveria Catterina, which is well documented in the record of this investigation. It suggests your complicity in her abduction, motivated by your love for her." (Braccesi's ear for detail perhaps noted Rossi's omission of the other common accusations.)

"I don't know any other truth beyond what I've told you already." (Braccesi's dropping "my lord" signaled new disrespect.) "I'm amazed that you can find individuals so omniscient that they dare to claim that I continually visited the convent out of love for Suor Silveria Catterina," Braccesi continued, perhaps with a hint of scorn, "when it is something that could *so easily be verified*, both by means of my servants and, I daresay, by means of everybody else in Romagna." Seven months had only fortified his righteous indignation. "I was certainly no stranger to this city—everyone noticed me in the streets, especially when I had the honor to serve Cardinal Antonio Barberini. Furthermore, I was far too occupied with his business to have time to waste loitering at some nuns' grated windows. I could never leave the house without a crowd about me. I therefore fail to see how anybody could ever prove that a person like me, walking streets known to everyone in Bologna, frequented someplace as public as a convent."[8]

"Desist from such subterfuge! As you must know, common, public knowledge, among both the convertite and the people of Bologna, has always implicated you in the nuns' abduction!" (Braccesi would not know how hard investigators worked to plant his name at the Convertite before nuns began to parrot it back. Among the public, Braccesi came to be mentioned in the same breath with Possenti only after his notorious arrest and imprisonment.)

"I no longer have the courage to undo the evil fancies about honorable men that grow rank in the minds of those motivated by personal ambition or ill will." Braccesi summoned an unwavering, accusatory stare. (Perhaps he *had* heard about Rossi's promotion.) "But nobody who is not telling the greatest falsehoods can impugn my actions in any manner whatever, particularly with regard to the nuns, because when the blessed Lord permits the truth to come out, it will reveal that I have been unjustly persecuted by someone determined to defame me before the world."

Unfazed by Braccesi's novel antagonism, Rossi shifted focus. "Why persist in such stubbornness? Freely admit your part in this sorry business. Face the fact that many other proofs demonstrate that you were party to the crime. Notably, that after Possenti's arrest you feigned illness, an illness confirmed neither by your appearance nor by your actions, and no disease was going around the city at that time."

"I don't know what more to add. While still in Rome I already named to you the doctor who treated me and the apothecary who administered medicines to me." As he paused for breath, Braccesi's look was a challenge. "It seems to me that in these last ten months the truth could have been discovered *by the simple step of consulting them*. But I now see that this accusation is like all the others—it is being put forward and zealously overstated in order to indict me for crimes I find despicable and would never commit!"

Again Rossi shifted tactics in search of an opening. "You try to persuade this tribunal that you became Possenti's friend only after these crimes. Evidence from the investigation refutes that."

"Whenever someone *finally questions Signor Cornelio Malvasia*, he will tell him precisely when Don Carlo started to visit my house: after Signor Cornelio no longer had anything to do with him, which was after the nuns' escape."

"The investigation establishes all the time you spent alone with Carlo Possenti," Rossi broke in. "This argues all the more strongly for your guilt of the crimes for which he stands convicted." (Braccesi would not know that Possenti had died without confessing and technically could not have been convicted.)

"I don't know what is in your investigation, but I do know that there are men in this world of such ill will that they are governed totally by their passions." After another tactical hesitation, Braccesi continued. "If any deduce my participation in these crimes from Possenti's having spent time with me, that is nothing but an assumption spawned by my present disgrace. But I thank God for having formed me always to behave honorably. There would be few today who would take me for such a criminal if they had not seen me treated for more than ten months as if I were the wickedest man on this earth."[9]

Braccesi paused, slightly breathless. With an air of grim despair, he awaited Rossi's next assault.

"Take him back to his cell."

Guards conducted Braccesi from the auditor's apartments back underground to Le Segrete. And with that, he vanished. No further trace of

Giovanni Braccesi survives in official records of the case of the murdered convertite.

On May 27 the governor immediately replied to Giandomenico Rossi's description of this latest fruitless encounter. "Lest your efforts to have B in the palm of your hand impede the dispatch of the entire case, I believe you would do well to execute the order given you against Guarnieri, so that you can then use this against the other prisoners."[10] The cryptic B could only be Giovanni Braccesi. Who were these "other prisoners" the governor mentioned? By late May the cells of the Torrone and the archiepiscopal prison, once filled to capacity, were virtually empty. Less than two days after Possenti's death, Dionisio Tomassini had been the last remaining person of interest to be released on bond (for the second time). Only Braccesi and Guarnieri apparently still waited below in Le Segrete.

"I KNOW NOTHING, MY LORD"

Giandomenico Rossi wasted no time. On June 2, for the first time in nearly six months, Donato Guarnieri came face-to-face with the prosecutor. Not, however, in the auditor's apartments.

"Are you ready, at last, to speak the truth in these matters, which is to say, that you ordered the abduction of Suor Laura Vittoria, the convertita?" (As the Roman governor stipulated, Rossi made no mention of the other crimes.)

"I can say nothing more than I've already said: I did not have Suor Laura Vittoria abducted."

"The time has come to abandon your hardheadedness. You've heard the enormity of the accusations launched against you."

"I dare to reiterate that I did not do this evil falsely attributed to me. And I never had that nun abducted or removed from the convent." (Significantly, Donato no longer claimed not to know La Rossa.)

"It seems, then, that to encourage you to tell the truth," Rossi continued, with an edge in his voice, "we must adopt those further remedies the court has stipulated."

"I have done no wrong. And if I am to receive the strappado, get on with it."

Prosecutor and guards reenacted the grim ritual of undressing, binding, and kindly exhortation, followed by the inevitable pause.

"I did not arrange to have any crime committed," Guarnieri responded, with an air of resignation. "I can say nothing beyond what I've said already."

When guards promptly did their duty, Guarnieri's hoisting up provoked not a word.

"Speak the truth!"

"I ordered no crime, my lord. Most Holy Madonna, help me!"

"Speak the truth! What do you know about these allegations?"

"I know nothing, my lord."

"If you show remorse for your wrongdoing, you need not endure further torment!"

"I know nothing, my lord."[11]

Rossi slumped in his seat and looked away.

Guarnieri hung by his wrists, uncomplaining, waiting out the hourglass, as the requisite hour passed.

At last guards let him down and the barber surgeon twisted his arms back into place. After he struggled into his clothes, they led him out.

Donato shuffled down the familiar route toward Le Segrete, but a guard nudged him another way: up the stairs, then through an unfamiliar door into a spacious vaulted cell, lit on two sides by large grated windows. Groups of curious prisoners turned from the windows to gawk at the shabby bearded figure as a guard fumbled with Guarnieri's shackles and manacles. After almost a year, Donato was finally free from solitary confinement.

He was still far from freedom. Weeks passed into months a bit more quickly, perhaps, with life to observe on Bologna's busy streets, with people to call out to below the Torrone's barred windows, and with other prisoners to help pass endless hours of boredom. Everyone eagerly shared information and misinformation, all of it news to Captain Donato: the flight of the Barberini, the pitiful end of Don Carlo Possenti five months earlier, Giandomenico Rossi's promotion. Nobody had anything to say about Giovanni Braccesi.

Word of events in the wider world also must have reached Donato Guarnieri once he was set at large in the public prison: how Innocent X first remained intransigent in the face of French demands, and how fortune eventually turned against the French fleet, which raised its siege of Orbetello and retreated in mid-July 1646. But the French were back in early fall, once again threatening the Tuscan coast and raising anxiety in Rome to its highest level. This time Innocent X blinked: on September 17 he agreed to grant the Barberini brothers a full pardon, to restore all their properties, and to let bygones be bygones. Bologna's ambassador informed the Senate two days later, "Please God that sorting out this matter will ensure that we may be permanently delivered from this painful business." How this papal amnesty might affect any less illustrious figures previously caught in the Pamphili-Barberini crossfire, nobody seemed to know or much care.[12]

Because of the contumacious Count Ferdinando Ranuzzi, negotiations about Ranuzzi family indemnity continued in the meantime. Rossi hoped at least to recover the costs of tracking him down (just as authorities had tried to dun Lucrezia Regi for similar costs to find her daughter two years earlier). "Their portion will perhaps not be so great that they cannot tolerate it," the Senate reported. Ranuzzi had disappeared from Rome immediately after Braccesi's arrest, allegedly headed for Venice. He was last spotted in Livorno, on the coast. Perhaps Ranuzzi hoped to catch a boat to somewhere safer. If so, he was not quick enough about it.

In November 1646, Count Girolamo Ranuzzi-Manzoli appeared before Bolognese authorities to declare that Count Ferdinando, his cousin, had passed to a better life a few months earlier in Livorno. Count Girolamo wished to claim his inheritance as next of kin. By then the family had performed the requisite funeral rites, visits of condolence, "and all the other accustomed practices among cavaliers," as a fellow aristocrat recalled years later. Long before then, others whispered that this had not been the full extent of his relatives' participation in Count Ferdinando's death: the Ranuzzi had supposedly arranged to have him poisoned, "for fear of the disgrace of a public spectacle. Well aware of the pope's evil intentions in the matter, they removed Count Ferdinando from this world and also covered up the evidence of his death." Or so one Bolognese chronicler alleged.[13]

Five weeks later, on December 19, 1646, Donato Guarnieri was brought for the last time before Giandomenico Rossi, who could not convict him without a confession. Rossi therefore exiled him from the Papal States in perpetuity. Should Guarnieri ever be caught on the wrong side of the border, he would be condemned to the papal galleys for ten years, even for a first offense. (Given his treatment at apostolic hands, Captain Donato presumably found such banishment easy enough to bear.)

Shortly before 9:00 that night, a corporal of the guard and eight mounted sbirri escorted Guarnieri from the Torrone,[14] through the deserted streets of Bologna, and out the city gate of San Felice. Although the party kept the prisoner loosely encircled as they made their way southward along the river Reno toward the border with Tuscany, the tension must have been considerably less than on the voyage from Venice to Bologna sixteen months earlier. Soon the Apennines loomed ahead, hedging in the river and the party following the

FIGURE 27. Sambuca Pistoiese (Tuscany). The facade of the Grand Duke of Tuscany's customs house (dated 1641 on the lintel), now hidden inside a nineteenth-century structure. Note the loophole to the right of the door. Photo: Luca Salvucci, Bologna.

road above its bank. The path was not difficult to navigate, thanks to a moon waxing nearly full above the mountains toward the west and a bright dusting of snow silvering the mountainsides, which stood out with an unnatural clarity behind skeletal forests.[15]

As the sky eventually brightened in early morning, the route along the river entered a broader valley. After splashing across the shallow, rocky riverbed, the party continued a few hundred yards toward a long, narrow edifice of rough gray sandstone, with strategically placed loopholes for harquebuses piercing its walls. It was the Grand Duke of Tuscany's border checkpoint, rising three stories above a few ruder stone cottages nearby.[16] A tall, narrow doorway with 1641 carved into the lintel faced the path (fig. 27; 44.1272° N, 10.9986° E). Guarnieri's escorts left him there but lingered until he vanished across the frontier into Tuscany. The company retraced its path and late in the day informed Bolognese authorities of their prisoner's successful release with orders never to return.

We might imagine Giulia Ragazzi, La Fratina, in her fetching monk's cloth, perhaps with bodice slightly ripped to reveal a hint of ruddiness in the frosty morning air, awaiting Captain Donato on the rise above the river, just across the border. (Or, who knows, instead of La Fratina, even Sergeant

Major Benedetto Machiavelli, astride his horse, picnic basket at the ready.) It is less fanciful, however, to imagine young Ottavio Agosti dutifully waiting to escort his cousin home. Given how quickly Donato's cousin had dashed off to Venice after his arrest, and how earnestly Ottavio had interceded on his behalf during his imprisonment in the Torrone, this scenario does not seem so implausible. In any event, whether he traveled in company or alone, we can be quite certain that Captain Donato Guarnieri reached Bergamo and his extended family in Gorlago—everyone, that is, but Colonel Alessandro—just in time for Christmas.

Epilogue

Donato Guarnieri's disappearance across the border on December 20, 1646, went unnoticed in the wider world. By then, any mention of him had long since disappeared from the news of the day as reported in avvisi or ambassadorial dispatches. Braccesi, Possenti, and the case of the convertite were also largely forgotten, eclipsed by events of greater moment on the European stage.

"SO LITTLE REGARD TO HIS REPUTATION"

Negotiations for Antonio and Francesco Barberini's reintegration into papal favor advanced slowly. In March 1647 the pope granted Cardinal Francesco permission to return to Rome, but the cardinal reached the Eternal City only in February 1648. The pope greeted him warmly and found him much changed, as did all of Rome. Not only did he cut quite a different figure *alla franzese*, but according to the diarist Giacinto Gigli, he "returned all white-haired and wan, whereas when he left Rome he was blond."[1]

Final steps in papal reconciliation waited until spring and summer of 1653, when the late Taddeo Barberini's eldest son Carlo ceded rights of primogeniture to his younger brother Maffeo. On June 15 in the Sistine Chapel, ablaze with cardinals' robes, twenty-two-year-old Maffeo wed twelve-year-old Olimpia Giustiniani, Olimpia Maidalchini's granddaughter, with Great Uncle Innocent X officiating. A Barberini-Pamphili alliance was finally a reality. A week later Carlo Barberini arrived in Rome, and Innocent X promptly made him a cardinal.

On July 12, 1653, Cardinal Antonio too appeared in the Holy City, as unexpectedly as he had left it eight years earlier. He gradually resumed his various church offices, including that of papal chamberlain. This meant that when Innocent X passed to a better life in January 1655, Cardinal Antonio was the one to pronounce him dead, just as he had done for his uncle an eventful decade earlier.

Cardinal Antonio's return seems to have marked a time for amendment of life. During the reign of Alexander VII Chigi (1655–67) he was less in the public eye and, when possible, was back in France. The matter of the Bolognese convertite apparently lingered in Rome's collective memory, however. It did not escape the anonymous author of *The Scarlet Gown*, who stated firmly,

> And if any one hath traduced his good name, saying, that he was privy to the death of the convert Nunns of *Magdalene* in *Bologna*, he lyes. But indeed after the Delinquents were discovered, in stead of chastising, he favoured and protected them, and also kept the Archbishop of *Bologna* from proceeding against them, enjoyning him to speak no more thereof. I cannot deny but Antonio committed an error in having so little regard to his reputation; for as Legate Apostolicall, as General, and as the Pope's Nephew, he might with all rigour have taken information of the matter, and then arraigned and condemned them to the punishment, which the heinousness of their offence required and afterwards he might graciously have pardoned them; for so he had shewed himself a just Judge; and they too, as if they had been sufficiently chastised, had not incurred that, which arrived unto them.[2]

The author apparently gave no thought to Suor Silveria and Suor Laura and what had arrived unto them.

"COURAGE IS NOT ALWAYS FAVORED IN ITS RISKY UNDERTAKINGS"

Giandomenico Rossi stayed on in Bologna as auditor of the Torrone only until 1648. In recognition of a subsequent campaign against banditry in Piombino and Venosa, Rossi also received the fine-sounding title of vice prince of Piombino and Venosa. He faced his greatest challenge some years later as vicar general of Milan during Alfonso Litta's turbulent reign as archbishop. Rossi's fearless determination in fulfilling his superiors' commands aptly suited this inflexible, thin-skinned superior, perpetually at odds with Milan's Spanish government. When Litta threatened to excommunicate the Spanish governor, the intrepid Giandomenico Rossi delivered the declaration of excommunication in person. Exactly what happened next is unclear, but Rossi abandoned Milan shortly thereafter, "prudently reflecting that courage is not always favored in its risky undertakings, well considered though they may be" (as an early nineteenth-century biography put it). The sometime lieutenant governor of Rome, auditor of the Torrone in Bologna, vicar general of Milan, and vice prince of Piombino withdrew to the tranquility of his birthplace: Brissago (46.120998° N, 8.71145° E), a backwater just across the Swiss border, on Lago Maggiore. Far from the corridors of power, Rossi hoped "to finish his days in peace and quiet," an aspiration he achieved in 1674, at age seventy-six.[3]

"MANENTE"

After his final confrontation with Rossi in May 1646, Giovanni Braccesi vanished from the investigation. *The Scarlet Gown* suggested a dire outcome for both of the accused, "one being *Carlo Possente*, and the other *Manente* Cardinal Antonio's Secretary, being both of them sent Prisoners to *Bologna*, where they were put to death." Given what Braccesi had been through, such a fate would not seem surprising. Very curiously, however, Barberini's secretary (allegedly "put to death") is not called "Braccesi" but is described as "Manente," which seems to imply that he remained Cardinal Antonio's secretary—that he "endured."[4]

Despite his disappearance after May 1646, Braccesi did not succumb to his ill treatment at Rossi's hands. Then as now, however, popes did not make mistakes: the Braccesi problem had to go away for a while. Vittorio Siri's recounting in *Il mercurio* (1655) suggests the pontifical solution: "For want of sufficient evidence to subject him to torture, Braccesi was assigned the city of Pesaro for his confinement."[5] Beautifully sited, overlooking the Adriatic between Rimini and Ancona, Pesaro (fig. 4; 43.9062167° N, 12.9061° E) marked an obvious improvement over being chained to a wall beneath the Torrone in Bologna. By late 1647 Cardinal Antonio had begun sending Braccesi three hundred scudi a year to live on in exile, plus an occasional pair of silk hose. A year after the cardinal's return to Rome in 1653, Braccesi still remained in Pesaro, but the wave of reconciliation finally swept him up too. Innocent X acknowledged that he "had been deceived" regarding Braccesi's wartime financial administration. (The other matter that justified Braccesi's arrest, the convertite—well, that was best overlooked.) Cardinal Antonio Barberini welcomed Braccesi back into his Roman household.[6]

In 1656 Giovanni Braccesi got his wish "to travel through the world with others, a notion I've always had in my head," as he had remarked in 1645. He accompanied Barberini to France, where he hobnobbed with the likes of Queen Christina of Sweden and, by mail, with Ferdinando II, Grand Duke of Tuscany, who turned to Giovanni Braccesi to feed his tulipmania. Braccesi dispatched several boxes of tulip and hyacinth bulbs, "some from the king's gardens at the Louvre."[7]

Braccesi soon became Cardinal Mazarin's Roman connection, as their frequent correspondence reveals. Braccesi recruited cardinals to the French faction with the promise of a pension, though some perceived imperiousness in the way he went about it. "I saw Abbé Braccesi in great fits of rage because Your Eminence has yet to send the order to give one thousand pistoles to Cardinal Maidalchini," a Jesuit in Rome informed Mazarin in October 1658.[8]

As a virtuoso of taste, Braccesi brokered the sale to Louis XIV of tapestries that Cardinal Antonio no longer wanted, facilitated the commission of a painting by Pietro da Cortona that Mazarin was keen to acquire, and regularly brokered artworks and objets de vertu on Cardinal Antonio's behalf.[9]

After Mazarin's death in March 1661, however, Fortune turned on Braccesi. Enemies at the French court accused him of having received ten thousand scudi and two damask hangings as graft from Cardinal Francesco Maidalchini. Most unforgivable, they claimed he was revealing secrets to France's enemies. Louis XIV ordered his Roman agent to press for Braccesi's removal from Cardinal Antonio Barberini's household as someone "showing scant loyalty to his master and scant affection for His Majesty's service."[10]

Louis's agent offered a singular analysis of Barberini's reaction to the allegations: "Cardinal Antonio fears Braccesi more than he loves him."[11] When Barberini equivocated, probably out of resentment for his own loss of control, the agent assigned blame to Braccesi, whom he denounced as a proto-Rasputin. "As scatterbrained and malicious as he may be, Braccesi does whatever he wants with His Eminence. And it pains me immensely to see His Majesty's business committed to hands that are as dangerous as Braccesi's."[12] Then, on December 18, 1661, Giovanni Braccesi appeared to confirm the agent's accusations: he was seen entering the Spanish ambassador's residence.[13]

In March 1662 Braccesi composed an apologia, which he hoped might reach the king's ear. With accustomed logic, if not the most forthright language (recalling his prison responses sixteen years earlier), Braccesi first addressed his easiest target. "Everyone at the court of Rome would understand that Cardinal Maidalchini needed to consider how to keep his own head above water, not how to be handing out gifts to others. Far from being able to offer me damask hangings, he had nothing that was not someone else's property." Braccesi had to acknowledge, however, that appearances suggested his culpability in the matter of betraying confidences. "After I was considered French, even though I no longer attended His Holiness's audiences, I received so many positions, so many benefits, and so many pensions that it would be difficult to persuade anyone that I got them for any other reason except for having betrayed secrets."[14]

When the recipient of Braccesi's manifesto launched into a defense of Braccesi before Louis XIV, the king brusquely cut him off.[15] Braccesi turned his back on the perilous domains he had aspired to since he came to Rome as a teenager and requested that Cardinal Antonio relieve him of his official administrative burdens. In early April, Barberini reported to France that Braccesi intended to withdraw to Pesaro.[16] By September 1662 Braccesi appears to have moved out of Palazzo Barberini and had begun to receive an annual stipend of four hundred scudi, which continued until Cardinal Antonio's death. Otherwise his name rarely appears in the household accounts.[17]

In no time Braccesi's words reached Cardinal Maidalchini, whose acid response circulated widely. Maidalchini's view of Barberini's former secretary presumably reflects an opinion shared by other lordlings of the church, even after almost twenty years.

> Signor Braccesi should be warned not to count so readily upon the power of the king's justice by submitting himself to a formal judgment of his actions. I do not know if this time he will successfully find another Carlo Possenti, ready to die on the vigil so he can escape his obligation to die on a gallows. As a prisoner he was tried in Bologna for nothing other than having abducted two nuns from their convent, having abused them for a while, and then having barbarously murdered them. He should therefore recognize his good fortune in escaping from the hangman's hands only through the pertinacity of his partner in crime. If he now goes around asking for justice, he might vex divine goodness once too often, since he deluded her once before.[18]

For another twenty-five years, Giovanni Braccesi took consolation in the virtuous pastimes of semiretirement, most notably his artistic interests. By 1664 his collection, which eventually included works by Raphael, Titian, Bellini, Guercino, and Reni, was impressive enough to merit inclusion in a Roman guidebook.[19]

Although ill health never ceased to plague him, Giovanni Braccesi lived on. After Antonio Barberini's death in 1671, he passed under the protection of Cardinal Francesco, though at half his former stipend, characterized as "charity." On Cardinal Francesco's death in 1679, he was adopted by a new Barberini generation, Cardinal Carlo, with the (largely honorary) title of maggiordomo.[20]

By 1685 the certainty of impending death, if not its exact hour, could not be ignored. Braccesi now lived in Rome, in Rione I Monti, near the Basilica of Santa Maria Maggiore (41.897598° N, 12.49847° E). When his old ailments confined Braccesi to his bed, a cousin, Sforza Frosini, stepped in to supervise his care: Frosini's manservant became Braccesi's nurse. On January 13 Braccesi therefore resolved to put his house in order.[21] He stipulated that his body should be taken privately to his nearby parish church of Santa Prassede (41.896172° N, 12.498695° E), where his funeral should be conducted "without pomp. If my lord, His Eminence, Cardinal Carlo Barberini, whom I have the honor to serve as maggiordomo, would graciously send candles for my funeral, as he does for his ministers and gentlemen, I do not wish my heirs to set out other candles, but only those that it may please His Eminence to provide."

Pride of place among his bequests went to Cardinal Carlo Barberini, to whom Braccesi bequeathed "the porphyry bust with the head of metal of His Majesty, Urban VIII, the head being by the hand of Cavalier Bernini, as a token of the greatest reverence in which I have always held him." Braccesi's considerable fortune went to the solicitous relative who made sure he was well looked after in his final days. In subsequent years this cousin would come to be called Sforza Frosini Braccesi.[22]

Death came for Giovanni Braccesi in the early hours of January 25, 1685. Amid a flurry of masses, as he had stipulated, his corpse was conveyed to Santa Prassede. The church and catafalque were swathed in rented black drapery, with the Barberini coat of arms prominently displayed, and lit by 155 pounds of fine white Venetian wax candles, "by order of His Eminence."[23] Cardinal Carlo Barberini thus sent Giovanni Braccesi on his way to a better life with appropriate solemnity, "as he does for his ministers and gentlemen."[24]

"CONDEMNED TO SUFFER THEIR PAINS OF PURGATORY IN THIS WORLD"

Even if some claim that no one mourns the wicked, Suor Silveria and Suor Laura lingered awhile in public memory, thanks primarily to Antonio Barberini's possible implication in the crime. Even before Cardinal Antonio returned to Rome, the author of *La giusta statera* and its English translation, *The Scarlet Gown*, publicized their misfortune, though in the telling only Carlo Possenti remained a historical figure rather than a cryptic anonymity. Vittorio Siri retold the nuns' tragedy in detail and called them by their nicknames in the next volume of *Il mercurio* (1655). Stendhal probably noticed them there in the 1830s and turned their story into a brief "Delle monache di Bologna," surviving in manuscript materials related to his *Chroniques italiennes*. Stendhal's retelling eventually found its way into print as "Die Nonnen von Bologna," in an early twentieth-century German translation of his collected works.[25]

In Bologna, Suor Silveria and Suor Laura's memory lingered longest. The city's indefatigable chronicler, Antonio Francesco Ghiselli, who was entering his teens when the case played itself out, retold the tale with his own embellishments in the early 1700s. To hear him tell it, their presence could still be felt on via Santo Stefano, opposite the voltone del Baraccano: "It is certain that, right down to the present day, sixty years later, people still look upon that house with horror. And many have claimed to descry certain spirits and ghosts nearby. One might well take that as a sign of the release of those poor souls, who may have been condemned to suffer their pains of purgatory in this world."[26]

Were Silveria and Laura doomed for a certain term to walk the night? Then perhaps in the quietest hour, when buses no longer thunder along the narrow street, one might still glimpse something more than fantasy beneath the arcades (fig. 28; 44.4861° N, 11.3543° E). It could as likely be just a mote to trouble the mind's eye, however, for after hundreds of pages of this story, many questions remain unanswered.

Why did Suor Silveria, despite misgivings and ambivalence, let Possenti hector her into misadventures that spiraled fatally out of control? Did the free-spirited La Rossa take fantasy too far in her parlatorio dalliance with the callow Captain Donato, creating an unlooked-for problem that only a callous older brother could solve? Exactly how did Colonel Alessandro Guarnieri figure in the scheme? Did the lure of La Rossa herself as well as her possessions perhaps draw him into the conspiracy? If Count Alessandro Maria Pepoli

FIGURE 28. Bologna, via Santo Stefano. Houses opposite the voltone del Baraccano, where La Generona and La Rossa's bodies were discovered in June 1645.

claimed the nuns were dead by late April 1644, how could La Rossa have been standing at a window near the voltone dei Caccianemici in mid-May? Was the Roman tribunal right to exclude Possenti from the charge of murder? Did the violent young priest take to his bed shortly after the crime because he was literally sickened by the deed? What of Possenti's defensive claims: Did those he wronged collude to ensure that he received his just deserts? Did Giovanni Braccesi's eloquence and frankness disguise the truth in precise, logical arguments, which often skirted the accusations? (After all, his defense against French charges in 1662 betrayed similar strategies.) How correct was Innocent X about Cardinal Antonio's shielding his miscreant gentlemen in 1644? He had done so in the past, and this affair and its victims were of scant importance, after all.

FIGURE 29. Bologna, the church of SS. Filippo e Giacomo delle Convertite as it looks today.

The convent of SS. Filippo e Giacomo delle Convertite remained an asylum for former women of the world long after Silveria and Laura were forgotten. After the convent closed its doors in 1810, the church reopened to a more respectable congregation as Santa Maria del Buon Pastore. Quite confusingly, the chapel of the suppressed Capuchin convent down the block became the renamed parish church of SS. Filippo e Giacomo.

After Allied bombing leveled most of the neighborhood in 1943, the Convertite's old church was miraculously still standing. This curious throwback survives today, hedged in on all sides by stark mid-twentieth-century housing blocks (fig. 29; 44.500384° N, 11.33444° E). When the Roman Catholic parish eventually closed, the church passed to Bologna's Seventh-Day Adventists. After they moved out too, fortune smiled on the old church: it has been attractively rehabilitated, with a stark, modern interior within its restored eighteenth-century exterior, as a venue for weddings, art exhibitions, and similar events.

Had La Generona and La Rossa, once rehabilitated, piously attended only to their prayers in this old church, many life stories—even those of a great man or two—might have gone somewhat differently. In the familiar words not of a blonde bombshell but of a distinguished Harvard professor, "Well-behaved women seldom make history."[27] Perhaps by retelling Silveria and Laura's story, we can make a place for them in a history that was also their history.

Abbreviations

AAB Archivio Generale Arcivescovile, Bologna

ASB Archivio di Stato, Bologna

ASB, ABR Archivio di Stato, Bologna, Ambasciata Bolognese a Roma

ASB, ABR, Lettere Archivio di Stato, Bologna, Ambasciata Bolognese a Roma, Lettere del senato all'oratore

ASB, ArchMGPep Archivio di Stato, Bologna, Archivio Marchese Giuseppe Pepoli

ASB, ArchPep Archivio di Stato, Bologna, Archivio Pepoli

ASCR1244 Archivio Storico Capitolino, Rome, MS 1244 (cred. XIV, tomo 95)

ASF Archivio di Stato, Florence

ASF, MdP3373 Archivio di Stato, Florence, Mediceo del Principato MS 3373

ASM, AIR Archivio di Stato, Modena, Ambasciatori d'Italia, Roma, busta 243

ASR Archivio di Stato, Rome

ASV Archivio Segreto Vaticano

ASV, SS Archivio Segreto Vaticano, Segr. Stato

ASV, VR Archivio Segreto Vaticano, Sacra Congregazione dei Vescovi e Regolari

ASVe Archivio di Stato, Venice

BAV Biblioteca Apostolica Vaticano

BCB Biblioteca Comunale dell'Archiginnasio, Bologna

BUB Biblioteca Universitaria, Bologna

FazUrb Claudio Costantini, *Fazione Urbana: Sbandamento e ricomposizione di una grande clientela a metà seicento*. Quaderni.net editoria online. http://www.quaderni.net/WebFazione/000indexFazione.htm

Ghiselli BUB, MS 770, 92 vols. (plus volume number)

Gigli1 Giacinto Gigli, *Diario di Roma,* ed. Manlio Barberito, vol. 1 (Rome: Editore Colombo, 1994).

Gigli2 Giacinto Gigli, *Diario di Roma,* ed. Manlio Barberito, vol. 2 (Rome: Editore Colombo, 1994).

HRC Harry Ransom Center, University of Texas, Austin, Ranuzzi Family Papers

Manifesto1 ASF, Carte Strozziane, prim. ser., MS 239, fols. 27–34

Manifesto2 BAV, MS Vat. Lat. 12184, fols. 275–77

Manifesto3 HRC, MS Ph12884, fols. 332–39v

MdAER Ministère des Affaires Étrangères (Rome), Paris

Processo ASR, Tribunale Criminale del Governatore, Processi, vol. 393bis

Siri4 Vittorio Siri, *Il mercurio overo historia de' correnti tempi,* vol. 4, pt. 2 (Casale: Christoforo della Casa, 1644).

Siri5 Vittorio Siri, *Del mercurio, overo historia de' correnti tempi,* vol. 5, pt. 1 (Casale: Giorgio del Monte, 1655).

£ Italian lire (1 scudo = approximately £5 in seventeenth-century Bologna)

Notes

— INTRODUCTION —

1. BCB, MS B82, 37.

2. http://www.quaderni.net/WebFazione/000indexFazione.htm.

3. FazUrb, 2e, n11. An additional discussion of the fugitive convertite appears in Ermete Rossi, "La fuga del cardinale Antonio Barberini," *Archivio della Regia Deputazione Romana di Storia Patria* 59 (1936): 303–27.

4. See Irene Fosi's extremely useful *Papal Justice: Subjects and Courts in the Papal State, 1500–1750* (Washington, DC: Catholic University of America Press, 2011), esp. 61–66. Giancarlo Angelozzi and Cesarina Casanova, *La giustizia criminale in una città di antico regime: Il tribunale del Torrone di Bologna (secc. xvi–xvii)* (Bologna: CLUEB, 2009), 480–89, describes standardizing of testimony and the frequent omission of interrogations from Bolognese trial records.

5. Mario Infelise, "Roman *Avvisi*: Information and Politics in the Seventeenth Century," in *Court and Politics in Papal Rome, 1492–1700*, ed. Gianvittorio Signorotto and Maria Antonietta Visceglia (Cambridge: Cambridge University Press, 2002), 212–28; Valeria Sestieri Lee, "Avvisi a stampa e manoscritti nella Roma del '500," *Quaderni d'Italianistica* 12 (1991): 83–92.

6. Lucia Ferrante's extensive work on prostitution in seventeenth-century Bologna proved essential. See especially her "La sessualità come risorsa: Donne davanti al foro arcivescovile di Bologna (sec. xvii)," *Mélanges de l'École Française de Rome: Moyen-Âge,*

Temps Modernes 99 (1987): 989–1016; see also her "Pro mercede carnali. . . . Il giusto prezzo rivendicato in tribunale," *Memoria: Rivista di Storia delle Donne* 17 (1986): 42–58; and Ferrante, "Honor Regained: Women in the Casa del Soccorso di San Paolo in Sixteenth-Century Bologna," in *Sex and Gender in Historical Perspective*, ed. Edward Muir and Guido Ruggiero (Baltimore: Johns Hopkins University Press, 1990), 46–72. For a general study of convents of former prostitutes, see Sherrill Cohen, *The Evolution of Women's Asylums since 1500: From Refuges for Ex-Prostitutes to Shelters for Battered Women* (New York: Oxford University Press, 1992).

7. A clear explanation of legal principles appears in John H. Langbein, *Torture and the Law of Proof: Europe and England in the Ancien Régime* (Chicago: University of Chicago Press, 1976, 1977, 2006). See also Massimo Meccarelli, "Tortura e processo nei sistemi giuridici dei territori della Chiesa: Il punto di vista dottrinale (secolo xvi)," in *La torture judiciare: Approches historiques et juridiques*, ed. Bernard Durand (Paris: Centre d'Histoire Judiciaire Éditeur, 2002), 1:677–707. Bolognese practices are meticulously described in Angelozzi and Casanova, *Giustizia criminale*, 479–512.

8. See Angelozzi and Casanova, *Giustizia criminale*, 496 and 523. The Congregation of the Holy Office of the Inquisition was generally more successful in requiring notaries to record such nonverbal signs (Anne Schutte, personal communication).

9. For a discussion of this approach to writing history, see Alison Frazier, "'Lightly Fictionalized' Books about the Italian Renaissance," *Not Even Past* (https://notevenpast.org/lightly-fictionalized-books-about-italian-renaissance).

10. On the creation of SS. Filippo e Giacomo, see Gabriella Zarri, "I monasteri femminili a Bologna tra il xiii e il xvii secolo," *Deputazione di Storia Patria per le Province di Romagna: Atti e Memorie*, n.s., 24 (1973): 180–81. For the establishment of such institutions throughout Italy, see Cohen, *The Evolution of Women's Asylums since 1500*, esp. 17–21. On Bologna's Casa del Soccorso and other similar institutions in the city, see Ferrante, "Honor Regained."

11. ASV, VR, posizione 1588, AB (statistics for 1574); ASV, S. Congr. del Concilio, Visite ad Limina, 136A, fol. 55 (statistics for 1614).

12. Domenico Sella, *Italy in the Seventeenth Century* (London: Longman, 1997), 8.

13. Ludwig Pastor, *The History of the Popes*, trans. Ernest Graf (reprint, St. Louis, MO: Herder, 1952), 28:349n4; Henry Coville, *Étude sur Mazarin et ses démêles avec le Pape Innocent X (1644–1648)* (Paris: Champion, 1914), 125–26; Laurie Nussdorfer, *Civic Politics in the Rome of Urban VIII* (Princeton, NJ: Princeton University Press, 1992), 40; Giglii, 209–11.

14. Sheila Barker, "Pasquinades and Propaganda: The Reception of Urban VIII," in *The Papacy since 1500: From Italian Prince to Universal Pastor*, ed. James Corkery and Thomas Worcester (Cambridge: Cambridge University Press, 2010), 71. On "Papa Gabella" see also Nussdorfer, *Civic Politics*, 247, which discusses a song with that title. Frederick Hammond, *Music and Spectacle in Baroque Rome: Barberini Patronage under Urban VIII* (New Haven, CT: Yale University Press, 1994), 24.

15. Realistic estimates of Barberini incomes appear in Hammond, *Music and Spectacle in Baroque Rome*, 4.

16. Examples of Barberini's youthful misbehavior with his friends appear in Pio Pecchiai, *I Barberini* (Rome: Biblioteca d'Arte Editrice, 1959), 191–96.

17. *The Scarlet Gown, or The History of All the Present Cardinals of Rome* (London: Humphrey Moselley, 1653), 89 [= 68].

18. Ibid.; Pastor, *History of the Popes*, 28:43. John Bargrave, *Pope Alexander the Seventh and the College of Cardinals*, ed. James Craigie Robertson (Westminster, UK: Nichols and Sons, for the Camden Society, 1867), 30. On later judgments of Cardinal Antonio's appearance, see chapter 13.

19. On Mazarin's service to the Barberini, see Georges Dethan, *The Young Mazarin* (London: Thames and Hudson, 1977), 47–61.

20. Hammond, *Music and Spectacle*, 8 (size of Antonio's entourage), 36 (fraternal rivalry).

21. This discussion of the war relies on Giovanni Battista Birago, *Mercurio veridico, overo annali universali d'Europa* (Venice: Matteo Leni, 1648), esp. 70–77; Antonio Frizzi, *Memorie per la storia di Ferrara*, vol. 5 (Ferrara: Eredi di Giuseppe Rinaldi, 1809), 94–107; Nussdorfer, *Civic Politics*, 205–27; Pastor, *History of the Popes*, 29: esp. 385–94; Frederick Hammond, *The Ruined Bridge: Studies in Barberini Patronage of Music and Spectacle, 1631–1679* (Sterling Heights, MI: Harmonie Park Press, 2010), esp. 103–4; HRC, MS Ph12811, fols. 222–33 ("Armamento del Duca di Parma contro lo Stato Ecclesiastico per la recuperazione di Castro, 1642"); and the exhaustively detailed three-volume manuscript history by Giovanni Battista Rinalducci, "Dell'una, e l'altra guerra di Castro," HRC, MSS Ph12919.i-iii (in fact, also a history of the papacy from Urban VIII's last years through Alexander VII's reign).

— CHAPTER ONE —

1. Processo, fol. 53 (warmer late March temperatures); ASB, ABR, Lettere, vol. 129, September 24, 1644 (barracks in Piazza Maggiore).

2. Girolamo Brusoni, *Della historia d'Italia . . . libri xxxviii. Riveduta dal medesimo autore, accresciuta, e continuata dall'anno 1625 fino al 1670* (Venice: Storti e Pancirutti, 1671), 399–400. Antonio Frizzi, *Memorie per la storia di Ferrara*, vol. 5 (Ferrara: Eredi di Giuseppe Rinaldi, 1809), 94–107. Although G. B. Rinalducci specifies March 31 as the treaty date (see HRC, MS Ph12919.i, fols. 395v–96v), other sources suggest March 30.

3. Processo, fols. 25–26v (Leonardo's observations and musings about the disruptions), 15 (character of abandoned habits), 672 (slipper ribbons).

4. Ibid., fols. 25v–26v (Leonardo's further observations).

5. Ibid., fols. 20v–21, 29v (Suor Paola Costanza Torosanti's observations; cracks in outer doors), 40 (muddy courtyard corner), 25v–26 (Leonardo Ortolano's comment).

6. Ibid., fols. 26 (Leonardo Ortolano), 14v–15 (Suor Paola Costanza and Prioress Lucina Conti's comments).

7. Ibid., fols. 664 (initials on wimples), 14v–15 (prioress's observations), 12 (prioress's unusual fury).

8. Ibid., fols. 3v–4 (notary's copies of letters; originals are bound into preliminary, unnumbered folios), 15v (prioress's inspection of nun's cell), 3–5 (contents of nuns' cells), 3v (prioress's inspection of letters).

9. Ibid., fols. 73–73v (Lucrezia Regi's response to news), 75v–76v (Giustina Regi's response to news).

10. Ibid., fols. 1v, 277–77v (initial archiepiscopal actions).

11. Ibid., fols. 1v–5v, 277v–79 (investigator's actions before interrogations).

12. AAB, Misc. Vecchia 226 (examples of convertite's misbehavior); ASB, Demaniale 54/6873 (SS. Filippo e Giacomo), "Ricordi à monsigr. vic.o delle monache per le suore convertite" (undated).

13. Processo, fols. 7v–9v (Suor Eufrasia Dioni's testimony).

14. Ibid., fols. 10–11v (Suor Innocenza Pazienza Serra's testimony).

15. Ibid., fols. 12–14 (Suor Clemenza Torti's testimony).

16. Ibid., fols. 14v–17v (Prioress Lucina Conti's testimony).

17. Ibid., fols. 18–19v (Leonora Rossi's testimony).

18. Ibid., fols. 37–39 (Galeazzo's biography), 28–28v (bargello Nicola Bartoli's comment; Galeazzo's escape), 428–28v (Galeazzo as "Monchino").

19. Ibid., fol. 45 (Suor Maria Diana Sturoli).

20. Ibid., fols. 67–69v (Suor Eufrasia), 53v (Suor Paola Emilia).

21. Craig A. Monson, *Nuns Behaving Badly: Tales of Music, Magic, Art, and Arson in the Convents of Italy* (Chicago: University of Chicago Press, 2010), 39.

22. Processo, fol. 768v (Lucrezia and Giustina Regi at the Torrone). Steven Hughes, "Fear and Loathing in Bologna and Rome: The Papal Police in Perspective," *Journal of Social History* 21 (1987): 101 (treatment of female prisoners).

23. Processo, fols. 73–75 (Lucrezia Regi).

24. Ibid., fols. 77–78 (Giustina Regi).

25. ASV, VR, sez. monache, 1644 (gennaio-maggio; luglio-dicembre) and 1645 (gennaio-febraio; aprile-luglio; novembre).

26. Processo, fols. 51 (Colonna), 182 (Colonna's recommendation).

— CHAPTER TWO —

1. On *publica vox et fama*, see Anne Jacobson Schutte, *By Force and Fear: Taking and Breaking Monastic Vows in Early Modern Europe* (Ithaca, NY: Cornell University Press, 2011), 160–62.

2. Processo, fols. 254 (guards at the palazzo), 133v (the reward), 185v, 855v (sighting near Bondeno), 134 (mistaken identity).

3. Ibid., fols. 134, 138v–39v, 180v–81, 187, 1029v–30 (sighting of La Rossa).

4. Ibid., fols. 222–23v, 617–20v (innkeeper's wife's observations), 632v–33v, 640–40v (innkeeper's observations), Siri5, 380, and Ghiselli29, 110 (nuns' possible flight to Venice).

5. Processo, fols. 178v, 321v, 415v (alleged locations of bodies).

6. Ghiselli28, 781 (snowstorm and depth); Processo, fol. 416 (the big freeze, May 9–13); Gigli1, 422 (icy Italian weather).

7. BAV, MS Barb. Lat. 6364, fol. 116v (peace proclamation); ASB, ABR, Lettere, vol. 129 (September 24, 1644).

8. Thomas Coryat, *Coryat's Crudities Hastily Gobbled up in Five Moneths Travels in France, Savoy, Italy . . .* (1611) (New York: Macmillan, 1905), 406.

9. The medieval aphorism is quoted in Graciela S. Daichman, "Misconduct in the Medieval Nunnery: Fact Not Fiction," in *That Gentle Strength: Historical Perspectives on Women in Christianity*, ed. Lynda L. Coon, Katherine J. Haldane, and Elisabeth W. Sommer (Charlottesville, NC: University of Virginia Press, 1990), 98. Pietro Aretino, *Sei giornate: Ragionamento della Nanna e della Antonia (1534)* and *Dialogo nel quale la Nanna insegna a la Pippa (1536)*, ed. Giovanni Aquilecchia (Bari: Laterza, 1969), 139. Guido Ruggiero, *Binding Passions: Tales of Magic, Marriage, and Power at the End of the Renaissance* (New York: Oxford University Press, 1993), esp. 24–26, which figures importantly in this discussion. For an excellent study of prostitution in Rome, see Tessa Storey, *Carnal Commerce in Counter-Reformation Rome* (Cambridge: Cambridge University Press, 2008).

10. Stefano D'Amico, "Shameful Mother: Poverty and Prostitution in Seventeenth-Century Milan," *Journal of Family History* 30 (2005): 109–11.

11. Lucia Ferrante, "La sessualità come risorsa: Donne davanti al foro arcivescovile di Bologna (sec. XVII)," *Mélanges de l'Ecole Française de Rome. Moyen-Âge, Temps Modernes* 99 (1987): 997–99.

12. Storey suggests a Roman prostitute could earn more in two sexual encounters than a woman engaged in "honest" work could earn in a month. See *Carnal Commerce*, 168. AAB, Reg. Batt. 55, fol. 182 (Giustina's baptism, September 25, 1616); Processo, fols. 436–36v (Regi women's alleged prostitution); Lucia Ferrante, "Pro mercede carnali. . . . Il giusto prezzo rivendicato in tribunale," *Memoria: Rivista di Storia delle Donne* 17 (1986): 45; ASB, Uffizio delle Bollette, Campioni delle meretrici, 1627–41, 1643–45.

13. AAB, Reg. Batt. 53, fol. 197 (Gentile's birth ca. November 28, 1614, to Domenico and Lucrezia Regi); Processo, fol. 39 (residence in Borgo delle Tovaglie).

14. Processo, fol. 26 (Borge delle Casse); see also Ghiselli29, 752. On mothers' roles in turning their daughters to prostitution, see Ferrante, "Pro mercede carnali," esp. 46. See also Storey, *Carnal Commerce*, 141–47.

15. Processo, fols. 69, 266 (Bentivoglio patronage), 917 (Giovanni Braccesi).

16. Ibid., fols. 116 (Suor Elena Federici), 415 (Andrea Pallada), 113v, 116, 117v (Gentile's white complexion).

17. Processo, fols. 103v, 105, 213v, 857, 857v (Gentile's scar).

18. Aretino, *Sei giornate*, 351. Sarah McPhee, *Bernini's Beloved: A Portrait of Costanza Piccolomini* (New Haven, CT: Yale University Press, 2012), 44–48 (discussion of the sfregio).

19. AAB, Reg. Batt. 55 (1604), fol. 38 (March 1, 1604, "Cornelia, filia Ludovici Pasini"); Processo, fol. 1046 (Silveria as "figlia del MM Ludovico Pasi").

20. Processo, fols. 78v, 89v, 95v, 100, 106, 108, 117v, 118v, 119v, 214 (Silveria's perfect teeth).

21. Ibid., fol. 184v (Peregrino Tori).

22. Ibid., fols. 165 (Suor Innocenza Pazienza Serra), 986 (Suor Giovanna Valeria Cortelli).

23. Ibid., fols. 3v (Silveria's painting), 36, 862 (Laura's borrowed spinet); Martelli is quoted in Tessa Storey, "Courtesan Culture: Manhood, Honour and Sociability," in *Erotic Cultures of Renaissance Italy*, ed. Sara F. Matthews-Grieco (Burlington, VT: Ashgate, 2010), 257.

24. Processo, fols. 1076v–84 (details of Catterina's parentage).

25. D'Amico, "Shameful Mother," 114–15; Storey, *Carnal Commerce*, 165–67.

26. Processo, fols. 112–112v, 791v–92 (Generoni provides for Suor Silveria Catterina), 57 (Leonora's encouragement to profess), 40v (Suor Paula Costanza Torosanti's sponsorship).

27. Ibid., fols. 143–43v (Silveria's baldness), 214 (pockmarks).

28. Giuseppe Guidicini, *Cose notabili della Città di Bologna* (Bologna: Stabilmento Tipografico Monti, 1869), 2:315–16.

29. ASB, Demaniale 62/6881 (SS. Filippo e Giacomo), "Estrato de li formenti," fol. 18 (dowry amount).

30. ASB, Demaniale 9/6828 (SS. Filippo e Giacomo), vacchetta for 1632–33; Processo, fol. 1046 (Suor Silveria Catterina's profession).

31. Processo, fols. 1082v (Catterina at the Convertite), 46v–47 (convent furnishings sent to San Lorenzo).

32. Ibid., fols. 791v (Generoni's parlatorio visits), 835 (Suor Maria Diana Sturoli); ASB, Demaniale 5/6824 and 6/6825 (SS. Filippo e Giacomo) (apothecaries' stock in trade).

33. ASB, Demaniale, 9/6828 (SS. Filippo e Giacomo), sacristan's logbook (Angela Ginevra's profession year); Processo, fol. 375v (Gonzino's assassination). On Gonzoni and Gnocchi's intended flight plan, see Processo, fols. 33v, 41v–42, 46.

34. Processo, fol. 1046 (Gentile Regi's profession); ASB Demaniale 9/6828 (SS. Filippo e Giacomo), sacristan's logbook; Processo, fols. 764v–65 (Laura's furniture).

35. Processo, fol. 103 (Suor Silveria as Suor Laura's maestra); ASB, Demaniale 9/6828 (SS. Filippo e Giacomo), sacristan's logbook.

36. Processo, fols. 14 (Suor Clemenza Torti), 71 (Suor Jacopa Rossi).

37. "Insaldan Manicini, e Collari / A' Prelati, à Preti, e à Secolari." The watercolors and rhymes appear in BCB MS B 3574 and are reproduced in Mario Fanti, *Abiti e lavori delle monache di Bologna* (Bologna: Tamari Editori, 1972).

38. Processo, fols. 169 (Suor Clara Maria Ansalori), 170v (Suor Violante Merigli).

39. Ibid., fols. 24v (Suor Steffana Peregrina Sforza), 12v–13 (Suor Clemenza Torti), 112v (Bernardino Generoni).

40. Ibid., fols. 654, 667v, 770v (running to parlatorio), 49 (Eufrasia speaks only to women).

41. Ibid., fol. 40v (Suor Paola Costanza Torosanti).

42. Ibid., fols. 996–97 (pay for shirts; other nuns' lacemaking), 508v (selling price for shirts), 999v–1002v (confusion about creators of needlework).

43. Ibid., fols. 670v (Silveria's doubloons), 647v–49, 657, 669v–70v, 827 (silver, jewelry, and linens), 792 (Bernardino Generoni), 670v (Suor Paola Costanza Torosanti).

44. Ibid., fols. 648v (Eufrasia's comment), 657, 670v–71 (Laura's other possessions).

45. Ibid., fols. 664v–65 (Suor Lucina Conti).

46. Ibid., fols. 44v–45, 833–34 (Suor Maria Diana Sturoli's comments and description of the fugitive nuns' behavior outside the parlatorio).

— CHAPTER THREE —

1. Niccolò Machiavelli, *Il Principe*, ed. Ettore Janni (Milan: Rizzoli, 1950), 55.

2. Pietro Aretino, *Sei giornate: Ragionamento della Nanna e della Antonia* (1534) and *Dialogo nel quale la Nanna insegna a la Pippa* (1536), ed. Giovanni Aquilecchia (Bari: Laterza, 1969), 139.

3. Processo, fol. 932v (Guarnieri's village); Thomas Hoby, *The Book of the Courtier*, http://extra.shu.ac.uk/emls/iemls/resour/mirrors/rbearold/courtier/courtier2.html.

4. Gigli, 361 (burning of Barberini abbeys), 370 (sack of Pieve); G. B. Rinalducci claims that Pieve was spared and Terra di Panicale was sacked—see HRC, MS Ph12919.i, fols. 177v, 193v–94 (Farnese's surprising retreat); Processo, fol. 576v (the Guarnieri's disgust at Farnese); see also HRC, MS Ph12811, fols. 222–33.

5. Processo, fols. 576v–79 (Guarnieri's move from Farnese to Barberini service; previous incarceration for murder).

6. Ibid., fols. 578–78v (Captain Donato's various residences).

7. Ibid., fols. 578v–79v (first Guarnieri residence), 591–92v (Guarnieri social circle and servants), 689v (Alessandro's acquaintanceship with Francesco Pepoli), 831, 961 (second Guarnieri residence).

8. Ibid., fols. 674v (Alessandro's appearance), 612v–13 (two letters a week, one in every post), 468–68v (Alessandro's fits of madness), 961v (infrequent beard trims); Emanuela and Maria Teresa Gozzini, personal communication (Guarnieri heavy builds).

9. Processo, fol. 762 (Donato Guarnieri).

10. Ibid., fols. 746v, 824 (Donato Guarnieri), 590v–91 (Donato's taste in prostitutes). The Turchetta is a dark-colored pigeon with red-ringed eyes and red feet; see Prideux John Selby, *Pigeons*, vol. 9 of *The Naturalist's Library* (Edinburgh: W. H. Lizars, n.d.), 164.

11. Processo, fols. 131v, 460, 674v, 688v, 837, 961 (Donato's appearance).

12. Ibid., fols. 459 (Donato's style alla franzese), 608v, 693–94 (Donato's wardrobe).

13. Ibid., fols. 596 (Donato's introduction to Convertite), 19, 593v, 771 (Guarnieri laundry), 1043–44v (fancy shirts), 35v–36, 862 (loaned spinet), 657–57v, 664 (Alessandro Guarnieri's multiple convent visits).

14. Ibid., fol. 45 (Suor Maria Diana Sturoli).

15. Ibid., fols. 19, 25, 45 (transmission of letters).

16. Ibid., fols. 13v, 20, 43, 764v (furniture to Casa Guarnieri), 829v (Suor Antonia Romea Stagnoli).

17. Hope B. Werness, *The Continuum Encyclopedia of Animal Symbolism in Art* (New York: Continuum International, 2004), 318.

18. Processo, fol. 839v (gifts of partridges and cows).

19. Ibid., fols. 773–73v (Suor Maria Giuliana Cochi), 667v (Suor Paola Costanza Torosanti).

20. Ibid., fols. 837v–38v (Suor Bianca Ignota).

21. Ibid., fols. 664v–65 (Suor Lucina Conti).

22. On convent romance after the Council of Trent, see Mary Laven, *Virgins of Venice: Broken Vows and Cloistered Lives in the Renaissance Convent* (New York: Viking, 2003), 167–85.

23. Processo, fols. 11v, 13, 647 (Donato's absence since Palm Sunday), 653 (Suor Laura confirms Donato's absence), 1053v–54 (observations by the staff at the Inn of the Two Keys).

24. Ibid., fols. 580v (Guarnieri ordered to Ferrara), 731v (Machiavelli's position at Fortezza Lagoscuro). On events of the war in 1643–44, see Antonio Frizzi, *Memorie per la storia di Ferrara raccolte da Antonio Frizzi*, vol. 5 (Ferrara: Eredi di Giuseppe Rinaldi, 1809), 94–107, and Girolamo Brusoni, *Della historia d'Italia . . . libri xxxviii: Riveduta dal medesimo autore, accresciuta, e continuata dall'anno 1625. Fino al 1670* (Venice: Heredi Francesco Storti, e Giovanni Maria Pancirutti, 1671), 399–400. Sergeant Major Machiavelli was the brother of Cardinal Francesco Maria Machiavelli, bishop of Ferrara, and cousin of Cardinal Antonio Barberini.

25. Processo, fols. 582 (rooming arrangements in Ferrara), 949v (gambling at the palazzo).

26. Antonio Frizzi, *Memorie per la storia di Ferrara* 5:105 (Venetians cross Po to assault Copparo).

27. AAB, Reg. Batt. 73 (1622), fol. 61 (Ranuzzi's birth to an ignoble mother). A useful discussion of *virtù* and its seventeenth-century interpretations appears in Andrew Dell'Antonio, *Listening as Spiritual Practice in Early Modern Italy* (Berkeley: University of California Press, 2011), esp. 95–98.

28. Processo, fols. 456–58v, 465–65v, 582v, 804v–7, 931v–32 (excursion to Copparo).

29. Ibid., fols. 685v–86 (picnic on horseback).

30. Ibid., fols. 685–85v (Guarnieri's dinner, treatment of his men, and shared bed), 931–31v (soldiers' warming feet; overcast skies). For an excellent discussion of male sociability across social classes, including their sexual implications, see Guido Ruggiero, "Mean Streets, Familiar Streets, or The Fat Woodcarver and the Masculine Spaces of Renaissance Florence," in *Renaissance Florence: A Social History*, ed. Roger J. Crum and John T. Paleotti (Cambridge: Cambridge University Press, 2006), 295–310.

31. Processo, fols. 703v–4, 743, 852v–53 (Guarnieri's Ferrara activities).

32. Ibid., fols. 589–90v (Donato's return to Ravenna), 1031v (early June departure).

33. Giovanni Della Casa, *Galatea, or A Treatise on Politeness and Delicacy of Manners Addressed to Young Noblemen* (London: J. Dodsley, 1774), 72.

34. Processo, fol. 77v (Giustina Regi); ASF, MdP3373, fol. 542 (Possenti's Accademia membership).

35. George McGill Vogt, "Gleanings for the History of a Sentiment: Generositas Virtus, Non Sanguis," *Journal of English and Germanic Philology* 24 (1925): 102–24.

36. AAB, Reg. Batt. 64 (1613), fol. 59 (March 29, 1613); Processo, fols. 286v, 462v (Lorenzo Possenti's property); ASB, Demaniale 45/45 (Santa Maria Maggiore), 39; ASB, Demaniale, 46/46 (Santa Maria Maggiore), unnumbered folio (Giovanni Battista Possenti at Santa Maria Maggiore).

37. Processo, fols. 462v–64 (Possenti's positions and earnings), 380 (Lorenzo Possenti's confinement to bed); ASB, Demaniale 45/45 (Santa Maria Maggiore), 40 (Possenti's canonry).

38. Processo, fols. 285v (Possenti's ordination ca. 1637), 869 (neglecting to say daily mass); Ghiselli29, 107 (reading *Pastor fido*).

39. Processo, fols. 228v (Possenti at bookstore), 236 (Carlo Manolesi).

40. Ghiselli29, 106 (utility of poetry to Possenti's advancement). *L'architettura: Panegirico di Carlo Possenti* (Bologna: Ferroni, 1633). See "Accademia dei Confusi" in Database of Italian Academies, http://www.bl.uk/catalogues/ItalianAcademies. *Il sogno d'Armindo solitario idillo per lo ratto d'Helena di Guido* (Bologna: Monti, 1633), A2.

41. On *I furori di Venere*, see Claudia Di Luca, "Tra 'sperimentazione' e 'professionismo' teatrale: Pio Enea II Obizzi e lo spettacolo nel Seicento," *Teatro e Storia* 6 (1991): 272–75; see also BCB, MS A2175, fol. 213.

42. Carlo Possenti, *All'eccellentiss. Sig. Cornelio Malvasia invitandolo dalle tenerezze della villa del Sasso alle solite imprese marziale*. My thanks to Riccardo James Vargiu for securing a copy of the print for me. On Malvasia, see Giuseppe Guidicini, *I riformatori dello stato di libertà della città di Bologna dal 1394 al 1797* (Bologna: Regia Tipografia, 1876), 92–94.

43. Processo, fols. 285–85v (Possenti enters military service).

44. BUB, MS 1706, fols. 100–101v (Possenti's unpublished poem). Possenti's name is not otherwise connected with the Accademia della Notte. See "Accademia della Notte" in Database of Italian Academies http://www.bl.uk/catalogues/ItalianAcademies. An exhaustive study of Italian early modern erotic double meanings appears in Jean Toscan, *Le carnaval du langage: Le lexique érotique des poètes de l'équivoque de Burchiello à Marino (xve–xviie siècles)* (Lille: Presses Universitaires de Lille, 1981).

45. Processo, fol. 435v (Possenti visits San Lorenzo with Malvasia).

46. Baldassare Castiglione, *Book of the Courtier*, trans. George Bull (London: Penguin, 2004), 56.

47. Processo, fols. 461, 496, 525v, 637v, 772, 996v (Possenti's wardrobe).

48. Ibid., fols. 530–31 (Braccesi's comments on Possenti's self-promotion), 814 (Carlo Possenti).

49. Ibid., fol. 239 (Bartolomea Galliani quoting Possenti).

50. Ibid., fols. 58v (Possenti declares his love at the grates), 231 (Possenti commissions Suor Silveria's red outfit).

51. ASB, Demaniale 88/88 bis (Santa Maria Maggiore), 16 (Possenti in prison); Processo, fols. 813, 1070 (attempted assassination of dall'Aglio and sentence).

52. Processo, fols. 473v, 634v, 1071 (Possenti's second banishment to Ferrara).

53. Ibid., fols. 227–28v (Mariani's description of his wounding), 369 (Mariani quotation), 678v–79v (tavern owner's description). On the dangerous complexities of cross-class sociability, see Ruggiero, "Mean Streets, Familiar Streets."

54. Ghiselli29, 109.

55. Processo, fols. 297v (Braccesi), 464 (Malvasia's discussion of rumors with Cardinal Antonio), 951 (Malvasia drops Possenti).

56. Ibid., fols. 286 (Possenti's version), 295v (Braccesi's version).

57. Ibid., fols. 517–18v (Possenti's trip to Rome at Braccesi's expense and his time there), 524–24v (need to leave Braccesi's servant behind), 497, 518v, 520v–21, 525 (Possenti at Ranuzzi's).

58. Ibid., fols. 282v (Possenti's departure for Segni), 286v (Possenti's description of his appointment), 287 (Possenti).

— CHAPTER FOUR —

1. Processo, fols. 816–20 (Francesco Maria dall'Aglio's attempted assassination and move to Florence), 1069 (location of property opposite the "voltone"), 83, 96v–97 (Isabella Machiavelli in Florence).

2. Ibid., fols. 83–83v, 810–10v (Isabella on housebreaking), 201 (Tedesco's age).

3. Ibid., fols. 83, 229v, 808v–11v (the state of the Machiavelli house and the discoveries there), 125v and 811 (Dionisio's furniture removal).

4. Ibid., fol. 82v (Giovanni Tedesco's investigation of the wine cellar and his testimony).

5. Steven Hughes, "Fear and Loathing in Bologna and Rome: The Papal Police in Perspective," *Journal of Social History* 21 (1987): 102 (sbirri's crowd control methods); Processo, fol. 95 (the neighbor Giovanni Battista Burrati on a helpless woman alone).

6. Ibid., fol. 83 (the assistant auditor).

7. Ibid., fol. 94 (the workman's remark).

8. Ibid., fols. 84v–100v (several references to the cadaver's red hair), 90, 91v, 100v (comments on nether red hair).

9. Ibid., fols. 86, 87v, 89–89v, 90v–91v, 93v, 95v, 98, 100 (nuns' measurements).

10. Ibid., fols. 89 (barber's comment), 88v and 90v (his colleagues' agreement).

11. Hughes, "Fear and Loathing," 110n5 (policemen's meager earnings).

12. Processo, fol. 78 (Francesco Navelli, the bargello).

13. Ibid., fols. 78–80 (archiepiscopal preliminary, somewhat muddled investigation; the initial announcement is dated June 21; the following description of the auditor's

visit is dated June 22; but the subsequent pair of depositions by the witnesses are dated June 21), 125v (another witness's claim to have seen a single cord).

14. Ibid., fols. 101–1v (Capitano Muzio, bargello of the Torrone).

15. Ibid., fols. 102–3v (Lucrezia Regi).

16. Ibid., fols. 104–5v (Giustina Regi).

17. Ibid., fols. 107 and 108 (Lucrezia Regi and Giustina Regi).

18. Ibid., fols. 107 and 108 (Lucrezia Regi and Giustina Regi).

19. Ibid., fol. 110 (Giovanni Battista Steffani, barber surgeon).

20. Ibid., fols. 108v–9 (Giustina Regi), 107v (Lucrezia's final remark).

21. Ibid., fol. 112v (Bernardino Generoni).

22. Ibid., fols. 269 (Leonora's death), 140 (Galeazzo's murder).

23. Ibid., fols. 115–20 (convent servants' identification of bodies).

24. Ibid., fols. 125, 915v (the city's visiting the corpses), 659v, 677 (transfer of bodies to the back garden).

25. Ghiselli29, 112 (Ghiselli on plaster).

26. Processo, fol. 811v (Isabella Machiavelli).

— CHAPTER FIVE —

1. BAV, MS Urb. Lat. 1109, fols. 132, 198v; ASB, ABR, Lettere, vol. 131, July 1, 1645 (Albergati-Ludovisi's trip to Bologna).

2. ASV, SS, Bologna 16, fols. 94–94v (Lelio Falconieri)

3. Processo, fols. 121–25 (Taddea Bertolotti's testimony).

4. ASV, SS, Bologna 188, fol. 33v (Camillo Pamphili).

5. Ibid., Bologna, 188, fol. 34 (Camillo Pamphili).

6. Processo, fols. 126–26v (Giulia Santi).

7. Athos Vianelli, *Le strade e i portici di Bologna* (Rome: Newton Compton, 1982), 236.

8. Processo, fols. 127–32 (Giulia Santi's testimony).

9. ASV, SS, Cardinali 14, fols. 29–29v (Albergati-Ludovisi).

10. Pompeo Dolfi, *Cronologia delle famiglie nobili di Bologna* (Bologna: Giovanni Battista Ferroni, 1670; repr., Bologna: Forni, n.d.), 602. ASB, MS B3298, 411 (infected line).

11. Baldassare Castiglione, *The Book of the Courtier*, trans. George Bull (London: Penguin, 2004), 137.

12. Processo, fols. 574–74v (Federico Panzacchi).

13. Ibid., fol. 249 (Dionisio Tomassini).

14. AAB, Reg. Batt 68, fol. 72 (Count Alessandro Maria's birth, April 3, 1617); BCB, MS B3298, 402 (relatives' deaths).

15. ASB, ArchMGPep, ser. VII/C, vol. 22 (Mazzi Volanti), "Sommario chiamato nelle ragioni del d. Conte" (Domenica as "più bella").

16. Ibid. (Taddea Bertolotti).

17. Processo, fasc. re: Pepoli scandal, fols. 14 (Angelo Campana), 22 (Alessandro Montanaro/Manzolini), 25v (Giulia Santi).

18. ASB, ArchMGPep, ser. VII/A, Instrumenti, 36, no. 1, 4 (Taddea Bertolotti); ibid., 35, no. 23 (Pepoli's will).

19. ASB, ArchPep, ser. III, busta 68, fasc. 6 (remarks attributed to Cesare).

20. BCB, MS B82, 35 and 42; Ghiselli28, 845–46; Ghiselli29, 333–55 (murder of Alessandro Maria Pepoli); BCB, Archivio Pepoli, busta 80, fasc. 11 and ASB, ArchPep, ser. I/B, busta 57, fasc. 10 (Dionisio Tomassini's hiding place). Giancarlo Angelozzi and Cesarina Casanova, *La giustizia criminale in una città di antico regime: Il tribunale del Torrone di Bologna (secc. xvi–xvii)* (Bologna: CLUEB, 2009), 265, quoting ASB, ABR, Lettere, vol. 129, October 1, 1644.

21. Processo, fol. 566 (Dionisio Tomassini's flight); ASB, Notarili, Pietro Bartolotti Instrumenti, 1640–46, II, fol. 92 (Diana as executor); ASB, ArchMGPep, ser. VII/A Instrumenti, no. 75 (registro), fols. 281v–82v (details of the case); ASB, ArchMGPep, ser. VII/A Instrumenti, vol. 36, nos. 1 and 2; BCB, ArchPep, busta 79, fasc. 23 (sentence against Roderico Pepoli).

22. Processo, fols. 143v (Diana Tomassini's arrest), 632 (her confinement "sù in Cima alla Torre"). On confinement of prostitutes in the Torre Prendiparte, see Lucia Ferrante, "La sessualità come risorsa: Donne davanti al foro arcivescovile di Bologna (sec. xvii)," *Mélanges de l'École Française de Rome. Moyen-Âge, Temps Modernes* 99 (1987): 997.

23. Processo, fols. 144–47 (Diana Tomassini's testimony).

24. Ibid., fol. 632 (Diana's explanation of her initial bluff).

25. Ibid., fols. 147–48, 625 (Diana Tomassini's testimony); Mario Fanti, *Le vie di Bologna saggio di toponomastica storica e di storia della toponomastica urbana*, 2nd ed. (Bologna: Istituto per la Storia di Bologna, 2000), 2:699 (identification of side street as via Sampieri).

26. Processo, fols. 623v and 148 (Diana Tomassini).

27. Ibid., fols. 148, 484, 623v–24v (Diana Tomassini).

28. Ibid, fols. 149–49v, 483 (Diana Tomassini).

29. Ibid., fols. 146–48v, 152–52v (Diana Tomassini's testimony).

30. Ibid., fol. 629 (Diana Tomassini).

31. Ibid., fols. 148v–49, 485v–86 (Diana Tomassini's testimony).

32. Ibid., fols. 628–28v.

33. Ibid., fols. 149v–50v, 631 (Diana Tomassini's testimony).

— CHAPTER SIX —

1. Processo, fol. 132v.

2. Ibid., fols. 133–35v (Nicola Bartoli, bargello).

3. ASV, SS, Cardinali 14, fols. 29–29v (Albergati-Ludovisi).

4. Processo, fols. 137v–39v (Maria Barbini).

5. Ibid., fols. 140v–43 (Suor Giovanna Valeria Cortelli and Suor Lucina Conti).

6. Ibid., fols. 163 (Suor Lodovica Bartolasia), 164 (Suor Alessandra Mattea Cerni), 164v–65 (Suor Isabetta Serafina Alberti), 167v (Suor Paola Lorenza Cantari).

7. Ibid., fol. 293 (Braccesi's arrest); Rome, Biblioteca Cassanatense MS 1832, fol. 164v (three hundred invaders); MdAER, 109 CP/87, fols. 205 (one hundred sbirri and twenty Corsicans), 153v (twenty-five Corsicans), 203, 205; Rafaelle Della Torre, *Fuga del Cardinale Antonio male interpretata e peggio caluniata* (Perugia [in fact, France], 1646), 97–98 (delay in requesting Barberini's permission, repeatedly confirmed in manuscript sources cited above; Braccesi's arrest in room adjoining the cardinal's bedchamber).

8. ASVe, DAS, Roma 122, fols. 414, 415–15v. My thanks to Anne Schutte for tracking down Angelo Contarini's letters and transmitting them to me.

9. ASF, MdP3373, fol. 572.

10. Processo, fols. 305–7v (Braccesi's early life and education). Braccesi family's listing among the nobility appears in http://it.wikipedia.org/wiki/Storia_di_Pisa.

11. Andrew Dell'Antonio coins the term "virtuoso of taste" in *Listening as Spiritual Practice in Early Modern Italy* (Berkeley: University of California Press, 2011), 39.

12. Processo, fol. 305v; Luigi Serafini, *Vetralla antica cognominata il foro di Cassio* (Viterbo: Mariano Diotallevi, 1648), 77–78 (Tondi's bureaucratic wanderings and Vatican connections).

13. *La giusta statera de Porporati, dove s'intende la vita la nascita, adherenza di ciascun cardinale hoggi vivente* (Geneva, 1650), 143.

14. Processo, fols. 179 (Giovanni Antonio Pera), 207 (Giovanni Torti), 176v (Giovanni Antonio Pera).

15. Ibid., fols. 176v (Giovanni Antonio Pera), 273v (Francesco Vincenzo Toffanelli).

16. Ibid., fols. 308–8v (Giovanni Braccesi); Carlo Cesare Malvasia, *Felsina pittrice: Vite de' pittori bolognesi*, ed. Giampietro Zanotti, vol. 2 (Bologna: Guidi all'Ancora, 1841), 266 (Braccesi's Guercino).

17. Processo, fols. 207v (Giovanni Torti), 176v (Giovanni Antonio Pera).

18. Ibid., fol. 467v (Braccesi's send-off).

19. ASR, CRM, Teatini, Sant'Andrea della Valle, busta 2162/161, int. 235, 10; ibid., int. 234, 65 (the refurbishing of Braccesi's rooms).

20. BAV, Archivio Barberini, Comp. 268, "3122" (description of the bed "nella stanza contigua parimente [alla stanza dove dorme S. Emza]"); Processo, fols. 913–14, 910v, 296v, 300–302 (Giovanni Braccesi).

21. Processo, fols. 151v (Diana Tomassini), 152v–54 (Catterina Monti).

22. Ibid., fols. 177v–78v (Giovanni Antonio Pera), 184 (Peregrino Turi), 219v–20 (Tomaso Bentuoli).

23. ASVe, DAS, Roma 122, fol. 436.

24. Ibid., fols. 416–16v; ASCR1244, fol. 122v.

25. Processo, fols. 180–82v (Bernardino Cattania).

26. Ibid., fols. 187–88 (Alfonso Arnaldi).

27. Ibid., fols. 326–32 (Domenica Barbini).

28. Ibid., fols. 350–50v.

29. Ibid., fol. 355 (Dorotea Gandolfi).

30. On *favor fidei*, see Kenneth Stow, "The Cruel Father: From Miracle to Murder," in

Studies in Medieval Intellectual and Social History: Festschrift in Honor of Robert Chazan, ed. David Engel, Lawrence H. Schiffman, and Elliot R. Wolfson (Leiden: Brill, 2012), esp. 264–73; and (especially) Marina Caffiero, *Forced Baptisms: Histories of Jews, Christians, and Converts in Papal Rome*, trans. Lydia G. Cochrane (Berkeley: University of California Press, 2012).

— CHAPTER SEVEN —

1. Processo, fols. 149–49v (Diana Tomassini).

2. ASV, SS, Cardinali 14, fol. 33 (Albergati-Ludovisi); BUB, MS 572, no. 1 (edict of August 4, 1645).

3. Processo, fols. 208v–10v (Margarita Mingati).

4. Ibid., fols. 213v–17 (Catterina Milani).

5. Ibid., fols. 217v–18 (Bartolomea Galliani and Catterina Milani).

6. Ibid., fols. 217v–18v.

7. Ibid., fols. 237v–41, 569v–71 (Bartolomea Galliani).

8. ASB, Archivio Ranuzzi, Instrumenti, XIX, no. 21 (layout of Ranuzzi's apartments); Processo, fols. 232–33 (raid on Palazzo Ranuzzi).

9. This is the location of Bologna's oldest bookshop, Libreria F. Veronese, dating from the nineteenth century (recently closed), near the voltone dei Caccianemici. Manolesi's shop would have been nearby.

10. Processo, fols. 234v–36v (Carlo Manolesi).

11. Ibid., fols. 159–60 (anonymous letter dated July 20, 1645).

12. ASV, SS, Cardinali 14, fols. 33, 43 (Albergati-Ludovisi). "Paolo da Zampone famoso Bargello di Ferrara" reappears in HRC, MSS Ph12892, fol. 182.

13. Processo, fols. 250v–51v (search of Casa Possenti and Casa Pallada).

14. Ibid., fols. 252 (Andrea Pallada), 256v (Doralice Pallada).

15. Ibid., fols. 559v–60v (Possenti's good deed), 546v (Carlino's death at Spoleto).

16. Ibid., fol. 252v (Andrea Pallada).

17. Ibid., fols. 560v (Catterina Milani), 257 (Doralice Pallada).

18. Ibid., fols. 260v, 394 (Doralice Pallada).

19. Ibid., fols. 257–57v (Doralice Pallada), 248v (nuns wearing swords).

20. Ibid., fol. 396 (Doralice Pallada, quoting Silveria).

21. Ibid., fols. 257v (Doralice Pallada), 253v, 421 (Andrea Pallada).

22. Ibid., fols. 399v–401v (Doralice Pallada's description), 254, 423 (Andrea Pallada's descriptions).

23. Ibid., fols. 258–58v, 396 (Doralice Pallada).

24. Ibid., fols. 421v–22 (Andrea Pallada).

25. Ibid., fols. 416–16v (Andrea Pallada), 420–20v (Doralice Pallada), 562 (Catterina Milani).

26. Ibid., fols. 443v–44.

27. Ibid., fols. 245–45v (Federico Panzacchi).

28. Ibid., fols. 254v–55 (Andrea Pallada quoting Possenti).

29. Ibid., fols. 424–24v (Andrea Pallada), 399 (Doralice Pallada), 445v–46.

30. Ibid., fols. 405v (Doralice Pallada), 417–17v (Andrea Pallada), 561 (Catterina Milani's gifts), 445, 975–76 (gifts), 984v (coral rosary).

31. Ibid., fols. 477–78 (Andrea Pallada), 396v–397, 444v, 947v–48 (Doralice Pallada), 246v (Doralice's epithet).

32. Ibid., fols. 255–55v (Andrea Pallada), 259 (Doralice Pallada).

33. Ibid., fols. 259v–60 (Doralice Pallada).

34. Ibid., fols. 255–55v, 477v (Andrea Pallada), 259 (Doralice Pallada).

35. Ibid., 975v–76v (Silveria's leavings), 417v–418 (prayerbook), 561 (pocket watch).

36. Ibid., fols. 410v–12v (Andrea Pallada).

37. Ibid., fol. 948 (Bartolomea's meager snack), 948v (Bartolomea's visits).

38. Ibid., fols. 418 (Andrea Pallada), 406 (Doralice Pallada), 247.

39. Ibid., fols. 413–14 (nuns' hideouts).

40. Ibid., fols. 415–16 (Andrea Pallada).

— CHAPTER EIGHT —

1. Processo, fols. 372v (letter's cover), 281–81v (letter signed C. R.), 288 (Possenti receives and scans the letter and leaves it on desk), 958 (Raguzzi on Possenti's inability to help).

2. Ibid., fols. 282–84, 492, 499, 512, 526v (Possenti's preparations and move).

3. Ferdinando Gregorovius, *Passeggiate per l'Italia*, trans. Mario Corsi, vol. 1 (Rome: Ulisse Carboni, 1906), 143–65. http://www.gutenberg.org/files/29955/29955-h/29955-h.htm (Segni and the environs).

4. Processo, fol. 283v (manservant's appearance at the moment of the bull's death).

5. Ibid., fol. 283v (Carlo Possenti); MdAER, 109 CP/87, fol. 153v (posse size).

6. Processo, fol. 284 (flight as far as the Portella). My thanks to Federica Colaiacomo and Francesco Cifarelli from the Museo Archeologico Comunale di Segni for identifying the probable location of the Portella.

7. MdAER, 109 CP/87, fols. 153v (Possenti's church refuge and the commissioner's search for a renegade priest), 236v (search for a bandit); Processo, fol. 284 (Carlo Possenti).

8. Processo, fol. 282 (Carlo Possenti).

9. ASVe, DAS, Roma 122, fols. 414–15, 416.

10. Processo, fols. 592–93v, 687v–88v, 850–52, 933–35v, 1031v–34 (Donato's post-Bologna activities, Venetian mission, and illness).

11. Ibid., fols. 722–26 (innkeeper).

12. Ibid., fols. 1012v–13v (Carlo Raguzzi).

13. Ibid., fols. 850–52, 932–35 (jailbreak).

14. Ibid., fols. 687v–88 (communication with Colonel Alessandro).

15. ASV, SS, Bologna 16, fol. 94 (Cardinal Falconieri, June 25, 1645).

16. Processo, fols. 786v–90v (Ottavio Agosti in Venice).

17. Ottavio Agosti's confiscated expense lists survive near the beginning of the Processo.

18. ASV, SS, Venezia 69, fol. 104; ASCR1244, fol. 171v.

19. Processo, fol. 787, and ASV, SS, Venezia 68, fols. 334 and 395 (Alessandro Guarnieri's possible whereabouts).

20. Processo, fol. 309; ASV, SS, Venezia 69, fol. 104.

21. ASV, SS, Cardinali 14, fols. 72, 75 (Guarnieri's transfer arrangements).

22. Processo, fols. 786v, 787v, 790–90v (Ottavio Agosti on Donato's transfer).

— CHAPTER NINE —

1. On the Tor di Nona prison, see Carlo Cirillo Fornili, *Delinquenti e carcerati a Roma alla metà del '600: Opera dei papi nella riforma carceria* (Rome: Editrice Ponteficia Università Gregoriana, 1991), esp. 83–99; Vincenzo Paglia, "*La pietà dei carcerati*": *Confraternite e società a Roma nei secoli xvi–xviii* (Rome: Edizioni di Storia e Letteratura, 1980), esp. 24–39; Michele Di Sivo, "Sulle carceri dei tribunali penali a Roma: Campidoglio e Tor di Nona," in *Carceri, carcerieri, carcerati: Dall'antico regime all'Ottocento*, ed. Livio Antonielli (Soveria Mannelli: Rubbettino Editori, 2006), 9–22.

2. MdAER, 109 CP/87, fol. 160v (the five hundred scudi); Processo, fol. 1080 (the twenty-seven scudi).

3. Processo, unnumbered preliminary folio dated September 2, 1645 (Braccesi's imprisonment in Le Segrete, despite illness).

4. ASCR1244, fol. 135v; MdAER, 109 CP/87, fol. 265 (the rooftop communicator).

5. ASCR1244, fol. 122v.

6. Processo, fol. 338v (Lomellini's residence at Palazzo Fava); MdAER, 109 CP/87, fols. 203, 234 (delays in Braccesi's arrest).

7. Gian Alfonso Oldelli, *Dizionario storico-ragionato degli uomini illustri del canton Ticino* (Lugano: Francesco Veladini, 1807), 1:158–59; Ghiselli29, 114–15.

8. MdAER, 109 CP/87, fol. 159v ("di assai buon stomaco"); ASCR1224, fol. 231v ("di complessione feroce").

9. Processo, fols. 285, 284v, 287 (Possenti).

10. Ibid., fols. 287v–92 (Possenti's testimony).

11. Ibid., fols. 301v–2 (Braccesi's excursion to visit Cardinal Sacchetti and other unnamed cardinals).

12. Ibid., fols. 294–96 (Braccesi's testimony).

13. ASCR1224, fols. 121–21v.

14. Processo, fols. 296–300v (Braccesi's testimony).

15. MdAER, 109 CP/87, fol. 265 (Possenti's comment).

16. Processo, fols. 313–24v (Possenti's testimony).

17. Ibid., fols. 333–40 (Braccesi's testimony).

CHAPTER TEN

1. ASCR1224, fols. 120v–21.

2. ASF, MdP3373, fols. 542v–43, 600–600v.

3. ASV, SS, Bologna 188, fol. 40.

4. MdAER, 109 CP/87, fols. 158v–59 (June 24, 1645).

5. ASF, MdP3373, fols. 545–45v; ASCR1224, fols. 129–29v (August 5), 223 (September 23). For some discussion of the song, see Amy Brosius, "'Il suon, lo sguardo, il canto': *Virtuose* of the Roman *Conversazioni* in the Mid-Seventeenth Century" (PhD diss., New York University, 2009), 147–48, 188–92. Yale, Beinecke Lib., Ital. Castle Arch. GEN MSS 110, v. 89 (original anti-Urban VIII version).

6. MdAER,109 CP/87, fols. 219–19v.

7. Ibid., fol. 219v (Domenico Vagnozzi). The suffix *-accio* implies "bad," while *-one* suggests "big"; fol. 231.

8. ASV, SS, Bologna 188, fols. 40–40v.

9. Ibid., Cardinali 14, fols. 32–32v.

10. ASCR1244, fols. 135 (August 9), 139 (August 12).

11. MdAER, 109 CP/87, fol. 285.

12. ASF, MdP3373, fol. 636v.

13. ASV, SS, Bologna 188, fol. 46v (August 12, 1645, Rossi's audience with Innocent X); ASCR1244, fol. 168v (August 26, 1645, five hundred scudi cost).

14. ASF, MdP3373, fol. 630 (the nighttime departure); http://astropixels.com/ephemeris/phasescat/phases1601.html (moon phases).

15. ASM, AIR (August 30, 1645); an almost identical account appears in ASCR1244, fol. 171; MdAER, 109 CP/87, fol. 296 (August 28, 1645).

16. ASM, AIR (August 30); largely identical text in ASCR1244, fols. 171–71v.

17. MdAER, 109 CP/87, fol. 313v.

18. Processo, fol. 358v (number of escorts; crowds); MdAER, 109 CP/87, fol. 313v.

19. Processo, fol. 358v (prisoners' confinement); BCB, MS B82, 38, and BUB MS 3847, 25 Agosto [1645] (prisoners' alleged detention at Palazzo Bargellini).

20. ASCR1244, fol. 179v.

— CHAPTER ELEVEN —

1. Processo, unfoliated protest by Guarnieri's lawyer, November 6, 1645 (prisoners' treatment).

2. ASV, SS, Cardinali 14, fols. 51, 64v, 69, 71 (Albergati-Ludovisi's accommodations to Rossi's authority and his vacation).

3. ASCR1244, fols. 187v, 194v (Auditor Argoli's detention).

4. The palace's well-known portal was completed only in subsequent decades.

5. Processo, fols. 229v–30, 365v–69 (Mariani).

6. Ibid., fols. 224v (Tomassini's incarceration), 373–75 (Dionisio Tomassini).

7. Ibid., fols. 250, 566–68v (Dionisio Tomassini), fascicle of bond postings (Tomassini's first bond, September 14).

8. Ibid., fols. 289, 383 (Possenti).

9. Ibid., fols. 379, 431 (Possenti).

10. Ibid., fols. 432–36v (Possenti's testimony).

11. Ibid., fols. 469, 507v (Possenti).

12. Ibid., fols. 387–90, 500 (Possenti).

13. Ibid., fols. 503–4 (Possenti).

14. Ibid., fols. 542v–43 (Possenti).

15. Ibid., fols. 543–44v (Possenti).

16. Ibid., fols. 549v–50 (Possenti).

17. Ibid., fols. 545v–47 (Possenti).

18. Ibid., fols. 542v–49v (Possenti's testimony).

19. Ibid., fols. 550–51 (Rossi).

20. Ibid., fols. 551–51v (Rossi and Possenti).

21. Ibid., fols. 551–54 (Andrea Pallada and Possenti).

22. Ibid., fols. 554–56v (Doralice Pallada and Possenti).

23. Ibid., fols. 245v (Panzacchi), 600–602v (Panzacchi and Possenti).

24. Ibid., fols. 634v–38v (Possenti).

25. Ibid., fols. 639–41 (Ferrarese innkeeper and Possenti).

26. Ibid., unnumbered petition dated September 16, 1645.

27. Ibid., fol. 642v (Pallada). On this practice, see Giancarlo Angelozzi and Cesarina Casanova, *La giustizia criminale in una città di antico regime: Il tribunale del Torrone di Bologna (secc. xvi–xvii)* (Bologna: CLUEB, 2009), 543.

28. Processo, fols. 642v–44 (Pallada); Thomas Coryat, *Coryat's Crudities Hastily Gobbled up in Five Moneths Travels in France, Savoy, Italy . . .* (1611) (New York: Macmillan, 1905), 392–93 (description of strappado).

29. Processo, fols. 644–44v (Pallada and Possenti; the length of Pallada's torture; his release on bond).

30. ACSR1244, fols. 194v–95 (after September 9, 1645).

31. Processo, fols. 783 (Rossi and Possenti), 572v (Bartolomea Galliani).

32. Ibid., fols. 783v–85 (Galliani and Possenti).

— CHAPTER TWELVE —

1. Details of Guarnieri's extradition appear in ASV, SS, Cardinali 14, fols. 51–51v, 65, 67, 68, 75, 78–79v; ibid., Bologna 188, fols. 48v–49, 56v–57; ibid., Venezia 68, fols. 309–11v, 319, 321; ibid., Ferrara 21, fol. 208v; Processo, fols. 786v, 787v. Full moon occurred on September 6 in 1645 (http://astropixels.com/ephemeris/phasescat/phases1601.html).

2. Processo, fols. 785v–86 and Agosti's unfoliated lists of expenses (details of Agosti's journey to Bologna).

3. Processo, fols. 576, 586 (Guarnieri's arrival and first examination); ASV, SS, Cardinali 14, fol. 78 (Albergati-Ludovisi to Cardinal Pamphili, September 13).

4. ASV, SS, Bologna 188, fol. 48v (Pamphili to Albergati-Ludovisi); ibid., Cardinali 14, fol. 71 (Albergati-Ludovisi to Pamphili); ibid., Venezia, vol. 68, fol. 334 (nuncio of Venice to Pamphili).

5. Cliff Eisen et al., *In Mozart's Words*, letter 170, http://letters.mozartways.com, Version 1.0, published by HRI Online, 2011, ISBN 978-0-955-78767-6.

6. Processo, fols. 788–91, Agosti's unfoliated expense lists, petition from Guarnieri's lawyer (November 6, 1645) (Agosti's actions at the Torrone).

7. Ibid., fol. 575v (Federico Panzacchi).

8. Ibid., fols. 567 (Dionisio Tomassini), 574 (Federico Panzacchi), 482 (Diana Tomassini), 157v (Pietro Zani on the Guarnieri brothers), 177 (Giovanni Antonio Pera on the Guarnieri brothers).

9. See chapter 5.

10. Processo, fols. 576, 579v–80 (Guarnieri).

11. Ibid., fols. 580–80v, 583v–85 (Guarnieri).

12. Ibid., fols. 590v–91; La Frattina and La Turchetta appear in bond postings (September 18).

13. Ibid., fol. 593v (Guarnieri's blush).

14. Ibid., fols. 593v–99v (Guarnieri's shirts, claimed ignorance of La Rossa, and torture).

15. Ibid., fols. 613v–15v (Guarnieri's further pleas of ignorance).

16. Ibid., petition (September 15, 1645). In Bologna, the age of full majority was twenty-five.

17. Ibid., fols. 695–95v (Guarnieri).

18. Ibid., fols. 204v, 694v–95 (Boschino).

19. Ibid., fols. 693–94 (Boschino).

20. Ibid., fols. 696v–97 (concluding exchanges with Boschino).

21. Ibid., fols. 696v–98v (Rossi's accusations and Guarnieri's denials).

22. Ibid., fol. 824 (Guarnieri).

23. Ibid., fols. 699, 748v, 749v, 750, 796v, 797v, 800, 801, 798 (Guarnieri's denials).

24. Ibid., fols. 781v–82 (Galliani).

25. Ibid., fols. 571v–72 (Galliani).

26. Ibid., fols. 782v–83 (Guarnieri and Galliani).

27. Ibid., fols. 848–49 (Caccini).

28. Ibid., fol. 864v (Guarnieri).

29. Ibid., Agosti's unfoliated expense lists document these actions. He recorded the payment to "S. Gio. Batta. Guardiano delle Priggioni."

30. Ibid., fols. 789v–91 (Agosti's testimony).

31. Ibid., bond postings (September 29, 1645).

32. Ibid., unfoliated petition (November 6, 1645), fols. 680v–81 (Guarnieri).

CHAPTER THIRTEEN

1. MdAER, 109 CP/87, fol. 296v (August 28, 1645).

2. [Gregorio Leti], *The Ceremonies of the Vacant See, or A True Relation of What Passes at Rome upon the Pope's Death*, trans. John Davis (London: Thomas Basset, 1671), 5; Gigli1, 424–25 (insults to Francesco Barberini), 426 (Campidoglio); Siri4, 567.

3. Gigli1, 427 (smell of decay); Gigli2, 427 [*sic*] (opening of conclave); Ludwig Pastor, *The History of the Popes* (reprint, St. Louis, MO: B. Herder, 1952), 30:15 (physicians' warnings); Laurie Nussdorfer, *Civic Politics in the Rome of Urban VIII* (Princeton, NJ: Princeton University Press, 1992), 249.

4. Gigli2, 427 (Francesco Barberini's behavior and strategy). Urban VIII had elevated Sacchetti to the cardinalate; he was perceived as a strong Barberini ally. Pastor, *History of the Popes*, 30:20–21; FazUrb, 2a.

5. Siri4, 638 (Barberini to French ambassador, August 19, 1644).

6. FazUrb, 2a, nn. 37–40.

7. On the marriage prospects, see ibid., 2a, esp. nn. 41–44. Siri4, 635 (Barberini to French ambassador, August 19, 1644).

8. Siri4, 651 (French ambassador to Barberini, August 27, 1644).

9. Gigli2, 428, 430 (ailing cardinals).

10. Henry Coville, *Étude sur Mazarin et ses démèles avec le pape Innocent X (1644–1648)* (Paris: Champion, 1914), 23; Pastor, *History of the Popes*, 30:23, claims only five dissenters; Gigli2, 433 (break in the weather); Galeazzo conte Gualdo, *Scena d'huomini illustri d'Italia, conosciuti da lui singolari per nascità, per virtù e per fortuna* (Venice: Andrea Giuliani, 1659), "Antonio Barberino Cardinale, &c," A[6].

11. Siri4, 758; Coville, *Étude sur Mazarin*, 39–40 (encounter with Barberini); BUB, MS 1706, fols. 168–71v; HRC, MS Ph12854, fols. 397–402 (Louis XIV's letter to the French ambassador and the ambassador's letter to Antonio Barberini); HRC, MS Ph12895, fols. 173–75 (description of Barberini's encounter with the French ambassador's representative).

12. Siri4, 759–61 (Louis XIV regarding Cardinal Antonio).

13. Girolamo Brusoni, *Della historia d'Italia . . . libri xxxviii. Riveduta dal medesimo autore, accresciuta, e continuata dall'anno 1625 fino al 1670* (Venice: Heredi Francesco Storti e Giovanni Maria Pancirutti, 1671), 403.

14. Nicolas Goulas, *Mémoires*, ed. Charles Constant (Paris: Librairie Renouard, 1879), 2:118 ("L'ho nel cul tutta la notte, che mi lasci il giorno!"). An alternative explanation appears in BAV, MS Barb. Lat. 5102, fols. 45v–49, which suggests that Gualtieri was banished for repeatedly bedding one of Cardinal Antonio's lady friends under the cardinal's roof. See FazUrb, ga58htm, n. 116 (17–19). HRC, MS Ph12854, fol. 458v claims that Cardinal Antonio "enjoyed the most intimate and close familiarity" with Gualtieri.

15. The most complete discussion of Gualtieri appears in Ermete Rossi, "La fuga del cardinale Antonio Barberini," *Archivio della Regia Deputazione Romana di Storia Patria* 59 (1936): 308–15, which questions Brusoni's statement and does not mention Goulas's

memoir, or BAV, MS Barb. Lat. 5102, which offers one description of Gualtieri's murder north of the Alps.

16. Gigli2, 437.

17. FazUrb, 2c (Venetian ambassador to the Senate, January 21 and March 11, 1645).

18. FazUrb, 2e; Pastor, *History of the Popes*, 30:52n (Florentine envoy, July 5, 1645).

19. ASF, MdP3373, fol. 543 (July 23, 1645, Malagigi's implication); MdAER, 109 CP/87, fols. 160 (July 24, 1645, Malagigi and multiple arrests), 203 (Pasqualini's innocence, July 31, 1645), 180 (July 30, 1645).

20. MdAER, 109 CP/87, fol. 285v (August 21, 1645); ASF, MdP3373, fol. 573v (July 30, 1645).

21. MdAER, 109 CP/87, fol. 313v (September 4, 1645).

22. ASCR1244, fols. 167v, 229v. On Nina Barcarola, see Amy Brosius, "'Il suon, lo sguardo, il canto': *Virtuose* of the Roman *Conversazioni* in the Mid-Seventeenth Century" (PhD diss., New York University, 2009).

23. ASM, AIR (October 18, 1645); MdAER, 109 CP/87, fol. 357v (police respect for Cardinal Barberini).

24. On the possibly sexual character of Cardinal Antonio's relationship with Pasqualini, see Frederick Hammond, *Music and Spectacle in Baroque Rome: Barberini Patronage under Urban VIII* (New Haven, CT: Yale University Press, 1994), 250, and Roger Freitas, "The Eroticism of Emasculation: Confronting the Baroque Body of the Castrato," *Journal of Musicology* 20 (2003): 196–249.

25. ASCR1244, fol. 257 (October 11, 1645); MdAER, 109 CP/87, 399v (Barberini's proposed Loretto excursion, October 2, 1645).

26. Details of Barberini's flight from Siri5, 394–95; Brusoni, *Della Historia d'Italia*, 416; FazUrb 2e; MdAER, 109 CP/87, fols. 399–400; HRC, MS Ph12919.ii, fols. 492–93v, which suggests that in Livorno Barberini hid out in the depths of the ship for twenty-four hours.

27. MdAER, 109 CP/87, fols. 428–29v (two letters of October 9, 1645). A similar letter from Antonio Barberini, signed and dated from Genoa on October 4, was printed and widely circulated; copy in BAV, MS Barb. Lat. 8800, fol. 42; see also his self-defense in Ghiselli 29, fols. 134a-34i and HRC, MS Ph12874, fols. 551–53v, which mentions Gualtiero Gualtieri but not the nuns, and BUB, MS 1706, fol. 172; ASF, MdP3373, fol. 797 (October 7, 1645, Barberini's implication in the case).

28. Mazarin's published correspondence after March 25, 1645, reveals the on-again, off-again character of negotiations. See Jules Mazarin, *Lettres du Cardinal Mazarin pendant son ministère*, vol. 2, ed. M. A. Chéruel (Paris: Imprimerie Nationale, 1879), 130, 157–59, 218–22.

29. MdAER, 109 CP/87, fol. 417 (October 6, 1645).

30. Ibid., fols. 443 (October 16, 1645), 460, 463v–64 (October 16, 1645); see also Gigli2, 456.

31. FazUrb, 2h.

32. Goulas, *Mémoires*, 139; *Journal d'Olivier Lefèvre d'Ormesson et extraits des mémoires*

d'André Lefèvre d'Ormesson, ed. M. Chéruel (Paris: Imprimerie Impériale, 1860), 1:343; See also Coville, *Étude sur Mazarin*, 103–4.

33. *Journal d'Olivier Lefevre d'Ormesson*, 1:328.

— CHAPTER FOURTEEN —

1. Processo, fols. 178v (Braccesi not friends with Alessandro Maria Pepoli), 185 (saw the Guarnieri brothers only on business), 208 (Guarnieri brothers never visited).
2. Ibid., unfoliated legal petitions at the beginning of the volume.
3. Ibid., fols. 518–18v (Braccesi's testimony).
4. Ibid., fols. 526–26v (Braccesi's testimony).
5. Ibid., fols. 528–31 (Braccesi's testimony).
6. ASV, SS, Cardinali 14, fol. 52v (Albergati-Ludovisi to Cardinal Pamphili).
7. Processo, fols. 448v–49 (Castelbarco on Maddalena Ponti).
8. ASCR1244, fols. 225–25v (September 27, 1645).
9. ASV, SS, Cardinali 14, fol. 74 (Albergati-Ludovisi to Pamphili).
10. Processo, fols. 534–36v (Braccesi's testimony).
11. ASCR1244, fols. 195, 213v.
12. Ibid., fol. 224v.
13. MdAER, 109 CP/87, fol. 332.
14. Processo, fols. 913–13v (Braccesi).
15. Ibid., fols. 914v–15 (Braccesi's testimony).
16. Ibid., fols. 521 (La Fiorentina), 917 (La Rossa), 177 (Giovanni Antonio Pera on La Romana).
17. Ibid., fol. 917v (Braccesi).
18. Ibid., fols. 920–20v (Braccesi's testimony).
19. ASCR1244, fol. 284.
20. Processo, fol. 950 (Braccesi).
21. ASM, AIR (November 1, 1645).

— CHAPTER FIFTEEN —

1. Processo, fol. 985v (tribunal under cloister arcade).
2. Ibid., fols. 883 (Suor Paola Costanza Torosanti), 888–88v and 897v–98 (lineups).
3. Ibid., fols. 836v–38v (Suor Bianca Ignota's testimony).
4. Ibid., fol. 882 (Donato Guarnieri and Suor Bianca Ignota).
5. Ibid., fols. 653v–56v (Suor Clemenza Torti's testimony), 882v (Guarnieri).
6. Ibid., fol. 835 (Suor Maria Diana Sturoli).
7. Ibid., fols. 675 (Suor Innocenza Pazienza Serra), 829v (Suor Antonia Romea Stagnoli).
8. Ibid., fols. 667v–68 (Suor Paola Costanza Torosanti).

9. Ibid., fol. 890v (Suor Giovanna Valeria Cortelli).

10. Ibid., fols. 960–66 (Guarnieri and Zucchini).

11. Ibid., fols. 838v–39 (Suor Bianca Ignota), 977v–78 (Possenti and Suor Bianca Ignota).

12. Ibid., fols. 978v–79v (Possenti and Suor Clemenza Torti).

13. Ibid., fols. 771v–72 (Suor Maria Giuliana Cocchi).

14. Ibid., fols. 33–33v (Suor Giovanna Valeria Cortelli), 985v (Possenti and Suor Giovanna Valeria Cortelli).

15. Ibid., fols. 49–49v (Suor Eufrasia Dioni).

16. Ibid., fols. 665v, 142v–43 (Suor Lucina Conti).

17. Ibid., fols. 994, 1006 (Possenti).

18. Ibid., fols. 173v–74v (Suor Palma Vittoria Ferri).

19. Ibid., fols. 955–59v, 1009v–16 (Raguzzi).

20. Ibid., fols. 1020–23 (Possenti).

21. Ibid., fols. 1023–24 (Guarnieri and Possenti).

22. Ibid., fols. 846–48v (Caccini).

23. Ibid., fols. 1026v–27 (Caccini and Possenti).

24. Ibid., fol. 1047 (receipt for mailing transcript to Rome).

— CHAPTER SIXTEEN —

1. ASM, AIR (December 20, 1645, and December 30, 1645).

2. Jules Mazarin, *Lettres du Cardinal Mazarin pendant son ministère*, vol. 2, ed. M. A. Chéruel (Paris: Imprimerie Nationale, 1879), 255; Gigli2, 456.

3. Gigli2, 458, 463; FazUrb, 2g.

4. BUB, MS 1706, fol. 253v (Francesco Barberini's explanatory letter); Ghiselli29, 120 (Francesco Barberini's ill-health ruse).

5. Gigli2, 462–63.

6. Ibid., 463; Henry Coville, *Études sur Mazarin e ses démèles avec le pape Innocent X (1644–1648)* (Paris: Champion, 1914), 105–7; Ghiselli29, 121; Ludovico Frati, "Una fuga storica," *Antologia di Lettere, Scienze ed Arti*, ser. 5, 154 (1911): 469–72; the original account appears in BUB, MS 1706, fols. 248–53v, and HRC, MS Ph12921.ix, fols. 1–9. For another very detailed, slightly different account, see HRC, MS Ph12919.ii, fols. 499v–502v.

7. Processo, fols. 510–11, 513v–14 (Possenti's jewelry), 669v–70, 829 (La Generona's jewelry).

8. Ibid., fols. 1076v–77v (Suor Jacopa Rossi).

9. Ibid., fols. 1078–78v (Suor Prudenza Prosperi).

10. Ibid., fols. 1079–80 (Matteo Bonnio).

11. Ibid., fols. 1080–82 (Possenti).

12. Ibid., fols. 1082–84 (Catterina Pasi's testimony).

13. Ibid., fols. 1084–85 (Possenti).

14. Ibid., fols. 1085–86v (accusations against Possenti).

15. Ibid., fols. 1086v–87 (Possenti).

16. Ibid., fols. 1087–90v (Rossi's summary of the accusations against Possenti).

17. Ibid., fol. 1090v (Possenti).

18. ASV, SS, Bologna 17, fol. 31 (Falconieri to Pamphili).

19. Processo, fols. 1091–91v.

20. At the Torrone, a half hour of torture was customarily followed on the second day by a full hour. See Giancarlo Angelozzi and Cesarina Casanova, *La giustizia criminale in una città di antico regime: Il tribunale del Torrone di Bologna (secc. xvi–xvii)* (Bologna: CLUEB, 2009), 478.

21. BCB, MS B915, 340–41 (time of the session); Processo, fols. 1093–95 (Possenti).

22. Ibid., fols. 1095–96v (Rossi and Braccesi; the vigil); Giovanni Battista Scanaroli, *De visitatione carceratorum libri tres* (Rome: Typis Reverendae Camerae Apostolicae, 1675), summarized in Angelozzi and Casanova, *Giustizia criminale*, 535–42; Jean Baptiste Labat, *Voyages du P. Labat en Espagne et en Italie*, quoted in A. Ademollo, *Le annotazioni di Mastro Titta Carnefice romano* (Città di Castello: S. Lapi, 1886), 24–28; Piero Fiorelli, *La tortura giudiziaria nel diritto commune,* vol. 1 (Milan: Giuffrè, 1953–54), 195–203.

23. Processo, fols. 1095v–96 (Possenti).

24. Ibid., fols. 1096–96v (Possenti's last moments).

25. BCB, MS B82, 38, and MS B915, 340–41 (Possenti's burial at the Celestini); ibid., MS B911, 495, 507, 513–14, 522 (Possenti vault at Santa Maria Maggiore and family burials: uncle Giovanni Battista, 1623; brother Jacopo, 1641; father Lorenzo, 1648; mother Catterina, 1668).

26. ASM, AIR (February 17, 1646).

27. ASV, SS, Bologna 188, fol. 86v (Pamphili to Falconieri, February 7, 1646); ibid., 17, fol. 49 (Falconieri to Pamphili, February 14, 1646); ASB, ABR, Lettere, vol. 132 (February 12, 1646).

— CHAPTER SEVENTEEN —

1. FazUrb, 3d (Venetian envoy); ASM, AIR (February 21, 1646).

2. BCB, MS B82, 38.

3. ASM, AIR (February 21, 1646).

4. Processo, fol. 1105 (letter from Rome); the penalties are stipulated on an opening, unnumbered folio; ASB, ABR, Lettere, vol. 132 (March 24, 1646) (date and promulgation of Rossi's decree); ASB, ABR, Posiz. 263, no. 83 (copy of printed decree).

5. ASB, ABR, Registrum 30, fols. 52v–54, 59, 60v, 63v–64, 70v, 80, 85v–86, 91v, 93, 99v.

6. Gigli2, 463–64.

7. Jules Mazarin, *Lettres du Cardinal Mazarin pendant son ministère*, vol. 2, ed. M. A. Chéruel (Paris: Imprimerie Nationale, 1879), 302 (Mazarin to Cardinal Grimaldi, May 8, 1646).

8. Processo, fols. 1096v–98 (Braccesi).

9. Ibid., fols. 1098–1104v (Braccesi).

10. Ibid., fol. 1107 (Lomellini to Rossi, May 27, 1646).

11. Ibid., fols. 1109–10v (Guarnieri).

12. ASB, ABR, Registrum 30, fol. 73.

13. ASB, ABR, Lettere, vol. 132 (April 28, 1646) (Ranuzzi family indemnity); ASCR1244, fol. 155; ASV, SS, Cardinali 14, fol. 104, and ASV, SS, Bologna 16, fol. 250 (Ranuzzi's flight); ASV, Fondo Ranuzzi, Instrumenti, vol. 25, no. 18 (claimed inheritance); ASV, Fondo Ranuzzi, Instrumenti, vol. 44, no. 13 (death in Livorno and funeral rites); Ghiselli30, 216–17 (Ranuzzi's alleged murder).

14. Processo, fol. 1111 (departure at "Hora 4 noctis circiteri"); Antonio di Paolo Masini, *Bologna Perlustrata*, 3rd printing (Bologna: Erede di Vittorio Benacci, 1666), 539 (midnight on December 1 at 7:31 after sunset).

15. Processo, fols. 1110v–11v (Guarnieri's banishment). Full moon fell on December 22, 1646; the moon, which rose at 10:25 a.m., had traversed most of the sky by this hour. (http://astropixels.com/ephemeris/phasescat/phases1601.html).

16. Renzo Zagnoni, "La strada 'Francesca della Sambuca' o 'Maestra di Saragozza' a nord di Pavana lungo la valle del Reno nel secolo xiii," *Bollettino Storico Pistoiese*, ser. 3, 21 (1996): 78 (papal and Tuscan customs houses, the latter dated 1641). A nearby sign identifies a building complex as the customs house built in 1641. Processo, fol. 1111v indicates only that Guarnieri was accompanied "usque ad confinia status [illeg.]tinae in loco detto il fiume Pavano [= Pavana]." My thanks to the owner of the building for permission to explore the lowest level, where I located the customs house facade inside another structure attached to it in the nineteenth century.

— EPILOGUE —

1. Gigli2, 522.

2. *The Scarlet Gown, or The History of All the Present Cardinals of Rome* (London: Humphrey Mosseley, 1653), 44–48 [=45].

3. BCB, MS B36, fol. 163 (Rossi's time as auditor). On Litta's reign in Milan, see Gianvittorio Signorotto, *Milano Spagnola: Guerra, istituzioni, uomini di governo (1635–1660)* (Milan: Sansoni, 1996), 247–55, which makes no mention of Rossi. See also Gian-Alfonso Oldelli, *Dizionario storico-ragionato degli uomini illustri del canton Ticino* (Lugano: Francesco Veladini, 1807), 158–59 (other biographical details).

4. *Scarlet Gown*, 48 [=45]; *Manente*, the ablative of *manens*, used as an adjective, means "enduring" or "remaining."

5. Siri5, 381.

6. BAV, Archivio Barberini, Comp. 226, 119 (Braccesi in Pesaro, 1647), 268 (silk hose); ibid., Comp. 227, 148 (Braccesi in Pesaro, 1654); Manifesto1, fol. 29, Manifesto2, fol. 275, Manifesto3, fol. 332 (pope's remark); BAV, Archivio Barberini, Comp. 228–30 (yearly payments to Braccesi until 1671).

7. ASF, Mediceo del Principato 5237, fols. 276–76v, 278–79, 282–82v (quotation), 291–92 (Braccesi's French sojourn). My thanks to Shannon McHugh for tracking down these documents and acquiring copies for me.

8. Jules Mazarin, *Lettres du Cardinal Mazarin pendant son ministère*, vol. 7, ed. G. D'Avenel (Paris: Imprimerie Nationale, 1893), 533–34, 558, 568, 581 (early correspondence with Mazarin). Charles Gérin, *Louis XIV et le saint-siège*, vol. 1 (Paris: Victor Lecoffre, 1894), 217 (letter from Père François Duneau to Mazarin). Further details gleaned from *Lettres du Cardinal Mazarin*, vols. 8–9, ed. G. D'Avenel (1894–96). "Abbate" and "abbé" indicate someone of considerable learning, venerability, and influence, not simply someone in holy orders.

9. *Lettres du Cardinal Mazarin*, 7:533, 568, and 8:685–86; BAV, Archivio Barberini, Comp. 228, 28, 83, 84, 168, 175, 179, 180, 319, 321 (Braccesi's artistic enterprises).

10. *Mémoriaux du Conseil de 1661*, vol. 1, ed. Jean de Boislisle (Paris: Renouard, 1905), 255.

11. MdAER (Mémoires et Documents), 24, fol. 57. My thanks to Antonia Banducci for tracking down and copying the documents relevant to the crisis of 1661–62; MdAER, 142, fols. 42–43.

12. MdAER, 142, fols. 349–50; MdAER (Mémoires et Documents), 24, fol. 84 (Braccesi as Cardinal Antonio's "gouverneur").

13. Ibid., fol. 82v.

14. Manifesto1, fols. 29v, 32; Manifesto2, fols. 275–75v, 277; Manifesto3, fols. 332v–33, 336; other copies in BUB, MS 2, fols. 216–25, and BUB, MS 1841, fols. 290ff.

15. MdAER (Mémoires et Documents), 24, fols. 108–108v. The gentleman in question was Seigneur de Fargues.

16. Manifesto1, fols. 27–28; Manifesto2, fols. 277A-277Av; Manifesto3, fols. 338v–39v. *Recueil des instructions données aux ambassadeurs et ministres de France depuis les traités de Westphalie jusqu'à la Révolution française, Rome*, vol. 1, ed. Gabriel Hanotaux (Paris: Germer Baillière, 1888), 133 and 223.

17. BAV, Archivio Barberini, Comp. 228–30, passim (Braccesi's stipend).

18. ASF, Carte Strozziane, prim. ser. 239, fols. 38v–39; HRC, MS Ph12884, fols. 343–43v.

19. *Nota delli musei, librerie, galerie et ornamenti di statue e pitture ne' palazzi, nelle case e ne' giardini di Roma* (Rome: Falco, 1664), 13–14; *Nuova raccolta di lettere sulla pittura, scultura ed architettura scritta dai più celebri personaggi dei secoli xv a xix*, ed. Michelangelo Gualandi (Bologna: Gualandi, 1856), 3:232–36, 248; Giulia de Marchi, *Mostre di quadri a S. Salvatore in Lauro (1682–1725): Stime di collezioni Romane* (Rome: Società alla Biblioteca Vallicelliana, 1987), 14–18; *I marmi vivi: Bernini e la nascità del ritratto barocco*, ed. A. Bacchi, T. Montanari, B. Paolozzi Strozzi, and D. Zikos (Florence: Giunti, 2009), 254–59; my thanks to Tomaso Montanari for bringing the Bernini bust to my attention. The correct collocation number for Braccesi's will is ASR, Trenta Notai Capitolini, Ufficio 2, vol. 316, fol. 216.

20. BAV, Archivio Barberini, Comp. 75, 459, 601, 721 (stipend from Cardinal Fran-

cesco); ibid., Comp. 298, 277, and Comp. 298, 22, 43, 66, 76, 110, 177, 217 (stipend from Cardinal Carlo).

21. Braccesi's will appears in ASR, Trenta Notai Capitolini, Ufficio 2, vol. 316, fols. 216–18v, 231, 232v.

22. Pietro Tommaso Cacciari, *Della vita, virtù e doni sopranaturali del venerabile servo di Dio P. Angiolo Paoli Carmelitano* (Rome: Giuseppe Collini, 1756), 173, where "Signore Abbate Sforza Frosini Bracese" is described as director of the Conservatorio dell'Immacolata Concezzione detto il Conservatorio delle Viperesche in the 1690s. He died in January 1720 (ibid., 99). Frosini may have used some of his newfound wealth to enlarge and improve the conservatorio. See Ignazio Orsolini, *Vita della Signora Livia Vipereschi vergine nobile romana, fondatrice del Conservatorio delle Zitelle dette dell'Immacolata Concezzione della Beatiss. Vergine presso l'Arco di San Vito di Roma* (Rome: Francesco Gonzaga, 1718), 161–62.

23. BAV, Archivio Barberini, Comp. 29, 276 (Braccesi's funeral).

24. Pio Pecchiai, *I Barberini* (Rome: Biblioteca d'Arte Editrice, 1959), 196–200, describes in detail a "Relatione del ratto fatto nel Monastero di Monte Magnanapoli li 11 marzo 1640" in Rome, involving a Giovanni Braccesi and two nuns, removed from the convent; Pecchiai bases his account on Rome, Archivio Caetani, Miscellanee, nn. 1111/1173, fols. 991–1018. FazUrb, 2e, n12, calls attention to another source for the same story, ASV, Fondo Bolognetti 87, 727–93. A summary appears in BAV, MSS Vat. Lat. 8632, fols. 241–42. Although Braccesi returned to Rome briefly in 1640 with Cardinal Durazzo, he was not yet connected with Antonio Barberini, and certainly was neither the cardinal's "maestro" nor "il dispotico del Cardinale Antonio," as the story claims, nor in a position to expropriate 250,000 scudi. The Duke of Créquy, mentioned as French ambassador to Rome, served there in 1633, not 1640. The narrative also refers to Braccesi's interactions with a courtesan on Fat Tuesday 1646 (when he was imprisoned in the Torrone in Bologna). The story also claims that after Braccesi fled to Venice (which sounds like Ferdinando Ranuzzi) and returned to the Papal States, Urban VIII [*sic*] confined him to the city of Pesaro. Given that Giandomenico Rossi uncovered Possenti and Guarnieri's previous criminal histories, it seems unlikely he would have failed to mention this crime if it were in fact genuine. Perhaps the story was subsequently concocted based on the "real" abduction of 1644. The inventories of the Tribunale Criminale del Governatore, Processi in the ASR make no mention of such a case in the years around 1640. By an interesting coincidence, however, Braccesi stipulated that at his death, five masses should be said at the same convent, Santa Catterina a Magnanapoli.

25. It appears in Paris, Bibliothèque Nationale, MS Ital. 297, fols. 323–34. See *Chroniques italiennes*, vol. 2 Appendice, ed. Victor Del Litto, new edition (Geneva: Edito-Service S.A., 1968), 84. The German translation appears in Stendahl [Henri Beyle], *Chroniken aus der italienischen Renaissance und nachgelassene Novellen*, trans. Friedrich von Oppeln-Bronikowski (Jena: Eugen Diederichs, 1908), 91–93.

26. Ghiselli28, 884–85. Ghiselli's account also includes "lightly fictionalized" descrip-

tions of the nuns' removal from the Convertite (which only Ranuzzi or Negrini would have known) and of their murder (with details only perpetrators of the crime would have known).

27. Laurel Thatcher Ulrich, "Vertuous Women Found: New England Ministerial Literature, 1668–1735," *American Quarterly* 28 (1976): 20; Ulrich, *Well-Behaved Women Seldom Make History* (New York: Knopf, 2007). The comment is regularly attributed to other transgressive women (e.g., Marilyn Monroe, Eleanor Roosevelt, Anne Boleyn).

Selected Bibliography

Angelozzi, Giancarlo, and Cesarina Casanova. *La giustizia criminale in una città di antico regime: Il tribunale del Torrone di Bologna (secc. xvi–xvii)*. Bologna: CLUEB, 2009.

Aretino, Pietro. *Sei giornate: Ragionamento della Nanna e della Antonia* (1534) and *Dialogo nel quale la Nanna insegna a la Pippa* (1536), edited by Giovanni Aquilecchia. Bari: Laterza, 1969.

Brosius, Amy. "'Il suon, lo sguardo, il canto': *Virtuose* of the Roman *Conversazioni* in the Mid-Seventeenth Century." PhD diss., New York University, 2009.

Castiglione, Baldassare. *The Book of the Courtier*. Translated by George Bull. London: Penguin, 2004.

Cohen, Sherrill. *The Evolution of Women's Asylums since 1500: From Refuges for Ex-Prostitutes to Shelters for Battered Women*. New York: Oxford University Press, 1992.

Costantini, Claudio. *Fazione Urbana: Sbandamento e ricomposizione di una grande clientela a metà seicento*. Quaderni.net editoria online. http://www.quaderni.net/WebFazione/000indexFazione.htm.

Coville, Henry. *Étude sur Mazarin et ses démêles avec le Pape Innocent X (1644–1648)*. Paris: Champion, 1914.

D'Amico, Stefano. "Shameful Mother: Poverty and Prostitution in Seventeenth-Century Milan." *Journal of Family History* 30 (2005): 109–20.

Ferrante, Lucia. "Honor Regained: Women in the Casa del Soccorso di San Paolo in Sixteenth-Century Bologna." In *Sex and Gender in Historical Perspective*, edited by

Edward Muir and Guido Ruggiero, 46–72. Baltimore: Johns Hopkins University Press, 1990.

———. "Pro mercede carnali. . . . Il giusto prezzo rivendicato in tribunale." *Memoria: Rivista di Storia delle Donne* 17 (1986): 42–58.

———. "La sessualità come risorsa: Donne davanti al foro arcivescovile di Bologna (sec. xvii)." *Mélanges de l'École Française de Rome: Moyen-Âge, Temps Modernes* 99 (1987): 989–1016.

Fiorelli, Piero. *La tortura giudiziaria nel diritto commune*. 2 vols. Milan: Giuffrè, 1953–54.

Fosi, Irene. *Papal Justice: Subjects and Courts in the Papal State, 1500–1750*. Washington, DC: Catholic University of America Press, 2011.

Hammond, Frederick. *Music and Spectacle in Baroque Rome: Barberini Patronage under Urban VIII*. New Haven, CT: Yale University Press, 1994.

———. *The Ruined Bridge: Studies in Barberini Patronage of Music and Spectacle, 1631–1679*. Sterling Heights, MI: Harmonie Park Press, 2010.

Hughes, Steven. "Fear and Loathing in Bologna and Rome: The Papal Police in Perspective." *Journal of Social History* 21 (1987): 97–116.

Infelise, Mario. "Roman *Avvisi*: Information and Politics in the Seventeenth Century." In *Court and Politics in Papal Rome, 1492–1700*, edited by Gianvittorio Signorotto and Maria Antonietta Visceglia, 212–28. Cambridge: Cambridge University Press, 2002.

Langbein, John H. *Torture and the Law of Proof: Europe and England in the Ancien Régime*. Chicago: University of Chicago Press, 1976, 1977, 2006.

Laven, Mary. *Virgins of Venice: Broken Vows and Cloistered Lives in the Renaissance Convent*. New York: Viking, 2003.

Mazarin, Jules. *Lettres du Cardinal Mazarin pendant son ministère*, 9 vols. Edited by G. D'Avenel and A. Chéruel. Paris: Imprimerie Nationale, 1872–1906.

Monson, Craig A. *Divas in the Convent: Nuns, Music, and Defiance in Seventeenth-Century Italy*. Chicago: University of Chicago Press, 2012.

———. *Nuns Behaving Badly: Tales of Music, Magic, Art, and Arson in the Convents of Italy*. Chicago: University of Chicago Press, 2010.

Nussdorfer, Laurie. *Civic Politics in the Rome of Urban VIII*. Princeton, NJ: Princeton University Press, 1992.

Pastor, Ludwig. *The History of the Popes*. Translated by Ernest Graf. 34 vols. Reprint, St. Louis, MO: B. Herder, 1952.

Pecchiai, Pio. *I Barberini*. Rome: Biblioteca d'Arte Editrice, 1959.

Rosenthal, Margaret F. *The Honest Courtesan: Veronica Franco, Citizen and Writer in Sixteenth-Century Venice*. Chicago: University of Chicago Press, 1992.

Rossi, Ermete. "La fuga del cardinale Antonio Barberini." *Archivio della Regia Deputazione Romana di Storia Patria* 59 (1936): 303–27.

Ruggiero, Guido. *Binding Passions: Tales of Magic, Marriage, and Power at the End of the Renaissance*. New York: Oxford University Press, 1993.

———. "Mean Streets, Familiar Streets, or The Fat Woodcarver and the Masculine Spaces of Renaissance Florence." In *Renaissance Florence: A Social History*, edited by Roger J. Crum and John T. Paleotti, 295–310. Cambridge: Cambridge University Press, 2006.

The Scarlet Gown, or The History of All the Present Cardinals of Rome. London: Humphrey Moselley, 1653.

Schutte, Anne Jacobson. *By Force and Fear: Taking and Breaking Monastic Vows in Early Modern Europe*. Ithaca, NY: Cornell University Press, 2011.

Sella, Domenico. *Italy in the Seventeenth Century*. London: Longman, 1997.

Siri, Vittorio. *Il mercurio, overo historia de' correnti tempi*. 15 vols. Casale: Christoforo della Casa, 1644–82.

Storey, Tessa. *Carnal Commerce in Counter-Reformation Rome*. Cambridge: Cambridge University Press, 2008.

Weaver, Elissa. *Convent Theatre in Early Modern Italy: Spiritual Fun and Learning for Women*. Cambridge: Cambridge University Press, 2002.

Zarri, Gabriella. "I monasteri femminili a Bologna tra il xiii e il xvii secolo." *Deputazione di Storia Patria per le Province di Romagna: Atti e Memorie*, n.s., 24 (1973): 133–224.

Index

Note: Page numbers followed by *f* indicate a figure or a map.